ECONOMIC ANALYSIS OF GREEN DEVELOPMENT IN CHINA

ECONOMIC ANALYSIS OF GREEN DEVELOPMENT IN CHINA

ZHIQING LI
Fudan University, China

TRANSLATED BY LANJUN YANG
Fudan University, China

World Scientific

NEW JERSEY • LONDON • SINGAPORE • BEIJING • SHANGHAI • HONG KONG • TAIPEI • CHENNAI • TOKYO

Published by

World Scientific Publishing Co. Pte. Ltd.
5 Toh Tuck Link, Singapore 596224
USA office: 27 Warren Street, Suite 401-402, Hackensack, NJ 07601
UK office: 57 Shelton Street, Covent Garden, London WC2H 9HE

Library of Congress Cataloging-in-Publication Data
Names: Li, Zhiqing (Researcher on environmental economics), author.
Title: Economic analysis of green development in China / Zhiqing Li, Fudan University, China ; translated by Lanjun Yang, Fudan University, China.
Other titles: Lü se fa zhan de jing ji xue fen xi. English
Description: New Jersey : World Scientific, [2024] | Originally published in 2019 in Chinese by Fudan University Press Co., Ltd. | Includes bibliographical references and index.
Identifiers: LCCN 2022022548 | ISBN 9789811255052 (hardcover) | ISBN 9789811255069 (ebook) | ISBN 9789811255076 (ebook other)
Subjects: LCSH: Sustainable development--China. | Economic development--Environmental aspects--China. | Environmental policy--Economic aspects--China. | China--Economic policy.
Classification: LCC HC430.E5 L5282613 2024 | DDC 333.70951--dc23/eng/20220512
LC record available at https://lccn.loc.gov/2022022548

British Library Cataloguing-in-Publication Data
A catalogue record for this book is available from the British Library.

《绿色发展的经济学分析》
Originally published in Chinese by Fudan University Press Co., Ltd.

For any available supplementary material, please visit
https://www.worldscientific.com/worldscibooks/10.1142/12799#t=suppl

Translated by: Lanjun Yang
Desk Editors: Nimal Koliyat/Lixi Dong/Lai Ann

Typeset by Stallion Press
Email: enquiries@stallionpress.com

About the Author

Li Zhiqing Ph.D in Economics, is an associate professor in environmental economics and green finance at School of Economics in Fudan University. He works as the director of Center for Environmental Economic Studies at Fudan University and the deputy director of Shanghai Key Laboratory of Policy Simulation and Evaluation of Ecological and Environmental Governance. Professor Li worked at Yale University from October 2009 to January 2012 and worked at Konstanz University in Germany from January 2006 to August 2006 both as a visiting scholar after receiving Ph.D in environmental economics at Fudan University.

Professor Li does research focusing on environmental economics and green finance. He is also playing an active role in developing the environmental economics theory and practice in China. He is the author of several books and dozens of papers, articles, and reports.

Contents

List of Figures

List of Tables

Introduction

China's Environmental Protection Since the 1978 Reform and Opening Up

1. Review of China's 40 Years of Environmental Protection from the Perspective of Economic Development

In the 40 years since its implementation of the reform and opening-up policy in 1978, China has witnessed the simultaneous advancement of environmental protection and economic development to achieve positive progress. However, the effect of environmental protection is not as prominent as that of economic growth. The comparison of indicators even shows that environmental protection breaks with economic growth, namely they are neither coordinated nor consistent. Well then, how can we interpret the evolution of environmental quality in the past four decades? Especially in the context where economic development contradicts with environmental protection, how can we look at our decades of endeavor in environmental protection from the perspective of economic development? They are important topics that will help us fully understand the relationship between environment and economy, and enlighten Chinese policy-makers to do better in developing environmental and economic policies.

How can we divide the stages of China's environmental protection in the past 40 years? There are already rich studies in this regard, and most of them make a stage division from the evolution of the environmental protection work itself. For example, some studies trace the starting point of China's environmental protection back to 1972 when a Chinese delegation attended the United Nations Conference on the Environment in Stockholm; other studies make a stage division based on the setup (and several times of "upgrade") of China's environmental protection administration. These types of stage division are somewhat praiseworthy since they have summed up all the efforts and attempts that China has made in environmental protection in four decades. However, being made only from the perspective of environmental protection, such stage division can hardly explain the current situation — now that environmental protection is of great concern, how can the results remain so "undesirable" despite of decades of endeavor? According to China Environmental Status Bulletin, several areas, cities, and waters were still beset by serious eco-environmental degradation by 2017. In this sense, these types of stage division do have drawbacks, and in my opinion, their greatest weakness is to separate China's environmental protection from its economic development, which is the main reason for the "deviation between process and result."

Now let us shift our focus to China's economic development in the past 40 years. It is generally believed that the reform and opening-up initiated in 1978 was the starting point of the most recent long-lasting economic development cycle. This judgment does make sense since the year 1978 marks a watershed between two utterly different economic systems and development models, and it was since then that China's economic scale and growth pattern began to take on a new look.

China's economic development has gone through several stages since 1978. Based on its growth rate, China's 40-year economic development is roughly divided into three stages: 1978–1992 (flat growth), 1992–2012 (rapid growth), and 2012–present (flat growth).

Looking back at environmental protection, during the first stage spanning 1978–1992, China's environmental protection work had by and large kept pace with its economic development, and even surpassed its economic performance to a certain extent, which is mainly reflected in the establishment and improvement of various environmental management systems, and some of them were predecessors of existing systems. But why did China begin to introduce a set of systematic environmental management systems when its economic recovery was just stabilized? It could be explained from two aspects:

(1) There were signs that the industrialization and economic growth in the 1980s were destroying the ecological environment. In particular, the aggravating pollution caused by township and village industries in some areas had alarmed the Central Government.

(2) The socialist China has been instinctively alert to the Western development model of "treatment after pollution," but inclined to prioritize environmental protection over economic development. As a result, China was able to maintain a relative balance between environment and economy at this stage with its overall environmental quality free from serious deterioration.

The second stage spanning 1992–2012 was a golden period of China's economic development, registering a growth rate above 10% almost every year, which was mainly attributed to two factors:

(1) China decided to develop a socialist market economy, and made it as its basic economic system in 1993.
(2) China's accession to the World Trade Organization (WTO) in 2001 was a crucial step toward substantive opening-up.

Economic boom is a great challenge to environmental protection. On the one hand, industrialization and urbanization will impose mounting pressure on the environment, and gradually approach the environmental carrying capacity. On the other hand, the existing environmental management systems are no longer "rigid constraints" in the era of market economy, but become increasingly "flexible" in implementation. These two aspects indicate that the relationship between environment and economy, though it may remain balanced, is becoming increasingly unstable since any gain for one means a loss for the other. Therefore, although China vigorously improved its environmental management systems (e.g., the State Environmental Protection Administration was upgraded to the Ministry of Environmental Protection in 2008), its environmental quality kept deteriorating with pollution incidents occurring from time to time. At this stage featuring rapid economic growth, the efforts in environmental protection were far from enough to form effective constraints on pollution. The reasons for this can be found in literatures:

(1) The transition from a planned economy to a market economy has, to a certain extent, brought great difficulties to environmental protection at both the government and market levels. An objective manifestation of this is less competent government and overpowering market, thus making environmental protection increasingly "vulnerable."
(2) After economic growth became an overwhelming political task, the Chinese leadership no longer rejected the Western development

model of "treatment after pollution," and downplayed the importance of environmental protection.

It is these factors, both objective and subjective, that gradually imbalanced the relationship between environment and economy for two decades.

At the third stage from 2012 to date, Chinese economic growth plummeted by 10% and then leveled off again. The key reason for the flat economic growth is the lack of development momentum, which is mainly reflected in low efficiency and weak market vitality. To respond to this situation, the Central Government launched a new round of reform and opening up in 2012, and put environmental protection on the agenda again, showing a sign that the relationship between economy and environment will be rebalanced. This latest trend has not yet ended. Generally speaking, the new round of environmental protection has achieved certain results. The environmental protection work at this stage can be evaluated from three aspects:

(1) The economic slowdown has to some extent created an important "window period" for environmental protection. In short, the outcome of market saturation is that we can put forward higher requirements and standards for environmental protection.
(2) A profound understanding of the characteristics of market economy has motivated both the government and the market to take more active actions in environmental protection.
(3) Thanks to 40 years of reform and opening-up and technological advances such as the widespread access to the Internet, the cooperative engagement capability of various fields has greatly improved, and reform measures have become more systematic and integrated. Therefore, China is now performing better in the co-development of environment and economy.

In a nutshell, the evolution of China's environmental protection in the past 40 years is not in a separate institutional space, but highly coupled with economic growth and the progress of reform and opening-up. Therefore, only by starting from the dominant trend of economic development can we fully understand the significance of environmental protection in those decades.

2. Interpretation of the Current Environmental and Economic Situation

Through a review of the history of China's environmental protection, we can interpret the relationship between environment and economy in three stages:

Stage 1: "Imbalance" between a sound environment and a poor economic performance.
Stage 2: "Imbalance" between deteriorating environment and booming economy.
Stage 3: "Balance" between recovering environment and stable economic growth.

It can be seen that the long-lasting "imbalance" between environment and economy is a normal state. However, from a subjective perspective, the relationship between environment and economy is related to the degree of "acquired" efforts, which mainly refer to the efforts in environmental protection. At the initial stage, the objective "imbalance" between environment and economy is not caused by less efforts in environmental protection, implying that environment and economy are "balanced" subjectively. At the second stage, people often attribute the imbalanced relationship between environment and economy to "inaction" in environmental protection, thus leading to a kind of subjective "imbalance," which accords with objective "imbalance." At the third stage, the efforts made in environmental protection have improved environmental quality, forming a "balanced" relationship between environment and economy both subjectively and objectively. So, how can we interpret the latest relationship between environment and economy? This book, based on the premise that the existing environment–economy relationship remains imbalanced, offers the following viewpoints:

(1) *Both objectively and subjectively, the relationship between environment and economy remains "imbalanced" on the whole.* The relationship between environment and economy remains at the "climbing" section of the Environmental Kuznets Curve, which is a manifestation of the objective "imbalance" between the two. When will it reach the vertex of this curve? It might be 2030, according to the mainstream judgment in

academia, when China's carbon emissions reach the peak. However, there are still uncertainties such as the effect of economic transition and the macroeconomic cycle. In the short term, the imbalance between environment and economy will remain as the foremost factor that leads the environmental and economic development trend. Therefore, we must to continue environmental protection unwaveringly in the mid-to-long term.

The subjective "imbalance" mainly manifests in inadequate work in environmental protection in contrast to fast economic growth. First, the inertia of economic growth pattern in the past 40 years remains strong, with extensiveness and inefficiency remaining the main characteristics of current economic growth. Consequently, the continuous economic development keeps weighing on the eco-environment. Second, all walks of life have reached consensus on the seriousness of environmental problems and the urgency of solving them, and they have taken actions in all directions to address the environmental challenges. However, due to the strong inertia and pressure on the economic side, the current environmental protection actions are not "powerful" enough to thoroughly improve the environmental quality. The root cause is that we are still unable to mobilize enough economic forces to invest in environmental protection, including all sorts of "large-scaled" and "efficient" economic forces.

(2) *As for the environmental economic situation in the short term, it is characterized by weakening economic growth momentum and continuously mounting pressure from environmental protection policies*. According to the latest economic and environmental statistics, the economic growth momentum has been weakening, while the environmental quality has been improving constantly as result of stricter environmental protection policies. Is there any causality between the two aspects? Different people may give different answers. In this book, the author argues that the rigorous environmental protection policies mainly have a "marginal" impact on economy, which is supported by a large number of theoretical studies, and the changes in economic growth are mainly caused by non-environmental factors.

Moreover, in terms of the endogenous relationship between environment and economy, weak economic growth momentum may have a greater impact on environmental protection policies. This is because slow economic growth will affect the ability and determination of local governments and companies in environmental governance. From the perspective of the chief decision-maker — the Central Government, it is more urgent to implement stricter policies to carry on the environmental protection work. For example, the Ministry of Ecology and Environment (MEE) issued the *Opinions on Further Strengthening the Supervision and Law Enforcement of Eco-environmental Protection* in September 2018, pointing out that "The outstanding problems such as illegal pollution discharge still exist in some enterprises. We must conscientiously strengthen and innovate the eco-environmental supervision and law enforcement, resolutely curb the deep-rooted phenomenon of illegal pollution discharge, urge enterprises to earnestly fulfil their principal responsibility in eco-environmental protection, and promote environmental compliance to become normal."

In short, the pressure on the currently imbalanced environmental–economic relationship mainly comes from the economic side. On the one hand, the quality of economic quality needs to be improved in the mid-to-long term so as to achieve high-quality and sustainable economic development. On the other hand, the short-term economic growth momentum needs to be strengthened, and the "troika" of consumption, investment and export needs to advance side by side; otherwise, the environmental protection policies and work will bear increasing pressure from the economic side and become hard to sustain.

(3) *Environmental protection policy tools will be fully replaced by means of market economy*. In the process of balancing the environmental–economic relationship by implementing strict environmental protection policies, the choice of policies has obvious stage characteristics. For example, in the early days of environmental protection, the corresponding policies are developed from scratch, and great attention is paid to establishing and improving the legal system, which is evident in the latest round of environmental protection campaigns. As the old policies cannot satisfy the environmental protection requirements in the new age, the Central Government kicked off the reform of the environmental protection undertakings, making the reconstruction of the environmental protection legal system a top priority. Laws and regulations have come out one by one, including the law on air pollution prevention and control and the law on soil pollution prevention and control, showing that the environmental protection policy tools (highlighting the construction of administrative and legal systems) have so far become saturated, and their scale effect starts diminishing gradually. In this new round of environmental protection campaigns, after the quantity of policies has increased "from zero to one" and

then "from one to many," their quality should be upgraded; because only "high-quality" policies are able to support the subsequent environmental protection work.

What are "high-quality" environmental policies? They must be able to protect the environment and sustain the economic development concurrently, and the key to this is "efficiency." The effective environmental policy tools that can take both aspects into account are environmental economic policies. The essence of these policies is to take the environment as a product in the market and incorporate it into the market equilibrium analysis framework. For example, not all pollution discharge is "illegal," so it is necessary to price the "legal" pollution discharge, which is the task of environmental economic policies.

However, the effective use of environmental economic policies is far more complicated than the establishment of a legal system for environmental protection. The most important thing is to understand and follow the internal development laws of environment and economy, especially how to simultaneously "price" environmental products and realize their "mobility" by way of the market.

Take green financial policy tools as an example. At present, both the central and local governments have begun to allow the access of financial institutions and financial tools in environmental protection, and highlight their important role. Financial channels for environmental protection are on the way of being formed. However, it is extremely difficult to truly utilize the green financial policy tools, and the biggest challenge is how to create a win–win situation between the financial sector and the environmental sector in the two-way flow of "getting in" and "getting out." The existing green financial policy tools are obviously unable to play the role of a precise channel as "finance-environment-finance," hence showing the asymmetry of "pan-green" on the financial side and "de-financialization" on the environmental side. It is unfavorable to the role of green finance in balancing the relationship between environment and economy.

Considering both environmental and economic factors, especially certain factors on the economic side, environmental protection itself will face great difficulties in terms of policy and effectiveness, even if the relationship between environment and economy is becoming healthy and balanced. In order to solve this difficulty, the author recommends the use of scientific and reasonable environmental economic policy tools.

3. Divide Environmental Protection Policies into Two Types

So far, the intensity, breadth, and depth of environmental protection work has reached the peak since the reform and opening up. However, as the cyclical economic fluctuation approaches, we have to think about the problems such as adjusting the environmental protection policy tools by combining the intensity of environmental protection work with the needs of economic growth, so as to make environmental protection work a "means of macro-control" for overcoming cyclical economic fluctuations.

(1) *The cause of an imbalanced environmental–economic relationship should be "divided into two."* The essence of environmental problems is an "imbalanced relationship between environment and economy," which can be expressed as "highlighting economy and downplaying environment" (i.e., environmental conservatism); it can also be expressed as "highlighting environment and downplaying economy" (i.e., environmental radicalism). No matter which scenario it is, as long as the environmental–economic relationship is imbalanced, it will undermine the overall welfare of society. For most of human history, "environmental conservatism" makes us overestimate the importance of economic development, thus causing environmental problems. Therefore, people have started opposing "environmental conservatism," but lack vigilance to "environmental radicalism." In fact, at certain stages of development, "environmental radicalism" may cause greater damage to the economy.

(2) *The solution to an imbalanced environmental–economic relationship should be "divided into two."* There are two types of "imbalance" between environment and economy: One is a "static" imbalance between environmental quality and level of economic development (either environmental quality lags behind or keeps ahead of economic development), and the other is a "dynamic" imbalance between environmental quality and level of economic development (whether changing environmental quality is compatible with changing economic development in the process of dynamic development).

For this reason, the solution to an "imbalanced" relationship between environment and economy needs to be divided into two sides. For one thing, if environmental quality is not compatible with level of economic development, we have to implement appropriate policies to correct this imbalance in the mid-to-long term. For example, in the context of continuously deteriorating environmental quality, it is necessary to strengthen environmental constraints and vigorously improve environmental quality. For the other thing, in case of a dynamic imbalance between environmental protection and economic growth, it is necessary to tactically adjust relevant policy tools in a timely and flexible manner while sticking to the mid- to long-term strategies. For example, while following the guidelines for environmental protection in the mid-to-long term, the intensity of short-term environmental protection work can be adjusted to satisfy the needs of economic growth, and different policy tools can be adopted.

(3) *The environmental protection policies amid the economic downturn should be "divided into two."* No matter the economic growth keeps going up or slows down, the implementation of environmental protection policies shall be "divided into two," especially in the case of economic downturn.

First, we must unswervingly adhere to the guideline of sustainable development. For a long time to come, the relationship between environment and economy will remained imbalanced; to be specific, it is the imbalance between lower environmental quality and higher economic development level. Therefore, environmental protection as a basic national policy must be persevered in the mid-to-long term. It is only when environmental quality and level of economic development are basically balanced, the work of environmental protection may become less urgent. Given this, environmental protection will remain a long-last endeavor within 30 years. In both short term and mid-to-long term, higher emission standards, stricter environmental protection laws and regulations, and tighter pollution discharge capacity will become the norm.

Second, we must combine environmental protection with economic growth. In the short term, China is in the downward period of the economic cycle, and may even enter the "recession period," so environmental protection must be coordinated with economic growth. Specifically, as for the second type of imbalance between environment and economy, people's aspiration for environmental protection may be stronger than that for economic growth. Therefore, we must think about how to combine the needs of mid- to long-term environmental protection with the need to overcome periodical economic fluctuations. On the one hand, we may appropriately loosen the requirements of environmental protection (e.g., emissions reduction targets) to help companies withstand the impact of economic downturn. On the other hand, we may transform environmental governance into tools to reverse periodical economic fluctuations, and divert the environmental investment into the weak links of the economic system, so as to stimulate economic growth and increase employment opportunities, and realize the "green transformation and recovery of economy."

Third, we must adopt more flexible environmental protection policy tools. While implementing the environmental protection policies on basis of environmental standards, more market-based environmental protection policies shall be carried out. For example, with the help of green financing policies, we can vigorously implement the "Clear Water and Green Mountains" project in an aim to achieve the dynamic balance between intertemporal environmental investment and economic benefit.

Generally speaking, in the new stage of development, environmental protection work must promote green development, not only on the environmental side, but also on the economic side, so as to better serve the goal of high-quality development and achieve mid- to long-term sustainable development.

Part 1

Economic Analysis of Green Development

Chapter 1

Coordinate Economic Growth and Environmental Protection: An Economic Analysis of Environmental Kuznets Curve

1.1 Introduction

The natural environment and economic growth had remained in a state of harmonious coexistence for most of the time throughout the human history. Prior to the era of industrialization, human beings with little knowledge about nature had to depend on it both objectively and subjectively. In the agricultural society, the mode of production did no harm to the natural environment; instead, it was largely restricted by climatic and geographic conditions. This backward mode of production helped to realize the most primitive harmony between man and nature. However, since industrialized production became part of human life, social productivity has improved constantly. From an objective perspective, people first got rid of their dependence on nature, and then learned to explore it, conquer it, and even plunder it. From a subjective perspective, people were able to discontinue their worship of nature. Industrial civilization flourished unprecedentedly, industrial technology emerged as a new spiritual power, and technological development never stopped, which inspired people to turn to self-admiration. During this period, the relationship between man and nature was on the whole inharmonious. Economic growth was over-expanding, boosted by the highly developed social productivity, while the natural environment was gravely undermined, which constituted the most prominent contradiction at that time. Resource exhaustion, ecological imbalance, and environmental degradation had led to a tremendous conflict between nature and human beings that are a part of it. As a result, human development was caught in a dilemma of sustaining economic growth and protecting environment. However, both are vital for human beings, and they ought to be synchronized and harmonized. How can we choose only one of them? Should we return to the pre–Industrial era primitive harmony dominated by nature after the natural environment is ruined? Or should we stop blind development to pursue a new state of harmony dominated by mankind? The first option is what we want the least. Being highly civilized, self-conscious, and productive, we human beings must comprehend the logical relationship between economic growth and natural environmental protection, and on this basis, choose a scientific development path that leads to the harmonious coexistence between man and nature.

In the 1960s, people started paying attention to the relationship between economic growth and natural environmental protection dated back to the pre–Industrial Age. In the 200 years after the Industrial Revolution of the late 1700s, economic growth had continued accelerating as propelled by industrialization. However, the economic growth model was characterized by high input, high consumption, and high pollution, the resulting pressure upon the natural environment continued mounting and finally manifested in extreme ways. By the 1960s, some parts of the world had seen disappearance of forests, loss of biodiversity, soil degradation, air and water pollution, natural resource exhaustion, and environmental destruction. Living in a deteriorating environment, hundreds of thousands of people died from pollution. Amid this ecological crisis, the people who had been obsessed with economic growth were gradually awakened; they began to rethink the necessity of environmental protection and call for sustainable growth. The ensuing half a century had witnessed the environmental protection movement extend to all over the world. At the end of the 20th century, China worked out a strategic plan for sustainable development: *Agenda of 21st Century of China — Population, Environment and Development of China in the 21st Century.*

However, at the beginning of the 21st century, while environmental issues are becoming increasingly globalized, the relationship between economic growth and environmental protection has begun to diverge in regions with different levels of development. On one hand, in developed countries, the fruits of long-term economic achievements have begun to feed back the natural environment many years ago, and their economic growth has begun to jump out of the traditional model, which has led to a gradual improvement in the natural environment in some areas. On the other hand, in developing countries, the economy is still in the initial stage of development. Although they know the importance of environmental protection, their continuous industrialization and urbanization has objectively brought great pressure on the natural environment, leading to the degradation of their environment day by day. In addition, the severe environmental degradation in developing countries has aggravated the deterioration of the global natural environment through the transmission mechanism of the ecosystem, thus causing disputes between countries. The key question is how to view the economic growth of developing countries. With regard to developing countries, can they learn from the traditional economic growth model of "pollution first, treatment later" that developed countries have implemented, or can they bypass the traditional economic growth stage and directly implement a low-input, low-pollution, and low-cost growth model. In order to answer this question, we need to review the confrontation and coordination that developed countries have experienced in the relationship between economic growth and environmental quality, and determine the causes to provide reference for developing countries.

By starting from the Environmental Kuznets Curve (EKC) that reflects the empirical relationship between economic growth and environmental quality in Western developed countries, this book explores the inherent logic between economic growth and environmental protection in human society through the research methods of Marxist political economy, for the purpose of providing theoretical support and reference for China to realize the ultimate harmony between man and nature in the process of economic growth.

1.2 The Empirical Relationship Between Economic Growth and Environmental Quality: Proposal, Connotations, and Origin of EKC

1.2.1 *Proposal of EKC*

In the mid-1950s, Simon Kuznets put forward a hypothesis when studying economic growth and income differences: In the early stage of economic growth, income difference will increase with economic growth, and when economic growth reaches a certain point, this difference begins to shrink. In a two-dimensional space, with income difference as the ordinate and per capita income as the abscissa, this hypothesis is an inverted U-shaped relationship (see Figure 1.1). This relationship, which was later confirmed by the statistical data of a large number of empirical studies, was known as the Kuznets Curve.

In the past few decades, empirical studies have shown that the relationship between economic growth and environmental pollution also presents a U-shaped relationship to varying degrees. In the entire process of economic growth, the natural environment first deteriorated and then improved. For example, the level of environmental pollution in cities in developed countries continues to decrease with economic growth, and the level of environmental pollution in cities in developing countries continues to increase with economic growth. In the early stage of development, the economy is in a low-level maintenance state, and its impact on natural resources and the environment is relatively limited. The amount of waste discharged is not only limited, but also biodegradable, so the environmental degradation at this time is limited. However, the accelerated economic growth,

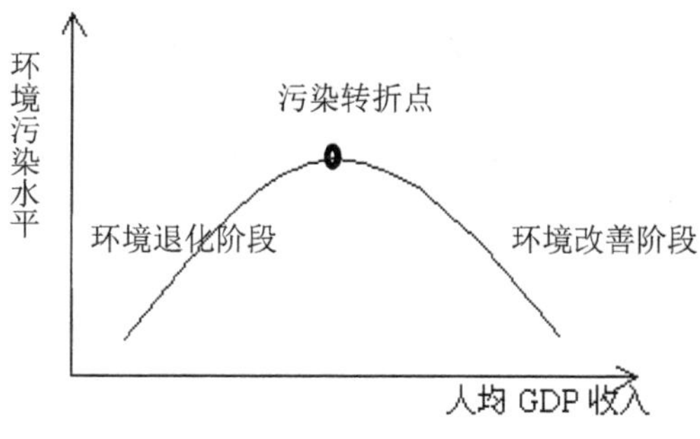

收入差异	Income difference
经济发展阶段	Developing stage
收入转折点	Turning point
经济发达阶段	Developed stage
人均 GDP 收入	Per capita GDP

Figure 1.1. Kuznets Curve.

modernization, and industrialization have caused the rate of resource consumption to exceed the rate of resource renewal, and the amount and toxicity of waste emissions have increased significantly, resulting in continuous environmental degradation. After the economic development reaches a high level, people's environmental awareness has been strengthened, environmental control measures have become more effective, technology has become more advanced, and environmental governance expenditure has further increased in order to curb environmental degradation.

Because this inverted U curve that may exist between economic growth and environmental pollution levels is similar to the inverted U curve proposed by Kuznets for depicting the relationship between economic growth and income difference, Panayotou (1993) named it as the Environmental Kuznets Curve (EKC).

1.2.2 *Connotations of EKC*

The core content of the EKC includes five aspects:

First, the degradation of environmental quality is inevitable to some extent at the economic take-off stage. Before the pollutant discharge reaches the turning point, economic growth and environmental pollution level will remain in a contradictory relationship, namely any gain for one must mean a loss for the other.

Second, as result of rapid economic growth, extensive natural resources are consumed, environmental quality is further deteriorated, and scarcity of environmental resources has become a prominent issue, thus requiring more investment to be poured into environmental protection. When economic development comes to a certain stage, it will create favorable conditions for improving environmental quality.

Third, the relationship between environmental pollution level and economic growth is, on the whole, characterized by an inverted U curve, as shown in Figure 1.2. Environmental pollution level can be evaluated by such metric as per capita pollutant discharge or pollutant concentration, while economic growth is generally assessed by the metric of per capita GDP. Since it takes a long time for a nation to transform from a less developed economy into a relatively developed one, the relationship between economic growth and environmental pollution level as depicted by the EKC will be of long existence.

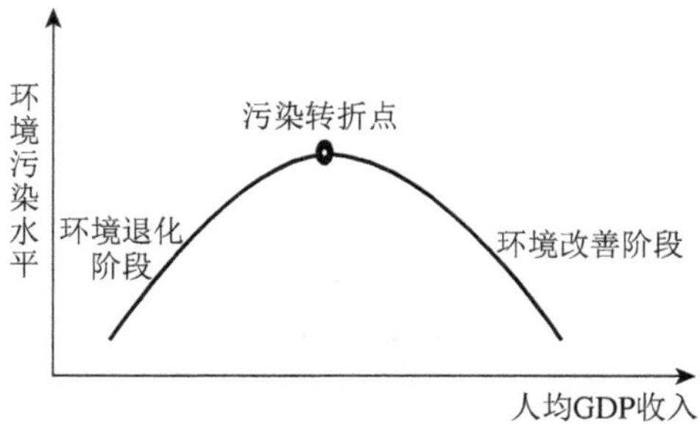

环境污染水平	Level of environmental pollution
环境退化阶段	Stage of environmental degradation
污染转折点	Turning point
环境改善阶段	Stage of environmental improvement
人均 GDP 收入	Per capita GDP

Figure 1.2. Environmental Kuznets Curve (EKC).

Fourth, institutional factors, including economic growth pattern and environmental policies, play an important role in altering the trend and shape of the EKC. As shown in Figure 1.3, the three EKCs under different environmental policies and institutional arrangements are different from one another.

- Curve A is irrespective of the costs of environmental destruction. If property rights are not clearly defined, pollution externality is not yet endogenous, or there are subsidies to the acts that harm resources and environment, then environmental degradation is likely to exceed the ecological threshold.
- Curve B takes into account some environmental costs. By employing certain policy means, such as developing environmental standards and removing harmful environmental subsidies, Curve B is somewhat flattened, with the peak of environmental degradation lowered.
- Curve C is free of most environmental costs. By clarifying property rights, internalizing costs, and removing harmful environmental subsidies, the peak of Curve C is further lowered, marking that the

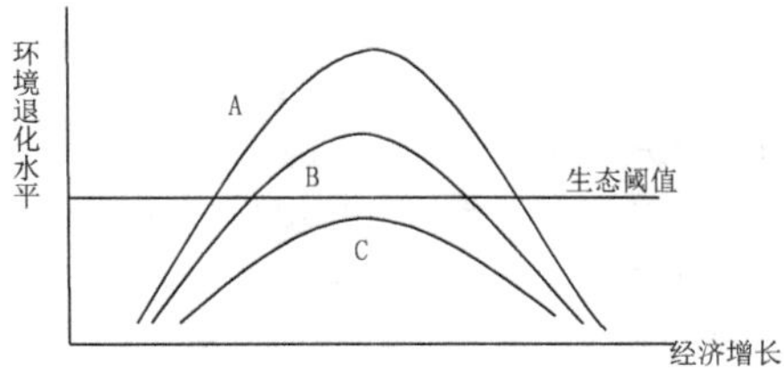

环境退化水平	Level of environmental degradation
生态阈值	Ecological threshold
经济增长	Economic growth

Figure 1.3. EKC under different environmental policies and institutional arrangements.

damage to environment caused by economic development is reduced to a relatively low level, namely the environmental destruction at the stage of economic take-off is effectively prevented.

Fifth, the EKC reveals the connection or transformation rule between economic growth and environmental quality, but this does not mean that developing countries are bound to improve their environment at a certain stage of economic development. When exceeding the ecological threshold, environmental degradation will become irreversible. Many critical resources, such as forest, fishery, and soil, have such a threshold. Suppose that these resources are gravely depleted or degraded at the stage of economic take-off, it will take a long time and a high cost to have them restored. In this case, even if the inverted U curve does exist, supporting policies and international assistance are needed to prevent the curve from exceeding the ecological threshold.

1.2.3 *Origin of EKC*

Since the EKC was proposed, environmental scholars in China and across the world have carried out empirical studies by nation and by region to prove this curve. To this end, they have employed various economic models, such as optimizing growth model, production factors' output model, endogenous growth model, and cross-generation model.

It is generally believed that the EKC is formed mainly on two theoretical bases in the realm of environmental protection:

One is payment preference theory, which holds that environmental quality is a luxury commodity, and high-income consumers have a higher effective demand for this commodity than low-income earners. Amid increasing resident income and continuous economic growth, environmental pollution is to be reduced and government is to be more capable of increasing investment in environmental protection.

The other is institution change theory, which holds that it is the changes in systems (including environmental policies and increased investment in environmental protection) that have led economic structure, technologies, and organizational forms to develop in the direction of pollution abatement along with economic growth.

1.2.4 *Significance and limitations of EKC*

The EKC is of great application value.

First, it shows that in the course of a country's development, especially at the take-off stage of industrialization, a certain degree of environmental degradation is inevitable.

Second, it shows that after per capita income reaches a certain level, economic growth will transform from the enemy of environment into its friend, even though economic growth can only compensate for the previous environmental damage over a long period of time. If economic growth does good to environment, then growth-stimulating endeavors, such as free trade, economic restructuring, and price reform, should also be environment friendly.

However, the EKC leads some people to misinterpret the relationship between economic growth and environmental quality. Some scholars even draw an extreme conclusion from this inverted U curve: There is no need to highlight environmental protection in either domestic policies or international assistance; sustainable development is simply a stage where we, by sustaining economic growth, transcend from the segment of environmental pollution in the curve to the segment of environmental improvement.

Of course, such a laissez-faire attitude toward environmental pollution can never be a best choice, because we need a very long time to get past the stage of environmental degradation, economic achievement and a cleaner environment in the future may hardly offset the current environmental damage. Therefore, it is more reasonable for us to start controlling pollutant discharge and resource depletion in the early stage of economic development.

From the perspective of economic input, earlier prevention and control of environmental pollution may be more cost-effective than doing so in the future. Moreover, certain types of environmental disruption at the early stage of economic development may lead to irreversible consequences at a later stage.

Economic growth is constrained by certain types of environmental disruption, such as soil erosion, inability to recover from natural disasters, reservoir sedimentation, deteriorating human health induced by respiratory diseases, lower productivity, and lost working hours caused by traffic congestion. Environmental degradation therefore ought to be directly controlled by implementing appropriate environmental policies and setting up an environment-specific investment, for the purpose of removing the obstacles to economic growth.

1.3 Logical and Causal Relationships Between Economic Growth and Environmental Quality: Theoretical Explanation

Based on the empirically discovered relationship between economic growth and environmental quality, economists have started exploring their logical and causal relationships. The focus of their discussion is placed on the change rule of environmental quality amid economic growth and on the role of economic growth in the changes of environmental quality (Hou, 2005). As for developing countries (including China), in the context of deteriorating environment, the hot topic of discussion is whether they should prioritize economy over environment or do the opposite. To figure out the logical and causal relationships between economic growth and environmental quality, we need to answer these questions: Is economic growth opposed to environmental quality as shown by the inverted U curve? What is the impact of economic growth on environmental quality?

1.3.1 *Different standpoints*

Regarding the impact of economic growth on environmental quality, there are two types of standpoints in the international academic community:

One is pessimistic, holding that economic growth is sure to seize more resources and services from the natural environment, and then cause pollution and resource depletion, thus bringing unavoidable damage to environmental quality. The typical supporters of this view are academics with the Club of Rome, which was set up in the 1960s. In their co-authored treatise on economics (Meadows *et al.*, 1972), they proposed to transform the traditional economic growth pattern and effectively control population and consumption, so as to achieve a relatively static state of balanced development across the world, which, according to them, was the only way resource and environmental disasters can be avoided.

The other is optimistic, believing that economic growth can harmoniously coexist with the environment since it is able to promote technological breakthrough, system rationalization, and resource conservation. Despite its temporary negative impact on the environment, economic growth itself will solve the problem of environmental pollution and become a friend of the environment. Beckman and Panayotou (1993) are representative scholars who are optimistic about the relationship between economic growth and environmental quality. According to Panayoutou's report submitted to the United Nations, when per capita income reaches a certain level, economic growth will transform from being an enemy of the environment into its friend. Such transformation means that we do not have to pay special attention to the environment; domestic policies or international pressure and assistance regarding the environment are totally unnecessary; and resources should be mainly consumed for achieving rapid economic growth so as to quickly transit from the stage where it goes against the environment to the stage where it is environment friendly.

So, which standpoint is more convincing? It is beyond doubt that economic growth, which is characterized by urbanization and industrialization, will exert some negative effects on the environment, but at the same time it creates material conditions for improving the environment, which is especially the case for developing countries where people's livelihood is the top priority. In order to shake off poverty and build a well-off society, these countries have no other way out but accelerate economic development and subordinate environmental improvement to economic growth. Nevertheless, as long as there is reasonable institutional guarantee, economic growth itself can still improve the environment to some extent.

1.3.2 *Economic basis for environmental protection*

Economic growth has both negative and positive effects on the environment:

The negative effect is mainly reflected in the pressure on resources and the environment from expansion of economic scale. No matter how economic structure and technologies are improved, the expanding production and consumption of mankind will inevitably lead to resource depletion and environmental pollution. That is why economic growth goes against the improvement of environmental quality.

However, economic growth also has a positive effect on the environment, which is mainly split into structural effect and technological effect:

(1) *Structural effect*. In the process of economic growth, the proportion of primary, secondary, and tertiary industries in the economy will gradually change. In the early stage, the secondary industry characterized by high input, high consumption, and high pollution develops at a rapid pace, and the economic structure mainly based on heavy industry will deteriorate environmental quality. In the later stage, the tertiary industry will gain prominence, fostering a less polluting economic structure.

(2) *Technological effect*. This will reduce pollutant discharge per unit of GDP through technological improvements, environmental policies, and economic restructuring. Economic growth will help increase capital investment and invent more effective and higher value-added technologies, all of which contribute to the reduction of pollutant discharge per unit of GDP. By replacing backward and inefficient technologies and industries with new ones, the absolute amount of pollutant discharge can be reduced. For example, Japan ascribes its economic success in the past 15 years to substantial reductions in energy use and pollutant discharge. Germany has not only maintained industrial growth but also considerably alleviated environmental pollution by implementing an emission trading system, phasing out old plants and equipment, and deploying new process and technologies. This shows that the technological progress brought about by economic growth has an enormous effect on improving the environment.

Considering the negative and positive effects of economic growth on the environment, we have to make a trade-off between them: When economic growth does more good than harm to the environment, it is better to vigorously develop the economy; otherwise, we should slow down the economic development and intensify efforts to protect the environment. As far as developing countries are concerned, they must abandon large-scale, resource-dependent growth patten without delay, and focus on economic restructuring and technological progress.

1.3.3 *Environmental basis for economic growth*

The above analysis, which shows different effects of economic growth on the environment, starts from economic growth itself, but ignores the importance of the natural environment from a purely logical perspective. In fact, environmental quality also plays a decisive role in economic growth. Karl Marx had made an in-depth analysis of this issue when expounding the development law of social productive forces.

According to Marx, there is a logical causal relationship between the natural environment and economic growth: The former is the cause and the latter is the result. He deemed productive force as a multi-level system composed of three parts, namely its source, itself and its result (Zhang, 1989). Regarding the source (or starting point) of productive force, Marx had split it into three levels: (1) Forces of nature; (2) Forces of humans and their surroundings; and (3) Forces of science and technology formed and accumulated by humans in transformation of nature. Among them, the forces of nature involve all the natural environmental systems on which humans depend for survival and production. The means of livelihood required for human survival, such as forests, water sources, atmosphere, and soil, come from the natural environment; and the means of production, such as biological resources and energy, also come from the natural environment. Hence, the natural environment plays a decisive role in promoting economic growth (including the productive force as manifested in labor force, means of labor and objects of labor, and the result of productive force as manifested in labor productivity). The process of economic growth must coexist with the natural environment. "Environmental protection is in essence to protect social productive force, and rational development of natural forces is to properly utilize all environmental resources for developing social productive force" (Zhang, 1989). In short, the protection and rational use of natural forces are actually creating an environmental foundation for economic growth.

On the surface, Marx's analysis tells us the importance of environmental foundations for economic growth, but its core is to explain the logical relationship between the two, that is, the causal relationship. Being a causal relationship, it logically means that at different stages, "effect" may become "cause." As Marx has analyzed, improved labor productivity (i.e., economic growth) is both the result of the development of productivity and the material basis for the further development of productivity. It can change from the result to the cause to get the internal driving force for the development of productivity, thereby promoting the further development of sources of productivity (natural force, labor force, science and technology) (Zhang, 1989). This explanation accurately grasps the essence of the EKC. In the process of economic development, the quality of resources and environment is not only the basis, source, and cause of economic development but also the result, goal, and purpose of economic development. Therefore, we can neither abandon the environment to develop the economy nor abandon economic growth to protect the environment.

1.4 Coordinating Economic Growth and Environmental Protection: Passage of EKC

The mutual causality and mutual influence of economic growth and environmental protection tells us that developing countries can learn lessons from the EKC's depiction of the economic growth path of Western developed countries, especially learn to coordinate economic growth and environmental protection through policy design and find out a way out from this inverted U curve.

1.4.1 *Theory of EKC passage*

Environmental economists believe that, by summarizing the experiences of developed countries with the EKC and taking account of their own national conditions, developing countries can design relevant systems to make up for the inherent shortcomings of economic policies and minimize the deviation between private decision-making and socially optimal decision-making, thereby promoting a benign interaction between economic development and environmental conditions, and changing the shape of their own inverted U curve.

Just as the Sri Lankan scholar Munasinghe (1995) pointed out, if the sustainable development strategy and the government's environmental policy are implemented in the process of economic growth, the arc of the inverted U curve can be reduced, and the inflection point may come earlier, so that a horizontal passage can be found on this inverted U curve (see Figure 1.4). This happens to be the theory of EKC passage.

To put it simply, the passage theory refers to the fact that developing countries adjust their own economic policies by learning from the

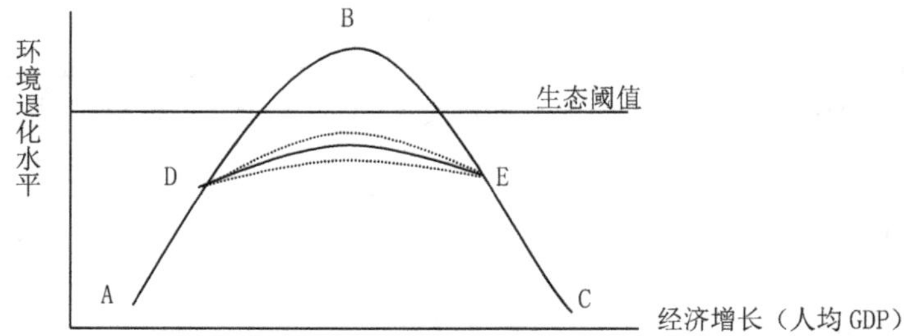

环境退化水平	Level of environmental degradation
生态阈值	Ecological threshold
经济增长	Economic growth (per capita GDP)

Figure 1.4. EKC passage.

experiences of developed countries, thus no longer repeating the old development path of "treatment comes after pollution."

1.4.2 *Construction of an EKC passage: Policy suggestions for coordinating economic growth and environmental protection*

The construction of an EKC passage in developing countries is essentially a question of how developing countries can effectively coordinate the relationship between economic growth and environmental protection, that is, how late-developing countries make use of their own favorable conditions to effectively protect the environment in the process of economic growth by formulating policies, and at the same time improve the "sources" of economic growth through environmental governance. Specifically, as a developing country, China should implement a sustainable development strategy in the following aspects:

(1) *Learn from the policy practices of developed countries, formulate systematic policies, and eliminate the negative environmental effects of growth-oriented economic policies*. The practices of developed countries show that the growth-oriented economic policies can easily cause overall

pressure on resources. However, to eliminate the negative effects of these policies, it is not necessary to deny the policies themselves. They can come up with supplementary policies to make up for the shortcomings and deficiencies of the original policies, improve the functions of the original policies, increase the social and environmental benefits of the policies, and raise the efficiency of economic operation.

It is particularly important for developing countries to use the synergy effect of policies to eliminate the inherent defects of the policies themselves. Economic development is the top priority of developing countries. Their economic growth rate must be high enough to create conditions for them to get rid of poverty and ease employment pressure. The experiences of developed countries have shown that economic development does not necessarily have to pay the cost and price of environmental degradation. By integrating the functions and effects of different policies, developing countries can achieve a win–win situation for the common development of economy and society.

Regarding how to eliminate the adverse effects of economic policies on the environment, in addition to the implementation of auxiliary policies, the timing of macroeconomic policies and sectoral policies needs to be adjusted to mitigate the adverse effects to a certain extent.

(2) *Learn from the pollution control experiences of developed countries and innovate environmental protection system, so as to create favorable external conditions for their own economic growth.* Looking at the evolution history of environmental protection systems in developed countries, the earliest system is likely to be the Pigovian tax, which was based on the analysis of externalities in classical economics. Since manufacturers have not thought about the environmental damage caused by their production, the marginal private cost line is lower than the marginal social cost line, their production at the equilibrium point where the marginal private cost line intersects with the price line is bound to generate higher output than the optimal level of social production, hence causing excessive pollution to society. Therefore, according to Pigou's proposition, as long as a pollution tax equal to the difference between the marginal private cost and the marginal social cost is imposed on the manufacturer, and the marginal private cost line of the manufacturer is forced to rise to the marginal social cost line, the pollution problem can be easily solved.

The collection of Pigovian tax was once considered the only effective pollution control system in the West, but in the mid-20th century, with the development of information economics, people had a new understanding of the limitations of this system. The prerequisite for the effective implementation of Pigovian tax is the correct determination of the marginal private cost of the manufacturer and the marginal social cost. However, in reality, due to the existence of information asymmetry and the lack of incentive mechanisms for business owners to provide this information, the government has to bear an extremely high cost to acquire marginal private cost. The marginal social cost is even more difficult to measure, because it involves physical damage caused by pollutants and people's reactions and feelings to such damage, as well as the process of monetary measurement (i.e., the "dose–response relationship"). Therefore, the Pigovian tax was either too low or too high in practice. If it was determined to be too low, it would not achieve the anticipated environmental protection effect; if it was too high, it would inevitably affect the enthusiasm of companies to invest, then the production scale of companies might be lower than the social optimal level, which would have an adverse effect on the overall social output level and economic growth. Therefore, since the 1970s to the 1980s, people have increasingly turned their attention to another institutional arrangement — emissions trading.

Compared with the Pigovian tax, emissions trading does not need to determine in advance the amount of emission tax that is difficult to measure. It only needs to determine the upper limit of the emission volume from the environmental-carrying capacity; and through the issuance of tradable emission rights, the trading price can be determined according to the condition of supply and demand. The advantage of this system also lies in that, with the entry or exit of enterprises and the change of social production scale, emissions trading can easily enable the government to make dynamic choices between economic scale and environmental protection.

Through emissions trading, the government can proceed from the local reality and formulate the most suitable local development strategy between the economy and the environment.

(3) *Introduce the environmental protection and pollution control technologies of developed countries to promote the development of their own environmental protection industry.* The progress of environmental

technology is the key to the effective implementation of various environmental protection policies and systems. The prerequisite for the collection of pollution taxes is the setting of environmental safety standards. For example, to ensure the smooth implementation of the emissions trading system, the first problem that needs to be solved is to scientifically and reasonably determine the upper limit of the emission volume and the pollution level of each enterprise. In addition, the advancement of environmental protection technology can also promote the country's economic development. Taking the emission rights trading system as an example, the advancement of environmental protection technology will increase the environmentally acceptable pollution emissions, thereby increasing the supply of emission rights. Therefore, under the same situation that the demand for emission rights remains unchanged, the price of emission rights that enterprises need to pay will decline, the scale of social investment will expand, and the level of welfare will be improved. Therefore, many countries regard the development of high-tech environmental protection technologies as one of their long-term development strategies. The US, Japan, and Germany are powerful countries in the global environmental protection industry, and their environmental protection industry has become a pillar in their domestic industries. They have developed a series of new techniques, new energy, and new materials, covering the process from production to consumption, and achieved the goal of saving energy and curbing pollution.

As a latecomer, developing countries have certain advantages in introducing these advanced technologies. They only need to pay a small amount of cost to import the technological results from developed countries that have consumed a huge amount of investment both tangible and intangible. Theoretically speaking, for countries that are latecomers in industrialization, there will be more technology stocks for them to utilize, allowing them to catch up with developed countries at a faster pace.

In short, economic growth and environmental protection are dilemmas faced by most developing countries. Economic backwardness gives the government a strong impulse for development, but this is often accompanied by the uncontrolled use and destruction of the country's resources and environment. The EKC passage theory provides us with another idea for overall development. Late-mover advantages also exist in the field of sustainable development. As long as developing countries are good at learning from advanced policies, systems, and technologies of developed countries, and drawing lessons from their experiences, they can blaze a path of leapfrog economic development and sustainable environmental development that suit their national conditions.

1.5 Summary

To sum up, economic growth and environmental protection are not categorically opposed and irreconcilable. As long as the two are included in the mission of sustainable development, they can be mutually restrictive and complementary.

On one hand, economic growth should become the core issue in sustainable development. Poverty has always been the greatest danger to environmental protection. Only by maintaining the continuous growth of the economy and the continuous improvement of the living standards of the members of the society can we provide the material basis for environmental protection and governance. On the other hand, economic growth should not be at the expense of greater damage or pollution to the environment. While implementing their economic growth policies, all countries shall seek as much social welfare as possible with minimal costs of resources and environment.

Even so, the current environmental effects of economic growth must be further studied from the following three aspects:

(1) There is still a lack of sufficient long-term and systematic follow-up research on the environmental impact of economic policies. Some economic policies, such as exchange rate changes and privatization issues in trade reforms, may have an impact on society, and there is still little research in this regard. At the same time, the innovation of new research methods and analytical frameworks is also the need for in-depth research in this field.

(2) Political management systems and systems should also be included in future work. Since the nature of environmental and social issues depends to a large extent on the distribution of government power and resources, each political reform will have a profound impact on the distribution of income and wealth, and the institutional impact cannot be ignored when economic policies are implemented.

(3) In order to better conduct systematic research on the environmental impact of economic policies, the value of resources and the environment and the design of sustainable development indicators are also issues worthy of further study, such as the construction of green GDP.

Chapter 2

Rethinking the Implications of Economics in Environmental Kuznets Curve

As mentioned in Chapter 1, there is an inverted U curve in environmental economics, namely Environmental Kuznets Curve (EKC), which is dedicated to describing the relationship between economic growth and environmental quality. However, with a variety of research techniques, the academic circle of economics has not yet drawn a final conclusion on this curve, but generally defines it as a hypothesis, which is to say that its authenticity cannot be verified. In spite of this, after EKC emerged in the last decade of the 20th century, it revolutionized the academic world of environmental economics, not only prospering subsequent studies in this regard but also becoming one of the most important theoretical creations since environmental economics was born in the middle of the 20th century.

This curve (or a hypothesis) has its origins: What kind of background and opportunity that promoted the emergence of this curve? Was there any theoretical basis that gave rise to this curve? Only when its origins are identified can we make further explorations to find out how does this curve, which appears simple and clear, benefit China's environmental protection practices.

In a word, EKC is used to describe the variation relationship between economic growth and environmental quality.

Prior to this, environmental problems had spread across Western developed countries a long time ago. By the early 1990s, people had "preconceived" economic growth as the culprit of environmental problems, arguing that it was rapid economic growth that resulted in high pollution and high emissions, and got them bogged down in wrong patterns of production and consumption, thus causing large-scale environmental pollution and deterioration of eco-environmental quality.

Because of this understanding, the pioneering environmentalists in Western developed countries took economic growth as an established exogenous condition, namely it is inevitable. Society must progress and economy must develop, but solving environmental problems are also a must-do. In this case, they had to turn to institutional arrangements, that is, adjust and improve all institutional arrangements for environmental protection. With institutional constraints, environmental degradation can be reversed to the greatest extent free from interrupting economic development.

This gave rise to the earliest theory of environmental economics which is based on property rights and internalization of externalities. Ronald H. Coase, one of the most innovative and provocative economists of the 20th century, has made great contributions to environmental protection. Based on the theory of Coase, the school of environmental economics at that time seemed to have found a solution to environmental problems, that is, eliminate "market failures" by internalizing "externalities," and let eco-environment serve as a kind of "factor" resource which can be reasonably allocated by market on the basis of maximized social welfare.

The above interpretation is apparently tenable since environmental problems indeed have their institutional origins. Many environmental protection practices have proved that as long as "shared property rights" are reasonably defined, the externalities of environmental pollution can be eliminated, thereby restoring environmental pollution to a socially optimal level.

According to the famous "Coase Theorem," the most representative and the most "confusing" viewpoint of Coase, as long as all transactions are carried out without friction or at zero cost, then the externalities can be addressed by the market itself, but in case of a friction or a high cost in the transaction process, the externalities need to be solved through government intervention or law enforcement. This theorem lays a theoretical basis for developing emissions trading market: since the market is able to address externalities, we can build a market for raising the allocation efficiency of eco-environmental resources, such as a carbon emissions trading market.

The theories of property rights and externalities once dominated the early study on environmental economics. Even the *Limits to Growth* theory (holding that resources and environment are probably more associated with economic growth, but failing to provide strong arguments or accurate predictions for various reasons) put forward by the Roman Club — another important school of environmental economics emerged in the 1970s — could not challenge the position of the theories of property rights and externalities in the field of environmental protection. It was during this period that environmental protection laws, regulations, and markets sprang up like mushrooms, stimulating Western countries to pin their hopes for environmental protection on institutional changes. This situation had remained so until the 1990s.

What happened in the 1990s was that Western countries had improved their environment. Both academia and industry ascribed this achievement to institutional changes and called on other countries to establish an environmental protection system. However, the reality was not encouraging. On one hand, while some developed countries had improved their environment, other countries and regions were seeing their environment deteriorate. On the other hand, carbon dioxide emissions had been increasing year by year, which threatened the development of human beings. Considering the pressing environmental concerns, the United Nations convened the first global environmental summit in 1990 to mainly discuss these two issues. This summit yielded two results: The motion of the "21st Century Agenda" was released to promote sustainable development; and the issue of tackling climate change was introduced. These two results implied that sustainable development was far from being realized; instead, it was ought to draw more attention. Now that the institutional origins of environmental problems were found and improved, why did new problems continue to crop up?

In fact, the early theories about the root causes of environmental problems had examined the causes beyond institution. For example, in a well-known paper "The Tragedy of the Commons" (Hardin, 1968) published in 1968, the author not only analyzed the overuse of resources and the resulting environmental destruction from the institutional perspective but also pointed out that the changes in "scarcity" of resources can also lead to their overexploitation. He observed that when resources are not scarce, there will be no problem of externalities or overuse of resources regardless of ambiguous property rights; however, in the case of a large population and extremely scarce resources, poorly defined property rights will cause serious externalities, and then result in environmental pollution and disruption.

The most valuable part of the above theories is to contend that, under the fixed institutional condition, the economic growth level — representing the degree of resource scarcity — also affects the eco-environment. Unfortunately, such an enlightening viewpoint was not taken seriously by the academia at that time. In other words, this viewpoint was not welcome at that time when economic growth was a task transcending all others (similar to the current situation in China).

In addition, in the 1990s, there was another factor, namely free trade, that motivated people to ascribe the evolution of environmental quality to economic growth. According to the previous theoretical hypothesis, free trade usually results in the transfer of environmental pollution industries from developed countries to developing countries. Many economists took interest in this hypothesis and devoted themselves into the research and demonstration in this regard. Among them, the American economists Grossman and Krueger came up with the EKC.

Grossman and Kruger had been used to studying free trade and the transnational transfer of environmental pollution, especially in the US and Mexico. However, in the process of research, they felt that if free trade has an impact on the transfer of environmental pollution, is environmental pollution also related to the economic growth behind free trade? In other words, the transfer of pollution and emissions is not determined by free trade, but by the factors such as economic growth and income level. As a result, they turned to studying the relationship between economic growth and environmental quality. Based on the data of various countries, they came to a basic conclusion that, with the economic growth of a country or region (mainly based on the indicator of per capita income), there will be mounting discharge of major pollutants and deteriorating environmental quality at the initial stage. However, after a certain period of time, if the economy continues to grow, then after the level of economic growth has passed a certain stage of development, the discharge of major pollutants will reach a peak and then start declining. This relationship between environment and economy could be illustrated by the EKC.

Why is this curve not named after the two economists themselves? This is because this curve is exactly in the same shape as the curve on income levels and the gap between the rich and the poor discovered by Simon Kuznets in the 1960s, so the two economists decided to name this curve as the "Environmental Kuznets Curve."

The emergence of EKC symbolizes that the development of environmental economics has begun to take a turning point: Researchers no longer try to look for the causes of environmental problems at the institutional level, but turn to identifying the causes from the perspective of economic growth and having them addressed. According to subsequent studies, there are several reasons why economic growth causes environmental problems.

(1) With the expansion of the scale of production and consumption, the absolute scarcity of resources and the environment has been created. According to the theory of "scarce rent," people generally develop resources or environments with good endowment conditions (e.g., good farmland) first, and then develop those with poor endowment conditions (e.g., thin farmland), In this way, with population growth and economic growth, the expansion of the overall development scale will inevitably cause marginal resources in areas with fragile eco-environments to be introduced into the economic system, that is, gradually break through the carrying capacity of the eco-environment, resulting in environmental degradation.
(2) In the process of economic growth, due to the development needs of urbanization, a large number of heavy chemical industries will inevitably be introduced. These industries are pollution-intensive, that is, at a certain stage of economic growth, the overall economic volume will appear to be "cumbersome" and the economic structure is not reasonable enough. This problem has caused double damage to the environment due to modern economic growth. In addition, some problems are brought about by industrial production methods, such as the dye industry. In *Toms River: A Story of Science and Salvation*, a book reflecting on industrial pollution (Fagin, 2013), the author introduces the serious harm caused by the pollution discharged by the chemical industry on rivers and residents' health.
(3) With the progress of globalization, trade liberalization will also bring new environmental problems, especially for developing countries that are disadvantaged in the international trade structure. This is because even if developing countries do not take over the polluting industries transferred from developed countries, they must objectively produce primary products for developed countries. These primary products are often resource- or environmental-pollution-intensive, and their environment obviously has to pay a huge price.

Now that the environmental problems are attributed to the economic side, they must be solved through economic means. This is also the reason why the advanced stage of economic growth may bring about the improvement of environmental quality.

(1) *The transition from absolute scale growth to scale effect.* With the economic growth, the scale of utilization of resources and environment is absolutely expanding and thus becoming scarce, is there any possibility of reducing resources and environmental inputs amid the expansion of the output scale? This is to achieve economic scale effect, which means that the scale of economic output is doubled, and input may only be expanded by 0.5 times or less. If this can be achieved, it means that we can expand the scale and develop the economy without increasing the burden on resources and environment, while the core is to improve the productivity of resources and environment.

(2) *Look for positive factors to improve environmental quality from technological progress.* There have been rich economic researches on technological progress, and many research results show that technological progress is a key contributor to economic growth. However, at the same time, technological progress itself is also affected by factors such as economic growth and population growth. However, technological progress is not directly linked to treatment of environmental pollution in the early stage. Why does economic growth improve environmental quality? The study on EKC has shown that economic growth and technological progress are mutually endogenous processes, that is, economic growth will promote technological progress, and technological progress will benefit the utilization efficiency of resources and environment, not only reducing the level of utilization but also helping the treatment of its end-of-pipe emissions. In this way, there is a big difference between the environmental quality under the scenarios with or without technological advancement.

(3) *Shift from an economic structure that relies on manufacturing industry to a structure that relies on service industry.* As mentioned earlier, since the high-polluting heavy chemical industry is a source of environmental problems, what if chemical production is reduced? Of course, a country cannot naturally or forcibly change its economic/industrial structure suddenly, and such change can only be dictated by the law of economic

growth. Because in the early stage of economic growth, the heavy chemical industry contributes more to economic growth, while in the later stage, the contribution of service and other industries will become greater (from the production side to the consumer side). At this time, with the change of economic structure, pollution will naturally decrease and environmental quality will get improved.

(4) *Shift from preference for material consumption to preference for environmental consumption.* As the economy grows and consumer income levels increase, after consumers have their basic material needs satisfied, they begin to pursue a healthy and high-quality life that is related to the eco-environment, and they are naturally more willing to pay for such a high-quality life, this is why a large number of studies have shown that ecological expenditures are occupying a greater share in the structure of resident payment.

To sum up, the above four reasons can be summarized by scale effect, technology effect, structure effect, and income effect, and all of these effects are related to the higher stage of economic growth. Basically, these four aspects are also the most valuable theoretical findings of the EKC theory.

Based on the above theoretical changes, we can summarize a few points which may be helpful to China's current environmental governance, and it can truly unify the "green waters and green mountains" and "golden mountains and silver mountains."

First of all, the EKC theoretical hypothesis was not put forward in the early stage of the outbreak of environmental problems. This is not accidental, because as mentioned above, even if it is put forward in the initial stage, it will not receive attention. The reason is very simple. The social economy needs to be developed, which is a major premise. Therefore, the early environmental economic theories only paid attention to institutional factors, which is similar to the current situation in China. In another way of thinking, in the process of solving environmental problems, institutional factors should indeed precede economic factors (scarcity factors). If there is no institutional change as a foreshadowing, the environment in Western countries is not necessarily going to be solved naturally with economic growth. This is not only a theoretical logic, but also a practical logic of environmental protection. In a specific stage of economic growth, we cannot protect the environment at the expense of economic growth.

Second, after the institutional factors are truly resolved, whether it is possible to directly transition to the level of economic solution is also a very heated issue at the moment — that is, the relationship between environmental protection and economic development. Looking at the development of theory and practice in the West, even after the institutional factors are resolved, the stage of economic solutions is not quickly reached. The reason is that the success of economic solutions depends on factors such as scale, technology, structure, and expenditure. After we have improved the environmental protection system, institutional factors will be reduced. Will it all be done? It is not necessarily so because there is a high probability that the process of institutional improvement and economic transformation cannot be absolutely unified. There is a time lag, or even a long time lag. Therefore, in order to shift the focus of environmental protection from institutional solutions to economic solutions, the key depends on whether conditions are ripe, rather than institutional factors themselves.

Finally, if we only focus on the institutional and economic aspects of environmental protection, it may seem to be consistent with the theories and practices of Western developed countries, but in fact, there is still an important issue that needs to be resolved, that is the system behind the institution and the economy — in layman's terms, it is the market. It should be understood that the above-mentioned institutional arrangements such as the internalization of property rights and externalities emerged to overcome the incompleteness of the market. In other words, these institutional arrangements are compatible with the standard market in the initial state. If our current local market is not the standard market in the initial state of Western countries, then all subsequent institutional arrangements designed to solve environmental problems and copy the Western economy will not be used to solve this so-called market failure. Similarly, the basis for the change of economic factors is also the initial standard market of Western developed countries. This means that if we cannot adjust the local market to that standard market state, then no change in institutional factors or economic factors can really solve our environmental problems on the basis of the EKC. This is precisely why the market must play a decisive role in resource allocation.

Chapter 3

Convergence of Environmental Quality and Economic Growth: On Natural Capital and Inequality in the 21st Century

3.1 Introduction

Since the 1990s, the international community of economists began to examine the relationship between economic development and environmental quality and came to several conclusions. The Environmental Kuznets Curve (EKC), which derives from the traditional Kuznets Curve depicting the relationship between income and inequality, emerged as the mainstream opinion. Most leading economists argued that environmental quality would first deteriorate and then improve as long as the economy could continue to develop, so the relationship between economy and environment could also be depicted by an inverted U curve (Grossman and Krueger, 1993), similar to such relationship between income and inequality. The EKC has been worshiped by environmental economists as a whole since then, and even become an "iron law" explaining the evolution of environmental quality in all countries after being refined and enriched by later scholars. Because of such knowledge, developed countries thought that they had climbed over the peak of environmental pollution, namely their environmental pollution was no longer "ascending" but "descending," so they started loosening environmental governance (i.e., both governments and citizens were passive in tackling climate change).

Likewise, developing countries were encouraged by the bright prospect, believing that as long as they could maintain economic growth momentum and create sufficient economic aggregate (i.e., reaching a critical point), their environmental quality, which was damaged in the early stage, would be bound to recover because of altered preference effect, technical effect, scale effect, and structure effect. Either affected or misled by this, the environmental protection measures adopted by developing countries had been existing in name only for a long time (e.g., ignoring environmental protection in exchange for large amounts of foreign investment).

However, the traditional Kuznets Curve, which has long been worshiped as a "truth," was questioned by the French economist Thomas Piketty in 2014 in his book *Capital in the Twenty-First Century*, who argued that:

(1) The Kuznets Curve on inequality is invalid. Under the condition of "return on invested capital larger than economic growth rate," inequality will not get alleviated with economic growth, but aggravate.
(2) Regarding the assertion that social inequality is an "irreconcilable contradiction," under the condition of technical progress and global dissemination of knowledge and technologies, and under the influence of mutual convergence of capital and labor income, inequality will not go to the extreme of "class struggle"; instead, the degree of inequality will go up, but largely converge within a certain range in the end.

The above analysis gives us a clue: Now that the Kuznets Curve illustrating the relationship between inequality and economic growth is not absolutely valid in the long run, is it possible that the EKC in the realm of environmental economics is not reliable? Suppose the global environmental quality failed to improve in the future with economic growth as previously expected, or even deteriorated to some extent in the long term, how would this development trend of resource and environment affect the existing hypotheses and conclusions on inequality? This book will, from the perspective of natural capital and some local characteristics of the evolution of environmental quality, explain and demonstrate the capital–labor relationship (i.e., inequality) that may occur in the 21st century.

3.2 Natural Capital

In previous studies, capital is mostly narrowly defined. In his book *Capital in the Twenty-First Century*, Piketty takes "land, air, resources, and energy" as a part of capital. In his opinion, there are both human capital and non-human capital; and non-human capital is not static, since it reflects the development trend of each society and the general social relations in that society (Piketty, 2014, p. 47). As for calculation of capital value, Piketty holds that the added value of land created by people can hardly be ruled out, and the same is true for the natural resources like oil, natural gas, and rare earth — namely, it is difficult for us to separate out the value put into exploration and extraction of natural resources and then calculate their pure value (Piketty, 2014, p. 48). These wealth data are defective since they fail to express natural capital and environmental disruption by numbers (Piketty, 2014, p. 58). In addition, with respect to the inequality in purchasing power, the author admits that the estimation of purchasing power parity is not entirely accurate, and even the comparison of countries with similar development levels has an error rate of more than 10% (Piketty, 2014, p. 65). In terms of public wealth accumulation, one of the reasons why the capital/income ratio has a long-term variation trend is that the Second Law ($\beta = s/g$) is invalid unless the focus of consideration is placed on the forms of capital that are accumulative. Even though a great portion of a country's national capital is purely natural resources (the value of these resources is irrelevant to human progress and past investments), β can still reach a high level without any help from savings. The importance of non-accumulative capital forms in reality is to be discussed later (Piketty, 2014, p. 172).

The above content shows that although many scholars (including Piketty) already know that natural capital, which is mainly embodied in natural resources and environment, somewhat affects the characteristics of capital, they have not conducted any separate and profound analysis of this issue. They have only split capital into divisible capital and non-divisible capital and human capital and non-human capital, but ignored the evolution of environmental quality since industrialization and its important impact on the forms of capital. Such impact is that capital can also be divided into positive capital and negative capital based on value appreciation.

For society as a whole, after externalities are addressed, general forms of capital are characterized with positive value appreciation, namely they are the traditional capital as talked about by Piketty, and he has incorporated "natural resources and environment" into this form of capital. On the basis of data statistics, Piketty draws basic conclusions such as long-term depreciation of land and gradual shrinking of public capital. How should we look at this definition and classification of capital? Does it make sense?

In fact, natural resources and environment, such as land, air, and water resources, are apparently different from traditional capital. Their differences mainly lie in two aspects:

(1) Natural resources and environment are not positive capital. They have peculiar accumulation process and forms; if externalities are taken into account, their total stock scale will show obvious characteristic of "value depreciation." In the case of absolutely limited natural resources and sound environment, all processes, which seem to utilize natural resources and environment to increase capital gain and wealth, are actually processes of consuming natural capital. Although owners of natural capital seem to gain payback in the form of factors, they only have added value from increased magnitude of value (to be further explained later), rather than increased stock of natural capital. In other words, value appreciation of natural capital in magnitude covers up its value depreciation in stock, and non-reproducible natural capital is equated with reproducible financial capital, which constitutes the "Hotelling's Law" — the most basic principle for resource utilization and allocation (Hotelling, 1990). By following Hotelling's Law, economists have incorporated resources and environment into production function and national accounts, making them an important source of capital and capital gains. With the advancement of industrialization and technological progress, resources and environment have been holding an increasingly lower proportion of the value chain formed by capital, with their marginal contribution becoming smaller and smaller, thus inspiring Piketty to draw a conclusion that land and other similar resources will depreciate in the long run (but capital will maintain a long-term fixed growth rate). However, such a conclusion runs counter to the feelings of people who are suffering from industrial pollution at the same time. The second characteristic of natural capital is therefore derived.

(2) Natural resources and environment are subjective value-based capital. According to the traditional definition of capital, the value of most capital forms is measured objectively, that is, after excluding price fluctuations, capital value is under objective influence of capital scale, and the most direct manifestation is the degree of marketization. The value of general capital is directly revealed through market transactions,

but the value of environmental capital is not the same case. Environmental economists have long discovered that environmental assets are factors or commodities with prominent public attributes, namely they cannot be marketized and their value is largely under the subjective influence of market players. That is why the value of natural capital is so unique. On one hand, like private capital, natural capital is valued according to its scarcity; on the other hand, unlike private capital, the total value of natural capital, which derives from its mounting subjective value, coexists with its diminishing stock scale.

According to the results of the Eighth National Forest Resources Inventory of China, by the end of 2012, the physical stock of forest land assets nationwide was 310 million hectares (ha), and that of forest assets was 16.074 billion cubic meters (m^3); the value of forest land assets and forest assets was 7.64 trillion yuan and 13.65 trillion yuan, respectively, totaling 21.29 trillion yuan. Compared with the seventh inventory, the results of the eighth inventory show that the physical stock of forest land assets increased from 304 million ha to 310 million ha (up by 2.0%), and their total value rose from 5.52 trillion yuan to 7.64 trillion yuan (up by 38.4%); the physical inventory of forest assets increased from 14.554 billion m^3 to 16.074 billion m^3 (up by 10.4%), and their total value rose from 9.47 trillion yuan to 13.65 trillion yuan (up by 44.1%). During the eighth inventory, the total value of key ecological services provided by the national forest ecosystem reached 12.68 trillion yuan annually (Jiang, 2014). These figures show that the value of environment significantly deviates from its stock.

In the opinion of the author, this deviation is the main reason why return on capital (ROC) has maintained a constant growth rate for a long time. To be specific, despite of diminishing stock (or growth rate) of natural capital, the ever-increasing subjective value of natural capital guarantees its soaring factor rents, which in turn contributes to the increase in total ROC.

3.3 Convergence Direction of Natural Capital

There are mainly two viewpoints on the convergence direction of natural capital.

As mentioned earlier, Kuznets Curve is one of the typical viewpoints. Its main idea is that, in the long run, as economic scale keeps expanding, environmental quality will improve gradually, resource utilization will become more efficient as result of technological progress, and population growth will slow down to stabilize on the whole, thus solving the ultimate development dilemma of mankind at one stroke. However, Malthus raised objections to Kuznets Curve as early as the 18th century (Malthus, 2008). In his debates with his opponents on the relationship between population and materials, Malthus denied that human beings have moral rationality to eliminate "surplus" population by themselves, but said that as long as the materials for survival are limited, the growth of population is bound to surpass that of materials, and people will be confined to poverty at a certain time point; they cannot get out of this dilemma unless they start wars or wait for breakout of plagues. This viewpoint of Malthus was later interpreted in the book *Limits to Growth* of the Club of Rome in the 1970s (Meadows *et al.*, 1972). The authors of this book speak out against the basic conclusion of Kuznets Curve, arguing that no matter in resources or in environment, human beings will fail to make ends meet and head toward the verge of collapse by the end of the 20th century. Although this prophecy has not come true to this day, the widening gap between supply and demand of natural capital is obvious to all.

Well, how should we look at the convergence trend of natural capital? In terms of developing countries, including China, which are suffering from smog and other environmental "diseases," can they finally converge toward better environmental quality through better governance? Or will the world finally fall into the abyss of environmental deterioration?

3.3.1 *Evidence No. 1 for the convergence direction of environmental quality: Practices of developed countries*

Regarding the convergence direction of environmental quality, the most convincing evidence to date is the practices of developed countries which have gradually entered the stage of post-industrialization, like the Northern European, Western European, and North American states, as well as Japan. These countries have common characteristics in evolution of environmental quality, namely they have experienced serious environmental degradation in the early stage (known as the "Eight Public Nuisance Events"), then they started environmental governance in the 1950s and 1960s, setting off a wave of global environmental protection for the first time (marked by the first United Nations global environmental summit held in Norway in 1972). The Club of Rome and many publications (e.g., *The Limits to Growth*) are products of this environmental protection campaign. Through decades of efforts, developed countries as a whole saw their environment gradually recover from the 1980s onwards, with a scene of devastation replaced by enjoyable landscape. So far, the environment in developed countries has largely returned to the livable state. Such outcome is the strongest support for environmental quality to gradually converge in the "positive" direction.

However, there was a significant change in the above-mentioned convergence trend in the early 1990s, that is, developed countries suddenly discovered that their environmental quality had not turned for the better on the whole (e.g., drought occurred in North America around 1987–1988): Although some traditional pollutant indicators had met the discharge standards, those non-traditional pollutant emissions, namely "greenhouse gases" (GHGs),[1] had kept mounting. By raising the average temperature, GHG emissions will lead to more ecological disasters. This discovery that has forced developed countries to pay great attention to climate change. In the early 1990s, they set off the second wave of global environmental protection with an aim of tackling climate change (marked by the Earth Summit held in Rio de Janeiro, Brazil, in 1991), and then adopted various response and governance measures. For example, the Intergovernmental Climate Change Response Organization (IPCC), established in 1988, releases climate change assessment reports in a regular manner, and a special agency was established under the framework of the United Nations Convention on Climate Change to promote the implementation of the international emission reduction framework (e.g., the Kyoto Protocol, aimed at reducing GHG emissions in developed countries, was passed in 1997). It should be said that developed countries have high hopes for the second wave of environmental protection, expecting to improve air quality like what they had achieved in the first environmental protection campaign. However, things were counterproductive. From the time Kyoto Protocol came into effect in 2008 to its expiration in 2013, the GHG emissions of developed countries had been increasing instead of falling (see Figure 3.1).

Before 1990, developed countries failed converge their GHG emissions in a positive direction owing to little knowledge in this regard, then

[1]It was not until May 2007 that GHGs were officially recognized as pollutants by the US Environmental Protection Agency.

Figure 3.1. US carbon dioxide emissions (Mt/a).

after they have gained better understanding of climate change and adopted positive responses, why has there been a trend of reverse convergence? How could two types of pollutant emissions converge in different directions? Which type of convergence trend is more representative? Before answering these questions, we need to look at the situation in developing countries.

3.3.2 *Evidence No. 2 for the convergence direction of environmental quality: Practices of developing countries*

According to demographic statistics, more than 80% of the world's population is concentrated in developing countries. For a long time, developing countries have modeled themselves on developed countries, learning their institutional, technological, and market policies and approaches, in order to accelerate their economic growth and catch up with developed nations. Under the influence of this objective, in the past decades, developing countries also introduced environmental governance practices from developed nations, and even taken their successful environmental transformation as an example, claiming to avoid the old path of "treatment after pollution," but the fact is that developing countries have exactly replicated the path taken by their developed counterparts.

China is the most typical developing country. Relevant statistics show that, in the past 30 years, China has seen all sorts of main pollutants keep increasing and even show a linear upward trend in recent years, with their total emissions much higher than they were in the early days of developed nations. Two types of facts can support such statistics. First, environmental incidents occur once in a while, and the frequency has been on the rise year by year. Second, in December 2013, severe smog covered 1.5 million square kilometers of North, East, and Northeast China, and its scope, severity, and duration far exceeded those of the similar incidents in London and Los Angeles in the 1950s. If expressed by a curve, we have evidence to prove that the environmental quality in development countries (at least in China) has not converged in a positive direction under the dual influences of emissions and governance. In other words, after the environmental quality of developed countries has converged in a positive direction, their experiences in economic development and environmental protection have not been fully transmitted to developing countries, resulting in the continued deterioration of the environmental quality of developing countries.

In addition, is there a positive convergence in the emission of new pollutants and GHGs in developing countries? Statistics show that, unlike the situation in developed countries, the development trend of GHG emissions in developing countries shows similar growth characteristics to traditional pollutants and has a faster growth rate than traditional pollutants. Today, the carbon emissions of large developing countries, including China and India, have far exceeded the average level of developed countries after just a few decades of industrialization. Even if calculated on a per capita level, China's carbon emissions have already surpassed that of the EU. These conclusions are supported by detailed data. According to this trend, the GHGs emitted by developing countries will soon account for the absolute majority of the stocks, which will have catastrophic environmental impacts on global climate change.

3.3.3 *Evidence No. 3 for the convergence direction of environmental quality: Global practices*

So far, there has been no systematic research on the quality, value stock, and changes of the global ecological environment. The vast majority of studies are limited to regions and countries, and various conclusions with greater limitations have been drawn. Regarding the global ecological environment quality, its convergence direction depends on two factors: the total scale of pollutant discharge (e) and the level of environmental governance. The latter is equivalent to the pollution elimination rate (m), which includes both natural emission and elimination processes (such as natural respiration processes, material attenuation or absorption), as well as man-made emissions and elimination processes (such as industrial production and sewage processing). If $g(e) > g(m)$, that is, the growth rate of pollution emissions exceeds the rate of pollution reduction, then global pollutants will gradually accumulate and the scale will continue to increase, thereby making the overall global environmental quality converge toward "deterioration"; vice versa, it will converge towards "improvement."

According to the above-mentioned investigation of environmental protection practices in developed and developing countries, it can be found that, in general, the growth rate of GHGs emissions as new pollutants far exceeds the elimination rate, and the atmospheric environment is continuously deteriorating, that is, at least the stock of this part of natural capital continues to decline.

Regarding the other part of natural capital, that is, the quality of eco-environment related to traditional pollutants, the global measurement of both emissions and governance are extremely challenging topics. To solve this problem, the most critical judgment is the extent to which the emission reduction of developed countries can offset the emission increase of developing countries. According to Thomas Piketty's conclusion that the global economic rate g converges to 1–2%, combined with the law of material circulation, the rate of emission of various environmental pollutants should be maintained at least within an interval greater than 0 and less than 2%. That is, increase at a slower or faster rate (the specific speed depends on the effectiveness of technological progress and environmental governance). To answer the question as to why in some developed countries and regions, there has been a phenomenon that the growth of pollution emissions is equal to zero, it is only the result of the transfer of pollutants between countries under the conditions of global trade and investment. If the economies of these countries and regions are closed, none of them will be able to achieve zero emissions. If this judgment is true, then from a global perspective, the quality of eco-environment, which is reflected in the level of traditional pollutant emissions, can only converge in the direction of "deterioration," but the rate of deterioration shows the characteristics of "faster and slower."

$$R \sim R_n > G > G_n$$

There are many details to be explored in the evolution of global natural capital, including whether active "governance" will change its convergence characteristics, how the discount level affects the timing and rhythm of "governance," and the relationship between the characteristics of global public goods and the evolution of global natural capital. In any case, under the condition that the rate of economic growth is converging, the rate of return on capital also tends to be stable. To maintain these two points, the natural capital stock must be declining, but not so fast that it undermines the core interest of return on capital itself. The evolution of the global natural capital stock will have an impact on economic growth and the rate of return on capital in the 21st century. The most direct impact is that, after deducting the loss of eco-environment, the economic growth rate will be lower than the previous level of convergence (1%~2%), that is, if measured by green GDP, which is different from the traditional national economic accounts, the scale of national income and economic growth will be reduced. In addition, the impact on the return on capital does not seem to be obvious. Taking oil as an example, looking at the trend of global oil prices in the past 150 years (see Figure 3.2), in the context of the general contraction of resource stocks, its actual price level has been rising, which means that even as the natural capital stock declines, its scarcity will still increase its value level, thereby ensuring that capital obtains the same rate of return as other assets (Hotelling, 1990). In this regard, we can roughly derive the general law of the evolution of the relationship between the rate of return on capital and the economic growth rate after incorporating the global natural capital convergence factors, that is:

$$R \sim R_n > G > G_n$$

Among them, R, R_n, G, and G_n are the rate of return on capital, the rate of return on natural capital, the rate of economic growth, and the rate of green economy, respectively (with the consumption of natural capital, its scarcity will increase the shadow price of natural capital year by year, and

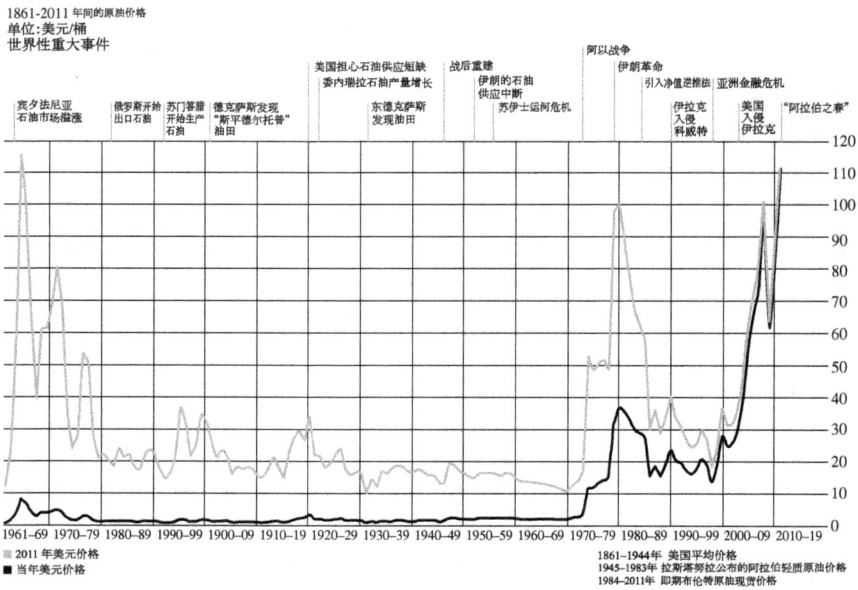

1861–2011 年间的原油价格	Crude oil prices over 1861–2011
单位:美元/桶	Unit: USD/barrel
世界性重大事件	World-class Events
宾夕法尼亚石油市场溢涨	Pennsylvanian oil market surges
俄罗斯开始出口石油	Russia begins to export oil
苏门答腊开始生产石油	Sumatra begins to produce oil
德克萨斯发现"斯平德尔托普"油田	Texas discovery of Spindletop oil field
美国担心石油供应短缺	US worries about oil supply shortage
委内瑞拉石油产量增长	Venezuela increases oil production
东德克萨斯发现油田	East Texas discovery of oil field
战后重建	Post-war reconstruction
伊朗的石油供应中断	Iran's oil supply gets disrupted
苏伊士运河危机	Suez Canal Crisis
阿以战争	Arab–Israel War
伊朗革命	Iranian Revolution

Figure 3.2. World crude oil prices over 1861–2011.

Source: BP Annual Report 2011.

expand the value of eco-environmental loss; if the prices of other sectors remain unchanged, the percentage of deductions from the total economic output will also increase year by year).

引入净值逆推法	Net worth reverse method is introduced
伊拉克入侵科威特	Iraq's invasion of Kuwait
亚洲金融危机	Asian financial crisis
美国入侵伊拉克	US invasion of Iraq
"阿拉伯之春"	"Arab Spring"
2011 年美元价格	2011 USD price
当年美元价格	US dollar price of the year
1861–1944年 美国平均价格	1861–1944 US average prices
1945–1983年 拉斯塔努拉公布的阿拉伯轻质原油价格	1945–1983 Ras Tanura's Arabian light crude oil prices
1984–2011年 即期布伦特原油现货价格	1984–2011 Spot Brent crude oil spot price

Figure 3.2. (*Continued*)

3.4 The Impact of Natural Capital Convergence on Income Equality

The next important question is to examine the impact of the convergence trend of natural capital on income equality.

The relationship between natural capital and equality generally has two dimensions, one is the time dimension, and the other is the space dimension. Although the difference between the two is obvious, there is an important common point, which is reflected in the income difference between groups. If the time span is limited to 30–50 years, it can almost overlap with the concept of equality in space. Therefore, in order to better connect with the previous research, we also mainly discuss the concept of equality based on space, that is, the income difference of different groups in the same time dimension.

Regarding natural capital and (income) equality, most of the previous literature focused on welfare, rather than limited to income, that is, the process of natural capital protection (sustainable development) can help the poor improve education, health care and transportation. The meaning is that "by improving the quality of eco-environment, fairness and equality in the sense of redistribution can be achieved to a certain extent" (UNDP, 2011). To extend this understanding, the premise is that "the process of using natural capital has different effects on different groups. Generally speaking, in the process of environmental degradation, the low- and middle-income groups are the first to suffer, and the damage to high-income groups is relatively low (UNDP, 2011)." The logic of this conclusion is that economic growth brings environmental pollution, as well as the decline of environmental quality. As a result, if the output effects of economic growth are divided into "capital (or wealth)" and "labor," the "labor" group with a lower income share is more vulnerable. Therefore, investment in environmental governance is more helpful to these groups. The above logic is actually used to understand the decline in environmental quality and the welfare and equity effects of environmental governance, but it does not respond to the impact of changes in natural capital on income distribution itself in the process of environmental pollution.

According to Thomas Piketty's definition, income should be divided into two parts: capital income (r) and labor income (l) according to its source. The contrast between them is usually expressed as $r > g > l$ (g is the economic growth rate). This is also the fundamental reason for the expansion of global income inequality. Then, as the composition of capital, what impact does natural capital have on the two parts of income?

One is the capital gains. This point has been analyzed before. While the natural capital stock decreases, its value increases because of its scarcity. Even if calculated at the same rate of return, natural capital will make a greater contribution to capital gains. That is to say, no matter how the quality of eco-environment declines, based on the need for the same return on assets, the owner of natural capital can always earn a return at least equivalent to that of other ordinary assets; otherwise, if it is lower, he will sell it, and if it is higher, he will buy it. Of course, in reality, natural capital, which is mainly reflected in the quality of eco-environment, cannot be bought and sold separately. Its circulation form is mainly dependent on other capitals for circulation, the most typical being dependent on landed property and real estate for circulation. It can be seen that the price of real estate with better eco-environment is generally higher, and the price difference reflects the value of eco-environment quality. Conversely, the eco-environmental quality with higher value forms a pushback effect on the low-yielding capital (such as manufacturing capital) and maintains its own high value. Therefore, the overall conclusion is that the "deteriorating" convergence trend of natural capital has little effect on the rate of return on capital, and even helps capital to ensure convergence to a higher rate of return in some cases.

The second is about labor income. According to the relationship between economic growth and labor income, discussing the impact of natural capital on labor income is essentially to explore the impact of natural capital evolution on economic growth. The primary direct effect of the decrease in natural capital stock is to increase the cost of economic growth. After the decline in the quality of eco-environment, in order to cope with this change, the social economy will bear various follow-up costs, which are mainly reflected in the loss of sanitation and health. Moreover, if the value of natural capital increases, the economy will gradually look for alternatives, that is, replacing the previous technologies with technologies with lower natural capital content, and the social economy will also pay for this transformation. In addition, in order to control the damaged eco-environment, the social economy has to pay additional costs. All these prices and costs must be deducted from economic growth in the end, which means that they must be deducted from labor income rather than capital gains. That is to say, compared with capital, labor appears to be less responsive to natural capital changes, and more passive. Whether the state increases the proportion of public capital before the first distribution for the need of environmental governance, or the private expenditure after the distribution for the need of prevention and control, it means that in the process of eco-environmental deterioration, the proportion of labor income in total income is on a downward trend. Similarly, in labor income, the gap between high-income groups and low-income groups will also be further widened. Of course, just as the quality of eco-environment will not deteriorate indefinitely, neither will the income gap in the above-mentioned two areas expand indefinitely (if it expands indefinitely, the two "inhibition" mechanisms that Malthus said will inevitably occur in the end).

The conclusion is that under the basic condition of $R \sim Rn > G > Gn$, the return on capital will not only be higher than labor income, but the gap will be further expanded. The deteriorating eco-environment erodes labor income, but at the same time, it will not harm the return on capital. In the 21st century, the degree of income inequality will further increase as the natural capital stock decreases.

3.5 Summary: Modern Significance of Malthus Conclusion

Malthus' research and investigation objects are concentrated on the population, but his judgments and conclusions on the growth of the means of living and the relationship between population and materials have considerable modern significance. One of the conclusions is that lower-class workers will be trapped in absolute poverty in the process, while capitalists are in a better position because they are in a more favorable position and are not restricted by the growth of means of subsistence. This conclusion is essentially equivalent to the inequality of social welfare caused by income inequality. In this regard, although Malthus ignored the huge impact of technological progress, he believed that the allocation of property rights is the key to solving this problem, that is, to allow the institutional environment to evolve in the direction that is most conducive to maximizing output and efficiency, rather than just solving fairness problems by fairness itself. The biggest inspiration for us from this conclusion is that even if the global progressive tax is the right direction to solve income inequality, in the process of global natural capital "deterioration" and convergence, we cannot forget to maximize the global allocation of eco-environmental resources through integrated markets and effective regulations, so as to give full play to its productivity.

Chapter 4

Social Capital, Technology Diffusion, and Sustainable Development

4.1 Introduction

The history of the Industrial Revolution is not only that of glorious era of wealth creation by mankind but also one that has witnessed extensive environmental destruction. After experiencing countless "acts of revenge" by nature, since the middle of the 20th century, mankind finally began to awaken to the need to protect the environment while pursuing economic development. This idea is fully reflected in the definition of "sustainable development" in the *Our Common Future — Report of the World Commission on Environment and Development* (1987): "Sustainable development is development that meets the needs of the present without compromising the ability of future generations to meet their needs." Apparently, the "needs" here are not only for the growth of material wealth but also for the quantity of natural resources and environmental services that are enough to ensure the growth of material wealth. Undoubtedly, this is an either/or dilemma for the traditional economic growth model that has always "ignored" the constraints of the quantity of natural resources and environmental services, because "the traditional development model, which simply consumes resources and pursues economic growth, is seriously threatening the sustainable use of natural resources" (Zhang, 2001). This phenomenon is especially prominent in developing countries. Therefore, we must "achieve a higher level of development at lower resource cost and social cost."

So, how can we guarantee intertemporal economic growth without harming the environment?[1]

There are obviously two meanings behind this goal: Reducing the consumption of natural resources while maintaining the current level of economic growth, or maintaining the current level of natural resource consumption, but achieving faster economic growth. The meaning of sustainable development is also reflected in these two relatively unified meanings.[2] However, both mean that economic growth is less dependent on natural resources, that is, the level of natural resource consumption[3] for economic growth is reduced, which means that we have taken a step toward the goal of sustainable development. To this end, which is more critical? The transformation of the government-led economic structure and institutional framework or the low-consumption and high-output technological progress? With this question as a starting point, this chapter goes on to analyze the relationship between social capital, technology diffusion, and sustainable development under the framework of sustainable development in the context of continuous technological progress.

4.2 Technology Diffusion and Sustainable Development

According to Lewis (1954), Kuznets (1965), and Chenery and Taylor (1968), the transformation of economic structure is essential for a country to move away from a development model that is highly dependent on natural resources; only when knowledge- and technology-intensive service industries and manufacturing replace agriculture and natural-resource–intensive industrial sectors can it be possible to reduce the consumption of natural resources. In addition, North (1990) argues that an effective institutional environment can promote the implementation of environmental protection policies, thereby reducing the consumption of natural resources. In the opinion of the author, the explanation for lower

[1] We must not only consider the coordination of current economic growth and environmental protection, but also the relationship between intertemporal economic growth and environmental protection.

[2] It mainly refers to the growth per capita.

[3] It refers to the natural resource consumption rate, that is, the proportion of a country's natural resource consumption in GDP.

dependence on natural resources for economic growth based on the transformation of economic structure and institutional framework is simply ignoring the role of technological progress; or most developing countries that are not competent enough in independent R&D, such explanation ignores the effect of the diffusion of new technologies.

For all countries, especially for developing countries, the reduction of natural resource consumption depends to a large extent on their ability to apply low-consumption production technologies. It is because only when it is possible to replace the old natural-resource–intensive technologies with new technologies[4] that require fewer natural resources and environmental services, the transformation of economic structure can be truly realized, and the policies designed to protect the environment by eliminating distortions in pricing for natural resources are likely, or more likely, to make a real difference.

Technological progress essentially has the characteristics of reducing resource input and increasing output. Marx (1953) stated, "As far as the means of labor are concerned, if the labor productivity of the sector that produces these means of labor develops … Old machines, tools, appliances, etc., are replaced by machines, tools, and appliances that are more efficient and less expensive … Old capital will also be reproduced in a more productive form. In terms of objects of labor, each advance in chemistry not only increases the number of useful substances and the uses of known substances … it also teaches people to put wastes from the production and consumption processes back into the recycling process of reproduction, so that new capital materials can be created without the need for prepayment of capital." This shows that, under the circumstance that other conditions remain unchanged, we can reduce the consumption of natural resources and environmental services through technological progress, while at the same time ensuring the level of economic development, that is, achieving sustainable economic development. Therefore, "(We) need to vigorously develop low-input, high-output, low-polluting and high-tech industries, and at the same time reduce pollution from traditional industries through technological progress, so that industrial development will benefit both economic development and environmental protection" (Zhu, 1997). At present, for most developing countries that are still in the first half of the EKC, the specific content of technological progress not only

[4]In this book, "new technologies" refer to low-consumption and high-output technologies, while "old technologies" indicate natural-resource–intensive technologies.

contains the enhancement of their own development capability but also the improvement of the ability to use new technologies with low consumption and high output, that is, the process of technology diffusion, which is the focus of this chapter.

4.3 Supply and Demand in the Process of Technology Diffusion

The diffusion of new technologies characterized by low consumption and high output will play an important role in sustaining economic development. However, we do not have enough knowledge about the factors that affect technology diffusion. Although the main macro-models dealing with the sustainable growth have taken into account of the importance of technological progress, there are no in-depth analyses of the technology diffusion process. On one hand, most models treat technological progress as an exogenous given factor of sustainable development after introducing natural capital factors. This actually ignores the substitutability of capital, labor, and natural resources (taking the standard production function as an example), especially the substitutability of natural resources in the context of technological progress, and the conclusion drawn from this is can satisfy the weak sustainable development criteria. On the other hand, those studies that try to endogenize technological progress usually exclude the process of technological diffusion (Goulder and Mathai, 2010), which is obviously impractical for most developing countries[5] that do not have sufficient technological development capability. The greatest obstacle they (including technology users in developed countries) face is how to obtain low-consumption and high-output new technologies and use them effectively. Therefore, governments and researchers, who are advocating sustainable development, should care about the technology diffusion process.

In the process of technology diffusion, there are two issues worthy of attention: One is technology supply, that is, research and development, the importance of which is known to all. The other is technology demand, that is, technology application — the academic community has not carried out

[5]Developed countries are also included here, because even in developed countries with development capability, the promotion and application of new technologies is still an important process for technological progress.

any in-depth research on the process of technology application and the corresponding incentives. In terms of some recent technology diffusion models (Messner, 1997; Goulder and Mathai, 2010; Meijers, 1994; Grubler and Gritsevskii, 1998), their focus is on the "on the supply process of technology diffusion," that is, on "Learning by Doing" and the reduction of uncertainties of cost and benefit. Eliminating the externality of technology development is obviously the focal point of their concern. At the same time, they seldom pay attention to the demand process of technology diffusion, especially neglecting the effect of the quantity and quality of information obtained by potential technology users through social interaction on technology diffusion during the demand process. The empirical model of technology diffusion (Mansfield, 1961) also fails to provide an explanatory analysis of the influence mechanism of the technological demand process. The traditional input–output benefit analysis obviously cannot justify the explanation of the incentive mechanism of the technological application process.

However, empirical research has shown that, in developing countries, an important factor in explaining the probability of adopting new technologies is the size of the social network of potential users (Boahene *et al*., 1999). This research implies that the learning process of technology demanders embedded in social interactions is not only the fundamental driving force for the diffusion of new technologies in developing countries but also another important source of uncertainties and externalities. Therefore, there is a close connection between social capital and technology diffusion, embodied as "social networks, norms and institutions that determine the process of social interaction."

4.4 Demand for Social Capital and Technology Diffusion

In traditional individualistic economic analysis methods, the behavioral choices of economic individuals (including manufacturers and consumers) are made on the basis of individual resource endowments, and he (she) does not need to consider the influence of other individual behavioral choices in the group. However, in fact, each economic individual is in a different group network, and their behavior is affected by the social interaction between individuals to varying degrees, which may deviate from their original choice. This is also reflected in the adoption of technology in the process of technology diffusion. Under the conditions of interaction, the impact of social capital on technology diffusion is not only reflected in the fact that it can promote the use of new technologies but also in that it sets obstacles to the transformation of old technologies.[6]

Boahene *et al.* (1999) used Ghanaian hybrid cocoa as an example to explore the role of social capital in the spread of agricultural technology in developing countries. In the end, they conclude that the social network of farmers has an important impact on the cost of acquiring and adopting technical information. "Research shows that the adoption of hybrid cocoa is a process of integrating different mechanisms and factors — including economic and social ..., empirical evidence shows that in the process of adopting hybrid cocoa, small farmers are more likely to obtain support through social networks than large farmers who take advantage of their farms to obtain support ..." In addition, a recent empirical survey[7] on the entrepreneurship of college students conducted in Shanghai also verifies the impact of social capital on technology diffusion based on entrepreneurs' evaluation of their own environment.

Broadly speaking, social capital refers to a series of social networks, norms, and institutions that determine the process of individual interaction in a given economic system, including formal and informal systems that influence individual behavioral choices by acting on individual interaction, and ultimately affect the evolution of the economic system.

In this extremely broad definition, its structural part is embodied in the social network of social connections (Kedzie, 1997) and social diversity (Fedderke and Klitgaard, 1998). The former is constructed on the basis of indicators such as the number of telephones per capita and network nodes per capita, while the latter is a combination of the three indicators proposed by Easterly and Levin (1997); it was originally used to measure the possibility that two randomly selected individuals belong to different ethnic groups and language groups, here, it explains the diversity of individuals in the network. The degree of social connections and the level of social diversity in different social networks are different.

In the author's opinion, the importance of social capital as defined above to the process of technology diffusion is embodied in the following two aspects.

---

[6]This actually means that social capital is a "double-edged sword," which is conducive to the diffusion of technology at a certain level, but it hinders the diffusion of new technologies if it exceeds a certain level.

[7]Yangpu District University Town Knowledge Economy Research Group, 2001.

On one hand, the process of social interaction itself has a fundamental impact on individual economic decision-making. Social interaction is the source of the externality[8] of individual behavior, that is, individual behavioral choices will be affected by the choices of others under interactive conditions, which may deviate from their original optimal choice path. This is reflected in the process of technology diffusion, which means that an individual's technological choices are influenced by the spillover effect of the choices of others that interact with him.

On the other hand, social networks affect the distribution of information within the economic system and the level of cooperation between individuals. The former includes the quantity and quality of information flow, and the degree of knowledge spillover that affects the adoption of new technologies. The latter refers to the level of coordination and consistency of economic individuals' behavioral choices. By changing the distribution of information and the level of cooperation, the structural part of social capital affects the expectations of individuals on the changes in different aspects of the economy (cost and benefit of purchasing new technologies), as well as the transaction cost and use cost associated with the adoption of new technologies. Therefore, one of the important reasons why countries with similar technological structure, human capital, natural capital, and productive capital endowments have different levels of development is the difference in their internal social network structure.

4.5 Conclusions and Issues for Further Study

4.5.1 *Basic framework*

Based on the above analysis, the author believes that the technology diffusion process affected by social capital has an endogenous decisive effect on sustainable development. In this way, the three core factors as social capital, technology diffusion, and sustainable development are organically integrated. The relationship between them is shown in Figure 4.1, which is the basic framework of sustainable development amid technological progress.

[8] The "externality" here does not refer to the positive or negative external influence of the individual behavioral results on the external society in the traditional sense, but that individual behavioral choices are affected by the spillover effect of the choices of others, such as the phenomenon of following the general trend.

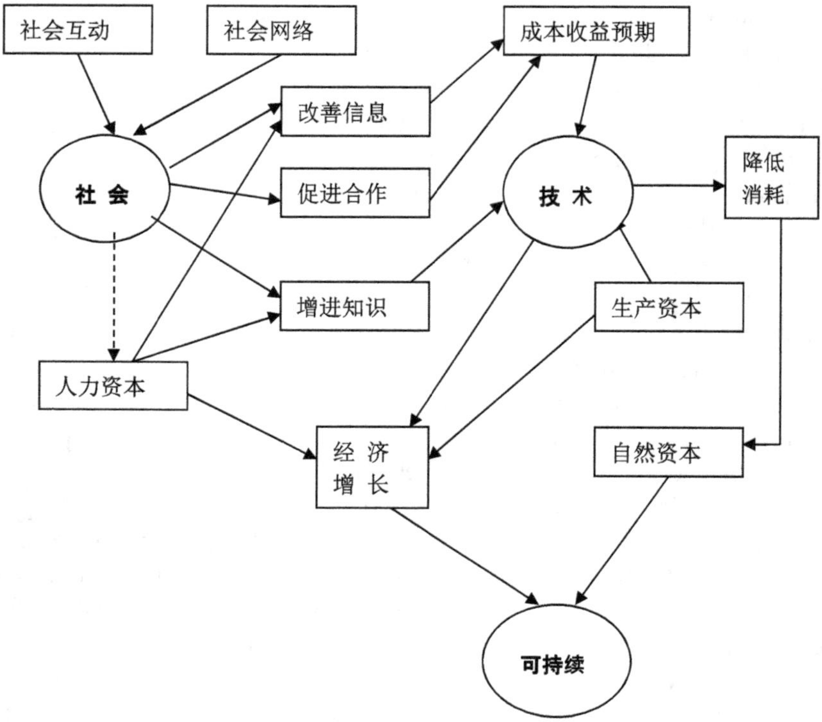

社会互动	Social interaction
社会资本	Social capital
人力资本	Human capital
社会网络	Social network
改善信息	Improve information exchange
促进合作	Promote cooperation
增进知识	Enrich knowledge
经济增长	Economic growth
成本收益预期	Cost-benefit expectation
技术扩散	Technology diffusion
降低消耗	Reduce consumption
生产资本	Production capital
自然资本	Natural capital
可持续发展	Sustainable development

Figure 4.1. Basic sustainable development framework amid technological progress.

4.5.2 *Summary*

The sustainable development process is not only a process in which human capital, production capital, and natural capital are coordinated but also a dynamic process of endogenous technology diffusion. This process is also indirectly affected by the interaction between economic individuals. Constructing a sustainable growth analysis framework, which emphasizes the endogenous technology diffusion of social capital factors, can better integrate the above different factors and help us better understand the decision-making mechanism of the sustainable development process.

The analysis of the sustainable development framework amid technological progress shows that sustainable development is the optimal intertemporal allocation process of endogenous human capital, production capital, and natural capital, which means that we can influence this allocation process by adopting many policy tools to achieve real development in the sense of strong sustainability. In fact, any type of policy intervention (e.g., trade policies, social security and welfare reforms, tax reforms, debt restructuring, monetary and fiscal policies, and minimum wage policies) can obviously affect consumption, savings and natural resource demand and further affect economic growth and sustainable development. Therefore, based on a detailed analysis of the overall space of many policy tools and policy choices applicable to decision-makers, a comprehensive policy framework is built to ensure of sustainable economic development.

4.5.3 *Important issues for further study*

Starting from the sustainable development framework amid technological progress as established above, there are mainly three issues that need to be further studied:

(1) With regard to developing countries, analyze the determinants of achieving sustainable economic development, especially the determinants of natural resource consumption rate[9] that are related to strong sustainable development. The overall environmental indicator of natural resource consumption rate is extremely necessary for the

[9]It refers to the total amount of natural resources and environmental services (NRES) that must be consumed in order to produce one unit of GDP.

formulation and evaluation of environmental policies in all countries. Its function is somewhat similar to the overall economic indicators (e.g., GDP) or social indicators (e.g., average lifespan).

(2) Introduce the concept of social capital into the analysis of the technology diffusion process and study how social interaction fundamentally changes the behavioral choices of economic individuals and how the structure of social networks affects economic individuals' choices of new technologies by changing their expectations.

(3) By constructing a macro-economic model of the optimal intertemporal allocation of human capital, production capital, and natural capital based on endogenous technology diffusion, a policy framework can be built to promote sustainable development.

Chapter 5

"Strong" and "Weak" Sustainable Development

5.1 Introduction

Among the viewpoints on sustainable development, a popular one stands for strengthening environmental protection by creating statistical indicators of green national economy (e.g., green GDP), that is, measure the real GDP by deducting the cost of environmental damage, which is similar to the net national income after deducting the depreciation of fixed assets. Through "green filtering," such national economic statistical indicators seem to make people sober-minded: If our economic growth, after deducting the losses caused by environmental damage, is slow growth, zero growth, or even negative growth, it means that our economy has been developing at the cost of environmental disruption, and therefore our economic development is unsustainable; conversely, our economic development can be sustained. The premise for this reasoning to be established is that natural resources can be completely substituted by other resources, meaning that we can inject enormous natural resources into economic development, and ignore the ecological limit of natural resource consumption. However, this is in fact an idea of "weak" sustainable development. Guided by this idea, a country tends to purposely lower the prices of natural resources to promote economic growth, because the low prices of natural resource prices (even if this part of environmental cost is deducted) will not weigh on economic growth rate. However, the problem is that the sustainable development of any economy is bound to be restricted by the ecological limit of natural resource consumption. Given this, the international environmental economists distinguished between "strong" sustainable development and "weak" sustainable development in the early 1990s, although different opinions remain in existence.

5.2 Controversy Between "Economical" and "Ecological" Sustainable Development

So far, there has not been a simple and generally accepted standpoint on the definition, measurement, and promotion of sustainable development, because there are two opposite views on this issue in the theoretical community: On one hand, ecologists hold that sustainable development should be linked to the protection of ecosystems. On the other hand, economists believe that the priority of sustainable development is to maintain and improve people's living standards, just like what Solow (1999) has said, "sustainable development ... is a plan to reserve total production capacity for future generations." In the opinion of ecologists, natural resources have uses other than production and cannot be replaced by other forms of capital (e.g., production capital, human capital, and social capital), but economists contend that as long as the capital stock left to the next generation is not less than the possession of contemporary people, then natural resources can be replaced by other forms of capital and consumed (Pearce, 1989, 1996).

Toman (1997) has a proper description of the different views of economists and ecologists on the concept of sustainable development: "If you think that contemporary people should take responsibility for their future generations, what kind of capital needs to be transferred between generations to fulfill this obligation? A view shared by many economists is that all kinds of capital — including natural capital, physical capital, and human capital — are mutually replaceable sources of welfare. Based on this point of view, large-scale destruction of ecosystems, such as environmental pollution, species extinction, forest destruction, or global warming, is no longer unacceptable ... However, most ecologists and certain economists hold a different view, believing that compensatory investment, like moral restraint, is usually infeasible, and natural laws have restrained other resources from offsetting ecological damage. Healthy ecosystems, including those that provide genetic diversity, are the best way to resist changes and preserve choices for future generations."

In response to this controversy, the World Commission on Environment and Development (WCED), also known as the "Brundtland Commission," proposed a more comprehensive definition of "sustainable development" in 1987. In the *Brundtland Report*, the WCED presents that "Sustainable development is development that meets the needs of the present without compromising the ability of future generations to meet their own needs." One of the views contained in this definition is that human development requires intergenerational equity; our future generations cannot express themselves in any political and economic forums presently, so it is unfair to lay down policies that hurt their interests for the time being. The second view is that we must acknowledge ecological constraints, and carry out economic activities within the scope of ecological permits, similar to how Turner (1991) points out that "protection has become the only basis for determining whether the allocation criteria of natural resources are appropriate." The third view is that all economic activities must be somewhat restricted so that environmental services or waste discharge will have an insurmountable limit. It can be seen that the WCED definition is a good synthesis of the different views of ecologists and economists. The following discussions about sustainability indexes are based on this definition.

5.3 Discussions on Creating Sustainability Indexes

The above-mentioned definition of sustainable development is only an abstract theoretical paradigm. In order to transform this theoretical paradigm into realistic and operable sustainability indexes, economic analysis tools must be employed. Putting sustainability indexes inside the framework of neoclassical economics can help us intuitively understand the essential differences between different viewpoints.

An effective way to integrate the viewpoints of economists and ecologists is, according to neoclassical welfare economics theory, to assume that individuals increase their welfare from spending, consumption of environmental products and services, and the resulting benign operation of the society; in this way, the complete substitution between natural resources and other capital can be ruled out. According to Gillis *et al.* (1992), if social welfare is an Aggregate Production Function (APF) that integrates spending, consumption of environmental products and services, and social stability, then a sustainable development path can be defined as a development path that maximizes the present value of an Intertemporal

Production Function (IPF). The biggest difference between sustainable development path and the non-sustainable development path is that the latter maximizes the present value of current utility (i.e., utility of contemporary people). In other words, along the path of sustainable development, the level of resource input should depend on the conditions required to maximize the present value of the IPF, including economic, environmental, and social conditions. By transforming the abstract sustainable development paradigm into specific conditions for maximizing the production function, we can integrate the given economic, environmental and social indicators into a single output indicator, which means that sustainable development can be measured uniformly, and the corresponding development policies will become a matter of how to influence this indicator.

In terms of sustainability indexes, Human Development Index (HDI), which was presented by the United Nations Development Program (UNDP) in 1990, is a typical index covering average life expectancy, literacy rate, and per capita income. It is published in the UNDP's Human Development Report every year. Besides, there are also Index of Sustainable Economic Welfare (ISEW) (Cobb and Daly, 1989), Net Primary Productivity Index (NPPI), and Carrying Capacity Index (CCI) (Moffat, 2002). According to Murray and Lopez Alan (1996), these indexes are often used by governments and international organizations as the basis for formulating policies and allocating public resources, which makes the indexes such as HDI a representative and normative measuring standard.

However, the problem is that these indexes only reflect the "preferences" of the methods that create the given indexes, and these preferences are apparently not social universal "preferences." For example, the maximization of HDI does not mean that the average life expectancy, literacy rate, and per capita income calculated with other measurement methods are also maximized. What is worse, the existing measurement methods do not even include those factors (which are of vital importance and ought to be included into any sustainability index), while one of these factors is environment.

In a nutshell, in order to put forward a sustainable APF that integrates all factors, a large number of assumptions must be made on various preferences and functional forms. However, as Goodin (1986) has pointed out, it is impossible to propose an APF that integrates all forms of preference, and this function can only be constructed on the basis of generally accepted preferences. As far as the sustainability of development is concerned, Pearce (1989) divides it into weak sustainability and strong sustainability based on different viewpoints and different measurement standards derived from this.

5.4 "Weak" and "Strong" Sustainable Development

5.4.1 *Weak sustainability*

Serageldin and Steer (1994) and Toman (1997) once put forward a general view on sustainable development, saying that sustainability is judged by the criterion as the ability to "maintain and increase the level of welfare available to economic individuals," and this level of welfare depends on the degree of wealth accumulated by all countries. Here, "wealth" is composed of three parts: production capital stock, natural capital stock, and human capital stock.[1] This leads to the criterion for judging the weak sustainability of development, that is, sustainable development requires that the total capital stock transferred from the present to future generations is not less than the existing stock (Hartwick, 1978; Solow, 1986). Sustainability based on this criterion is usually referred to as Solow–Hartwick Sustainability. Evidently, weak sustainability is only concerned with the total capital stock composed of three forms of capital. As long as the total capital stock available to future generations is not less than that of contemporary people, then the development is sustainable. The premise of this view is that natural capital and other capital are completely substitutable, meaning that we do not have to care about the specific forms of the total capital stock transferred to future generations. In Solow's words, "the previous generations have the right to use the capital in the pool, as long as they replenish the pool of renewable capital stock" (Solow, 1974). If we use savings to represent the capital stock, then economic development is sustainable when the level of real savings (after deduction of production capital depreciation and natural capital consumption) is non-negative, because the total amount of capital available to future generations is greater than that of contemporary people. Based on the conclusions of Solow and others, Serageldin and Steer (1994), further present that the sustainable development path needs to maintain not only the necessary production capacity but also the minimum level of environmental services and ecological diversity.

[1]The most recent view is that another form of capital — social capital — should be counted in the wealth of a country.

Based on the above framework, the criterion for measuring the weak sustainability of development can be derived from the real savings rate of a country given by the following formula:

$$S_t = \frac{\text{GDP} * (1 - c_t) - K_t\delta_k + (N_t R - n_t) + h_t}{\text{GDP}_t} \tag{5.1}$$

in which:

S_t	The real savings rate;
c_t	The proportion of consumption in GDP;
$K_t\delta_k$	Depreciation of production capital stock in period t;
N_t	Natural capital stock;
n_t	The amount of natural resources and environmental services consumed in period t;
R	Regeneration rate;
h	Human capital investment.

The weak sustainability criterion for development is that when a country's is greater than or equal to zero, it means that its development is sustainable, that is, it meets the minimum conditions for sustainability.

This criterion inspires countries to make better preparations for the future. Following this development path of weak sustainability, countries can create enough total capital to replace the consumption of natural resources while sustaining their productive capacity; that is to say, they can fix or even increase the total wealth while reducing natural resources. Assuming that a country's net savings rate (without deduction of production capital depreciation and natural resource consumption) is 15%, the production capital depreciation rate is 10%, the natural resource consumption rate is 10%, and the investment in human capital is zero, then according to the criterion of weak sustainability, its wealth will decrease by 5% every year ($S_t = -0.05$). However, this does not necessarily mean that the development of this country is unsustainable. In fact, it may trade the optimal natural resource depletion rate for economic stability in a certain period of time. A negative S_t is undoubtedly a warning sign for economic growth, meaning that the current growth strategy cannot be maintained in the long run.

5.4.2 *Strong sustainability*

In fact, the substitution between natural resources and other forms of capital has certain limitations. For example, when natural resources (renewable and non-renewable) are exhausted, it is impossible for us to talk about sustainable development. Since "natural capital is essentially not interchangeable with other forms of capital, and various forms of natural capital themselves cannot completely replace each other," many ecological economists conclude that to achieve truly sustainable development, stocks of natural resources (at least critical ones) must be kept above certain limits, otherwise it will not be a sustainable development path (Turner, 1991; Pearce, 1993). This leads to the second criterion of economic development: strong sustainability.

Considering the development path of strong sustainability, the stock of both total capital and natural capital must be maintained between generations. In other words, there are additional requirements for the natural capital consumption on the basis of weak sustainable development. Of course, these requirements do not mean that natural resources should be preserved as they are; instead, renewable resources shall be developed while non-renewable resources are being consumed so as to maintain the level of the total stock of natural resources. Moreover, certain important natural resources must be specially maintained because of their irreplaceability, that is, the use of these natural resources cannot exceed their substitution limit and regeneration capacity, which are referred to as "ecological limit."

The development path of strong sustainability stresses the capital structure that is transferred to our future generations. Since various forms of capital cannot be completely replaced, special attention must be paid to the environment in addition to the total capital. The reality also shows that the major threat to the development needs of our future generations is none other than environmental degradation.

Compared with the development path of strong sustainability, weak sustainability appears to have multiple development paths. Among them there is a path that can maximize per capita intertemporal consumption, and this maximum consumption is also an indicator that measures the total output of a society. We can use several functions to measure the utility that individuals obtain from their intertemporal consumption. Here is a utility function often used in macroeconomic research (Blanchard and Fisher, 1989):

$$U(C_t) = L_t \frac{(C_t / L_t)^{1-\tau}}{1-\tau} \tag{5.2}$$

in which:

C Consumption;

L Population;

τ Coefficient of relative risk aversion.

The development path of strong sustainability is to maximize the intertemporal utility function, namely:

$$V(C_t) = \sum^{t} (1+r)^{T-t} \left\{ L_t \frac{(C^t / L^t)^{1-\tau}}{1-\tau} \right\} \tag{5.3}$$

in which:

r Discount rate;

T The last phase of the planning period.

The maximum consumption in the infinite period means that we need to maintain certain production capacity in this period. Since natural resources cannot be completely replaced by other forms of capital, the optimal intertemporal allocation of natural resources sufficient to maintain certain production capacity constitutes a necessary condition for strong sustainability of development, meaning that we must pay special attention to the level of natural capital consumption.

5.5 Summary

The above analysis shows that different understandings of the substitutability between various forms of capital have led to two criteria for measuring the sustainability of development: One is weak sustainability ("replaceable development paradigm"), and the other is strong sustainability ("irreplaceable development paradigm"). Their biggest difference is whether we need to consider the ecological limit of natural resource consumption while ensuring that the output capacity of future generations is not lower than that of contemporary people. According to the development paradigm of weak sustainability, we do not need to care about the ecological limit, but create green GDP statistical indicators to ensure the intergenerational equity of development, which is utterly inadvisable, and it goes against the law of environmental development in the development paradigm of strong sustainability.

Chapter 6

An Economic Analysis of Urban "Carrying Capacity" — How Big Can a City be?

6.1 Introduction

Since the second half of 2012, China has successively introduced the strategies and policies on urbanization,[1] which not only increased related discussions and reports but also stimulated a new wave of "urban construction" across the nation. Townships, counties, prefecture cities, separate or major cities, and metropolises invariably harbor ambitions to be upgraded. In the era of "urban construction," such a passion and ideal is understandable. Many examples in history tell us that as long as the Central Government allows, even a small fishing village is likely to be transformed into a metropolis under the effect of resource accumulation.

However, the "urban construction" plan is so far no longer sustainable. Most things are attainable with a plan, for example, the land can be "enclosed," the level can be "upgraded," the population can be "moved," and even "fairness" can be expected, but the "carrying capacity" is an exception. To be more specific, it is the "population carrying capacity"[2] based on the eco-environment. Even if the development of human

[1]The Central Economic Work Conference was convened in Beijing (December 17, 2012). Retrieved from http://politics.people.com.cn/n/2012/1217/c1024-19913897.html.

[2]For the definition of "carrying capacity," see Rees (2019), Cohen (1995), and Newman (2006).

civilization so far is sufficient for us to overcome all obstacles in progress, the only thing that makes us feel powerless is the carrying capacity. The disappearance of many splendid civilizations and ancient cities tells us that no matter how much we have possessed, the environmental disasters that hit the bottom line of the "carrying capacity," such as desert sands, sudden climate change, and saline intrusion, can deprive us of everything in an instant. Therefore, on one hand, we must keep employing various planning and market means to promote the urbanization process; on the other hand, we need to explore the objective impact of "carrying capacity" on city size, making our new-type urbanization operate within the range of carrying capacity.

6.2 Beautyism: The Economic Paradigm Under the Challenge of "Carrying Capacity"

As far as the existing relationship between city size and carrying capacity is concerned, we can intuitively observe the occurrence of various urban ecological disasters and their disastrous effects. Before that, we have little idea of the existence of carrying capacity. Although the propositions of ecological disasters and their consequences seem to be out of the research scope of economics, they have been under the influence of various economic growth philosophies for a long time.

For example, in the agricultural society, only areas with arable land and water resources can enable human beings to reproduce. Affected by spontaneous small-scale peasant economic thinking, people are firmly entrenched in extensive farming (not caring about intensive and meticulous farming) and increasing the "labor force" through childbirth. Consequently, the total population approaches and breaks through the carrying capacity of land, thus leading to the "Malthusian Catastrophe."[3] It should be clarified that there is nothing wrong with an economic development philosophy or thought that stands for raising agricultural output by increasing labor force within the scope of carrying capacity. It also accords with the modern economic theories that highlight factor endowment. However, no matter whether it is static small-scale peasant

[3]That is, the growth rate of population outpaces that of arable land and other materials, resulting in absolute poverty, thereby inhibiting further expansion of the population.

economic thinking or dynamic modern economics (from classicism to neoclassicism), they delimit the production-possibility frontier (PPF) within the individual scope of behavioral agents, that is, they calculate the maximum PPF under various technical conditions from a country/region, or from the scale and structure of the factors owned by enterprises or individuals (see Figure 6.1).

In Figure 6.1, horizontal axis (X) and vertical axis (Y), respectively, represent different production factors, while each point on the curve represents a combination of factors, and also the position where there are optimal social output and welfare. Theoretically, it is possible for one factor to completely replace the other one, which explains the reason why the output remains unchanged after an expensive factor is substituted by a cheap one.

Figure 6.1 seems to contain the meaning of carrying capacity, that is, individuals cannot produce beyond the boundary of carrying capacity of their factors, but in fact, this calculation only expresses a possibility that the factors required for social and economic development (mainly covering land, food, water resources, minerals and energy that are related to eco-environment) have an upper limit. Intuitively, this upper limit is manifested as the eco-environmental carrying capacity in the sense of population size.

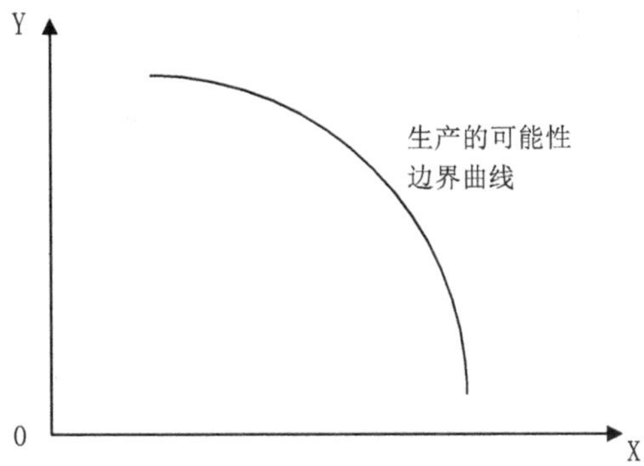

生产的可能性边界曲线	PPF curve

Figure 6.1. PPF determined by production factors.

On the basis of Figure 6.1, we add two straight lines in Figure 6.2 to represent the factors C1 and C2 that determine the eco-environmental carrying capacity. Beyond all doubt, their size constrains the scope of PPF and gives production an upper limit. In fact, this upper limit is exactly the eco-environmental system that produces all the factors with carrying capacity. The components of this system intersect with each other in cycles both on a local scale and on a global scale.

In the pre-industrial era, prosperous regions, which were guided by the above economic thoughts, broke through the constraints of local eco-environment in a short period of time, but they were unable to effectively transfer their carrying capacity constraints through the interaction with the economic system, hence the outcome of collapsed civilization and cities. In the age of industrialization, this cycle of rise and fall seems to have been lengthened. In some regions, such as developed countries or cities with a large population, the constraints of carrying capacity are unperceivable over a long period of time. Even so, this does not mean that our development capability has fully relieved us of the worries about carrying capacity. It is just because the globalization allows the transfer of the constraints and consequences of carrying capacity from one place to another, which is attributed to the possible interactivity between eco-environment

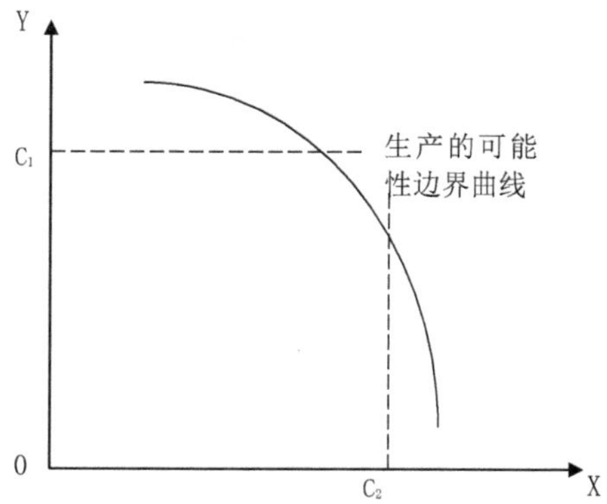

生产的可能性边界曲线	PPF curve

Figure 6.2. PPF under the constraint of eco-environmental carrying capacity.

and economic system. Such transfer, which is structural transfer, has built up the carrying capacity of regions, but failed to expand the global carrying capacity. In case of developed countries and regions, their carrying capacity has increased in nominal terms at the price of rapidly shrinking carrying capacity of underdeveloped countries and regions; some of them are even in a desperate situation, for example, certain island countries have retreated to inland areas due to rising sea level as affected by climate change.

Some countries and regions can modify their local boundaries of carrying capacity through technical means or terms of trade, so as to continue to use the theories of modern economics to guide their economic development, but for other countries and regions, the possibility of doing so is remote. On one hand, the carrying capacity constraints of these countries and regions are quite strong, and their eco-environmental foundation is relatively fragile. On the other hand, these countries and regions cannot import the carrying capacity of other countries and regions, but export their own carrying capacity. The final result is the gradual erosion of the carrying capacity of these countries and regions. From the perspective of global eco-environment interaction, the decline in the carrying capacity of some countries and regions is not a good thing, because it will gradually spread and affect those countries and regions who are "starters" or possess higher-level carrying capacity.

In sum, the enlightenment of the carrying capacity constraints to the research on modern economics is that, by employing the existing methods, we need to further increase the importance of eco-environment system in production function and development decision-making. Otherwise, the economic system will be implicated by the eco-environment. From areas with fragile eco-environment to areas with better eco-environment, various symptoms related to carrying capacity will gradually spread out and ultimately harm the overall welfare of society. If we regard the natural capital (standing for eco-environment) as "beautiful,"[4] then restoring the price relationship between natural capital and other forms of capital and increasing the proportion of natural capital in economic development will become "beautyism" paradigm and system of economics research (Li, 2013b).

---

[4]From the aesthetic perspective.

6.3 Carrying Capacity and City Size

As far as urban development is concerned, is there any reference value in the "beautyism" economic research paradigm? In the urban–rural structure, cities seem like "starters." At the beginning of their development, cities have a higher-level carrying capacity, and it is on this basis that cities can survive and develop. However, from the perspective of development process and results, the size of different cities (city size in the sense of population density) can be large or small. Even for the same city, its size is not fixed; some have grown from small to large, while others have been shrinking (UN Habitat, 2008). Why do these differences arise? According to *The World Cities Report* published by the UN Habitat (2008), the possible reasons for the increase in the size of cities mainly include "urban primacy, economic and industrial policies, changes in the quality of life, and administrative promotion." In contrast, the decrease in the size of cities results from the natural selection in aspects such as eco-environmental quality (UN Habitat, 2008). This may provide us with an enlightenment: If the city is compared to a wooden barrel, then its carrying capacity will be the shortest board, and this board ultimately determines the limit value of the city size. Before drawing up a conclusion, we need to answer two questions: First, what is the impact of the carrying capacity of eco-environment on the development of cities? Second, how does the development of cities affect the quality of eco-environment?

The first question is related to the origin of cities. As mentioned above, in history, the earliest settlements (predecessors of cities) are mostly located in areas with fertile soil and water sources. From the perspective of eco-environmental quality, the climate in these areas is more suitable for human beings to gather, dwell, and reproduce. At the same time, the rich natural resources can satisfy various consumer needs. In addition, there is another important condition, that is, convenient transportation, especially waterway transportation. These characteristics mean that the development of cities in pre-industrial era is attributed to their high-level natural carrying capacity. Putting aside the concepts of employment, price, and currency developed by modern economics, it can be found that the original starting point for mankind to settle in an area and expand their place of residence is to have their survival needs satisfied. In this regard, the carrying capacity determines the output boundary of cities in an absolute sense and indirectly determines the size of cities. Of course, there is some possibility of "spillover," that is, through convenient waterway transportation, pre-industrial cities can have a certain degree of economic interaction (i.e., trade) with the outside world. In the Chinese Song Dynasty (960–1279), the population size of a metropolis (Dongjing, present-day Kaifeng City in Henan Province) reached 1 million, as astonishing as an "astronomical figure," which is mainly attributed to the Beijing–Hangzhou Canal running through the north and south. A large number of southern products were continuously imported to the north through the canal, thus supporting the size of a metropolis beyond the local carrying capacity. From the perspective of eco-environment, the opening of the canal itself is also a manifestation of the city's carrying capacity, that is, with advanced technological means, the city's eco-environmental conditions can support a large-scale water conservancy project (see the details below). This is the origin of urban development in pre-industrial times, then what happened after industrialization?

Since 1776, along with the process of industrialization, modern economics emerged and the interpretation of the origin of modern cities has become increasingly systematic, that is, to demonstrate the agglomeration effect brought about by urban development from the perspective of improving efficiency, and take the method of marginal analysis as the constraint condition of urban development. To put it simply, through creation of employment opportunities and welfare treatment, cities have been increasing their attractiveness and enhancing their absorptive capacity in an economic sense, thereby promoting their own expansion step by step. Later, when their marginal scale effect continues to diminish, and when the increase in size can no longer raise their marginal output, the growth of urban size will soon come to a halt.

In this theory, economic variables such as employment and prices are of vital importance. For one thing, cities rely on industries to drive employment and create output. For another, cities rely on output to stabilize prices and maintain welfare. Therefore, the two major processes of industrialization and urbanization are dependent on each other. Why? It is because industrialization is the only way to create large-scale employment and support urban development. It is from the stage of industrialization that the population has shown a trend of explosive growth. According to the research on the relationship between population size and the development of industrialization driven by innovation (Kremer, 1993), when other conditions are more or less the same, the base of population size is an important factor in determining the level of innovation. Therefore, mankind has a development path that is very different from the "Malthusian Trap," that is, to promote urbanization through industrialization under the continuous pressure of expanding population size, and then break through the constraints of output and improve the level of welfare.

In such an analysis path, carrying capacity seems to be no longer important, or the development of industrialized cities is no longer constrained by carrying capacity, but in fact, even in the cases of urbanization driven by industrialization, we can still find cities of different sizes in different regions. In terms of urbanization driven by industrialization, varied city sizes reflect different degrees of industrialization, but why does industrialization have different degrees? Or what are the conditions for industrialization? From the perspective of geoeconomics, in comparing the distribution of highly industrialized cities or regions across the world with that of major cities in the agrarian age, they have at least one common characteristic, that is, convenient transportation. Nowadays, modern cities have diversified choices for external transportation — in addition to waterways, there are also expressways, railways, and aviation. Because of the robust development of various forms of modern transportation, which are the main achievements of industrialization, the scope of trade has been expanding globally and cities have become more capable of economic interaction between each other. This means that the production capacity and scale of the industrial society can be highly dependent on the outside world by means of modern transportation, which is greatly different from the agricultural society. For this reason, transportation or terms of trade becomes the main cause for different degrees of industrialization.

The next question is: Why do some industrialized regions or cities have stronger transportation capacity than others? The key determinant is also the carrying capacity represented by the quality of eco-environment. From the perspective of system interaction, whether it is water, land, or air transportation, their effectiveness is closely linked to the quality of eco-environment. In an area with a harsh environment, no matter how many transportation facilities are built, they are hardly used very often. Or in an ecologically fragile area which can only carry a small population size and a small industry scale, although there are beautiful mountains and rivers, how can it develop into a large city?

Based on the above analysis, we can partly answer the question "how big a city can be?" That is, in principle, the scale of urban development must be planned within the carrying capacity of eco-environment. This carrying capacity includes the eco-environmental conditions that support the local direct output, such as the quality of air, water, and soil, and also various natural conditions or foundations that support the city to conduct economic interactions with the outside world.

Generally speaking, traditional theories often define the shortest piece of wood in a wooden barrel as water or food (Cohen, 1995; Li Z. Q., 2013a). However, considering the uniqueness of cities, the weakest link in the carrying capacity that supports the urban development is the eco-environmental conditions that facilitate external transportation. Starting from this, we can answer the second question as mentioned above, that is, how do cities affect the quality of eco-environment? Or will the development of cities expand the boundary of their carrying capacity?

Mainstream theories, which start from the considerations of efficiency, care more about the positivity of urban development in all fields (UN Habitat, 2013), including the value of urban development in improving the quality of eco-environment. The two reasons are as follows: On one hand, cities have a kind of agglomeration function, meaning that they can reduce per capita eco-environmental depletion while increasing population density; as compared with rural areas with scattered population, the expansion of cities with the same population size is equivalent to the increase of the proportion of urban residents in the total population, thereby reducing the eco-environmental depletion by the total population. In economics, this can be summarized by scale economies effect, which has been thoroughly demonstrated in a considerable number of literatures (Lu *et al.*, 2013). On the other hand, in many literatures, especially in research reports on urbanization in developing countries (UN Habitat, 2013; World Bank, 2010), it is believed that cities, as a carrier of population, have a stronger learning ability than other ways of population settlement. For example, in cities there are complete infrastructures to ensure people's quality of life and endogenously beneficial organizations and systems to promote technological improvement and innovation. All these mean that cities naturally have the institutional endowment to improve the efficiency of using eco-environmental resources. More importantly, it is precisely because of this institutional endowment that the use efficiency of urban eco-environmental resources has been improved, which in turn has a strong "whirlpool" effect on surrounding and external eco-environmental resources, that is, a city seems like a huge whirlpool whose strong suction draws in the surrounding water and continuously strengthens its own energy (carrying capacity).

The earlier paragraph explains the reason why the traditional eco-environmental factors are no longer the boundary of urban carrying capacity as mentioned in Section 6.2. With the support of urban infrastructure and favorable socio-economic institutional arrangements, cities not only interact economically with the outside world through traffic and trade but also import external important eco-environmental resources with modern technological means. For example, Singapore and China's Hong Kong are typical cities that import eco-environmental resources (Newman, 2006). Their own carrying capacity is impossible to make them accommodate such a large population in this day and age. The process of urban development is tantamount to expanding the boundary of eco-environmental factors by borrowing external resources, which make other shortcomings of carrying capacity (such as geographical location) more prominent.

The above two points are the main reasons why urbanization is highly acclaimed. As far as the constraints of carrying capacity are concerned, the process of urbanization has not aggravated the deterioration of eco-environment where cities are located for a long time. Instead, driven by a series of city-building campaigns, the living environment in some cities is still being improved and even beautified. Such result may mislead people that cities can continuously expand their boundary and size and alleviate the contradiction between their own development and eco-environment. However, has the urban development, whether it is guided by the theory of "efficiency supreme" or any plan, got out of the predicament of sustainable development as in the past? Is it a kind of "beautyism" as described in Second 6.2?

In fact, the above arguments on the enthusiasm for urban development has overlooked at least two points:

(1) The traditional urban theories emphasize the marginal effect of scale. On one hand, in terms of overall scale, the increment in urban scale within a certain range does have a scale effect, that is, the same incremental scale can be achieved over time at a lower cost. However, even if the marginal cost of urban expansion is decreasing, the total cost of urban expansion is still increasing in terms of total scale. From the perspective of regional eco-environment, the marginal diminishing effect does not matter at all, and what matters is whether the total scale is gradually approaching the boundary of carrying capacity. In this regard, the absolute impact of urban development on eco-environment is undoubtedly increasing (Newman, 2006). On the other

hand, with regard to the per capita consumption of eco-environmental resources, it will decrease under the agglomeration effect brought about by urban development. However, population density is an important indicator of city size, therefore, when the increase in population density outpaces the decrease in per capita consumption of eco-environmental resources, the city is constantly approaching the maximum carrying capacity. In addition, another major misunderstanding is that people tend to ignore the rebound effect of eco-environmental resource consumption in the process of urban development, that is, when urban development is considered to benefit the protection of resources and environment, it may in turn increase the consumption of resources and environment. For example, if urbanization (or city cluster) is proven to be beneficial to energy conservation and emissions reduction (Lu, 2012), it will stimulate more regions to enter this rank, thereby cities will further increase burdens on resources and energy. The final result is that the average urban consumption of resources and environment will be higher than the initial state. Therefore, each increase in urban scale means the erosion of eco-environmental quality or carrying capacity. With limited carrying capacity, the development process of cities itself is constantly approaching the boundary of their carrying constraints. Take the air quality in cities as an example: Although there is evidence that the per capita PM2.5 concentration in cities is much lower than that in rural or other areas, cities are still caught in fog and haze. Given this, how can we defend statements that imply urban development is positive?

(2) The argument about the positivity of urban development has ignored the price factor. As mentioned above, in the development process of some cities, the extent of their scale expansion often breaks through the boundary of their own carrying capacity. Why? It is because cities can import carrying capacity from villages or other cities in the outside world, which is similar to the import of "carrying capacity" from developing countries through global trade. Here, the "carrying capacity" embodied in the comprehensive quality of eco-environment has become a tradable product. Although some cities have the advantages of "starters" in technology and institution, it is undeniable that these cities obtain cheap "eco-environmental" goods through unequal institutional arrangements, which has created favorable conditions for low-cost expansion of scale. Especially in areas where the dual structure of urban and rural areas is obvious, it is extremely common to see

the price scissors between "industrial products" and "environmental products," that is, the former is more expensive than the latter. And cities are using such price scissors to carry out long-term primitive accumulation, making their scale increase rapidly in the name of "efficiency."

Well then, why is there such a phenomenon of "anti-marketization" even when the market system is so widespread and the concept of fairness is deeply rooted in the hearts of people? The reason is that "the market is selectively malfunctioning," that is to say, market malfunctions based on externalities are well known — while some market malfunctions, which are noticed by "planners," are quickly corrected, such as healthcare, education, transportation, and national defense, some are deliberately ignored, such as the destruction of eco-environment. It is precisely because of this effect that the terms of trade for tradable eco-environmental resources are distorted: The "planned" market price is too low and there is no legal protection. Therefore, cities are able to absorb a large amount of eco-environmental resources from the outside world in a very short time. As a result, the carrying capacity boundary of cities has been greatly expanded, but the eco-environmental quality in their surroundings and other areas has been declining and approaching the constrained boundary. This is obvious to all. Take climate change as an example: The expansion of cities is absorbing the world's fossil energy at an accelerating rate, and cities themselves have basically achieved the goal of lower per capita carbon emissions. The per capita carbon emissions of cities in major developed countries are lower than their national per capita levels, and the per capita carbon emissions of urban population in developing countries are still higher than their national per capita levels (World Bank, 2010). However, countries and regions that are more vulnerable to climate change will suffer as a result, as climate change is likely to break through the carrying capacity of these countries and regions. This is the consequence of direct or indirect transfer of bearing capacity. However, that is not the end of it. In the interaction system of global eco-environment and economy, the decline or breakthrough of the carrying capacity of different regions will eventually affect cities, causing the size of cities to shrink. So far, we have found some evidence of urban shrinkage: One is the decline in the natural growth rate of the original urban population (UN Habitat, 2008), and the other is the suburbanization of urban population (UN Habitat, 2008; Zhu, 2013).

6.4 Summary

How big a city can be? Based on the above analysis, we can draw up the following conclusions: First, cities must reasonably plan their feasible scale level according to their own eco-environmental constraints. Second, cities also need to calculate the net inflow of tradable eco-environment resources and limit their size to a level no higher than the per capita consumption of resources and environment in both urban and rural areas What is important is to correct the disadvantaged position of eco-environment resources in the market, eliminate the failure of selectivity, and pay more attention to the "beauty" of eco-environment. Otherwise, even if cities have achieved "leapfrog development" in a short period of time, this "fictitious" increment in city scale will be eventually "returned" in different ways, or returned even more.

Chapter 7

Economic Analysis of the Global Response to Climate Change: From the Cost-Benefit Perspective

7.1 Introduction

In 1988, the international community held the first Semipolitical Conference on Climate in Toronto, Canada. In 2012, the 18th United Nations Conference on Climate Change was convened in Doha, Qatar. This in-between period of more than 20 years has witnessed several rounds of international negotiations on the response to climate change. The Toronto Conference proposed a carbon emissions reduction target (known as the "Toronto Target"), that is, with the emissions in 1988 as a benchmark, the global emissions shall be cut by 20% by 2025.

This target now seems too idealistic. In fact, the final resolution of the Doha Conference does not contain any definite or compulsory goal for carbon emissions reduction despite of the efforts made by the international community; what we can only find are words such as "hope," "should," and "voluntary." This means that by the year 2025, although the global total carbon emissions will be much higher than the level in 1998, the international community can hardly make any dramatic progress in tackling climate change and reducing carbon emissions, and the possibility of retrogression cannot be ruled out. For this reason, we need to summarize and review all specific response strategies in the past and, more importantly, figure out what theories have been guiding the practice of the international community in coping with climate change in the past more than two decades.

To answer this question, we must first learn about the decision-making basis for all countries to participate, semi-participate (conditionally participate), or not participate in the framework and mechanism for global response to climate change. It is generally believed that the effectiveness of the climate change response framework depends on the participation of all countries. The reason why the international community can finally pass a resolution is precisely because the resolution reflects the participation of all countries to the greatest extent. Therefore, the entry-into-force conditions of the initial Kyoto Protocol — an important milestone in addressing global climate change — are set at 66% of global total emissions (Nordhaus, 2010), that is, the countries and regions (in the list of Annex 1 Countries) that have signed the protocol shall have combined emissions holding at least 66% of global total emissions. Well then, on what basis do countries decide to join in international climate change frameworks such as the Kyoto Protocol?

Take the US as an example. When discussing and voting on the accession to the Kyoto Protocol, the US Senate stated that any international agreement (on addressing climate change) will inevitably have a series of financial (economic) impacts on the domestic economy. In fact, the so-called "economic and financial impacts" indicate costs and benefits. Specifically, before signing any international agreement on climate change, the American politicians are eager to know what benefits the US will get and what costs it will pay. In other words, the US will not make decisions on whether to join this kind of agreement until such a cost-benefit relationship is clarified. At a hearing on tackling climate change in the US Congress, a senator explained why the US has not joined any international agreement in this regard, saying that "because we have not yet figured out the influences of these agreements on the American economy."

The above analysis shows that the cost-benefit comparison is the basis for the foreign policy-making of all countries, including the US, to deal with climate change. Only when the basic cost–benefit principles are met will countries endorse an international agreement to address climate change in their favor, if not, they will reject it. Well then, in an economic sense, how will the international climate change agreement bring benefits to countries?

7.2 The Cost-Benefit Calculation of the Global Climate Change Response Framework

Regarding the global climate change response framework, the relevant calculations made by the international academic community are mainly based on various economic models. The general equilibrium analysis, one of the representative economic analysis methods, incorporates multiple factors in a given period (e.g., by 2055 or 2100), such as economic growth, energy use, carbon emissions, climate change patterns, climate change impacts, and various policies on carbon emissions reduction and adaptation to climate change, as variables into these models, assigns parameters to each variable, and then calculates the prices for carbon emissions under different scenarios of emissions and emissions reduction, as well as the resulting costs and benefits.

Based on the study of Nordhaus (2010) with the Dynamic Integrated Climate-Economy Model (DICE), the author made a cost-benefit analysis of the Copenhagen Accord reached by the international community in December 2009 (see Table 7.1), in an aim to discuss a new plan for addressing climate change after the Phase-1 commitment of the Kyoto Protocol expires.

In Table 7.1, there are three bases for calculating the costs and benefits of the Copenhagen Accord:

(1) First, under the response path to climate change as proposed in the Copenhagen Accord, the entire world and different countries are suffering direct net losses[1] due to the impact of climate change. The meaning of net losses is associated with both costs and benefits.

(2) The paths for emissions reduction as proposed in the Copenhagen Accord will impose additional costs to the entire world and different countries. The extent of such costs is closely related to the provisions of the accord, because technological transformation, economic growth, and social welfare will be greatly affected by the process of emissions reduction.

---

[1]"Net losses" refer to the gains under the influence of climate change minus losses. Since countries are affected by climate change in different degrees and attributes, net losses are shown in utterly different forms across the world.

Table 7.1. Costs and benefits of the Copenhagen Accord (by 2055) (billion US$, present value).

Country/region	Change in loss	Cost of missions reduction	Spending on carbon emissions allowances	Net cost
US	−5.1	32.8	22.8	50.5
Europe	−5.6	16	1.71	27.5
Japan	−1.2	4.4	6.4	9.6
Russia	−0.5	9.2	−17.6	−8.9
Central Asia	−0.4	6.2	−15	−9.2
China	−5.2	65.5	−26.8	33.5
India	−5.4	18.5	−0.1	13
Middle East	−4.7	12.3	−13.4	−5.8
Africa	−4.1	0	0	−4.1
Latin America	−3.3	12.7	15.4	24.8
Other high-income countries	−1.8	9.6	4.8	12.6
Others	−4.2	18.8	6.4	21
World	−41.3	20.6	0	164.7

Note: All figures in the above table are discounted values, and the discount rate is the world real interest rate after capital weighting.
Source: Nordhaus (2010).

(3) Under the framework of the Copenhagen Accord, based on the carbon emissions prices (including carbon tax and purchase prices for carbon emissions allowances) simulated by the author with the same model, as well as the additional carbon emissions bought by countries for meeting their respective emissions quotas, the cost of paying for additional carbon emissions allowances in different countries and the world at large is calculated in the end. Here, under the framework of the Copenhagen Accord, the distribution of carbon emissions reduction allowances among countries is not even. Considering their emissions reduction capability, different countries will see the scenario of either "surplus" or "insufficiency." This cost is thus positive for some countries and negative for others. Of course, the total cost is zero from a global perspective.

Under this calculation framework, Nordhaus concludes that the global direct expenditure on addressing climate change will add up to

US$1,647 billion by 2055, the deadline set by the Copenhagen Accord. Is this a high-level expenditure or not? In his earlier studies in this regard, Nordhaus (2008) calculated the total expenditure costs for tackling climate change under different scenarios[2] by employing the same model. He divided these costs into two parts in light of their different properties:

(1) The first part includes the losses from climate impact and the cost of emissions reduction. Nordhaus compared the low costs under the optimal response scenarios with the high costs under the scenarios without any measures or with overhigh targets for emissions reduction or temperature control.
(2) The second part of the costs comes from the purchase of carbon emissions allowances. Carbon emissions price determines the final purchase expenditure, while different response scenarios for climate change will lead to different carbon emissions prices.

After sorting out the response strategies for climate change, Nordhaus (2008) found that if a more radical strategy is implemented, the international community will share a higher carbon emissions price in the future, meaning that each country will pay more for buying additional carbon emissions allowances in order to fulfill the emissions reduction target.

Due to the great uncertainties in scientific research and socio-economic development, it is possible that the calculations by Nordhaus and other international economists and climate-change research groups (such as IPCC, 2007a; Stern, 2007) on the costs and benefits of a global response to climate change are not mathematically accurate. However, the permutation of different scenarios shows that their conclusions are logically tenable, that is, in different scenarios for climate change response and for economic development, the international community will share different costs and benefits. So, from the cost-benefit perspective, how can we interpret the main differences between different climate change response and development scenarios? And what key factors are affecting the costs and benefits of the global climate change response framework? Understanding these issues will help us construct an international climate change response model in the sense of cost-benefit economics.

[2]In his studies, Nordhaus (2008) sets the possible paths for global climate change response to eight categories and a total of 15 scenarios.

7.3 Carbon Emissions Prices, Participation, and Cost-Benefit Analysis

According to the analysis on the economic impact of climate change by Nordhaus (2008, 2010) and Tol (2002, 2009), the impact from the climate change response on the net cost mainly has three sources: The direct impact from climate change, the impact from the process of carbon emissions reduction, and the impact from carbon emissions prices. Globally, the impact from the first two sources is manifested in the form of a positive net cost, while the impact from carbon emissions prices on the net cost is nominally zero after being offset by countries. In fact, there are two sources of global carbon emission prices: Carbon tax and carbon trading. If all carbon prices are embodied in the form of a carbon tax, then the carbon emissions prices in an equilibrium state should be equivalent to the marginal cost of carbon emissions reduction, meaning that the country pays for the carbon emissions beyond its emissions quota. If the global impact of climate change is also included in the calculation of carbon emissions prices, that is, if the external effects of climate change are fully internalized into the carbon prices, then the prices can be used as an indicator to measure the costs and benefits of the global climate change response framework. In this regard, under the different paths for tackling global climate change, a variety of carbon prices will be generated, showing the level of global net cost paid for these different climate change response frameworks.

If carbon emissions prices are endowed with a new meaning — that is, converting the two costs (impact of climate change and expenditure on carbon emissions reduction) into carbon emissions prices and taking the prices as a landmark indicator to measure the costs and benefits of the global climate change response framework — then we can recombine and rearrange the previous cost-benefit comparison results obtained in general equilibrium state. Take the 15 climate change response scenarios set by Nordhaus (2008) as an example: In a given period of time and with other conditions remaining fixed, we can rearrange the 15 scenarios in a high-to-low order (Figure 7.1). This new arrangement shows that, only from the perspective of time series, irrespective of what emission reductions strategies and paths are adopted by the international community, the carbon emissions prices will unanimously go up from the lowest point at the

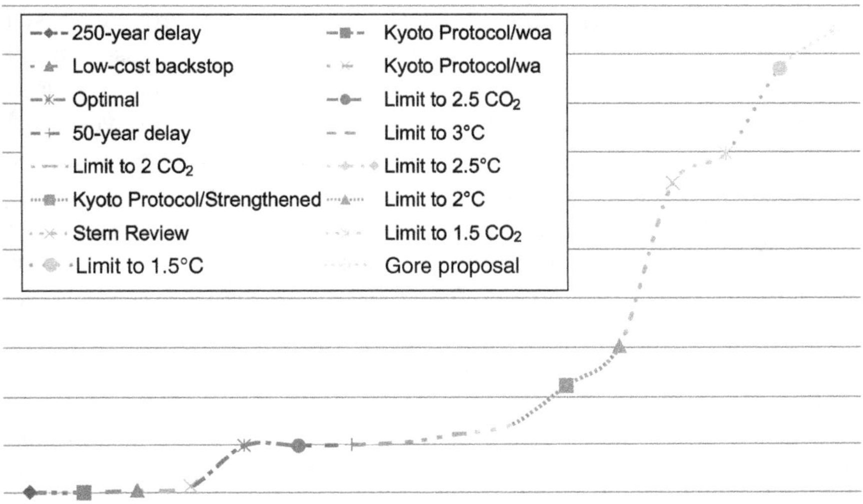

Figure 7.1. Carbon emissions prices under different response scenarios.
Source: Nordhaus (2008).

initial stage. However, a cross-sectional comparison clearly shows the differences between different climate change response scenarios. According to the previous analysis, the differences in carbon emissions prices actually represent the differences in the costs and benefits of various climate change response mechanisms.

We can draw two basic conclusions from Figure 7.1:

(1) The higher carbon prices a climate-change response mechanism imposes, the more costly it will be. For example, compared with the Kyoto-Protocol–based response mechanism, the mechanism that controls global temperature rise within 2°C obviously has a higher cost. Moreover, the KP that covers the US carbon emissions costs much than the one exclusive of the US carbon emissions.
(2) Countries' participation determines the carbon emissions prices and the cost-benefit level of the response mechanism. Through further comparison of various response scenarios that lead to different carbon emissions prices, we can find that the biggest difference between them lies in the participation of countries, that is, the coverage of

global carbon emissions. Whether it is the Kyoto-Protocol based response mechanism or the setting of a temperature increase limit at 2°C, its essence lies in the extent to which global carbon emissions fall into the scope of control. In an absolute sense, larger coverage of the response mechanism means higher prices for carbon emissions, and more effective response. However, the problem is that in the international community, the coverage of the response mechanism does not depend on the carbon emissions prices or the effectiveness of the response, but on the degree of recognition of the response mechanism by countries or the degree of their participation. Based on the official statements made by all countries, we can divide their "participation" into three types: participation, non-participation, and conditional participation. Taking KP as an example, the US is in the group of "conditional participation," the EU is in the group of "participation," while developing countries such as China and India are in the group of "non-participation." Taking the Copenhagen Accord as another example, both China and India are in the group of "conditional participation." In addition, from an unofficial point of view, the measurement of participation is more complicated, because it is possible that the participation of market, sector, or region is not consistent with the official statement, which makes the actual participation seem to be either higher or lower. However, it is the carbon emission prices finally formed in the market that can reflect the actual participation. By this standard, we can replace the vertical axis in Figure 7.1 with "participation" to describe the differences between 15 response mechanisms and scenarios in different ways. The degree of participation, from the lowest to the highest, determines the response mechanisms and scenarios with different attributes.

If the above relationship between participation and response mechanism is applied to the practices of global climate change response mechanisms, then we can find that, by selecting some important points in time from 1988 when the international community kicked off the negotiations and consultations on climate change response to 2012 when the Doha Conference was convened, it is the differences in the actual participation of countries in addressing climate change based on their carbon emissions coverage and the subsequent changes that determine the ups and downs of response mechanisms and targets.

Although the response scenario to control the temperature rise by 2°C requires a higher degree of participation (approximately 100% coverage), and it is confirmed in the Copenhagen Accord, such target has failed in practice, and the global participation (embodied in carbon emissions coverage in the Copenhagen Accord) has not improved, but rather declined due to the implementation of the emissions reduction mechanism.

Therefore, the number of participating countries in global climate change response has kept falling since 1988. During the same period, the carbon prices in the international market has also remained at downside (Li, 2012), indicating that the international community on the whole is becoming less willing to cope with climate change and reduce carbon emissions. This also provides circumstantial evidence for the evolutionary impact on the net cost from the global climate change response mechanism in different stages and based on the cost-benefit measurement.

7.4 Cost-Benefit Model of the Global Climate Change Response Framework

$$\text{Cost function: Cost} = \sum f(\text{Commitment}_i)e^{rt} \quad (7.1)$$

With given factors, such as technological progress, climate change trend, and economic development, the cost (present value, the same below) for the international cooperation in climate change response depends on the degree of countries' participation/commitment. Previous studies have shown that the international community pays greater incremental costs in the case of low participation (in the early stage), but the growth of costs will slow down in the case of high participation (in the later stage), meaning that the cost function curve is incremental and convex, that is, it increases rapidly at the beginning and then slows down (see Figure 7.2). In the end, if all countries in the world join in the cooperation framework, then the costs will be fixed at a certain maximum point instead of increasing endlessly. This is because once a globally effective cooperation mechanism is established to control carbon emissions and control temperature rise within a bearable range, then the carbon emissions prices

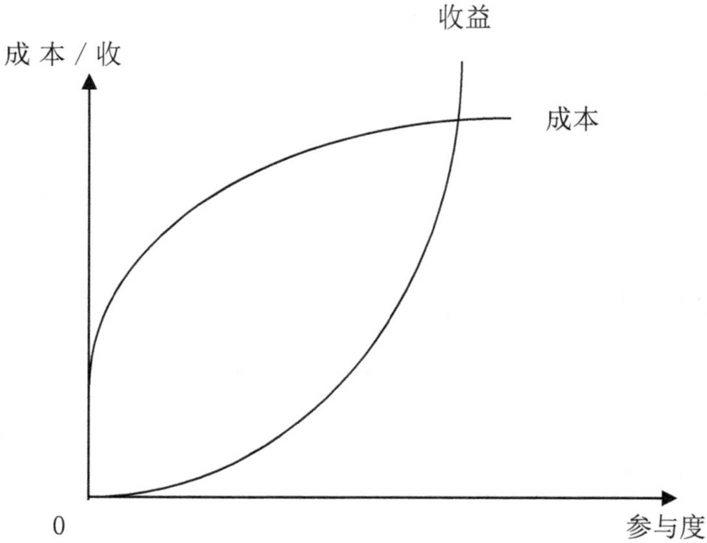

成本/收益	Cost/benefit
收益	Benefit
成本	Cost
参与度	Commitment

Figure 7.2. Cost and benefit of commitment to international climate change response (1).

will cease going up further (see Figure 7.2) and the costs of climate change response will come to a standstill.

$$\text{Benefit function: Benefit} = \sum f(\text{Commitment}_i)e^{rt} \qquad (7.2)$$

Similarly, with other given conditions, the benefits of the international cooperation in climate change response also depend on the participation of countries. According to relevant studies and the above analysis, higher participation will bring more benefits to the world. Of course, the characteristics of the benefit curve are different from those of the cost curve.

(1) In the early stage, the global benefits arising from intensified participation (cooperation) grow slowly because of the leakage effect; once the

participation reaches a certain high level, the effectiveness of global policies on reducing carbon emissions will be strengthened significantly as the leakage effect weakens notably, such as a carbon tax and carbon trading. At this time, the entire world will gain greater benefits from countries' participation and see their rapid growth, meaning that the benefit curve will demonstrate an incremental increase, that is, to increase slowly at first and then speed up (see Figure 7.2).

(2) The second characteristic of the benefit curve is that due to the low participation of countries in the early stage, the benefits from international cooperation are lower than the costs, and the benefits may be negative in some extreme cases — that is why the benefit curve is below the cost curve. However, in the later stage, the benefit curve will climb up faster and go beyond the cost curve after the participation reaches a certain level. This level of participation is exactly the participation in a state of equilibrium.

(3) The third characteristic of the benefit curve is that, after the participation of countries has increased, the growth rate of benefits is most likely to decline, that is, the benefit curve will climb up slowly and gradually approach the cost curve (see Figure 7.3). In this way, the relationship between the cost and benefit curves will change, and two points of equilibrium will show up. The first point (Q1) is the low-level participation equilibrium, and the second point (Q2) is the high-level participation equilibrium.

The conditions for equilibrium are as follows:

(1) The circumstance where the cost curve is above the benefit curve is known as "under commitment." At this time, the whole world will pay a net cost for this, thereby promoting the continuous increase of commitment until the cost and benefit are equivalent to each other.
(2) The circumstance where the cost curve is lower than the benefit curve is known as "over commitment." At this time, the whole world will gain a net benefit from a higher level of commitment. Nevertheless, commitment will not continue to increase, but begin to decline until the net benefit drops to zero. This is mainly because when commitment is too high, on the one hand, the increase in the

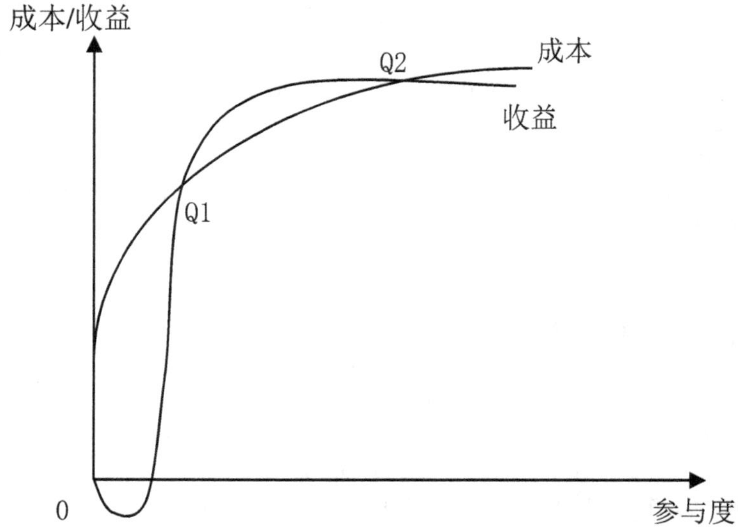

成本/收益	Cost/benefit
收益	Benefit
成本	Cost
参与度	Commitment

Figure 7.3. Cost and benefit of commitment to international climate change response (2).

net benefit of the climate change response organization itself will dampen the continuous investment and participation enthusiasm of countries, highlighting the inadequate investment from other organizations and the overspending of the climate change response organization. On the other hand, although the global total benefit continues to increase, the regional distribution of such benefit is apparently uneven. As a result, there will be various political and economic barriers that hinder the growth of net benefit from increased commitment.

(3) Comparison of the two equilibrium levels: According to the above analysis, if the benefit curve is simulated, it will be concave at first and then turn to be convex, which will lead to two levels of equilibrium (low and high) in contrast to the fixed cost curve. When the conditions for equilibrium are established, the two levels of equilibrium can help the international community optimize the

"commitment," that is, at the high and low levels of equilibrium, a relatively stable state can be formed at least within the climate change response organization. Evidently, although the equilibrium at low-level commitment has realized internal stability of the organization, its benefit to the global total output and total welfare are lower than that at high-level commitment.

(4) The fourth condition needs to be introduced here, that is, the general equilibrium condition as shown in the following formula:

$$Y = \sum f(\text{Commitment}_i)e^{rt} \tag{7.3}$$

In other words, if the commitment of countries to climate change response is included in the overall welfare considerations, it will affect the internal cost and benefit of the organization, those of other organizations, and finally the overall welfare level. Generally speaking, given the current scientific cognition and development stage, the commitment of countries to climate change response has a growing impact on the present value of the total economic welfare. However, based on the existing general equilibrium analysis, we have reason to believe that the commitment to climate change response does not increase the total economic welfare in an absolute sense. This is because once the commitment is higher than a certain level, no matter how the net benefit within the organization changes, it will adversely affect the overall economic welfare, thus causing their relationship to develop in the opposite direction. In this regard, Figure 7.4 is shown below to depict the relationship between climate change response and economic welfare.

In this way, the commitment at two levels of equilibrium has different impacts on welfare: The low-level one brings a lower level of output, while the high-level one brings a higher level of output. Therefore, from the perspective of output, the former is low-benefit equilibrium which is not what we want, while the latter can bring us better benefit. The development process of global climate change response is actually a process of seeking a balance between cost and benefit and achieving a higher level of output. Relatively speaking, if the current international climate change response framework is to be classified, then we should say it is quite close to low-benefit equilibrium, that is, countries "freely" determine their own

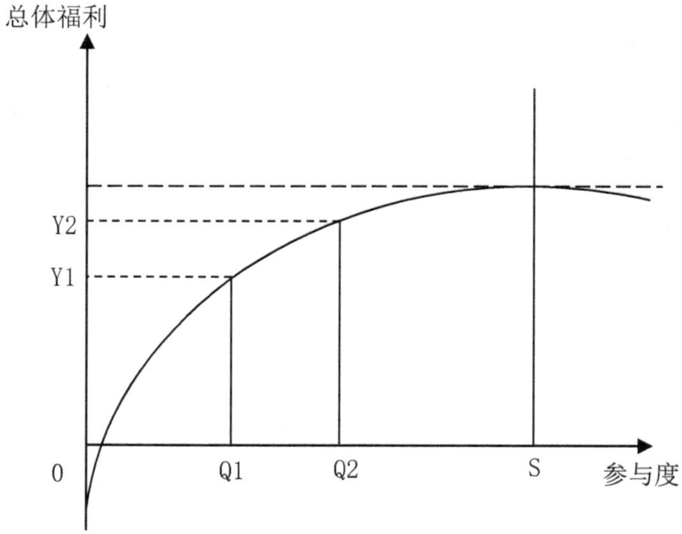

总体福利	Overall benefit
参与度	Commitment

Figure 7.4. International commitment to climate change response and economic benefit.

level of commitment on the basis of their own cost-benefit accounting. It was first confirmed at the Doha Conference in 2012, and then subject to feedback and summarization in 2015 before a new international response framework was formed to further strengthen and fix the equilibrium within the climate change response organization.

However, from a global perspective, such equilibrium is not optimal, because Figure 7.4 shows that there may be higher-level overall output and benefit in case of higher degree of commitment. The problem is that once we have reinforced and even fixed the equilibrium state of low-benefit commitment in the following years, how can we break this state and increase commitment to further optimize the level of output and benefit?

There may be two circumstances for more countries to commit to addressing global climate change:

(1) Changes in external conditions, such as intensified climate change, increased social preference for coping with climate change, government approval of more climate change control policies, and

technological progress, will simultaneously increase the cost of different degrees of commitment to climate change response (or reduce the benefit), which will make the cost curve move up (or make the benefit curve move down), thereby forcing the optimal equilibrium state of commitment to extend to the right. In this case, the valuation level of the climate change response organization will be raised, thereby increasing the relative value of various inputs, making the opportunity cost of commitment to the climate change response get lower, and the total output and benefit get higher.

(2) The endogenous mechanism promotes the increase of commitment, and the most important thing is the demonstration effect brought by participating countries/regions/organizations. Across the world, the commitment of countries/regions/organizations to climate change response is extremely uneven. Some of them are volunteers, and some are just followers. Therefore, it is possible to see slight changes in the degree of commitment. However, because of various endogenous reasons and incentive factors, the degree of commitment will continue to increase, and such an increase itself will bring benefit and costs. Once the participants get a net profit from it, such demonstration effect will attract an increasing number of non-participants in the next period. As mentioned above, because of the conditions for equilibrium, the additional net benefit of higher commitment brought about by the demonstration effect in the initial stage may not continue to increase commitment; instead, the degree of commitment will fall back to the state of equilibrium. There is a "tipping point." After certain key countries/regions/sectors join the climate change response process or implement certain landmark emissions reduction policies, the increase in commitment will have irreversible results, which will accelerate convergence to the next equilibrium point (i.e., high-benefit equilibrium) and gradually stabilize at this equilibrium point.

There is an important assumption for the output function, that is, 100% commitment cannot bring maximum output, which is based on the law of diminishing commitment marginal output. As described in the UN Intergovernmental Panel on Climate Change (IPCC) Fourth Assessment Report (2007a), the international community is faced with a variety of alternative emissions and emissions reduction scenarios, ranging from the "business as usual" scenario to the most positive response scenario, and they are arranged in an order from the lowest degree of commitment (≥ 0) to the highest degree of commitment ($<100\%$). In fact, the scenario selected

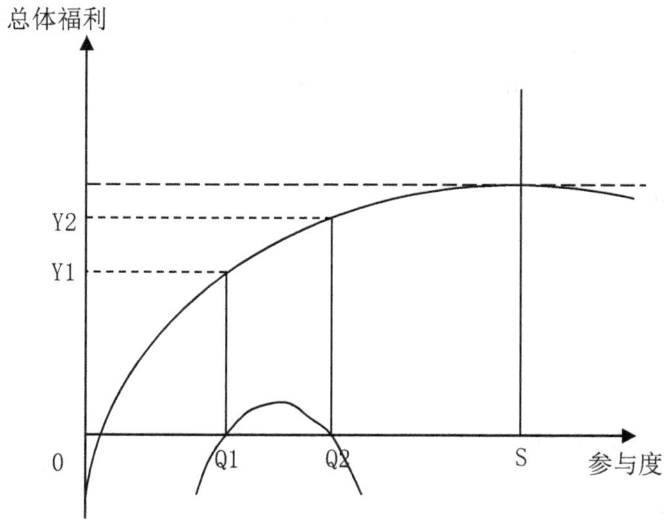

总体福利	Overall benefit
参与度	Commitment

Figure 7.5. International commitment to climate change response and economic benefit with 2 constraints.

by the international community is neither the lowest nor the highest commitment. This proves that neither the lowest nor the highest commitment is what we need from both the perspectives of cost-benefit and output. The disadvantage of low-degree commitment is that it cannot achieve intra-sectoral equilibrium, while the biggest disadvantage of high-degree commitment (or even "over commitment") is that excessive global investment in climate change response will cause distortions in resource allocation, which is depicted by the benefit curve that the level of benefit start declining after reaching a certain point as the degree of commitment keeps going up. Therefore, from the perspective of benefit and regardless of low- or high-degree equilibrium, countries' commitment to global climate change response cannot cross a certain limit, namely Point S in Figure 7.5.

7.5 Application of the Analysis Model

The significance of the above analysis model to the current practice of the international community in tackling climate change lies in the following two points.

7.5.1 *Two constraints of the development paths for international climate change response*

(1) The development path moves along the net benefit curve within the sector. As more countries commit to climate change response, the net benefit of the corresponding international emissions reduction framework will change accordingly (see Figure 7.5). Based on the existence of dual equilibrium, this curve will show an inverted U shape, and there will be two intersections (Q′, Q″) with the horizontal axis (commitment), meaning that the possible degree of commitment will only remain between these two points.

(2) For the sake of achieving equilibrium, the range between Q1 and Q2 is the most likely degree of commitment after stabilization. Therefore, the climate change response framework measured by the degree of commitment will fluctuate around these two points; at the same time, under the influence of internal and external conditions, a transition can be made between the two points. In other words, the selection of the degree of commitment will be finally limited between Q1 and Q2.

7.5.2 *The above constraints are fit for the current realistic choices of countries in tackling climate change*

(1) All countries/regions/sectors have joined in the climate change response framework to varying degrees, which will be eventually reflected in a moderate and balanced degree of commitment on a global scale ($Q1 \leq Q \leq Q2$). This properly explains that although some major carbon emitters have not signed any international agreement on climate change response or emissions reduction, they have already started coping with climate change through voluntary emissions reduction. On one hand, this comes from the endogenous emissions reduction need of these countries/regions/sectors based on their own costs and benefits. On the other hand, they are motivated to a certain extent by other countries/regions to respond to climate change and reduce emissions.

(2) The international community has made slow progress in responding to climate change in the past 25 years and has even regressed. This proves that, from a general equilibrium perspective, although increased commitment is conducive to higher output, the degree of response also depends on the balanced costs and benefits within the sector. Before the "tipping

point" is broken, it will be difficult for the international community to respond to climate change not on the basis of low-level equilibrium. In this context, all sorts of positive or negative policy fluctuations are found in different countries.

(3) If the international community wants to get out of the current dilemma in climate change response and break out of the low-level equilibrium, it must search and study the "critical mass" and its "critical level" that affect countries' commitment. The possible "critical mass" includes more accurate scientific knowledge of climate change, greater climate disaster, more systematic social mobilization, and more effective and feasible policy tools. Of course, in order to find this "critical mass" and its "critical level," the international community needs to have them verified through trial and error.

7.6 Summary

If the commitment of countries is used as a measure of the progress of the global climate change response framework, then the limited results of the Doha Conference show that such progress has almost come to a halt, reaching the lowest point since 1988 when the international community began negotiating and designing the response framework. Nevertheless, from the cost-benefit perspective, the analysis in this chapter indicates that this low point may have realized the equilibrium state determined by commitment. However, this is a low-level equilibrium point that can only bring low-level benefit and welfare. In the process of global response to climate change, there is bound to be high-level equilibrium that can bring high benefit and high welfare, that is, high-degree commitment can help to tackle climate change, reduce carbon emissions, and obtain better efficiency (output). However, for the global climate change response framework, we must find the corresponding "tipping point" and achieve a breakthrough, only in this way can we jump out of a low-level equilibrium state and enter a high-level equilibrium state.

Part 2

Analysis of Green Development Governance and Policies

Chapter 8

Evaluation and Analysis of Environmental Economic Policies in Jiangsu Province*

8.1 Introduction

According to the latest *Bulletin on the State of Environment of Jiangsu Province* (Monitoring and Information Center, 2016), the overall environmental quality of Jiangsu has remained stable, with some indicators improved and environmental protection work making positive progress. In recent years, Jiangsu has kept pressing ahead with environment-friendly projects, intensifying efforts in pollution control and emissions reduction, strengthening environmental supervision and law enforcement, deepening the reform of the environmental protection system, and fulfilling the annual tasks for reducing total emissions of major pollutants, air pollution prevention and control, and governance of key river basins. For example, in 2015, the environmental quality of surface water in Jiangsu was generally slightly polluted; although the ambient air quality of 13 provincially administered cities did not meet the national secondary standards, that of the whole province had improved compared with 2014. In the same period, Jiangsu realized a landmark transformation of industrial structure (the development of tertiary industry outpaced that of secondary industry); compared with 2010, the province saw its energy consumption per GDP drop by 22%, and construction land scale per GDP drop by 33%;

*This chapter is co-authored by Feng Yuanping, Fei Yeqi and Xu Jinwei.

it allocated 1.5 billion yuan as the annual provincial ecological compensation fund, and overfulfilled the national obligatory targets for the reduction of major pollutants:

According to incomplete statistics,[1] in 2015, Jiangsu Province introduced more than 30 environmental economic policies in accordance with national policies or on its own, covering five major fields such as environmental public finance, green finance, emissions trading and market, environmental protection industries, and related supporting policies, marking that the province would promote environmental protection work in an all-round way. In 2016, Jiangsu kept working on policy-making; by the time this book was finished, the province had issued more than 30 environmental economic policies related to the afore-mentioned five fields, hence continuing its previous year's efforts. The statistics also show that, from 2015 to 2016, Jiangsu directly forwarded and implemented more than 40 national environmental economic policies, which is indeed a substantial outcome, although no provincial-level policies were put into force in this period.

This chapter analyzes and evaluates the environmental economic policies formulated and implemented in Jiangsu Province from 2015 to 2016. The evaluation results show that Jiangsu has been doing a good job in policy-making for environmental and economic affairs, such as timely promulgation of corresponding policies, in line with provincial conditions and within the scope authorized by the State, and adjustment of resource tax rates. These policies are characterized with clear objectives, rich content, and strong executive power. Jiangsu is determined to actively play its role as a major developed province, vigorously develop Public–Private Partnership (PPP) and other green financial programs, further improve its investment climate, and earnestly implement the national environmental economic policies.

This chapter is made up of five sections. Section 8.1 is a general introduction. Section 8.2 is an overview of environmental economic policy evaluation, including a research review, evaluation methods, and indicators. Section 8.3 evaluates and analyzes Jiangsu's environmental economic policies and draws conclusions on the evaluation results.

[1] See Appendix A. This chapter mainly introduces the environmental economic policies and official public data of Jiangsu Province from 2015 to 2016. If there is no provincial policy in Jiangsu Province, the national policies shall prevail. All the data come from the official websites of administrative agencies, research papers, and mainstream media reports.

Section 8.4 analyzes the categories and SWOT of Jiangsu's policies. Section 8.5 sums up the content of this chapter.

8.2 Overview of Environmental Economic Policy Evaluation

8.2.1 *Overall progress*

Environmental economic policies refer to a series of "market-based" tools and means that are employed for environmental protection. They belong to the category of economic policies in the entire environmental policy framework, thus making them differ from other environmental regulatory tools based on laws or administrative regulations (Panayotou, 1994; Stavins, 2003; Tietenberg, 1990; Li, 2017). According to previous studies, market-based environmental economic policies, which mainly include traditional policy tools and means such as taxes, subsidies, emissions trading and deposit refund, have played an important role in regulating and improving the environmental quality in many countries (Barde, 1994).

After countries started implementing environmental economic policies, many countries have put policy evaluation on the agenda. According to Wang *et al.* (2016), "Environmental policy evaluation is important for improving policy design, overcoming the drawbacks and obstacles in policy implementation, and increasing the vitality and benefits of environmental policies." The policy evaluation can "serve as a useful reference for developing other environmental policies in the future, thereby improving the effect of policy implementation" (Song *et al.*, 2003).

Through decades of development, the international environmental economic policy evaluation has become increasingly systematic, both theoretically and practically. Based on different criteria, different evaluation models have been created, such as evaluation by time (*ex-ante*, in-progress, and *ex-post* evaluation), evaluation by objects (macro-evaluation and micro-evaluation), and evaluation by objectives (cost-benefit evaluation and procedure evaluation, Song *et al.*, 2011). In the research on environmental economic policy evaluation, a critical issue is to define the evaluation criteria, because the multiple criteria of different latitudes (i.e., relevance, effectiveness, fairness, flexibility, and consistency) play a vital role in environmental economic policy evaluation (Mickwitz, 2006).

Compared with international academic circles, the Chinese academic circle started late in environmental economic policy evaluation, because environmental economic policy tools were not employed in China over the years, and the policy evaluation itself is underdeveloped. In recent years, environmental economists have embarked on the research of related theories and practices, or even attempted policy evaluation at both macro (national policies) and micro (individual policies) levels, and have made substantial progress in Dong both theoretical study and practical application (Dong *et al.*, 2010, 2012; National Environmental Economic Policy Research and Pilot Project Technical Team, 2015a, 2015b, 2016).

At the same time, the Chinese academic circle began evaluating the provincial environmental economic policies (at the meso level). Provincial governments, as the most critical link in China's central–local environmental decentralization system, play a vital role in the formulation, implementation and delivery of environmental economic policies. The evaluation and research of provincial environmental economic policies can help us better understand the development trend of these policies and environmental protection system at the national level. For this reason, many scholars have devoted themselves into the evaluation of the environmental economic policies in Jiangsu and Guangdong provinces as well as in Tianjin Municipality (a provincial-level administrative region) (Chen *et al.*, 2015; Tian *et al.*, 2014; Zheng *et al.*, 2007).

8.2.2 *Evaluation of environmental economic policies in Jiangsu Province*

In terms of the research on Jiangsu's environmental economic policies, there are summarization and evaluation of the overall policy implementation during a certain period and interpretation of the implementation effect of specific single policies. The research literature mainly analyzes the price system for main pollutant emissions, environmental supervision, environmental liability insurance, and PPP-based green finance.

Regarding the overall evaluation of environmental economic policies, Zhang Bing, Zhang Yongliang and Bi Jun systematically combed and analyzed the existing environmental economic policies in Jiangsu, summarized its experiences and main problems in the process of policy implementation, and proposed specific suggestions for making improvements. According to Zhang *et al.* (2012) and Wang Wei, because of factors such as local protectionism, the effectiveness of Jiangsu's environmental economic policies has been restricted, so they recommended to use the policy mix instead of single policies.

With respect to the evaluation of specific single policies, Jin Haobo pointed out that the emission indicators should follow four principles (including gradual reduction); moreover, he also explored the method for determining the initial trial price of sulfur oxide emissions trading, and proposed suggestions for creating a secondary market for sulfur dioxide emissions trading. Tang Zhenya reviewed Jiangsu's environmental supervision, summed up its achievements and challenges in this regard, and put forward suggestions for improvement. He Zhen explained the reasons why Jiangsu could succeed in practicing environmental liability insurance. According to Li Jingzhao, the "green credit," as a kind of economic means, can help small and micro companies obtain bank loans through the development of low-carbon businesses and facilitate the upgrading of industrial structure; and on this basis, he demonstrated the need for further legalization and standardization of green credit. Tang Man and Lu Fengan generated statistics on the development trend and status of Jiangsu's PPP projects (with financial support) from 2013 to 2015, spoke highly of its achievements in this field, and came up with suggestions for improvement since the financial investment is not yet perfect.

To sum up, scholars have already conducted research on the overall environmental economic policies of Jiangsu Province and offered their suggestions. In addition, there are also rich studies on Jiangsu's specific policies which are relatively mature, such as the policies for public finance and for emissions trading and supervision. Green finance — one of the most dynamic fields — is another research topic. Although there are plenty of studies on China's policies for environmental protection industry, a special study on Jiangsu's environmental protection industry has not yet manifested.

8.2.3 *Evaluation methods and indicators*

The policy evaluation in this chapter is successively performed using the Content Analysis Method, AHP Method, and SWOT Analysis Method.

The entire evaluation process with the Content Analysis Method is divided into two parts: One is to analyze the policy content, and the other is to score the evaluation of the policy category. In order to make the policy evaluation more precise, the Experts Grading Method is adopted for quantification. The evaluation is made on basis of five indicators, that is, integrity, specificity, enforceability, coordination, and result. Among them, "integrity" denotes the quantity of policies (whether there are documents issued by upper-level departments and whether the policies are applicable at all levels); "specificity" means that policies shall have definite goals, detailed content, criteria or quantitative method; "enforceability" indicates that whether policies contain scheduling, clear division of responsibilities, implementation rules or associative directories for reference, rewards, and punishments; "coordination" means that whether the content of a policy matches up with the policies issued by upper-level departments or other departments, or whether their contents contradict with each other; "result" tells about whether the system is perfect and whether the effect of policy implementation is satisfactory. The full score of each indicator is 5 points (1 point stands for totally unsatisfying, and 5 points stand for totally satisfying) which are figured out by the evaluators after reviewing the contents of all policies.[2]

With varying importance, the above five indicators undergo weighted evaluation in combination with the AHP Method.[3] The evaluation process is as follows: the five indicators are compared in pairs to construct a judgment matrix, relative weight is to be scored by experts, the indicator weight is obtained after synthetic calculation, and the final evaluation result is obtained by integrating the indicator weight (see Figure 8.1).[4]

In order to depict the full picture of Jiangsu's environmental economic policies, including both their potentials and problems, a SWOT

---

[2]The evaluators reviewed and scored 15 sub-categories of policies, and the scores of the five categories of policies were averaged based on their respective sub-categories.

[3]The AHP (Analytical Hierarchy Process) Method was proposed in the early 1970s by T.L. Saaty, American operations researcher and professor of the University of Pittsburgh. In 1971, Saaty used this method to study the "Emergency Planning" developed by the US Department of Defense. In 1972, he applied this method to the study on electric power distribution in industrial sectors for the National Science Foundation. The AHP Method is essentially a way of thinking that breaks down a complex issue into several constituent factors, then groups these factors into a hierarchical structure according to the dominant relationship, and finally determines the relative importance of these factors in the hierarchy through pairwise comparison. The AHP combines qualitative and quantitative methods to express and process people's subjective judgments in a quantitative form.

[4]See Appendix B.

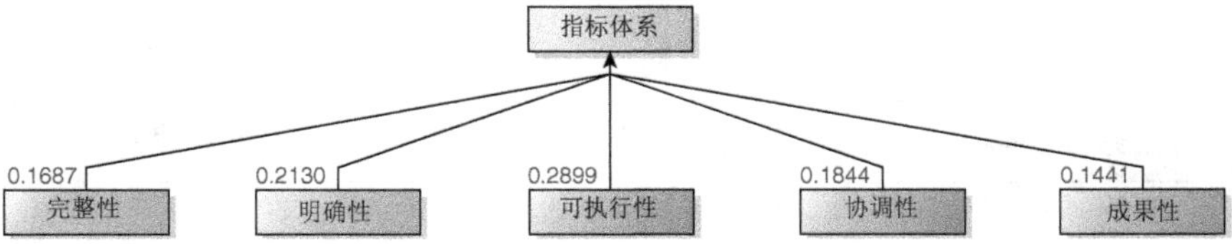

指标体系	Indicator system
完整性	Integrity
明确性	Specificity
可执行性	Enforceability
协调性	Coordination
成果性	Result

Figure 8.1. Weight of evaluation indicators.

Analysis is performed (see Section 8.4.2) to identify their Strength, Weakness, Opportunity, and Threat.

8.3 Analysis of Environmental Economic Policies in Jiangsu

In this chapter, environmental economic policies are divided into five categories[5] and 15 sub-categories (see Figure 8.2). The policies of sub-categories are respectively analyzed and scored, and then on basis of their weight, the five categories of policies are to be scored one by one.

8.3.1 *Analysis and evaluation of policy content*

8.3.1.1 *Public fiscal policies*

(1) *Public investment in environmental protection*. In terms of public investment in environmental protection, the governments at all levels in Jiangsu Province have been active in implementing national policies, with their investment in environmental protection increasing year after year and implementation of such investment remaining quite effective.

[5] Public fiscal policy, green financial policy, emissions trading and market policy, environmental protection industry policy, other supporting and supervisory measures.

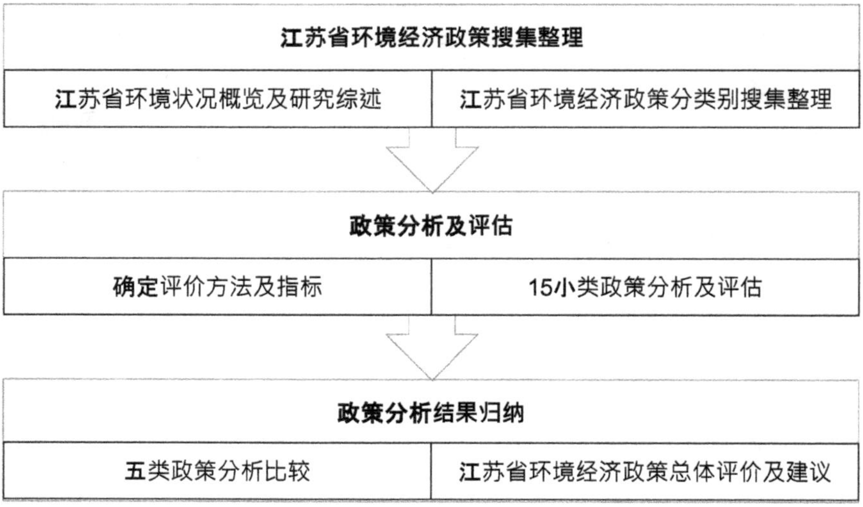

江苏省环境经济政策搜集整理	**Collect and sort out Jiangsu's environmental economic policies**
江苏省环境状况概览及研究综述	Overview of Jiangsu's environmental conditions and research summary
江苏省环境经济政策分类别搜集整理	Collect and sort out Jiangsu's environmental economic policies by category
政策分析及评估	**Policy analysis and evaluation**
确定评价方法及指标	Determine evaluation methods and indicators
15 小类政策分析及评估	Evaluate 15 sub-category policies
政策分析结果归纳	**Summarize policy evaluation results**
5 大类政策分析比较	Analyze and compare five categories of policies
江苏省环境经济政策总体评价及建议	Overall evaluation of and suggestions for Jiangsu's environmental economic policies

Figure 8.2. Research framework.

According to the statistics of the Jiangsu Provincial Bureau of Statistics, from 2011 to 2015, both the revenue in the general public budgets and the special budgetary expenditure on energy saving and environmental protection had kept increasing steadily, and the growth rate of fiscal revenue and provincial GDP had remained stable at around 10%. During this period, the annual growth rate of the investment in energy saving and environmental protection was 16% on average.[6]

[6] Jiangsu Provincial Bureau of Statistics. *Jiangsu Statistical Yearbook* (2016).

In terms of policy-making for public investment, Jiangsu Province has been actively developing provincial-level policies within the scope of authorization while earnestly implementing national policies. The policy-making of Jiangsu features wide coverage and high-level standardization:

(i) In specific areas, from 2015 to 2016, Jiangsu newly formulated or updated seven policies for special fiscal funds, covering transportation, construction, renewable resources, comprehensive utilization of crop straw, land reclamation, and comprehensive management of marine fishery,[7] with an aim to provide a reliable financial guarantee for environmental protection investment in different directions. The applicable scope and conditions of each policy are specified, requiring that funds must be used for special purposes and executive agencies must clearly define their powers and responsibilities.

(ii) In terms of the overall management of environmental funds, in 2016, Jiangsu issued the *Administrative Measures for the Use of Provincial Environmental Protection Guide Funds*,[8] which designate the administrative departments (the Department of Finance and the Department of Environmental Protection) and define their responsibilities, as well as specify the applicable scope of the funds, project application and review, funds allocation, standards, use and management, supervision and inspection, and performance assessment. The introduction of these measures is to cooperate with existing national and provincial budget management policies[9] and put forward regulations for green financial

---

[7] *Administrative Measures for Special Guide Funds for Provincial Energy Conservation and Emissions Reduction (Energy Conservation of Buildings and Modernization of Construction Industry) in Jiangsu Province, Administrative Measures for Special Funds for Energy Conservation and Emissions Reduction of Provincial Transportation in Jiangsu Province, Administrative Measures for Special Funds for Cyclic Utilization of Agricultural Renewable Resources in Jiangsu Province, Administrative Measures for Special Funds for Comprehensive Utilization of Crop Straws in Jiangsu Province, Administrative Measures for Special Funds for Provincial Land Reclamation in Jiangsu Province, Provincial Marine and Fishery Integrated Management and Administrative Measures for Special Funds for Resources and Environmental Protection in Jiangsu Province.*

[8] *Budget Law of the People's Republic of China, Regulations on Penalties for Financial Violations, Administrative Measures for Provincial Financial Special Funds in Jiangsu Province.*

[9] *Budget Law of the People's Republic of China, Administrative Measures for Provincial Financial Special Funds in Jiangsu Province.*

management at a macro level, so as to further standardize public financial policies.

In general, the public investment policies in Jiangsu, which are formulated on the basis of higher-level documents, are characterized by systematic and complete contents (covering almost all aspects of people's livelihood); definite and detailed objectives; unambiguous standards, procedures and supervision mechanism for the use of special funds; specific implementation rules by industry (such as marine and transportation); designated executive and supervisory agencies; and better coordination with other relevant policies. According to *Jiangsu Statistical Yearbook* (2016), the province increased public investment in environmental protection in 2015, but it failed to update the policies of sub-categories in a timely manner after new regulations came out in 2016.

(2) *Collection of environmental protection taxes and fees*. In terms of environmental protection taxes and fees, Jiangsu has been actively carrying out national policies in this regard and has issued provincial-level policies on resource tax, pollutant discharge fee, and energy-saving subsidy within the scope of authorization. According to the disclosed statistical data[10] of Jiangsu, from 2015 to 2016, the provincial resource tax and preferential vehicle purchase tax yielded substantial results, and Jiangsu was far ahead of other provinces in terms of collecting pollutant discharge fee.

With respect to green taxation, China stepped up the pace of green taxation reform since 2015. On one hand, breakthroughs have been made in the greening of consumption tax and value-added tax (VAT).[11] The State has introduced policies for levying consumption tax on batteries and

[10] See the detailed analysis below.

[11] In 2015, the Ministry of Finance (MOF) and the State Administration of Taxation (SAT) jointly issued the *Notice on Collection of Consumption Tax on Batteries and Coatings*. Then the two authorities jointly issued the *VAT Preferential Catalogue for Products and Labor Services Based on Integrated Use of Resources*, and at the same time announced to implement a 50% VAT refund policy for new-type wall materials to encourage integrated use of resources. Also in 2015, the MOF, the SAT and the General Administration of Customs (GAC) issued a notice to resume the collection of VAT on chemical fertilizers to restrict their excessive use. Besides, for the purpose of reducing or exempting VAT, the MOF and the SAT also issued the *Notice on the Implementation of the VAT Policy for Wind Power Generation* in 2015 and the *Notice on the Continuous Implementation of the VAT Policy for Photovoltaic Power Generation* in 2016.

coatings, and for collection, abatement, and exemption of VAT on wind power, new-type wall materials, and photovoltaic power generation. On the other hand, important progress has been made in resource tax reform, and the State has introduced policies for resource tax reform and collection.[12] In 2016, the State allowed provinces to set certain mineral resource tax rates within the scope of national policies,[13] in an aim to promote resource tax reform. In this context, the *Notice on Adjusting Certain Mineral Resource Tax Rates in Jiangsu Province* was released. In addition, Jiangsu has been actively implementing national preferential policies for vehicle purchase tax.[14] According to the statistics from the Jiangsu Provincial State Taxation Administration,[15] in the first three quarters of 2015, China's domestic VAT reached 248.5 billion yuan, while consumption tax and vehicle purchase tax were respectively 50.9 billion yuan and 18.8 billion yuan. In the first three quarters of 2016, domestic VAT rose to 29.8 billion yuan, while consumption tax and vehicle purchase tax were, respectively, 53.7 billion yuan and 17.2 billion yuan; both VAT and consumption tax rose from the same period of 2015, but vehicle purchase tax dropped significantly. According to the statistics from local taxation bureaus in Jiangsu Province,[16] the resource tax revenue of the province totaled 1.5 billion yuan from January to June of 2015, but plummeted to 900 million yuan in the same period of 2016, showing that Jiangsu's resource tax reform has produced initial results.

---

[12] In 2015, the MOF and the SAT jointly issued the *Notice on Implementing the Ad Valorem Taxation Reform of the Resource Tax on Rare Earth, Tungsten and Molybdenum*, the *Notice on Adjusting the Applicable Tax Standards for Iron Ore Resource Tax* (80% of the prescribed tax rate is adjusted down to 40%), and the *Administrative Measures for Coal Resource Tax Collection (Trial)* for further standardizing the management of coal resource tax.

[13] In 2016, the MOF and the SAT jointly issued the *Notice on Comprehensively Promoting Resource Tax Reform*, requiring provinces and cities to submit proposals for local mineral resource tax rates according to the requirements of the notice before May 31, 2016.

[14] In 2015, the MOF and the SAT jointly issued the *Notice on Reducing the Purchase Tax for Passenger Cars with Displacement of 1.6 Liters and Below*. In 2016, the two authorities jointly issued the *Notice on the Exemption of Vehicle Purchase Tax on Public Automobile and Electric Vehicles Purchased by Urban Public Transport Enterprises*.

[15] *Jiangsu's national taxation by tax types and by region in the first three quarters of 2015* (October 14, 2015); *Jiangsu's national taxation by tax types and by region in the first three quarters of 2016* (November 18, 2016).

[16] *Jiangsu's local tax revenue from January to June 2015* (July 13, 2015); *Jiangsu's local tax revenue from January to June 2016* (July 15, 2016).

In terms of energy-saving subsidies, Jiangsu attaches great attention to subsidizing photovoltaic power generation. On the basis of the national on-grid benchmark price of 1 yuan/kWh for photovoltaic power generation, Jiangsu subsides 0.15 yuan/kWh to the newly operated photovoltaic power projects in 2015, which is specified in the *Administrative Measures for Provincial Electricity Tariff Subsidies to Photovoltaic Power Generation Projects*.

With respect to pollutant discharge fees, Jiangsu issued two notices on adjusting the collection of pollutant discharge fees[17] in 2015, in an aim to adjust the benchmark collection standards for certain pollutant discharge fees, implement a differentiated charging policy, and set standards for certain pollutant discharge fees in the Taihu Lake Basin. In 2016, Jiangsu unveiled a new policy for charging volatile organic compounds (VOCs) emissions,[18] specifying the calculation of VOCs emissions, charging standards, reporting, payment, supervision, and management, in order to promote the standardization of VOCs emissions charges. In the same year, Jiangsu promulgated a sewage treatment charging policy,[19] which specifies the calculation, payment, and supervision of sewage treatment fees. In 2015, Jiangsu collected 2.218 billion yuan of pollutant discharge fees, ranking first in China for 15 consecutive years (Monitoring and Information Center, 2016). According to the statistics published by Jiangsu Provincial Bureau of Statistics,[20] the waste water, waste gas, and industrial solid waste discharges of Jiangsu maintained a downward trend in 2015, proving that the pollutant discharge fees are practicable and effective.

In general, the policies for collecting environmental protection taxes and fees in Jiangsu Province are not complete and systematic enough, because its tax policies only focus on specific fields and its pollution

---

[17] *Notice on Adjusting the Collection Standards for Pollutant Discharge Fees and Other Related Issues, Notice on Further Clarifying Issues Concerning the Collection of Pollutant Discharge Fees.*

[18] The *Measures of Jiangsu Province for Pilot Implementation of Volatile Organic Compounds Discharge Fees* developed on basis of the national *Measures for Pilot Implementation of Volatile Organic Compounds Discharge Fees.*

[19] The *Implementation Measures for the Collection, Use and Management of Sewage Treatment Fees* developed on basis of the national policies such as the *Notice on the Setting and Adjustment of the Charging Standards for Sewage Treatment Fees and Other Related Issues.*

[20] Jiangsu Provincial Bureau of Statistics. *Jiangsu Statistical Yearbook* (2016).

charging policies (formulated on basis of higher-level policies) only deal with VOCs emissions and wastewater discharge. Despite these shortcomings, these policies of Jiangsu Province have (i) definite objectives and rich contents, with each policy having its own objectives and standards; (ii) highly enforceable specific measures, with detailed and explicit implementation rules, specific charging standards, and calculation formulas available and executive and supervisory agencies specified; (iii) local policies that are highly consistent with national policies free from any contradiction; and (iv) preferential resource taxes that have yielded prominent results (i.e., Jiangsu saw its pollutant discharge keep decreasing in 2015, proving the significant effect of collecting pollutant discharge fees).

(3) In terms of ecological compensation and transfer payment, Jiangsu has issued more than 11 policies at all levels since 2015. In this province, the exploration and practice of ecological compensation policies mainly involve three aspects: public-good forests, river basin, and key functional districts.

(i) *Ecological compensation for forests*. Since the *Administrative Measures for the Provincial Compensation Funds for Forest Ecological Benefits* were introduced in 2007, Jiangsu has specified the ecological compensation standards and financial sources for public-good forests. As of 2013, the provincial fiscal budget for subsidizing public-good forests above the provincial level was adjusted up to 25 yuan per mu (1 mu ≈ 0.067 hectare) (Jiang *et al*., 2014). The Administrative Measures were revised in 2016 to define the minimum compensation standards for each city and county. The key public-good forests of Jiangsu cover a total area of 384,000 hectares, including 69,200 hectares of national public-good forests and 314,800 hectares of provincial public-good forests (Jiangsu Provincial Forestry Bureau, 2016).

(ii) *Ecological compensation for water environment*. The ecological compensation for water environment in Jiangsu is mainly for river basins. In 2013, based on the pilot ecological compensation for the Taihu Lake Basin and Tongyu River Area, Jiangsu issued the *Implementation Measures for Water Environment Ecological Compensation (Trial)*, becoming the first province in China that implements the water environment ecological compensation system, and set up 30 monitoring sections[21] to carry out the work. The three indexes — chemical oxygen demand (COD), ammonia nitrogen (NH_3-N) and total phosphorus (TP) — are monitored and calculated for compensation. To date, the practical cases of ecological compensation for river basins in China remain limited; while the water right trade in Yiwu of Zhejiang Province has created a precedent and become a typical model of market-based operation of river basin ecological compensation in China, no official announcement shows that Jiangsu has made such attempt.

(iii) *Ecological compensation for key functional districts*. In 2009, Jiangsu promulgated the *Regional Planning for Key Ecological Functional Conservation Districts*, which divides ecological protection into 12 major categories, involving a total of 569 key ecological functional conservation districts. This planning provides basic conditions for ecological compensation in natural reserves and key functional districts, and all cities at prefecture level or above have made explorations one after another. In 2015, the *Implementation Opinions of the General Office of Nanjing Municipal Government on Establishing an Ecological Compensation Mechanism for Water Conservancy Scenic Spots* and the *Administrative Measures for Ecological Compensation Funds in the Main Functional Districts of Zhenjiang City (Interim)* were released.

In general, Jiangsu has introduced a large number of ecological compensation policies which have already formed a complete system. These policies properly link with higher-level policies; contain explicit and detailed rules and standards; designate both executive and collaborate agencies and define their powers and responsibilities; facilitate cooperation between competent departments at different levels; and allow cities to make differentiated arrangement in light of their local situations.[22]

---

[21] Seven compensation sections and one comparison section were set up at the Wangyu River Basin. As for the other 14 rivers that flow into the Taihu Lake Basin, a total of 14 compensation and comparison sections were set up. At the Sunan Section of the Beijing–Hangzhou Grand Canal, there are five compensation sections and two comparison sections.

[22] The scope of ecological compensation in Suzhou City covers paddy fields, public-good forests, important wetlands, water sources, and scenic spots; that in Nanjing City includes ecological red-line zones, cultivated land, public-good forests, and water conservancy scenic spots.

Thanks to the implementation of these policies, Jiangsu has accumulated rich practical experiences in ecological compensation for public-good forests, cultivated land, wetlands, and other functional districts. Among them, the ecological compensation practices for public-good forests are the most fruitful; in contrast, although there are plenty of policies and regulations for water environment ecological compensation, the practical experiences in this field are far from enough.[23]

While ecological public welfare forests have achieved great results, there are many compensation policies and regulations in water environment basins, and there is less practical experience.

8.3.1.2 *Green financial policies*

(1) *Establishment of the green financial market.* Jiangsu has developed a green financial market by employing the PPP model. Since the Ministry of Finance (MOF) established the government-social capital cooperation center in 2014, Jiangsu has been actively taking part in introducing supporting policies, developing specific standards, and preparing for project declaration and implementation. According to incomplete statistics, from 2015 to 2016, China promulgated a total of nine green finance policies[24] at the national level, which have specified the PPP model in five aspects,

[23]The implementation of river basin ecological compensation policy has, to a certain extent, reduced the total pollutant discharge in the Taihu Lake Basin for years in a row; improved the water quality of key monitoring sections; promoted local industrial restructuring; and helped establish a long-term mechanism for coordinating environmental, economic, and social development. The ecological compensation for public-good forests has covered the entire province and yielded good results. However, Jiangsu is still a new hand in carrying out the ecological compensation policy, and mistakes and omissions are unavoidable; for example, the compensation standard for public-good forests remains low and over-simplified, the compensation mechanism for drinking water sources and ecologically vulnerable areas is not yet available, and the ecological compensation in rural areas has drawn little attention.

[24]*Guiding Opinions on Promoting the PPP Model in Public Service Field, Guidelines for PPP's VFM Evaluation (Trial), Interim Measures for the Financial Management of PPP Projects, Notice on Promoting the Work for PPP's Development Financing, Administrative Measures for Franchising of Infrastructure and Public Utilities, Notice on Regulating the Management of PPP Contracts, Guidelines for the Financial Affordability Demonstration of PPP Projects, Opinions on the Key Work for Deepening the Economic Structural Reform in 2015, Interim Measures for the Financial Management of PPP Projects.*

that is, overall direction, specific item identification, set-up operation, approval criteria, and fund guarantee mechanism. In response to this, Jiangsu worked out a series of provincial-level policies in combination with local actual situations, which has ensured the effective implementation of national policies. These provincial policies, including the *Implementation Measures for the PPP Financing Fund in Jiangsu Province (Trial)*, the *Implementation Opinions on Promoting the PPP Model in Public Service Field*, and the *Administrative Measures for the Rewards and Subsidies to PPP Projects (Trial)*, have further improved the standardization and enforceability of the PPP model. In 2015, the Department of Finance of Jiangsu Province initiated the establishment of the "Jiangsu Provincial PPP Financing Fund." In December of the same year, the first project sponsored by this fund was signed,[25] marking that Jiangsu will provide better services, in terms of operation and financing, to the PPP projects.

In terms of the implementation of PPP projects,[26] Jiangsu has been actively carrying out the submission, data entry, and pilot work of PPP projects and insisting on regular inspection and timely reporting of problems and results. In case any project fails to meet the pilot project requirements, the competent department will make public explanations in an open, fair, and transparent manner. All the procurement activities associated with the PPP projects are carried out in strict accordance with the specifications. Jiangsu has implemented a large number of PPP pilot projects and achieved fruitful results. These projects mainly deal with environmental remediation, sewage treatment, garbage treatment, and elderly care.

Presently, a total of 388 PPP projects are already included in Jiangsu's database, covering 17 fields and a total investment of 761.5 billion yuan. Among them, there are 315 new projects with a total investment of 641.8 billion yuan to be built 15 years later and 73 stock projects with a total investment of 119.7 billion yuan, basically realizing the full coverage of PPP projects in cities and counties across the province. According to the statistics from Jiangsu's Department of Finance, 75 projects with a total investment of 161 billion yuan have absorbed 125.3 billion yuan of social capital (the average share of social capital is 81%), with average length of cooperation of 19 years. Among the provincial-level PPP pilot projects,

[25]Retrieved from http://item.jschina.com.cn/ppp/

[26]Retrieved from http://czt.jiangsu.gov.cn/col/col7969/index.html

30 of the planned 73 projects are approved; their total investment is as much as 86.379 billion yuan, including 64.856 billion yuan of social capital.

In a nutshell, the green financial policies of Jiangsu are fairly complete, systematic, and executable. These policies, which are formulated on basis of higher-level policies, are characterized by scientific and reasonable contents as well as definite objectives. They play a guiding role in making full use of public funds and exploiting the advantages of financial institutions and social capital and propose to address financing problems by setting up a special fund. Thanks to the implementation of these policies, Jiangsu has launched a large number of highly standardized PPP projects that can attract huge investment from all sources, thus outperforming other provinces in China in this regard. However, the green financial policies of Jiangsu somewhat ignore the divisions of powers and responsibilities between competent departments, that is, the Department of Finance is too powerful, while the Environmental Protection Department and the Development and Reform Commission are too humble.

(2) *Construction and innovation of green financial products*. In Jiangsu Province, the category of green financial products is quite simple, that is, most of them are green-credit products, and the financial institutions that are involved in this business refer to banks. The green credit flows into almost all types of green projects, such as energy conservation, pollution prevention and control, clean transportation, and new energy utilization.

From 2015 to 2016, the State promulgated a number of energy efficiency credit policies.[27] In response to this, Jiangsu immediately embarked on formulating provincial policies and vigorously developing green credit

[27]In 2015, the China Banking Regulatory Commission (CBRC) and the National Development and Reform Commission (NDRC) jointly issued the *Energy Efficiency Credit Guidelines*, in an aim to encourage financial institutions to implement energy efficiency credit to support industrial restructuring and corporate technological transformation and upgrading. In 2016, the PBOC, together with other seven ministries and commissions, issued the *Opinions on Financial Support for the Stable Growth, Restructuring and Benefit Growth of Industries*, in order to implement differentiated industrial credit policies, and guide financial institutions to intensify support for strategic emerging industries and for technological transformation and upgrading of traditional industries. The PBOC also released the *Opinions on Supporting the Iron & Steel and Coal Industries to Resolve Overcapacity and Achieve Development Out of Difficulties*, for the purpose of encouraging financial institutions to support the "de-capacity" of iron & steel and coal industries through the implementation of differentiated credit policies.

in the province. In 2016, Jiangsu implemented the policy on offering financial support to manufacturing industry,[28] further increased the credit loan placement in manufacturing industry, and encouraged financial institutions to develop green financial services such as pollution emissions rights and carbon pledge loans and build up their ability to innovate green financial products and services.

The news on the website of the Nanjing Branch of the People's Bank of China (PBOC, The Nanjing Branch, 2016) show that Jiangsu has achieved remarkable results in credit business. The banks in Nanjing City have intensified financial support to local manufacturers by increasing their credit loans and implementing differentiated credit policies to promote the transformation and upgrading of the entire manufacturing industry.

According to the statistics from the Jiangsu Provincial Economic and Information Commission (2016), in 2016, the growth rate of industrial investment slowed down, and technological transformation became a powerful driving force for investment growth. Over January–August, Jiangsu completed an industrial investment of 1,531.49 billion yuan, registering an increase of 10.1% year-on-year, but the growth rate was 1.8% lower than the same period of the previous year. The investment structure has been continuously optimized with the investment in energy-intensive industries increasing slowly. Over January–August, the provincial energy-intensive industries completed an investment of 287.52 billion yuan, registering a year-on-year growth rate of 7.4%, which was 2.7% lower than that of industrial investment. To sum up, the effect of financial support for the transformation and upgrading of manufacturing industry was becoming apparent.

In general, the green financial product policies of Jiangsu are formulated based on higher-level policies. However, most of these policies are about green credit, which is why the insurance, securities, bonds, and carbon financial products of Jiangsu have been developing slowly. These green credit policies feature definite objectives, rich contents, and explicit quantitative regulations on the amount of financing and loan risk compensation fund pool. Moreover, these policies have specified the measures for credit implementation, designated executive and supervisory agencies and

---

[28] Jiangsu introduced the *Provincial Government's Opinions on Financial Support for the Development of Manufacturing Industry* on basis of relevant national policies, e.g., the *Opinions on Financial Support for the Stable Growth, Restructuring and Benefit Growth of Industries*.

divided their powers and responsibilities, and even set out specific requirements for the work in all links and designated responsible agencies. From 2015 to 2016, Jiangsu only laid down the policies on credit and loan, instead of updating the policies on other green financial products, hence the development achievements of green finance have not spread across the province.

(3) *Establishment and improvement of the financial market system.* In order to establish and improve the financial market system, Jiangsu has developed detailed policies on disclosure of blacklist for dishonesty, eco-environmental assessment, and supervision of venues for financial transactions.

From 2015 to 2016, Jiangsu issued only four policies on the establishment and improvement of the financial market system; they may be few but were effective. On one hand, Jiangsu introduced the publicity policy on the blacklist for serious dishonesty,[29] which specifies the information sources of the blacklist, content to be disclosed, validity period of the publicity, and objections, in order to further enhance the effect of the punishment mechanism for discreditable behaviors and guide the work of competent departments. On the other hand, Jiangsu came up with the policies on supervision of trading venues,[30] which specify the establishment, change, termination, operation, and supervision of the trading venues in the province and designate responsible agencies, in an aim to supervise all sorts of trading platforms that are legally established in Jiangsu and engaged in equity securities transaction. In 2015, the *County-level Financial Eco-environmental Assessment Indicator System in Jiangsu Province* was unveiled, covering 42 indicators in five categories (i.e., economic environment, financial operation, social credit, legal environment, and policy environment), to apply to the review of county-level financial ecology and comprehensive assessment of province-wide

---

[29]The *Administrative Measures for the Publicity of the Blacklist of Serious Dishonesty in Jiangsu Province (Trial)* were introduced on basis of relevant policies, e.g., the *Regulations on Government Information Disclosure*, and the *Punishment Measures for Dishonest Social Legal Persons in Jiangsu Province (Trial)*.

[30]The *Measures for Supervision and Administration of Trading Venues in Jiangsu Province (Revised)* were introduced on basis of relevant national policies, e.g., the *Decision of the State Council on Cleaning up and Rectifying Various Trading Venues and Guarding Against Financial Risks*.

financial ecology. In 2016, Jiangsu formulated and updated the supporting policies[31] for county-level financial ecological assessment, in order to upgrade the province-wide financial eco-environment in combination with new situations and new characteristics in this regard.

In sum, the policies of Jiangsu for construction and improvement of the financial market system are made up of three parts: publicity of the blacklist for dishonesty, supervision of financial trading venues, and financial eco-environmental assessment. These policies have definite and detailed objectives; classified and scored eco-environmental assessment indicators; and specific measures and corresponding rewards and punishments. However, they do have some shortcomings: Each policy itself is complete, but they are not closely correlated with each other; the latest policies on the implementation of eco-environmental assessment and responsible supervisory organs are still unavailable; and there are no higher-level policies for guiding financial eco-environmental assessment. Besides, the statistics about Jiangsu's financial market supervision and assessment over 2015–2016 are not explicit enough. Although the financial eco-environmental assessment indicator system has been updated in a timely manner, there is no annual report explaining the scores of each county.

8.3.1.3 *Policies for trading of pollution discharge rights*

(1) *Establish a system for paid use and trading of discharge rights.* Jiangsu started explorations into the paid use of pollution discharge rights since 2002. In the environmental protection policies promulgated by the province since 2003, there are explicit requirements for "paid use of initially allocated pollution discharge rights." In 2004, Jiangsu made public the *Study on the Pilot Paid Allocation and Trading of Water Pollutant Discharge Rights in Jiangsu Province*, and carried out pilot work on COD emissions trading in some key industries in Nantong and other cities. In 2007, the province issued the *Regulations on the Prevention and Control of Water Pollution in Taihu Lake of Jiangsu Province (Revised)*, stipulating that the Taihu Lake Basin shall, based on pilot projects, gradually implement the system for paid allocation and trading of major water

---

[31]*Financial Ecological Environment Construction Plan, Appraisal Measures for the Establishment of Financial Ecological Counties.*

pollutant discharge rights. In 2008, the MOF, MEP, and Jiangsu Provincial Government launched a pilot project for the paid use and trading of major water pollutant discharge rights in the Taihu Lake Basin in Wuxi City. Afterwards, Taizhou, Nanjing, Suzhou, and other cities have successively introduced discharge rights trading policies.[32]

At present, Jiangsu has four pollution factors (COD, sulfur dioxide, ammonia nitrogen, and nitrogen oxides) included into the paid use and trading of pollution discharge rights. In 2015 and 2016, the provincial-level pollution discharge rights trading was successively held in Taizhou and Suzhou; the trading volume in 2015 reached about 15 million yuan (Department of Ecology and Environment of Jiangsu Province, 2016). Jiangsu Property Rights Exchange Center and some companies co-founded Jiangsu (Suzhou) Environmental Resources Exchange Center and set up a special website to release information on the trading of carbon emissions, pollution discharge rights, and wastes.

In general, the policies on pollution emission trading in Jiangsu are relatively complete, and more and more policies are as concrete as city-based. These policies are highly executable with definite objectives, specifications for related indicators, and strict requirements for the qualifications of emission rights trading companies, as well as specific timelines. An increasing number of cities and companies have taken part in pollution emission trading and achieved positive results. However, Jiangsu still needs to overcome some shortcomings in this regard; for example, the pollution emission trading is not tied to project management and total emissions control. Under the background of total emissions reduction, the scope of pilot trading programs and tradable emission allowances are limited, the verification of pollutant emissions is not smooth enough, and public participation is far from active.

(2) *Market of resource-use rights*. To promote the development of a resource-use rights market, all levels of local governments of Jiangsu Province have brought forth more than 17 policies on water, electricity,

---

[32]Three local policies were promulgated in 2014, i.e., *Interim Measures for the Paid Use and Trading of Pollution Discharge Rights in Taizhou City*, *Notice of Nanjing Municipal People's Government on Issuing the Implementation Plan for the Establishment of a Regional Pollution Discharge Rights Trading Mechanism*, and *Notice of Suzhou Municipal Environmental Protection Bureau on Holding Activities for Trading Discharge Rights of Major Pollutants*.

natural gas, and other resources or resource markets, which are able to guide the assessment of water resources management system, water charge, differential electricity tariff, and marketization of electricity industry.

In terms of water resource reform, Jiangsu issued the *Implementation Opinions on Promoting the Comprehensive Reform of Agricultural Water Prices*[33] in 2016. Later, Xuzhou City released the opinions on comprehensive reform of agricultural water prices at the municipal level, and carried out pilot work to distribute agricultural water rights.

In terms of the reform of electricity industry, Jiangsu issued the *Implementation Rules for the Pilot Direct Transactions between Power Users and Power Generation Companies in Jiangsu Province (Trial)*[34] as early as 2012, and the contracted transaction volume that year reached 1.316 billion kWh. In 2014, Jiangsu issued the *Interim Measures for the Pilot Direct Transactions between Power Users and Power Generation Companies in Jiangsu Province* and the *Working Plan for Expanding the Pilot Direct Transactions between Power Users and Power Generation Companies in Jiangsu Province*, which specify the entry conditions, transaction mode and prices, and the rules for measurement and settlement in the direct trading market. In 2015, Jiangsu issued the *Notice on Further Expanding the Pilot Work for Direct Transactions of Electric Power in 2015*, marking that the third batch of large power users are allowed to join in the direct electricity transactions. In 2016, Jiangsu issued the *Notice on Further Expanding the Pilot Work for Direct Transactions of Electric Power in 2016* and established the Electricity Market Management Committee. In addition, Jiangsu-based companies are required to pay for differential electricity tariff based on their environmental protection credit.[35] In terms of natural gas reform, Jiangsu has come up with some

---

[33]These opinions of Jiangsu were formulated on basis of the *Opinions of the General Office of the State Council on Promoting the Comprehensive Reform of Agricultural Water Prices*.

[34]These rules of Jiangsu were formulated on basis of the *Notice of the SERC on Printing and Distributing the Basic Rules for Pilot Direct Transactions between Power Users and Power Generation Companies (Trial)*.

[35]*Notice of Jiangsu Provincial Price Bureau and Jiangsu Provincial Department of Environmental Protection on Issues Concerning Trial Implementation of Differential Electricity Tariffs Based on Environmental Credit Ratings*.

policies on price control, but there is yet no specific policy on the natural gas market.[36]

In general, Jiangsu has promulgated a large number of policies related to the market of resource use rights on basis of higher-level policies, but these policies are more specific and complete, and many of them focus on certain cities and counties. These policies contain explicit and enforceable requirements for differential water price, sewage treatment price, and electricity tariff, and they are linked up with the environmental credit system. Jiangsu Province closed 71 electricity deals in 2016, and saw the transaction volume increase by 50.5 billion kWh in 2017. Although the water power and natural gas markets have not yielded rich results, the resource markets in Jiangsu on the whole are changing for the better.

(3) *Construction of a third-party governance market.* In Jiangsu Province and on a national scale, the construction of a third-party governance market remains at an initial stage.

In 2014, the *Opinions of the General Office of the State Council on the Implementation of Third-party Governance of Environmental Pollution* were released, presenting the necessity and existing problems of third-party governance of environmental pollution, and also coming up with solutions. However, these opinions are more like a theoretical guide than practical guide. Since then, the national-level policies in this regard have been updated slowly, leading to hardly any increase in the number of follow-up policies at the local level. In 2015, the State promulgated the *Guiding Opinions on the Implementation of Third-Party Governance of Environmental Pollution in Coal-fired Power Plants*, providing for the third-party governance in the pollution control of coal-fired power plants in detail, such as division of responsibilities and selection criteria. Jiangsu fails to develop a great number of specific policies in response, and these policies do not have a broad coverage. However, they are quite executable and put into force as soon as they were introduced. From 2015 to 2016, Jiangsu unveiled the supporting policies on the disposal of waste electronic products[37] to strengthen the daily supervision of relevant

[36]The *Opinions on Accelerating the Utilization of Natural Gas*, issued by the Oil and Gas Department of the National Energy Administration in 2016, include Jiangsu as one of the pilot provinces, but it ends up with nothing definite.

[37]The *Measures for the Third-party Verification of the Dismantling and Disposal of Waste Electrical and Electronic Products in Jiangsu Province* were formulated on basis of the

companies; in terms of carbon emissions, Jiangsu has come up policies[38] to provide for the qualifications and methodologies of third-party verification agencies and inspectors, as well as regulators and penalties for violations of the regulations. In February 2016, the Jiangsu Provincial Development and Reform Commission issued a notice for the open selection of third-party carbon emissions verification agencies, and announced the list of eligible agencies (the first batch) on May 5.[39]

In general, the policies of Jiangsu related to the third-party governance market, which contain definite objectives, detailed implementation rules and measures, and rewards and punishments, are highly executive. Most of these policies focus on coal-fired power plants, waste electronic products, and carbon emissions, implying that their applicable scope needs to be further expanded. These provincial-level policies, which are based on higher-level policies (though not many), are mainly implemented by Jiangsu Provincial Development and Reform Commission. However, their implementation would be more effective if they were directly under the control of the Environmental Protection Department. Right after the promulgation of third-party governance policies, Jiangsu started the open selection of third-party verification agencies; the attitude is active enough, but the effect of these policies needs to stand the test of time.

8.3.1.4 *Policies for environmental protection industry*

(1) *Industry access policies*. Most of the industry access policies of Jiangsu are developed for coal power, industrial, and information industries. Such policies for other industries are too fragmented to form a

---

policies like the *Regulations on the Administration of Recycling and Disposal of Waste Electrical and Electronic Products*, and the *Notice on Carrying out the Review of the Dismantling and Disposal of Waste Electrical and Electronic Products in Jiangsu Province*.

[38]The *Administrative Measures for Third-party Verification Institutions of Carbon Emissions Trading in Jiangsu Province (Interim)* were formulated on basis of the policies like the *Notice of the General Office of the NDRC on Effectively Doing a Good Job to Fulfill the Key Tasks of Launching the National Carbon Emissions Trading Market*.

[39]The list is published on the website of Jiangsu Provincial Development and Reform Commission. Retrieved from http://fzggw.jiangsu.gov.cn/art/2016/4/6/art_319_6650769.html

system. Jiangsu issued the *Thirteenth Five-Year Plan for Energy Conservation* (2016–2020) and the *Thirteenth Five-Year Plan for Industrial Green Development* in 2016, putting forward definite tasks and indicators for the upgrading and adjustment of industrial and environmental protection industries in the province, but the implementation effect of these plans needs to be observed and evaluated.

From 2015 to 2016, Jiangsu first issued the *Notice on Producing the Directories of Structural Adjustment, Restrictions and Elimination for Industrial and Information Industry, and Imposing Energy Consumption Limits*, and then began producing the list for guiding the restructuring of industrial and information technology industries and the directories of the products to be restricted or eliminated. In these directories, 14 categories of products (e.g., coal, steel, and automobile) are to be restricted; a total of 137 products based on outdated production technology and equipment are to be phased out; 110 categories of key energy-using products are to be subject to energy consumption limits; and there are unambiguous definitions and standards for each product.

The regulatory policies for other industries were mentioned in the *Aquatic Eco-environmental Functional District Planning of the Taihu Lake Basin in Jiangsu Province (Trial)* (hereinafter referred to as the "Planning"), and the *Notice of the Provincial Government on Strengthening Eco-environmental Protection Work in the Yangtze River Basin* (hereinafter referred to as the "Notice"), which were both promulgated in 2016. According to the Planning document, the Jiangsu Provincial Government will manage these industries through grading, zoning, classification, and phased assessment and implement differentiated policies for industrial restructuring and access in river basins. According to the Notice, the Jiangsu Provincial Government will formulate and implement an annual elimination plan for backward production capacity, in an aim to resolve certain overcapacity and withdraw from certain fields characterized with low-end production capacity.

In general, most of the industry access policies of Jiangsu issued over 2015–2016, which are about coal power, industrial, and information industries, are fairly complete and standardized; but such policies for other industries are limited to the Taihu Lake and Yangtze River basins and not explicit enough. Regarding the directories of the products to be restricted or eliminated, they are fairly independent and short of the support from higher-level policies. As for the afore-said Planning and Notice, although they are fairly complete and closely linked up with the higher-level policies, their industrial regulations are inexplicit. According to the *Bulletin on the State of Environment of Jiangsu Province (2015)*,[40] the ecological governance of river and lake basins in Jiangsu has achieved certain results, but there are few statistics showing the implementation effect of industry access policies.

(2) *Industry supporting policies.* In 2016, Jiangsu introduced the *Thirteenth Five-Year Plan for Industrial Green Development* and the *Thirteenth Five-Year Plan for Energy Conservation*, both of which aim to vigorously develop green industries, new energy industries, and other emerging industries, but are not executable enough for lack of specific supporting or subsidizing measures. Over 2015–2016, Jiangsu had not come up with any policies dedicated to industrial support. In 2016, the Jiangsu Provincial Government issued the *Opinions on Promoting the Redevelopment of Inefficient Industrial Land*, proposing to classify the land supply policies for redeveloping inefficient industrial land, define the scope of VAT collection, and avoid double tax collection, which is taken as an indirect industry supporting policy. In the same year, the *Opinions of Jiangsu Provincial Government on Financial Support for the Development of Manufacturing Industry* was issued to guide financial institutions to intensify their support for strategic emerging industries, high-tech industries, technological transformation and upgrading of traditional industries, especially green industries.

In 2015, the State Council came up with the *Opinions on Promoting the Application of Advanced Photovoltaic Products and Industrial Upgrading*, which is an industry supporting policy at the national level, pointing out that fiscal funds and government procurement should play a role in supporting the progress of photovoltaic power generation technology, so that advanced photovoltaic products can get access to sufficient financial support.

In general, the industry-supporting policies of Jiangsu are not complete, with most of them focusing on the application of advanced photovoltaic technology and redevelopment of inefficient industrial land; and relevant policies are rarely updated. The existing policies have provided for development of different industrial lands and set standards for identifying and subsidizing advanced photovoltaic products, but they are not highly executable for lack of detailed implementation rules. All policies are implemented by

[40] Monitoring and Information Center, Environmental Protection Department of Jiangsu Province (May 30, 2016). *Bulletin on the state of environment of Jiangsu Province (2015)*.

competent authorities with powers and responsibilities clearly divided, but they do not have direct support from higher-level policies. Besides, the lack of publicity is partly blamed for few marked achievements of these policies.

(3) *Industry regulatory policies*. In terms of industry regulation, in 2015, Jiangsu was actively implementing the national and provincial policies under the guidance of the Twelfth Five-Year Plan (2011–2015), achieving remarkable results in the fields of energy-saving (coal-fired and photovoltaic power generation), petrochemistry, and green transportation.

In the petrochemical field, Jiangsu issued the *Planning and Layout Scheme for the Petrochemical Industry in Jiangsu Province*[41] in 2015, stating that the province should optimize and adjust the layout of the petrochemical industry, take account of resource and environmental constraints, guarantee safety production and environmental protection, and prevent hidden social risks.

In the field of green transportation, Jiangsu issued the *Implementation Opinions on Accelerating the Development of Green and Low-Carbon Circular Transportation*[42] in 2015, pointing out that the province should pay great attention to energy conservation, environmental protection, low-carbon emission and high efficiency in transportation infrastructure, organization, technologies, equipment and management capabilities, actively introduce new energy-saving and environmental protection technologies, and specify the specific work of organization and implementation.

In the field of energy, Jiangsu — one of the major provinces of energy in China — has been committed to upgrading and transformation of energy industry. In 2015, the *Action Plan for Upgrading and Transformation of Coal-fired Power Generation for Energy Conservation and Emissions*

---

[41] It was formulated on basis of the national policies such as the *Planning and Layout Scheme for the Petrochemical Industry* and the *Notice on Doing a Good Job in the Implementation of the "Planning and Layout Scheme for the Petrochemical Industry."*

[42] The opinions were formulated on basis of the *Framework Agreement for the Ministry of Transport and Jiangsu Provincial Government to Jointly Promote the Development of Jiangsu's Green and Low-Carbon Circular Transportation*, the *Notice on Printing and Distributing the Outline of the Transportation Modernization Plan in Jiangsu Province (2014–2020)*, and the *Notice on Printing and Distributing the Development Plan for the Green and Low-Carbon Circular Transportation in Jiangsu Province (2013–2020)*.

Reduction in Jiangsu Province (2014–2020) was introduced, requiring Jiangsu-based coal-fired power plants to improve their environmental protection policies and measures, in order to fully implement the national strategy of "clean energy, energy conservation, and pollution reduction." Jiangsu issued the *Notice on the Annual Newly-added Photovoltaic Power Generation Capacity*[43] consecutively in 2015 and 2016, in a bid to vigorously develop the photovoltaic power generation and promote energy conservation and environmental protection in energy industry. In 2016, the province issued the *Notice on Issuing the Implementation Plan of Newly-added Production Capacity and Organizational Structure of Photovoltaic Power Stations in 2016*, so as to implement differential electricity tariffs for companies with different environmental credit ratings. According to statistics from the Jiangsu Provincial Economic and Information Commission,[44] in 2015, the province saw the power source infrastructure construction complete an investment of 7.615 billion yuan, with newly-added solar power generation totaling 14.632 million kilowatts. Over January–November 2016, the power source infrastructure construction completed an investment of 7.595 billion yuan, with newly-added solar power generation totaling 10.682 million kilowatts. The development of photovoltaic power generation in Jiangsu Province is inarguably fruitful.

Besides, the *Work Program for the Prevention and Control of Water Pollution in Jiangsu Province* was issued in 2015, proposing to speed up the elimination of outdated production capacity and optimize the industrial layout to improve the water eco-environment of the whole province. In the same year, Jiangsu developed the *Industry Classification Table for Consulting Agencies That Join in Clean Production Audit of Key Companies in Jiangsu Province*, and forwarded two national-level clean

---

[43] It was formulated on basis of the national regulations on the management of photovoltaic power stations in recent years, like the *Notice of the National Energy Administration on Issuing the Implementation Plan for Construction of Photovoltaic Power Stations in 2015*, the *Guiding Opinions on Improving the Scale Management of Photovoltaic Power Generation and Selecting Investment Entities Through Competition*, and the *Notice on Issuing the Implementation Plan for Construction of Photovoltaic Power Stations in 2016*.

[44] Electricity and Energy Office under the Jiangsu Provincial Economic and Information Commission. *The Electricity Generation and Consumption in Jiangsu Province over January-December 2015* (January 6, 2016); *The Electricity Generation and Consumption in Jiangsu Province over January–December 2016* (December 6, 2016).

production evaluation indicator systems.[45] According to the information from the Environmental Protection Department of Jiangsu Province,[46] the *List of Key Companies under Clean Production Audit in Jiangsu Province* was made public consecutively in 2015 and 2016, in order to verify the status of clean production in the province, showing that Jiangsu has been actively implementing the national clean production policies.

In general, over 2015–2016, Jiangsu successively issued industry regulatory policies based on higher-level policies, covering a wide range of fields such as petrochemical, photovoltaic power generation, and transportation. The regulatory policies for individual industries contain definite objectives, informative contents, and concrete measures, and they have specified executive and supervisory organs. Different policies are able to complement with each other. Jiangsu has effectively implemented the national evaluation indicator system for clean production and greatly improved its pollution discharge, but it is only able to update the data about photovoltaic power generation, with the data about other industries still unavailable.

8.3.1.5 *Other supporting and supervisory measures*

(1) *Environmental capital accounting*. Although Jiangsu has taken some actions in dealing with environmental capital accounting, the available national policies for reference can be counted on one's fingers.

According to the *Notice of the General Office of the State Council on Printing and Distributing the Pilot Program for the Preparation of Natural Resources Balance Sheets (2015)* and the *Reform Program for Eco-environmental Protection System and Mechanism in Jiangsu Province (2016)*, ecological asset accounting should be promoted. Jiangsu took

[45] In 2015, the NDRC issued the *Announcement on the Issuance of Three Clean Production Evaluation Indicator Systems Including Electricity (Coal-Fired Power Generation Companies)*, and the *Announcement on the Issuance of Clean Production Evaluation Indicator Systems for Four Industries Including Batteries*, specifying the clean production evaluation indicator systems for coal power, battery, and other industries.

[46] Environmental Protection Department of Jiangsu Province. *Notice on announcement of the twelfth batch of key companies for clean production audit in Jiangsu Province* (February 25, 2016). *Notice on announcement of the eleventh batch of key companies for clean production audit in Jiangsu Province* (February 26, 2015).

actions before making policies in this regard. In 2013, Wuzhong District, which owns three-fifth of the waters of Taihu Lake, launched the project study "Preparation of Natural Resources Balance Sheets." However, the formal policies about natural resources balance sheets are still unavailable in either Wuzhong or the entire province.

In terms of pollution damage identification and assessment, the "Environmental Damage Assessment Report on Pollution of Drinking Water Sources in Changzhou and Other Places by Xinpu Chemical Industrial (Taixing) Co. Ltd." — the first report of this kind in Jiangsu Province — passed the expert review[47] in 2013. The State passed the "Report on the Pilot Reform of the Eco-environmental Damage Compensation System in Certain Provinces" in 2016, approving the implementation plan for this pilot reform in seven provinces and cities (including Jiangsu), but Jiangsu has not come up with detailed regulations.

In general, the policies of Jiangsu on environmental capital are fairly executable, because they contain specific requirements for cities and districts to carry out relevant pilot work, clearly divided powers and responsibilities of competent authorities, and unambiguous content for accounting. They are also consistent with the policies from the departments at the same and higher levels. Take Wuzhong District for example: Its study on preparation of natural resources balance sheets has yielded substantial results. However, these policies of Jiangsu on environmental capital are quite limited and far from complete.

(2) *Environmental credit and information*. In terms of environmental credit and information, Jiangsu has remained active in both taking actions and making policies. Its performance in policy-making in recent years is especially commendable.

In 2012, Wuxi City began to evaluate the environmental protection credit of companies.[48] In 2013, Jiangsu issued the *Interim Measures for Corporate Environmental Credit Evaluation and Credit Management in Jiangsu Province*, and then in 2015 issued the *Notice on the Issues Concerning the Trial Implementation of Differential Electricity Tariffs Based on Environmental Credit Evaluation Ratings*, becoming the first province in China that will implement a differential electricity tariff

[47] Environmental Protection Department of Jiangsu Province (March 1, 2013). Retrieved from http://hbt.jiangsu.gov.cn/art/2013/3/1/art_1564_4402213.html

[48] *Announcement of Wuxi Municipal Environmental Protection Bureau on the Results of Environmental Credit Evaluation of Some Companies in 2012*.

policy for certain high-polluting companies with annual environmental credit evaluation ratings marked in red and black: Their electricity tariff is to increase by 0.05 yuan/kWH and 0.1 yuan/kWH, respectively, on the basis of the current price. In 2016, the *Implementation Measures for the Collection and Use of Sewage Treatment Fees in Jiangsu Province* were released to set the sewage treatment charging standards in different grades: It is initially decided that the water price of "black" and "red" companies is to increase by 1 yuan/t and 0.6 yuan/t, respectively,

Besides, certain cities in Jiangsu have successively presented requirements for the disclosure of environmental monitoring data from the government and companies.[49] Environmental credit has a significant impact in the field of green credit in Jiangsu.[50] By the end of 2015, the major banks in the province reported that their loans to "green" and "blue" companies had increased by 53.453 billion yuan and 11.863 billion yuan, respectively, but the loans to "red" and "black" companies had decreased to 511 million yuan and 1,338 million yuan, respectively. In a word, the unbiased green credit policies and well-founded rewards and punishments have fully demonstrated the power of market supervision.[51] In 2015, a total of 22,542 polluting companies in Jiangsu participated in environmental credit evaluation; among the 878 state key monitoring companies, 280 were rated as "green," 415 as "blue," 118 as "yellow," 43 as "red," and 22 as "black."[52]

In general, Jiangsu has issued many policies on environmental credit and information which are fairly complete and consistent with the higher-level policies. With explicit regulations on environmental assessment, monitoring, information disclosure, green credit, sewage treatment, and electricity tariff, these policies are highly executable. The price bureau, environmental protection department, and construction bureau have been cooperating with each other in policy implementation. Every year, a directory of corporate environmental protection credit will be published, achieving substantial results.

---

[49] *Notice of Suzhou Municipal Environmental Protection Bureau on Strengthening the Self-monitoring and Information Disclosure of Newly-added State-controlled Enterprises in 2015.*

[50] See Section 8.2.2.

[51] Jiangsu announces the environmental credit evaluation results of 944 companies (September 21, 2016). Retrieved from http://jiangsu.sina.com.cn/city/csgz/2016-09-21/city-ifxvyqvy6954036.shtml

[52] *Ibid.*

(3) *Environmental rewards and punishments*. Jiangsu has been actively implementing national policies on environmental rewards and punishments, and promulgating provincial-level policies accordingly, including the specific policies for environmental supervision, accountability, and compensation for damages.

From 2015 to 2016, the State successively introduced a number of policies[53] on the investigation of the projects with falsified EIA report or environmental monitoring data, punishment of environmentally dishonest behaviors, interim and subsequent environmental supervision of construction projects, and accountability of party and government officials. Jiangsu successively promulgated the *Opinions on Implementing the Notice of the General Office of the State Council on Strengthening Enforcement of Environmental Supervision* and the *Opinions on the Pilot Program for the Reform of the Eco-environmental Damage Compensation System in Jiangsu Province (Draft for Solicitation of Comments)*, which specify the implementation rules to create a good atmosphere for environmental rewards and punishments in the province, with an aim to implement the national policies on environmental supervision and the environmental damage compensation system.

According to the data from the Environmental Protection Department of Jiangsu Province,[54] the environmental protection departments at all levels have inspected companies on site for a total of 236,000 times and filed and investigated 8,033 environmental violations with a total penalty of nearly 420 million yuan (see Table 8.1); 875 cases were handled by means as provided for in the *Environmental Protection Law*, the responsible persons were fined daily (97 cases), asked to curtail or halt production (340 cases), with assets seized or detained (362 cases), and held under administrative detention (76 cases); the 33 typical environmental

[53] *Notice on Further Strengthening the Accountability of Illegal Projects in Environmental Impact Assessment, Measures for the Accountability of Party and Government Officials for Environmental Damages (Trial), Measures for Judging and Handling Falsification of Environmental Monitoring Data, Memorandum of Cooperation on Joint Punishment of Untrustworthy Production and Business Units and Related Personnel in the Field of Environmental Protection, Administrative Measures for the Interim and Subsequent Supervision and Management of Environmental Protection in Construction Projects (Trial).*

[54] Monitoring and Information Center, Environmental Protection Department of Jiangsu Province (May 30, 2016). *Bulletin on the state of environment of Jiangsu Province (2015).*

Table 8.1. Evaluation scores of 15 sub-category policies.

Category No.	Category	Sub-category No.	Content	Integrity	Specificity	Enforceability	Coordination	Result	Weighted average
1	Public finance policy	1.1	Public investment in environmental protection	5.00	5.00	5.00	5.00	4.00	4.86
		1.2	Collection of environmental protection taxes and fees, including environmental tax, pollution discharge fees, and energy-saving subsidies	4.33	5.00	5.00	5.00	5.00	4.89
		1.3	Ecological environment compensation and transfer payment	4.00	4.67	5.00	4.67	4.33	4.60
2	Green finance policy	2.1	Encouragement and establishment of the green financial market, including the construction of market platforms and institutions, the cooperation between government and social capital, i.e., the PPP model	5.00	5.00	5.00	4.33	4.33	4.78
		2.2	Construction and innovation of green financial products	3.00	4.33	4.33	4.33	2.67	3.87

(*Continued*)

Table 8.1. (*Continued*)

Category No.	Category	Sub-category No.	Content	Integrity	Specificity	Enforceability	Coordination	Result	Weighted average
		2.3	Construction and improvement of financial market systems, including supervision and risk prevention and control, and corporate information disclosure	4.00	4.33	4.00	4.00	3.00	3.93
3	Emissions trading market policy	3.1	Establish a system of paid use and trading of emission rights	4.67	4.33	4.67	4.67	4.00	4.50
		3.2	Resource use rights market, such as the construction of water, electricity, gas and other markets	4.67	5.00	5.00	4.67	4.00	4.74
		3.3	Construction of the third-party governance market, such as third-party assessment of environmental pollution	3.33	4.00	4.00	4.00	3.33	3.79
4	Environmental protection industrial policy	4.1	Industry access policy	3.00	3.33	3.67	3.67	3.33	3.44
		4.2	Industrial support policies, including industrial technology (innovation) policy subsidies, and green consumption	2.67	3.67	3.33	3.67	3.33	3.35

		4.3	Industrial regulatory policy	4.67	4.33	4.67	4.33	4.00	4.44
5	Other supporting and monitoring measures	5.1	Environmental capital accounting, including environmental resourcc value accounting policies, natural resource accounts and balance sheets, and promotion of pollution damage appraisal and assessment	3.67	4.33	4.33	4.33	4.00	4.17
		5.2	Environmental credit and information, including comprehensive list of environmental products, comprehensive list of environmental pollutants, environmental credit evaluation system, local environmental information disclosure	4.67	5.00	5.00	5.00	4.00	4.80
		5.3	Environmental rewards and punishments, including daily penalties, post-event accountability systems	4.67	4.67	4.67	4.33	4.33	4.56

violation cases that were publicly exposed in the media have evoked great repercussions.

In general, the policies of Jiangsu Province on environmental protection rewards and punishments were promulgated promptly after the national policies came out. They are fairly complete, containing definite objectives, specific implementation rules for separate fields, interrelated measures for rewards and punishments, and detailed requirements for the objects of rewards and punishments and for executive and supervisory agencies. Jiangsu pays high attention to disclosing the information about environmental rewards and punishments. On the website of the Environmental Protection Department, there is a platform for exposing environmental violations, and a notice board showing permits and administrative penalties regarding environmental protection, which have facilitated the implementation of corresponding policies.

8.4 Overview of Jiangsu's Environmental Economic Policies

8.4.1 *Analysis by policy category*

8.4.1.1 *Five major categories of policies*

(1) *Public fiscal policies.* From 2015 to 2016, the performance of Jiangsu in formulating and implementing public fiscal policies was commendable (see Figure 8.3 and Table 8.2). Based on the national policies, Jiangsu came up with provincial-level policies in combination with local conditions. The public expenditure policies are complete and systematic, covering key fields such as ocean and land. Although the policies on pollution discharge fees are only applicable to volatile organic compounds, the policies on environmental compensation are fairly complete. All of these policies contain definite objectives, concrete regulations for individual industries, and explicit standards or formulas (e.g., for calculation of taxes and fees). They are highly executable (both cities and counties can effectively implement these policies) and conductive to cooperation between all competent authorities (e.g., executive and supervisory authorities). Consequently, the achievements of Jiangsu in implementing public fiscal

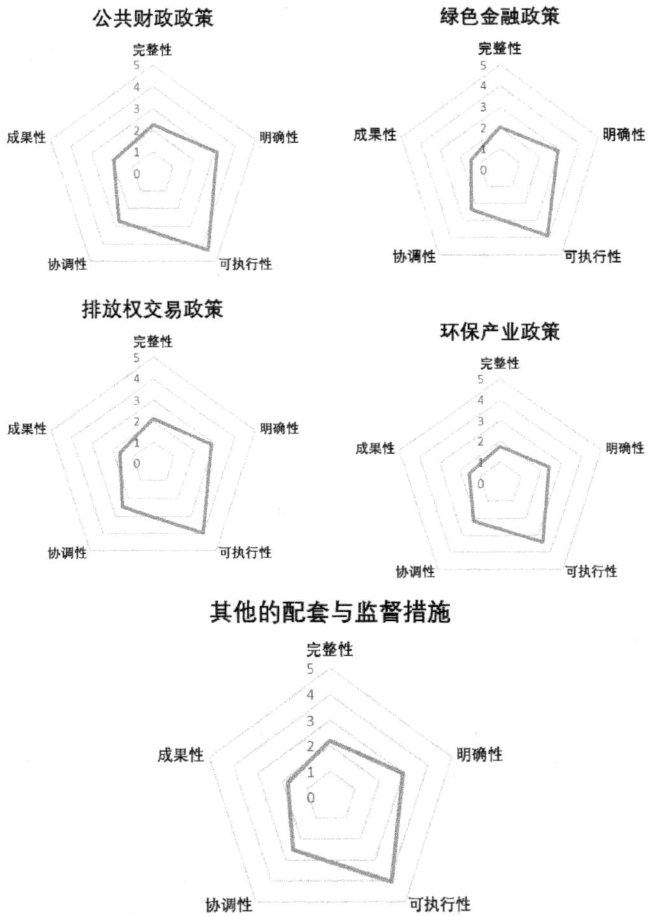

第一行的两幅图	公共财政政策	Public fiscal policy
	完整性	Integrity
	成果性	Result
	协调性	Coordination
	可执行性	Enforceability
	明确性	Specificity
	绿色金融政策	Green financial policy
第二行的两幅图	排放权交易政策	Emissions trading policy
	环保产业政策	Environmental protection industry policy
最下方的图	其他配套与监督措施	Other supporting and supervisory measures

Figure 8.3. Radar chart (after weighting).

Table 8.2. Evaluation scores: Five categories of policies.

No.	Policy	Integrity	Specificity	Enforceability	Coordination	Result	Total
1	Public finance policy	2.25	3.12	4.35	2.70	1.92	14.35
2	Green finance policy	2.02	2.91	3.87	2.34	1.44	12.58
3	Emissions trading and market policy	2.14	2.84	3.96	2.46	1.63	13.03
4	Environmental protection industry policy	1.74	2.41	3.38	2.15	1.54	11.23
5	Other supporting and monitoring measures	2.19	2.98	4.06	2.52	1.78	13.53

policies are obvious to all; for example, the amount of pollutant discharge has greatly decreased, and the public-good forests are well protected.

(2) *Green financial policies*. Jiangsu takes the lead in formulating and implementing green financial policies in China. It highlights the development of PPP and green credit and keeps improving market supervision. From 2015 to 2016, the green financial policies introduced by Jiangsu are complete, systematic and backed up by higher-level policies and supporting implementation rules. In order to promote the development of green finance, Jiangsu keeps promulgating policies with definite objectives and detailed requirements; for example, there are policies covering all links of PPP from planning to final operation. These policies are highly executable, with the sound implementation effect attributed to coordination between all competent authorities. Besides, based on the remarkable achievements in PPP, Jiangsu has built a special website to guide the further development of PPP. However, the shortcomings should not be overlooked; for example, the contents of the policies on green credit and financial market supervision are not rich enough, and the

eco-environmental assessment indicator system defines the specific indicators for assessment, but its responsibilities, supervision and implementation are somewhat mixed with those of PPP.

(3) *Emissions trading policies*. Although Jiangsu was not actively updating the policies on emissions trading over 2015–2016, the implementation effect of these policies was still significant. Jiangsu had already built the policy framework for emissions trading years ago, with the policy updates in recent years mainly at the municipal level, and free from major adjustment at the provincial level. All the available policies contain definite objectives and rich contents, and they are highly executable thanks to detailed implementation rules. The policies on resource-use rights, which are updated in a timely manner, involve both water and electricity. However, the policies on third-party governance are neither enough nor widely applicable. With respect to pollutant discharge rights, the coordination between competent authorities is poor. With respect to third-party governance, there are limited policies and fewer competent authorities at the provincial level. Although there are no public data showing the trial implementation effect of new policies on third-party governance, all policies on pollutant discharge and resources use rights have achieved substantial results as proven by specific data.

(4) *Eco-friendly industry policies*. Although Jiangsu had been dedicated to the transformation and upgrading of coal power, industrial and information industries over 2015–2016, the regulatory policies on high and new technologies (e.g., environmental protection technologies) are not updated. These industry policies are not complete, and those on industry access and support are not updated promptly. Jiangsu has introduced environmental protection technologies to promote industrial upgrading, and it has also developed directories with specified industry access standards. Both industry supporting policies and regulatory policies are highly executable, but the former is neither complementary enough nor fully endorsed by higher-up policies, while the latter boasts complementarity between each other and solid grounds. In terms of implementation effect, the effect of industry policies can only be inferred from environmental data indirectly, because there are no official statistics that can directly demonstrate their effect.

(5) *Other supporting and supervisory measures*. Jiangsu improved the supporting and supervisory measures over 2015–2016 and achieved

substantial results. There are complete and detailed regulations on environmental credit information disclosure, and on rewards and punishments. Although there are not many policies for environmental capital accounting to take reference, the available policies in this regard, at both the national and provincial levels, have explicit contents, clearly divided responsibilities, and strong executability. The environmental credit regulations can be combined with loaning and electricity tariff policies to play their due role, and the regulations on rewards and punishments are interlinked. These supporting and supervisory measures of Jiangsu are consistent with the policies from the Central Government and other authorities. The pilot projects of capital accounting have achieved good results; the environmental credit list has been made public in a timely manner; and the platform for disclosing the information about rewards and punishment is already available.

8.4.1.2 *Vertical comparison*

Over 2015–2016, all the five indicators of Jiangsu's public fiscal policies score the highest, demonstrating its preference and success in formulating environmental economic policies and in employing price tools, which are in line with the provincial economic development. In contrast, the average score of the five indicators of eco-friendly industry policies is the lowest. However, it should be noted that other policies can also promote the development of eco-friendly industries to a certain extent, meaning that a low score only reflects that the policies are not perfect. In fact, the indirect data have already proved the sound results of eco-friendly industry policies. In terms of green financial policies (most of which focus on green credit), their incompleteness has affected their overall score. Even so, all publicly available information shows that industry insiders remain optimistic about the prospect of green financial policies, and Jiangsu has been making efforts to expand green financial business. The scores of emissions trading policies and other supporting and monitoring measures are at an intermediate level; the two types of policies (and measures), though not complete, have achieved rich results. In short, the five types of environmental economic policies have a lot of room for improvement, that is, they must be improved to become more complete and more fruitful.

8.4.2 *SWOT analysis*

Strengths	Weaknesses
(1) With economic development at the forefront of the country and solid financial strength; (2) The environmental conditions are under control and likely to improve step by step; (3) Based on sound policies, the main work in the future is to make improvement; (4) Strong autonomy and a powerful reserve of professionals.	(1) The information disclosure mechanism is not good enough, and the output data are not transparent; (2) Green finance is too simplified to match the economic development; (3) There are few specific policies on eco-friendly industries, and the effect of these policies in promoting the transformation and upgrading of other industries remains to be tested.
Opportunities	**Threats**
(1) During the 13th Five-Year-Plan period, national and provincial policies are relatively new and have potential for development; (2) The prospect for the development of the national carbon emissions trading market is promising.	(1) Regional development is very different, and it is difficult to implement provincial policies; (2) Environmental resources are not abundant enough, and environmental protection responsibilities are becoming increasingly severe; (3) Mainly responsible for the governance of the Yangtze River Basin and Taihu Lake Basin, which is an arduous task.

8.5 Summary and Suggestions

Jiangsu Province has initially formed a policy system with the environmental price system as the core; the paid use of pollution discharge rights and the regional compensation of environmental resources as auxiliary means; and in combination with the fiscal, taxation, credit, and insurance methods. Jiangsu has been gradually increasing and extending the policy means and achieved certain results in raising funds, reducing pollutant emissions, and improving environmental quality by implementing environmental economic policies. However, some policies have failed to play their due role since they do not adapt to the provincial development situation or they do not have enough supporting measures. Some environmental economic policies, such as the paid use and trading of pollution discharge rights, have not been fully integrated with the existing environmental management system, and the compatibility between policy making and implementation needs to be improved. Over 2015–2016, the environmental economic policies of Jiangsu had maintained a good development momentum, but they were free from major innovations because of the transitional period between the 12th Five-Year Plan (2011–2015) and the 13th Five-Year Plan (2016–2020). However, Jiangsu still contributed an eye-catching performance in utilizing price tools which are updated frequently and timely, while exercising caution in introducing quantity tools, which conforms to its status as a major economic province. The policy disclosure is on the whole satisfying, but the information disclosure in some fields is not transparent enough, which is likely to cause loopholes in policy implementation.

To sum up, the author recommends that Jiangsu should make improvements in the following aspects:

(1) Lay down policies on specific fields within the scope of provincial power and pay special attention to updating policies so as to make provincial policies comply with national policies and reflect local economic development.
(2) Continue to develop price tools, use quantity tools in the fields where price tools do not perform well, and enable these tools to complement with each other. Pay particular attention to regional differences and carry out policies flexibly.
(3) Keep working hard in formulating green financial and emissions trading policies, give full play to the advantages of a major economic province, promote the formulation of eco-friendly industry policies, and fully display the role of eco-friendly industries in promoting the transformation and upgrading of other industries.
(4) Establish a complete information disclosure system, unify the channels for policy release and results disclosure, unblock information communication channels, and maintain smooth communication between the government and the people.

Appendix A: Jiangsu's Environmental Economic Policies

Table 8A.1. Summary sheet of Jiangsu's environmental economic policies over 2015–2016.

No.	Policy title	Issuing date	Issuing authority	Policy category
1	Administrative Measures for Special Funds for Energy Conservation and Emissions Reduction of Provincial Transportation in Jiangsu Province	2015/4/22	Jiangsu Financial Department	Environmental protection public investment
2	Administrative Measures for Special Guide Funds for Provincial Energy Conservation and Emissions Reduction (Energy Conservation of Buildings and Modernization of Construction Industry) in Jiangsu Province	2015/4/30	Jiangsu Financial Department	Environmental protection public investment
3	Administrative Measures for Special Funds for Provincial Environmental Protection of Marine and Fishery Resources in Jiangsu Province	2015/7/9	Jiangsu Financial Department	Environmental protection public investment
4	Administrative Measures for Special Funds for Cyclic Utilization of Agricultural Renewable Resources in Jiangsu Province	2015/8/5	Jiangsu Financial Department	Environmental protection public investment
5	Administrative Measures for Special Funds for Comprehensive Utilization of Crop Straws in Jiangsu Province	2015/8/5	Jiangsu Financial Department	Environmental protection public investment
6	Administrative Measures for the Use of Provincial Environmental Protection Guide Funds	2016/4/1	Jiangsu Financial Department	Environmental protection public investment

(*Continued*)

Table 8A.1. (*Continued*)

No.	Policy title	Issuing date	Issuing authority	Policy category
7	Administrative Measures for Special Funds for Provincial Land Reclamation in Jiangsu Province	2016/4/5	Jiangsu Financial Department	Environmental protection public investment
8	Provincial Marine and Fishery Integrated Management and Administrative Measures for Special Funds for Resources and Environmental Protection in Jiangsu Province	2016/4/29	Jiangsu Financial Department	Environmental protection public investment
9	Administrative Measures for Special Funds for Comprehensive Improvement of Provincial Urban and Rural Environment (Village Environment Improvement) in Jiangsu Province	2016/5/31	Jiangsu Financial Department	Environmental protection public investment
10	Notice on the Setting and Adjustment of the Charging Standards for Sewage Treatment Fees and Other Related Issues	2015/1/21	MOF, MOHURD, NDRC	Environmental tax and fees
11	Notice on Collection of Consumption Tax on Batteries and Coatings	2015/1/26	MOF, SAT	Environmental tax and fees
12	Announcement of the State Administration of Taxation and the National Energy Administration on Several Issues Concerning the Implementation of the Preferential Policy for Coal Resource Tax	2015/4/14	MOF, SAT	Environmental tax and fees
13	Notice on Adjusting the Applicable Tax Standards for Iron Ore Resource Tax	2015/4/27	MOF, SAT	Environmental tax and fees

Table 8A.1. (*Continued*)

14	Notice on Implementing the Ad Valorem Taxation Reform of the Resource Tax on Rare Earth, Tungsten and Molybdenum	2015/4/30	MOF, SAT	Environmental tax and fees
15	Notice on the Implementation of the VAT Policy for Wind Power Generation	2015/6/12	MOF, SAT	Environmental tax and fees
16	Notice on the Implementation of the VAT Policy for New Wall Materials	2015/6/12	MOF, SAT	Environmental tax and fees
17	VAT Preferential Catalogue for Products and Labor Services Based on Integrated Use of Resources	2015/6/12	MOF, SAT	Environmental tax and fees
18	Measures for Pilot Implementation of Volatile Organic Compounds Discharge Fees	2015/6/18	MOF, NDRC, MEP	Environmental tax and fees
19	Administrative Measures for Coal Resource Tax Collection (Trial)	2015/7/1	SAT	Environmental tax and fees
20	Notice on Reducing the Purchase Tax for Passenger Cars with Displacement of 1.6 Liters and Below	2015/9/29	MOF, SAT	Environmental tax and fees
21	Notice on Comprehensively Promoting Resource Tax Reform	2016/5/9	MOF, SAT	Environmental tax and fees
22	Notice on the Specific Policy Issues of Resource Tax Reform	2016/5/9	MOF, SAT	Environmental tax and fees
23	Notice on the Continuous Implementation of the VAT Policy for Photovoltaic Power Generation	2016/7/25	MOF, SAT	Environmental tax and fees
24	Notice on the Exemption of Vehicle Purchase Tax on Public Automobile and Electric Vehicles Purchased by Urban Public Transport Enterprises	2016/7/25	MOF, SAT	Environmental tax and fees

(*Continued*)

Table 8A.1. (*Continued*)

No.	Policy title	Issuing date	Issuing authority	Policy category
25	Administrative Measures for Provincial Electricity Tariff Subsidies to Photovoltaic Power Generation Projects	2014/10/17	Jiangsu Financial Department	Environmental tax and fees
26	Notice on Adjusting the Collection Standards for Pollutant Discharge Fees and Other Related Issues	2015/10/13	Jiangsu Price Bureau, Financial Department, Department of Environmental Protection	Environmental tax and fees
27	Notice on Further Clarifying Issues Concerning the Collection of Pollutant Discharge Fees	2015/12/28	Jiangsu Price Bureau, Financial Department, Department of Environmental Protection	Environmental tax and fees
28	Implementation Measures for the Collection and Use of Sewage Treatment Fees in Jiangsu Province	2016/2/16	Jiangsu Financial Department, Price Bureau, Department of Housing and Urban-Rural Development, Department of Water Resources, Department of Environmental Protection	Environmental tax and fees
29	Notice on Adjusting Certain Mineral Resource Tax Rates in Jiangsu Province	2016/7/1	Jiangsu Financial Department	Environmental tax and fees
30	Measures of Jiangsu Province for Pilot Implementation of Volatile Organic Compounds Discharge Fees	2016/9/28	Jiangsu Financial Department	Environmental tax and fees

Table 8A.1. (*Continued*)

31	Pilot Program for Reforming the Eco-environment Damage Compensation System	2015/12/3	CPC Central Committee, State Council	Ecological environment compensation and transfer payment
32	Opinions on Improving the Compensation Mechanism for Ecological Protection	2016/4/28	State Council	Ecological environment compensation and transfer payment
33	Opinions of the State Council on Reforming and Improving the Central-to-Local Transfer Payment System	2016/5/16	State Council	Ecological environment compensation and transfer payment
34	Interim Measures for the Management of Performance Targets of Special Transfer Payments from the Central Government to Local Governments	2015/9/29	MOF	Ecological environment compensation and transfer payment
35	Measures for the Administration of Special Transfer Payments from the Central Government to Local Governments	2015/12/31	MOF	Ecological environment compensation and transfer payment
36	Measures for Balanced Transfer Payments from the Central Government to Local Governments in 2016	2016/4/15	MOF	Ecological environment compensation and transfer payment
37	Measures for Transfer Payments from the Central Government to Local Governments	2016/6/30	MOF	Ecological environment compensation and transfer payment
38	Administrative Measures for the Provincial Compensation Funds for Forest Ecological Benefits	2016/5/10	Jiangsu Financial Department	Ecological environment compensation and transfer payment

(*Continued*)

Table 8A.1. (*Continued*)

No.	Policy title	Issuing date	Issuing authority	Policy category
39	Guiding Opinions on Promoting the PPP Model in Public Service Field	2015/5/19	MOF, NDRC, PBOC	Encouragement and establishment of a green financial market
40	Notice on Regulating the Management of PPP Contracts	2015/2/16	MOF	Encouragement and establishment of a green financial market
41	Notice on Promoting the Work for PPP's Development Financing	2015/3/17	NDRC, CDB	Encouragement and establishment of a green financial market
42	Administrative Measures for Franchising of Infrastructure and Public Utilities	2015/4/21	NDRC, MOF, MOHURD, MOT, MORC, PBOC	Encouragement and establishment of a green financial market
43	Guidelines for the Financial Affordability Demonstration of PPP Projects	2015/5/5	MOF	Encouragement and establishment of a green financial market
44	Notice on Key Work Opinions on Deepening the Reform of the Economic System in 2015	2015/5/8	NDRC	Encouragement and establishment of a green financial market

Table 8A.1. (*Continued*)

45	Implementation Opinions on Promoting the PPP Model in Public Service Field	2015/9/5	Jiangsu People's Government	Encouragement and establishment of a green financial market
46	Notice on the Implementation of the "Reward Replacing Subsidy" Policy for PPP Projects	2015/12/14	MOF	Encouragement and establishment of a green financial market
47	Guidelines for PPP's VFM Evaluation (Trial)	2015/12/18	MOF	Encouragement and establishment of a green financial market
48	Interim Measures for the Financial Management of PPP Projects	2016/11/14	MOF	Encouragement and establishment of a green financial market
49	Notice on the Relevant Issues about Promoting the PPP Model in Jiangsu Province	2014/12/12	Jiangsu Financial Department	Encouragement and establishment of a green financial market
50	Notice of the Department of Finance of Jiangsu Province on the Submission of PPP Projects in 2015	2015/4/8	Jiangsu Financial Department	Encouragement and establishment of a green financial market

(*Continued*)

Table 8A.1. (*Continued*)

No.	Policy title	Issuing date	Issuing authority	Policy category
51	Implementation Measures for the PPP Financing Fund in Jiangsu Province (Trial)	2015/6/5	Jiangsu Financial Department	Encouragement and establishment of a green financial market
52	Notice of the Department of Finance of Jiangsu Province on the Submission of the PPP Financing Support Fund	2015/10/26	Jiangsu Financial Department	Encouragement and establishment of a green financial market
53	Notice from the Department of Finance of Jiangsu Province on Doing a Good Job in the Storage and Pilot Work of PPP Projects in 2016	2016/3/31	Jiangsu Financial Department	Encouragement and establishment of a green financial market
54	Administrative Measures for the Rewards and Subsidies to PPP Projects (Trial)	2016/6/6	Jiangsu Financial Department	Encouragement and establishment of a green financial market
55	Notice of the Department of Finance of Jiangsu Province on Doing a Good Job in the Pilot PPP Projects in 2016	2016/7/14	Jiangsu Financial Department	Encouragement and establishment of a green financial market
56	Notice on the Application of the Reward-Replacing-Subsidy Fund for the Ministry of Finance's PPP Projects	2016/11/9	Jiangsu Financial Department	Encouragement and establishment of a green financial market

Table 8A.1. (*Continued*)

57	Notice on the Implementation of the Third-Batch National PPP Projects	2016/11/14	Jiangsu Financial Department	Encouragement and establishment of a green financial market
58	Energy Efficiency Credit Guidelines	2015/1/13	NDRC, CBRC	Construction and innovation of green financial products
59	Opinions on Financial Support for the Stable Growth, Restructuring and Benefit Growth of Industries	2016/2/14	PBOC, NDRC, MIIT, MOFCOM, CBRC, CSRC, CIRC	Construction and innovation of green financial products
60	Opinions on Supporting the Iron & Steel and Coal Industries to Resolve Overcapacity and Achieve Development Out of Difficulties	2016/7/12	The Nanjing Branch of the PBOC, CBRC	Construction and innovation of green financial products
61	Opinions of Jiangsu Provincial Government on Financial Support for the Development of Manufacturing Industry	2016/9/5	Jiangsu People's Government	Construction and innovation of green financial products
62	Administrative Measures for the Publicity of the Blacklist of Serious Dishonesty in Jiangsu Province (Trial)	2015/2/1	Jiangsu People's Government	Construction and perfection of financial market system

(*Continued*)

Table 8A.1. (*Continued*)

No.	Policy title	Issuing date	Issuing authority	Policy category
63	County-level Financial Eco-environmental Assessment Indicator System in Jiangsu Province	2015/6/12	Jiangsu Financial Stability Coordination Group	Construction and perfection of financial market system
64	Measures for Supervision and Administration of Trading Venues in Jiangsu Province (Revised)	2015/9/10	Financial Work Office in Jiangsu People's Government	Construction and perfection of financial market system
65	Appraisal Measures for the Establishment of Financial Ecological Counties	2016/1/20	Jiangsu Financial Stability Coordination Group	Construction and perfection of financial market system
66	Interim Measures for the Administration of Income from the Sale of Pollution Discharge Permits	2015/7/23	MOF, NDRC, MEP	Compensated use and trading system of emission rights
67	Interim Measures for the Administration of Greenhouse Gas Emission Reports from Key Units in Jiangsu Province	2015/4/17	Jiangsu People's Government	Compensated use and trading system of emission rights
68	Trial Measures for the Verification of Emission Rights of Major Pollutants in Jiangsu Province (Draft for Solicitation of Comments)	2015/9/11	Jiangsu Environmental Protection Department	Compensated use and trading system of emission rights

Table 8A.1. (*Continued*)

69	Administrative Measures for the Issuance of Pollution Discharge Permits in Jiangsu Province (for Trial)	2015/10/10	Jiangsu Environmental Protection Department	Compensated use and trading system of emission rights
70	Interim Measures for the Administration of Public Resources Trading Platform	2016/6/24	NDRC, SAT, MIIT, MOF, MLR, MEP, MOHURD, MOT, MORC, MOFCOM, NHFPC, SASAC, NFGA, NGOA	Resource use right market
71	Administrative Measures for the Project-based Energy Saving Transaction in Jiangsu Province (Trial)	2015/3/28	Jiangsu People's Government	Resource use right market
72	Implementation Opinions on Promoting the Comprehensive Reform of Agricultural Water Prices	2015/5/28	Jiangsu People's Government	Resource use right market
73	Notice on Stopping the Implementation of Differential Electricity Tariffs and Punitive Electricity Tariffs for Certain Enterprises	2015/8/12	Jiangsu Price Bureau, Jiangsu Economic and Information Commission	Resource use right market
74	Notice on Issues Concerning Trial Implementation of Differential Electricity Tariffs Based on Environmental Credit Ratings	2015/12/14	Jiangsu Provincial Price Bureau, Jiangsu Provincial Department of Environmental Protection	Resource use right market, environmental credit and information

(*Continued*)

Table 8A.1. (*Continued*)

No.	Policy title	Issuing date	Issuing authority	Policy category
75	Opinions on the Implementation of Third-party Governance of Environmental Pollution	2014/12/27	State Council	Construction of the third-party governance market
76	Guiding Opinions on the Implementation of Third-Party Governance of Environmental Pollution in Coal-fired Power Plants	2015/12/31	NDRC, MEP, NEA	Construction of the third-party governance market
77	Notice on Carrying out Pilot Demonstration Work for Third-party Governance of Environmental Pollution	2016/8/22	NDRC	Construction of the third-party governance market
78	Measures for the Third-party Verification of the Dismantling and Disposal of Waste Electrical and Electronic Products in Jiangsu Province	2015/3/9	Jiangsu Department of Environmental Protection	Construction of the third-party governance market
79	Administrative Measures for Third-party Verification Institutions of Carbon Emissions Trading in Jiangsu Province (Interim)	2016/6/15	Jiangsu DRC	Construction of the third-party governance market
80	High-efficiency and Energy-saving Boiler Promotion Catalog (First Batch)	2015/12/30	NDRC, AQSIQ	Industry access policy
81	National Key Energy-saving and Low-carbon Technology Promotion Catalog (2015)	2015/12/30	NDRC	Industry access policy
82	Action Plan for Upgrading and Transformation of Coal-fired Power Generation for Energy Conservation and Emissions Reduction in Jiangsu Province (2014–2020)	2014/11/10	Jiangsu People's Government	Industry access policy

Table 8A.1. (*Continued*)

83	Notice on Producing the Directories of Structural Adjustment, Restrictions and Elimination for Industrial and Information Industry, and Imposing Energy Consumption Limits	2015/11/23	Jiangsu People's Government	Industry access policy
84	Aquatic Eco-environmental Functional District Planning of the Taihu Lake Basin in Jiangsu Province (Trial)	2016/4/17	Jiangsu People's Government	Industry access policy
85	Notice of the Provincial Government on Strengthening Eco-environmental Protection Work in the Yangtze River Basin	2016/7/22	Jiangsu People's Government	Industry access policy
86	Opinions on Promoting the Application of Advanced Photovoltaic Products and Industrial Upgrading	2015/6/1	NEA, MIIT, CNCA	Industry supporting policy
87	Implementation Opinions on Accelerating the Development of Energy Conservation and Environmental Protection Industries	2013/11/26	Jiangsu People's Government	Industry supporting policy
88	Opinions on Promoting the Redevelopment of Inefficient Industrial Land	2016/3/24	Jiangsu People's Government	Industry supporting policy
89	Announcement on the Issuance of Three Clean Production Evaluation Indicator Systems Including Electricity (Coal-Fired Power Generation Companies)	2015/4/20	NDRC	Industry supporting policy
90	Announcement on the Issuance of Clean Production Evaluation Indicator Systems for Four Industries Including Batteries	2015/12/31	NDRC, MEP, MIIT	Industrial regulatory policy

(*Continued*)

Table 8A.1. (*Continued*)

No.	Policy title	Issuing date	Issuing authority	Policy category
91	Clean Production Audit Measures	2016/5/16	NDRC, MEP	Industrial regulatory policy
92	Implementation Opinions on Promoting the Construction of Multi-energy Complementary Integration and Optimization Demonstration Projects	2016/7/4	NDRC, NEA	Industrial regulatory policy
93	Action Plan for Upgrading and Transformation of Coal-fired Power Generation for Energy Conservation and Emissions Reduction in Jiangsu Province (2014–2020)	2014/11/10	Jiangsu People's Government	Industrial regulatory policy
94	Industry Classification Table for Clean Production Review and Consultation Institutions for Key Enterprises in Jiangsu Province	2015/4/9	Jiangsu Environmental Protection Department	Industrial regulatory policy
95	Notice on the Annual Newly-added Photovoltaic Power Generation Capacity in 2015	2015/4/17	Jiangsu DRC	Industrial regulatory policy
96	Implementation Opinions on Accelerating the Development of Green and Low-Carbon Circular Transportation	2015/11/26	Jiangsu People's Government	Industrial regulatory policy
97	Notice on Issues Concerning Trial Implementation of Differential Electricity Tariffs Based on Environmental Credit Ratings	2015/12/14	Jiangsu Price Bureau, Jiangsu Department of Environmental Protection	Industrial regulatory policy
98	Planning and Layout Scheme for the Petrochemical Industry in Jiangsu Province	2015/12/25	Jiangsu DRC, Jiangsu Economic and Information Commission	Industrial regulatory policy

Table 8A.1. (*Continued*)

99	Work Program for the Prevention and Control of Water Pollution in Jiangsu Province	2015/12/28	Jiangsu People's Government	Industrial regulatory policy
100	Notice on Issuing the Implementation Plan of Newly-added Production Capacity and Organizational Structure of Photovoltaic Power Stations in 2016	2016/7/20	Jiangsu DRC	Industrial regulatory policy
101	Thirteenth Five-Year Plan for Industrial Green Development	2016/8/16	Jiangsu Economic and Information Commission	Industrial regulatory policy
102	Thirteenth Five-Year Plan for Energy Conservation	2016/8/16	Jiangsu Economic and Information Commission	Industrial regulatory policy
103	Notice on Printing and Distributing the Pilot Program for the Preparation of Natural Resources Balance Sheets	2015/11/08	State Council	Environmental capital accounting
104	The Third Batch of Greenhouse Gas Accounting Methods and Reporting Guidelines for Enterprises in Ten Industries (Trial)	2015/7/6	NDRC	Environmental capital accounting
105	Guiding Opinions on Planning Environmental Impact Assessment to Strengthen Space Control, Total Control and Environmental Access (for Trial)	2016/2/24	MEP	Environmental capital accounting
106	General Outline of Technical Guidelines for Eco-environmental Damage Appraisal and Assessment	2016/6/29	MEP	Environmental capital accounting

(*Continued*)

Table 8A.1. (*Continued*)

No.	Policy title	Issuing date	Issuing authority	Policy category
107	Eco-environmental Damage Identification and Assessment Technical Guidelines for Damage Investigation	2016/6/29	MEP	Environmental capital accounting
108	Notice on Soliciting Opinions on the "Technical Guidelines for Accounting of Volatile Organic Compound Emissions in Key Industries in Jiangsu Province (Trial)" (Draft for Solicitation of Comments)	2016/5/23	Jiangsu Environmental Protection Department	Environmental capital accounting
109	Administrative Measures for the Recordation of Emergency Response Plans for Environmental Incidents of Enterprises and Institutions (Trial)	2015/1/8	MEP	Environmental credit and information
110	Guiding Opinions on Strengthening the Construction of Corporate Environmental Credit System	2015/11/27	MEP, NDRC	Environmental credit and information
111	Information Disclosure Mechanism Plan for Environmental Impact Assessment of Construction Projects	2015/12/10	MEP	Environmental credit and information
112	Guiding Opinions on Strengthening the Construction of Corporate Environmental Credit System	2015/12/16	MEP, NDRC	Environmental credit and information
113	Administrative Measures for Regional Approval of Environmental Impact Assessment of Construction Projects (Trial)	2015/12/18	MEP	Environmental credit and information

Table 8A.1. (*Continued*)

114	Letter from the General Office of the Ministry of Environmental Protection on Forwarding the Policy Documents of Jiangsu Province on Implementing Differential Electricity Tariffs and Sewage Treatment Charges Based on Environmental Credit Rating	2016/5/3	MEP	Environmental credit and information
115	Notice on Matters Concerning the Pilot Work of Compiling the Inventory of Air Pollutant Sources	2015/3/27	MEP	Environmental credit and information
116	Notice on Holding Advanced Seminar on Air Pollutant Emission Inventory	2015/4/28	MEP	Environmental credit and information
117	Announcement on the Issuance of the "Technical Guidelines for the Comprehensive Treatment of Civil Coal Combustion Pollution (Trial)" and the "Technical Guidelines for the Compilation of Civil Coal Air Pollutant Emission Inventories (Trial)"	2016/10/22	MEP	Environmental credit and information
118	Notice on Starting the Dynamic Management of Enterprise Environmental Credit	2015/1/7	Jiangsu Environmental Protection Department	Environmental credit and information
119	Opinions on Further Deepening Price Reform and Effectively Strengthening Price Supervision	2015/1/28	Jiangsu People's Government	Environmental credit and information

(*Continued*)

Table 8A.1. (*Continued*)

No.	Policy title	Issuing date	Issuing authority	Policy category
120	Planning Outline for the Construction of Environmental Credit System of Jiangsu Province (2015–2020)	2015/12/24	Jiangsu Environmental Protection Department, Office of the Leading Group of Jiangsu Provincial Social Credit System Construction	Environmental credit and information
121	Planning Outline for the Construction of Environmental Credit System of Jiangsu Province (2016–2020)	2016/1/19	Jiangsu Environmental Protection Department, Office of the Leading Group of Jiangsu Provincial Social Credit System Construction	Environmental credit and information
122	Notice on Issuing the Administrative Measures for the Graded Examination and Approval of Environmental Impact Assessment Documents for Construction Projects in Jiangsu Province	2016/10/9	Jiangsu People's Government	Environmental credit and information
123	Notice on Further Strengthening the Accountability of Illegal Projects in Environmental Impact Assessment	2015/3/18	MEP	Environmental rewards and punishments

Table 8A.1. (*Continued*)

124	Measures for the Accountability of Party and Government Officials for Environmental Damages (Trial)	2015/8/9	CPC Central Committee, State Council	Environmental rewards and punishments
125	Administrative Measures for the Interim and Subsequent Supervision and Management of Environmental Protection in Construction Projects (Trial)	2015/12/10	MEP	Environmental rewards and punishments
126	Measures for Judging and Handling Falsification of Environmental Monitoring Data	2015/12/28	MEP	Environmental rewards and punishments
127	Memorandum of Cooperation on Joint Punishment of Untrustworthy Production and Business Units and Related Personnel in the Field of Environmental Protection	2016/7/20	NDRC	Environmental rewards and punishments
128	Opinions on the Pilot Program for the Reform of the Eco-environmental Damage Compensation System in Jiangsu Province (Draft for Solicitation of Comments)	2016/6/6	Jiangsu Environmental Protection Department	Environmental rewards and punishments
129	Opinions on Implementing the Notice of the General Office of the State Council on Strengthening Enforcement of Environmental Supervision	2015/5/25	Jiangsu People's Government	Environmental rewards and punishments

Appendix B: Explanations for Data Evaluation

Table 8B.1. Scale table for judgment matrix.

Intensity of importance	Definition
1	*i* and *j* are equally important
2	Relatively weak (between 1 and 3)
3	*i* is slightly more important than *j*
4	Relatively weak (between 3 and 5)
5	*i* is apparently more important than *j*
6	Relatively weak (between 5 and 7)
7	*i* is strongly more important than *j*
8	Relatively weak (between 7 and 9)
9	*i* is extremely more important than *j*
Reciprocal of the above scale	*i* has one of the above non-zero values, when compared with *j*, their values are reciprocal of each other

Table 8B.2. Schematic table for judgment matrix.

Indicator system	Integrity	Specificity	Enforceability	Coordination	Result
Integrity	1	M12	M13	M14	M15
Specificity	/	1	M23	M24	M25
Enforceability	/	/	1	M34	M35
Coordination	/	/	/	1	M*ij*
Result	/	/	/	/	1

Note: "M*ij*" represents the ratio of importance of Factor *i* to Factor *j*. For example, "M12" represents the ratio of importance of the two factors as "integrity" and "specificity."

Table 8B.3. Indicator weight.

Indicator	Integrity	Specificity	Enforceability	Coordination	Result
Weight	0.1687	0.213	0.2899	0.1844	0.1441

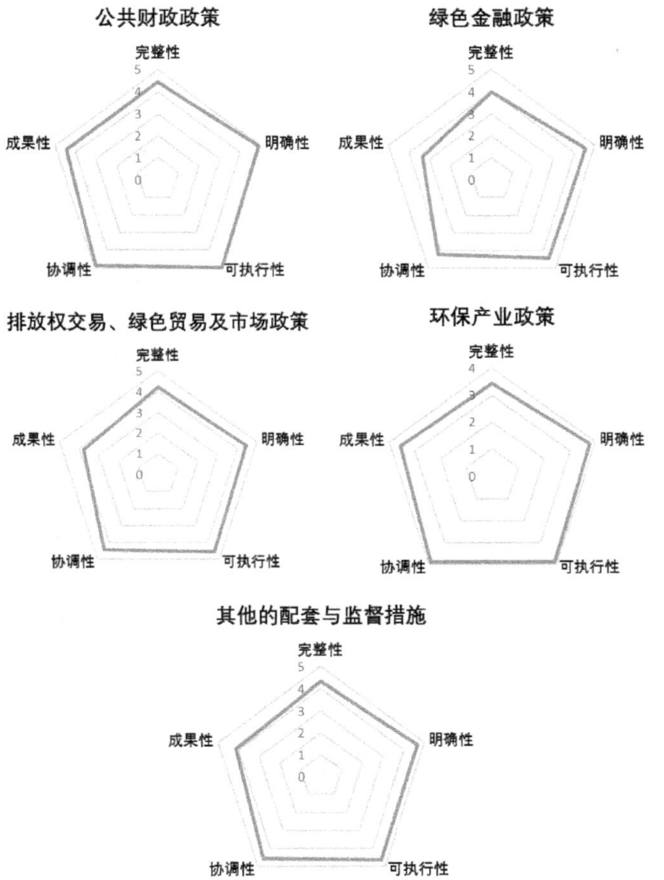

第一行的两幅图	公共财政政策	Public fiscal policy
	完整性	Integrity
	成果性	Result
	协调性	Coordination
	可执行性	Enforceability
	明确性	Specificity
	绿色金融政策	Green financial policy
第二行的两幅图	排放权交易政策	Emissions trading policy
	环保产业政策	Environmental protection industry policy
最下方的图	其他配套与监督措施	Other supporting and supervisory measures

Figure 8B.1. Evaluation scores of policies in five categories (unweighted).

Chapter 9

Analysis of the Green Investment Effect of Environmental Tax and Fees — A Research Based on Provincial Panel Data*

9.1 Introduction

While promoting the rapid development of productive forces, the modern industrial society is also destroying the environment, on which mankind depends for survival, at an unprecedented speed. Although China, as the largest developing country in the world, has experienced robust economic growth in recent years, the condition of its environment is cause for concern. In terms of water pollution, 75% of lakes across China suffer from eutrophication to varying degrees, and 90% of its urban waters are seriously polluted. A survey of groundwater quality in 118 large- and medium-sized cities in China shows that 115 cities suffer from polluted groundwater, of which 40% of those cities. The Annual Report on Enterprise Citizenship in China states that industrial enterprises are the main source of ecological damage and environmental pollution, and that 70% of China's pollution is caused by industrial enterprises. As a basic natural resource for the survival and development of the human society, water resources are important not only for the sustainable development of the economy and society but also the survival and living quality of people.

*This chapter is co-authored by Zhong Yiwen.

Therefore, protecting water resources and reducing water pollution are not only economic and ecological issues but also social issues involving people's lives.

The Chinese government has issued numerous policies and measures to protect water resources and reduce water pollution, one of them being the water pollution tax and fee system. The system of pollution charges has been instituted to levy pollutant discharge fees on organizations and individuals (polluters) that discharge pollutants in accordance with laws and regulations. Environmental tax mainly refers to a type of tax that is levied or reduced (or exempted) on organizations and individuals that develop, protect, and use environmental resources according to the extent of their development, utilization, protection, pollution, and destruction of such environmental resources. Pollution charges and environmental tax are the main means of government environmental regulation.

Green investment is the investment quota for the main body of investment in R&D, and services for environmental protection to reap economic and environmental benefits. Green investment is a new type of investment that is accompanied by environmental protection, government regulation, and sustainable development. It plays an important role in both green production at the micro level and in environmental protection at the macro level.

So, what about the changes and current status of China's existing water pollution tax and fee system? What is the impact of pollution charges on heavily polluting companies? Does it promote green investment by companies? Does it motivate companies to standardize wastewater treatment and discharge? This chapter combs through the historical changes of China's water pollution charge system and explores the impact of pollution tax and fees on China's heavily polluting companies. A conclusion is drawn that the pollution charge system plays a significant role in promoting corporate green investment behavior through government environmental regulation, represented by environmental tax and fees. Therefore, improving the environmental tax and fee system plays a highly significant role in China's quest to reduce pollution.

9.2 Literature Review and Concept Definition

In recent years, China has been subjected to the pressure of international public opinion on energy conservation and emissions reduction, as well as the domestic pressure due to water pollution, haze weather, and people's appeal for environmental protection after their living standards greatly improved. The internal and external environments have become increasingly mature for the Chinese government to introduce the environmental tax. Compared with the slightly backward domestic policy-making and legislation on environmental protection and green investment, the relevant research was started a long time ago.

9.2.1 *Environmental tax*

Environmental tax mainly refers to a type of tax that is levied or reduced (or exempted) on organizations and individuals that develop, protect, and use environmental resources according to the extent of their development, utilization, protection, pollution, and destruction of environmental resources. Environmental pollution governance requires government regulation, and levying environmental tax is one of the most efficient and equitable regulatory means (Liang, 2010). Compared with several commonly used environmental protection measures such as direct government control, pollution charge, emission rights trading, and fiscal subsidy, environmental tax has obvious advantages in realizing ecological protection and promoting sustainable social and economic development.

Chinese scholars have conducted extensive research on environmental tax, fees, and costs but most of these analyses are undertaken from a theoretical perspective. They analyze the necessity of environmental tax and fees from Marshall's theories of externality and market failure, and Arthur Pigou's "Internalization of Environmental Cost" and "Pigovian tax." The "Internalization of Environmental Cost" and "Polluter Pays Principle" (PPP) provide a theoretical basis for determining the objects of environmental tax collection. Other theoretical analyses probe into the meaning of environmental tax and fee system from the perspectives of the environmental signal theory of information economics and the sustainable development theory of development economics. In terms of the system design and taxation standard of environmental tax, Chinese scholars generally agree that the actual emissions of pollutants should be used as the basis for tax calculation, that is, environmental tax should be a specific duty. China's current pollution charge system is also based on the specific charge mode. As for the benefit analysis of environmental tax, there have been comprehensive analyses, from the macro-economic development to the impact on micro-economic individuals. In terms of environmental costs and tax rates, scholars have brought forth various calculation methods, but they all agree that China's existing collection standard for water pollution fee is far lower than the negative environment cost caused by companies to the society, that is, the pollution charge is far from enough to make up for the environmental losses caused by industrial production and also far from enough to cover the treatment cost, rendering the failure of Chinese water pollution companies to pay great attention to environmental cost accounting and pollutant treatment and discharge. Therefore, the urgent reform of environmental tax and fees is of significance.

Regarding the empirical analysis of the impact and benefit of environmental tax, Chinese scholars usually use macro-level data and the Computable General Equilibrium (CGE) method to measure the impact of environmental tax on China's economic development and emissions reduction effect. There are few studies on meso- and micro-level data. To date, Chinese scholars have achieved significant results in the analysis of the macro-economic impact of environmental tax, which provides a policy basis for promoting the national environmental tax reform and improving the environmental tax system.

9.2.2 *Green investment*

Foreign research on corporate green investment began earlier, and the research content includes legal factors, incentives, informal factors (e.g., religion and culture), and supervision mechanisms. Paul Ekins and Stefan Speck conducted an empirical study on the relationship between environmental tax and green growth in Europe and found the environmental tax reform within Europe to be an effective economic means in achieving the 2020 emissions reduction target in the European Union, since it not only costs less but also helps to solve the problems in employment, technological innovation, and long-term economic development. Domestic research has shown that green investment is closely related to the growth of the national economy (Wang 2009) and has a positive effect on the reduction of exhaust emissions and water pollution COD discharge by industries, and on the development of environmental protection industries. At present, China's green investment has problems such as insufficient investment, low efficiency, and unreasonable structure.

Green investment is a new type of investment that has emerged in recent decades. Due to different research perspectives, the theoretical community has different definitions of green investment. The main research classifications are shown in Table 9.1.

Table 9.1. Definition of green investment.

Chinese scholars	Macro-level	An investment that, with the government as the main investor, benefits the sustainable development of green GDP; an investment activity that is designed to obtain expected economic benefits and protect the environment.
	Micro-level	An investment that, with companies as the main investor, sponsors the companies' R&D and services in environmental protection in order to enhance their environmental governance effect.
Western scholars		An investment that is to perform the corporate economic, environmental, and social responsibilities.

"Green investment" refers to the amount of investment in R&D, and services in environmental protection at the corporate or government levels. Here "green investment" refers to the micro-level corporate green investment. The environmental protection investment disclosed in the financial statements of Chinese-listed heavily polluting companies is consistent with the green investment as defined by the research group. However, due to the ambiguous regulations on corporate environmental information disclosure (EID) in China, the disclosure of green investment quotas in the afore-said financial statements are relatively vague and broad, and most companies only provide a value of their green investment without explaining its concrete use.

Therefore, based on the availability of research data, the research group has combined Chinese scholars' research on "green investment" at both the macro and micro levels when collecting data, and reached a consensus on the "meso-level" corporate green investment, that is, the total green investment of heavily polluting companies at the provincial level.

9.2.3 *Environmental tax and green investment*

Regarding the impact of environmental tax and fees on corporate green investment, the research of Chinese scholars is mainly concentrated on the following aspects:

(1) *Some scholars believe that the government environmental regulation is the fundamental motivation for heavily polluting companies to invest in environmental protection.* The externality of environmental issues determines the passivity of free-riding when companies face environmental governance. The core of green investment is to create environmental benefit; however, such vague characterization determines the low initiative of environmental protection investment. Based on rational assumptions, corporate decision-makers tend to take free-riding decisions. In this context, environmental regulation by the government, represented by environmental tax and fees, becomes the decisive factor in corporate green investment decision-making. From the perspective of corporate governance, if a company ignores environmental regulation, any potential environmental litigation or penalty may affect its operational cash flow in the future (Liu and Yang, 2010). Therefore, companies are forced to do a good job with regard to corporate environmental governance in the early stages and increase the corresponding investment. The collection of environmental tax, which is the successor to the "pollutant charge," will increase the tax burden of companies, but the guiding role of taxation will force them to adjust production (Bi and Yu, 2016b). On one hand, in order to seek profit margins for polluting products and production lines that are heavily taxed, companies must improve their existing products and production scale, increase resource utilization and production efficiency, highlight the production of energy-saving products, and enhance their market competitiveness. On the other hand, thanks to the incentive of environmental tax, companies continue to transform and innovate technologies that can improve production efficiency, introduce energy-saving and emissions reduction equipment, and achieve pollution control and R&D of new energy through technological innovation. This will undoubtedly promote companies to broaden the scale of green investment.

(2) *Research on the degree of impact of environmental regulation on corporate green investment.* Some scholars believe that there is an inverted U-shaped relationship between environmental regulation and the intensity of corporate environmental investment, and the intensity of the former's impact on the latter first increases and then decreases. In addition, companies with different property rights have different levels of response to environmental regulation. Some scholars have analyzed the green investment of Chinese listed companies and argue that, compared to

non-state-owned companies, state-owned companies are generally more active in responding to environmental regulation such as environmental tax and allocate more funds for more green investment (Bi and Yu, 2016). Other scholars believe that, under the same degree of environmental regulation, private companies are more inclined to adjust environmental investment strategies in time to satisfy the government requirements for environmental governance.

Contrary to the conclusions of the positive impact of government environmental regulation on corporate green investment, some scholars have found that government intervention has no significant impact on corporate environmental investment. Through panel data regression, these scholars have found a negative correlation between corporate green investment and environmental regulation by the government, showing that companies prefer fines to green investment in the face of environmental regulation. As an extension of pollution charge, environmental tax will soon become an important means of government environmental regulation in China, so it has also attracted the attention of scholars.

Through the above literature review on environmental tax and corporate green investment, it can be found that Chinese scholars are very active in the research of environmental tax and fee policies, and the conclusions they have drawn have their own merits, although some of them are completely opposite.

9.2.4 *China's policies on water pollution control and current situation of green investment*

From the long-standing pollutant charge system to the *Law of the People's Republic of China on Environmental Protection Tax* that was put into force as of January 1, 2018, China's policies on pollutant charge have continued to change and improve. The pollutant charge system is a way for government departments to collect fees for the external environmental losses caused by the pollution discharge so as to internalize the environmental external cost of the pollutant discharge units. The pollution charge system, implemented since the late 1970s, is a basic environmental management system in China. In 1978, the *Key Points of Environmental Protection Work Report* proposed, for the first time, to implement a pollution charge system. The *Environmental Protection Law* (*Trial*) of 1979 specifies that "the pollutants discharged in excess of the national standard shall be charged according to the quantity and concentration of the discharged pollutants, and the pollution discharge fee shall be charged according to the regulations."

By the end of 1981, 27 provinces, autonomous regions, and municipalities directly under the Central Government had gradually launched pilot projects for pollutant charge. In February 1982, the State Council promulgated the *Interim Measures for the Collection of Pollutant Discharge Fees*, which set out detailed regulations on the purpose, objects, charging standards, management, and use of pollution fees, marking the official establishment of the pollution charge system in China. The *Law on Water Pollution Prevention and Control* of 1984 stipulates that sewage discharge fees should be levied at the same time as the levy of excessive discharge fees. Article 18 of the *Environmental Protection Law* revised in 1989 stipulates that "Companies and institutions that discharge pollutants in excess of the national or local pollutant discharge standards shall pay fees for excessive discharge of pollutants in accordance with national regulations and be responsible for governance."

In 2003, the State Council promulgated the *Regulations on the Collection and Use of Pollutant Discharge Fees*, which was a milestone in the comprehensive reform of the pollution charge system, bringing significant changes to the collection objects, charging standards, management, and use of the fees, and specifying that pollutant discharge fees are levied on the basis of the total amount of pollutants discharged and the pollutant discharge standards. The Regulations came into effect on July 1, 2003. At the same time, the *Administrative Measures for the Collection Standards of Pollution Discharge Fees*, the *Administrative Measures for the Collection and Use of Pollutant Discharge Fees* and other supporting regulations were issued, which comprehensively and systematically established the pollution charge system under the conditions of market economy in China.

The reform in 2003 realized the transition from charging for excessive pollution to charging for pollutant discharge and double charging for excessive discharge, from concentration-based charging to concentration- and total-amount based charging, and from single-factor charging to multi-factor charging. The collection, use, and management of pollutant discharge fees have become so strict that all collected fees must be turned over to the government to be incorporated into the special fund for environmental protection.

On September 1, 2014, the NDRC, MOF, and MEP jointly issued the *Notice on Adjusting the Collection Standards for Pollutant Discharge Fees and Other Related Issues* to raise the charging standards for discharge of certain pollutants. The core content is that, by the end of June 2015, the price administration, fiscal, and environmental protection departments of all provinces (cities and districts) shall adjust the pollution charge for sulfur dioxide and nitrogen oxides in exhaust gas to no less than 1.2 yuan/CO_2e and adjust the pollution charge for the pollutants as COD, ammonia nitrogen, and five major heavy metals (lead, cadmium, chromium, mercury, metal-like arsenic) in sewage to not less than 1.4 yuan/CO_2e. Besides, at each sewage discharge outlet, sewage charges shall be levied on five major heavy metals; other pollutants are sorted in descending order of pollution equivalent, and pollutant discharge fees are levied on no more than three pollutants.

On December 25, 2016, the 25th meeting of the Standing Committee of the NPC passed the *Law on Environmental Protection Tax*, which came into effect on January 1, 2018. This Law consists of five chapters (general rules, tax calculation basis and tax amount payable, tax reduction and exemption, collection management, and supplementary rules) and 28 articles. This is China's first single tax law that specifically embodies the "green tax system" and promotes the construction of ecological civilization. The *Regulations on the Collection and Use of Pollutant Discharge Fees* and the *Notice on Adjusting the Collection Standards for Pollutant Discharge Fees and Other Related Issues* constitute the current pollution charge policies, which have the following characteristics:

(1) *Raise the standards for pollutant discharge fees significantly and further internalize external environmental costs*. The cost averaging method is used to determine the charging standards for air and water pollutant discharge fees. Taking into account the economic development level and the affordability of companies at that time, the charging standards determined by the 2003 pollution charge reform are based on the halving of the average pollution treatment cost of a sampling of companies. The new pollution charge standard will "regress" the four major pollutants and five heavy metals in the sewage to the level of the average pollution control cost, which will significantly increase the pollution control cost of companies and stimulate them to further improve the effect of pollution control.

(2) *Strengthen the control of major pollutants in the new era.* It is mainly reflected in two aspects: On one hand, these policies raise the charging standards for four pollutants as sulfur dioxide, nitrogen oxides, COD, and ammonia nitrogen, which need to be treated as important pollutants, and use economic means to encourage companies to independently install and operate pollution control facilities. On the other hand, they have fully considered the costs for pollution control costs and environmental loss, and gradually increased the charging standards of heavy metal discharge by industry and by pollutant type, so as to encourage companies to upgrade and transform technologies and actively reduce pollutant emissions.

(3) *Establish a differentiated policy, reward companies with good performance in environmental protection and punish those with environmental violations.* In addition to raising the pollution charging standards, a differentiated policy for the pollution charge system is also established, marking a major progress in the development of the pollution charge system.

(4) *Adjust measures to local conditions and leave full autonomy to local governments.* "The Notice on Adjusting the Collection Standards for Pollutant Discharge Fees and Other Related Issues" clearly state that all localities "may adjust the standards for the discharge of major pollutants while adjusting the standards for the discharge of other pollutants in light of local actual conditions." It not only encourages provinces and cities to formulate higher charging standards but also entrusts them with full autonomy to decide when and how much to raise the standards based on their development characteristics and management level.

(5) *The level of pollution charges is generally low, making it hard to cover the environmental costs of corporate production.* As shown in Figure 9.1, China's current COD (one of the main pollutants in industrial wastewater) discharge fee is generally low. Except for Beijing (10 yuan/CO_2e), Tianjin (7.5 yuan/CO_2e), Jiangsu (5.6 yuan/CO_2e), and Shanghai (4 yuan/CO_2e), all the pollution charge standards in the other provinces (municipalities) are at a low level. There are altogether 21 provinces (municipalities) with a COD discharge fee at the national minimum standard.

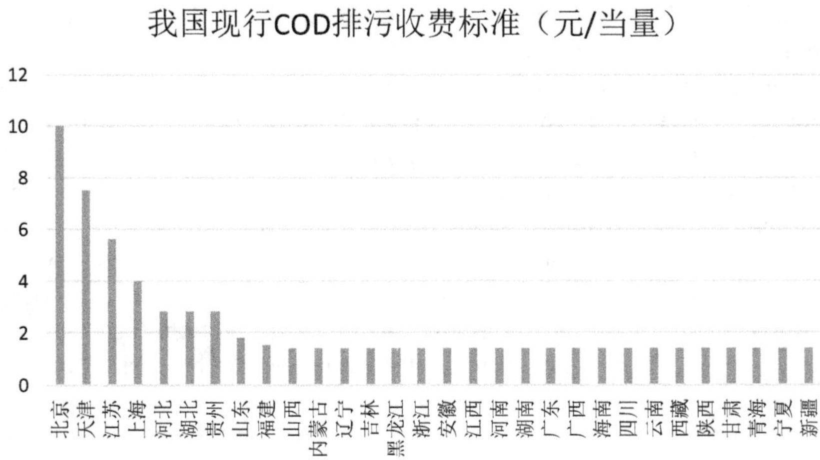

北京	Beijing	安徽	Anhui
天津	Tianjin	江西	Jiangxi
江苏	Jiangsu	河南	Henan
上海	Shanghai	湖南	Hunan
河北	Hebei	广东	Guangdong
湖北	Hubei	广西	Guangxi
贵州	Guizhou	海南	Hainan
山东	Shandong	四川	Sichuan
福建	Fujian	云南	Yunnan
山西	Shanxi	西藏	Tibet
内蒙古	Inner Mongolia	陕西	Shaanxi
辽宁	Liaoning	甘肃	Gansu
吉林	Jilin	青海	Qinghai
黑龙江	Heilongjiang	宁夏	Ningxia
浙江	Zhejiang	新疆	Xinjiang

Figure 9.1. China's current COD discharge fee by province/municipality (yuan/CO_2e).
Source: News reports, website of MEP.

The ultimate goal of environmental tax and pollution charge is to protect environment and resources. There is no essential difference between the two in terms of economic significance. Their main goal is to internalize the negative external effects of ecological damage. As far as China is concerned, the current pollutant discharge fee is a kind of pollution charge, and the environmental tax is the product of the reform of the pollution charge system.

However, there is a certain difference between environmental tax and pollutant discharge fee. From the legal perspective, pollutant discharge fee is an administrative charge, and environmental tax is prescribed law. From the perspective of their formulation duration, that of environmental tax goes through a long period, while pollutant discharge fee is relatively flexible and takes a short time. From the perspective of enforcement, environmental tax is more mandatory and standardized, while pollutant discharge fee is relatively loosely enforced. From the perspective of implementation effect, environmental tax is more conducive to promoting companies to actively carry out environmental protection, technological innovation, and improve environmental awareness. A comparison of their differences can be found in Table 9.2.

As shown in Figure 9.2, the amount of investment in industrial wastewater treatment across China in 2015 differed greatly. The green investment in wastewater treatment in Guangdong Province (top investor) reached 1.64 billion yuan, accounting for 5.64% of the provincial fixed asset investment. Hainan Province, the lowest ranked, had an investment of only 8.93 million yuan, accounting for only 0.38% of the provincial fixed asset investment. The industrial structure of Hainan is dominated by tertiary industries such as tourism, so the green investment on the treatment of industrial wastewater is naturally low. However, from a national perspective, the green investment in industrial wastewater treatment in all provinces is not high on the whole and account for a relatively small proportion of their respective fixed asset investment. Across China, only four provinces (Fujian, Zhejiang, Jiangxi, and Guangdong) saw their green

Table 9.2. Comparison between pollutant discharge fee and environmental tax.

Item	Pollutant discharge fee	Environmental tax
Procedures for establishment	To go through administrative procedures, easy to be adjusted	To go through strict legislative procedures, hard to be adjusted
Approval department	NDRC, MOF, or provincial government	NPC, MOF
Object	Environmental polluter	Universal
Intensify of enforcement	Weak	Mandatory
To be returned or not	To be returned	Not to be returned

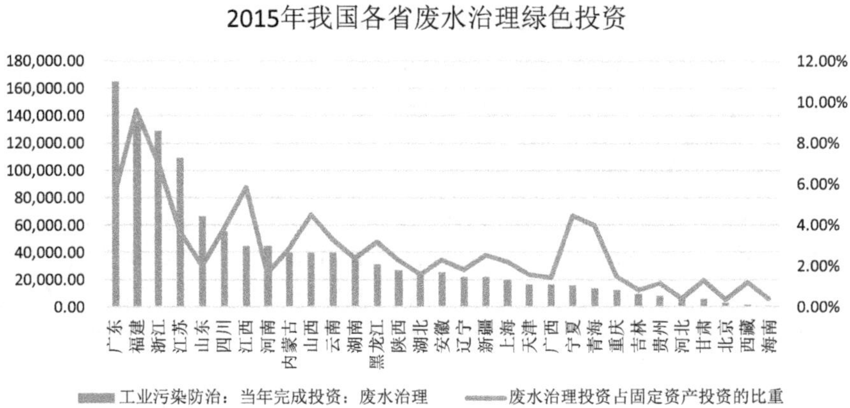

工业污染防治：当年完成投资：废水治理	Industrial pollution prevention and control: Investment completed in the same year: Wastewater treatment		
废水治理投资占固定资产投资的比重	Proportion of investment in wastewater treatment in fixed asset investment		
广东	Guangdong	辽宁	Liaoning
福建	Fujian	新疆	Xinjiang
浙江	Zhejiang	上海	Shanghai
江苏	Jiangsu	天津	Tianjin
山东	Shandong	广西	Guangxi
四川	Sichuan	宁夏	Ningxia
江西	Jiangxi	青海	Qinghai
河南	Henan	重庆	Chongqing
内蒙古	Inner Mongolia	吉林	Jilin
山西	Shanxi	贵州	Guizhou
云南	Yunnan	河北	Hebei
湖南	Hunan	甘肃	Gansu
黑龙江	Heilongjiang	北京	Beijing
陕西	Shaanxi	西藏	Tibet
湖北	Hubei	海南	Hainan
安徽	Anhui		

Figure 9.2. Green investment in wastewater treatment in provinces (autonomous regions and municipalities) across China in 2015.

Source: News reports, website of MEP.

investment in industrial wastewater treatment hold 5% or above in their respective fixed asset investment, and such proportions in other provinces (municipalities) were all below 5%. In Jilin, Hebei, and Hainan provinces and Beijing Municipality, the proportion was even lower than 1%.

9.3 An Empirical Analysis of the Impact of Pollutant Discharge Fee on Corporate Green Investment

9.3.1 *Regression model*

In order to empirically test the impact of government environmental regulation, which is represented by environmental tax and fees, on corporate green investment, we constructed the following linear regression model and selected inter-provincial panel data from 30 provinces (municipalities) across China for regression:

$$\ln GI_{i,t} = \beta_1 * \ln PG_{i,t} + \beta_2 * SIA_{i,t} + \beta_3 * PW_{i,t} + C, \tag{9.1}$$

in which, the meaning of specific variables is as follows:

ln*GI* The log value of the province's green investment amount (ten thousand yuan) in that year;

ln*PG* The log value of the province's per capita GDP (yuan/person) in that year;

SIA Industrial structure: The proportion of the province's secondary industry output value that year;

PW Per unit pollutant discharge fee (100 million yuan/ton): Pollutant discharge fee/the province's sewage discharge volume in that year.

This study is based on the data of 30 provinces (and municipalities) in China over the years 2002–2014 (excluding the data of Tibet), that is, the data of $T = 14$ and $N = 30$ are used for regression. The data have a total of 420 observed values and are obtained from the website of the environmental protection department of each province (and municipality) and compiled by the research team. The software Eviews 9.0 is used for statistical analysis, first assuming that a random effect model is used and then performing the Hausman test on the results. The results are as follows:

Redundant fixed effects tests
Pool: Untitled
Test cross-section fixed effects

Effects test	Statistic	d.f.	Prob.
Cross-section *F*	24.559096	(29,387)	0.0000
Cross-section Chi-square	438.448818	29	0.0000

Through the Hausman test, the individual effect in null hypothesis has nothing to do regression variables, and a random effect model should be established. Judging from the test results, the null hypothesis can be rejected, so a fixed effect model should be established. The regression results are as follows:

Dependent Variable: GI				
Method: Pooled Least Squares				
Included observations: 14				
Cross-sections included: 30				
Total pool (balanced) observations: 420				
Swamy and Arora estimator of component variances				
Variable	Coefficient	Std. Error	*t*-Statistic	Prob.
C	6.541891	0.620857	10.53688	0.0000
ln*PG*	0.115368	0.056143	2.054901	0.0406
SIA	0.048740	0.009105	5.352927	0.0000
PW	0.242722	0.062703	3.870994	0.0001
	Effects Specification			
Cross-section fixed (dummy variables)				
R-squared	0.746463	Mean dependent var		10.17697
Adjusted *R*-squared	0.725498	S.D. dependent var		1.219537
S.E. of regression	0.638951	Akaike info criterion		2.017335
Sum squared residual	157.9960	Schwarz criterion		2.334783
Log likelihood	−390.6403	Hannan–Quinn criterion		2.142805
F-statistic	35.60635	Durbin–Watson statistic		1.155492
Prob (F-statistic)	0.000000			

Judging from the significance of each estimator, the partial regression coefficients are all significant at a higher level, indicating that each explanatory variable has a significant impact on the explained variable.

From the point of view of the significance of the equation, the *p*-value of the F test is very small, indicating that the overall linear relationship of the equation is significant. The linear relationship among ln*GI* (log value of GDP per capita), *SIA* (proportion of secondary industry), and *PW* (per unit pollutant discharge fee) in the model is generally established.

9.3.2 *Analysis of regression result*

Looking at the regression results of the model, the coefficient of the pollution discharge fee per unit of wastewater discharge is 0.24, and has a very high level of significance, indicating that environmental tax and fees have a significant and positive impact on corporate green investment. The higher the pollution discharge fee per unit of wastewater discharge, the higher the environmental tax of the company, that is, the higher the corporate tax burden. However, the guiding role of environmental tax and fees will force companies to adjust production. As stimulated by environmental tax and fees, companies will introduce energy-saving and emission-reducing equipment and control pollution through technological innovation, which will vigorously promote them to increase green investment.

The coefficient of the log value of the per capita GDP of each province is 0.29, and has a significance level of 1%, indicating that the level of economic development has a significant impact on corporate green investment in each province. Provinces with a higher level of economic development pay more attention to the green production and environmental protection of companies, and higher per capita GDP has a significant positive impact on corporate green investment.

The industrial structure of each province also has a significant impact on corporate green investment. The higher the proportion of the secondary industry in the province, the higher the corporate green investment. This shows that the corporate green investment behavior is closely related to the environmental protection needs of provinces. It is the provinces with greater industrial pollution pressure that a larger amount of green investment.

9.4 Summary and Suggestion

This chapter combs the development history of government environmental regulation represented by the pollution charge system in China and uses the empirical data of pollutant discharge fees and green investment in most provinces across the nation over the years 2002–2014 to tentatively explore the impact of environmental tax on corporate green investment. The study has found that government environmental regulation represented by environmental tax and fees have a significant positive impact on corporate green investment; compared with the current pollution charge system, environmental tax is more conducive to promoting the environmental protection and green investment of companies, which reflects the necessity and importance of China's reform of environmental tax and fees.

The report of the Nineteenth CPC National Congress raises the "modernization with harmonious coexistence between man and nature," that is, we must not only create more material and spiritual wealth to meet the people's growing needs for a better life but also provide more high-quality ecological products to meet the people's ever-growing needs for a beautiful ecological environment. The report also points out four major measures for building a beautiful China: promote green development, vigorously solve outstanding environmental problems, intensify the protection of ecosystem, and reform the eco-environmental supervision system. This fully reflects China's attention and determination to promote eco-environmental protection and green development. Based on the importance and necessity of environmental protection and green investment as discussed above, we have derived two aspects of enlightenment and recommendations. On one hand, the Chinese government needs to further improve the environmental regulatory system, gradually establish a sound environmental taxation system, and strengthen the incentive effect of environmental tax on corporate green investment and energy conservation and emission reduction. At the same time, legislation should be strengthened to improve the environmental information disclosure mechanism of Chinese companies to make their environmental costs more transparent. On the other hand, in addition to the government legal environmental regulation, market incentives should also be added to gradually guide companies to voluntarily increase green investment, conduct green production, consciously carry out environmental protection, and meet the requirements of environmental regulation. From the corporate perspective, in order to adapt to the trend of green development and green consumption, green investment and environmental technology innovation should be strengthened. While reducing the pressure of environmental tax and fees on their own development, companies should enhance their core competitiveness through environmental technology innovation, thereby achieving a win–win situation for pollution control and corporate performance improvement.

The analysis in this chapter, mainly from the micro-level corporate perspective, explores the impact of environmental tax on heavily polluting companies. However, in China's environmental tax system, implemented since January 1, 2018, to date, there are only "pollutant discharge fees" (similar to "environmental tax") that can be inquired, the information disclosure of pollutant discharge fees of listed companies is in a mess, there is no systematic information disclosure system for environmental tax and fees, and the database of companies is not yet constructed. Therefore, the research team finally used inter-provincial panel data from heavily polluting companies. Compared with the micro-level corporate data, inter-provincial data can hardly reflect the response mechanism of companies; however, the data were collected from the website of the environmental protection department in each province, thus eliminating subjective factors.

After the official introduction of environmental tax on January 1, 2018, with relevant environmental tax data, we should continue to study the original intention of such tax, build an environmental tax and fee database of Chinese companies, and analyze the impact of environmental tax and fees on corporate behavioral choices.

Chapter 10

Environmental Protection Public Expenditure, Degree of Capitalization, and Economic Growth

10.1 Introduction

The ultimate goal of economic growth is to improve people's welfare. The development model of simply pursuing GDP growth at the expense of the environment has been increasingly questioned, and countries are paying increasing attention to the pursuit of sustainable economic development amid environmental protection. In fact, the more developed the economy is, the more attention it pays to environmental protection. To effectively protect the eco-environment, there must be resource input into corresponding governance. From an economic point of view, it involves the determining how to bear the cost of environmental control. The results of previous theoretical studies have shown that the environmental-protection–based regulatory measures will somewhat hurt economic growth. On one hand, the environmental control process itself requires resource input (including public and private resources), which will generate additional costs, thus causing a "crowding out effect" on other economic sectors that also need these resources, especially the private sector. On the other hand, environmental regulation also means to raise the access standards for production and consumption, including the restrictions of the original economic growth model in terms of technology and scale, resulting in a "leakage effect," thereby weakening domestic and local competitiveness and slowing down economic growth.

Does environmental protection necessarily harm economic growth? This is what all countries, especially developing countries, have been worried about for a long time. Take the case of China, a major developing country: Although it is currently engaged in transforming its economic development pattern, it has kept advancing industrialization and urbanization and still considers rapid development as an important task for a period of time to come. Therefore, the contradiction between environmental protection and economic growth seems more prominent in China. If we do not solve the problem of whether environmental protection and economic development are negatively related, it will not only hinder the progress of environmental protection but also harm economic growth itself and even endanger the sustainable development process on a global scale. Fortunately, contrary to the traditional theory, the fact is that after the Western developed countries greatly raised environmental control standards in the 1960s, so far, the economic growth and social welfare of European and American countries have not been significantly affected by environmental protection policies. This provides us with some enlightenment for studying the relationship between environmental protection and economic growth, that is, environmental protection and economic growth may be attainable at the same time. While environmental protection impacts economic output, it may promote economic growth through mechanisms such as stimulating demand and increasing investment in environmental protection, so that "one person can chase two rabbits at the same time."

This chapter mainly discusses the relationship between environmental protection and economic growth from three aspects. First is the role of government environmental public expenditure in promoting the relationship between environmental quality and economic growth. Specifically, this chapter analyzes the cause of Environmental Kuznets Curve (EKC) based on environmental public expenditure. Second, compared with private expenditure, it analyzes whether environmental public expenditure — as a part of social expenditure — is more conducive to economic growth, or on the contrary, environmental public expenditure is an unfavorable factor for economic growth. Third, in the process of modern economic growth, due to government budget constraints and other restrictive factors, it studies how can environmental public expenditure be unified with economic growth.

10.2 Environmental Public Expenditure and EKC

Regarding the relationship between environmental quality and economic growth, there have been a large number of studies in this regard, the most important of which is the inverted U-shaped EKC proposed by Grossman and Krueger in 1995, that is, when a country's economic development level is low, the degree of environmental pollution is relatively light, but with the increase of per capita income, the degree of environmental degradation will aggravate with economic growth; when the economic development reaches a certain turning point, as per capita income further increases, the degree of environmental pollution gradually slows down and the environmental quality gradually improves. Since then, a large number of scholars from various countries have devoted themselves into studying Environmental Kuznets Curve to further verify the inverted U-shaped relationship between environmental quality and economic growth in countries, regions, and cities, and further explain the underlying mechanism. In general, they have succeeded in identifying key explanatory variables including scale, structure, system, and technological progress.

According to Pearce *et al.*, the explanatory variables of EKC and their evolution can be summed up into four points:

(1) An increase in per capita income will absorb more resources and energy. At this time, if there is no government intervention, the environmental quality will continue to decline with the increase in income;
(2) After a certain point in time, the output structure changes, which will reduce the dependence of the unit output on pollutant emissions, and then under the conditions of trade permits, pollution-intensive industries will be exported to underdeveloped countries, that is, pollution is actually "exportable";
(3) If the environmental quality is income elastic, the change in the demand for environmental quality will be reflected in the policy change, and the strengthening of environmental regulation will put higher requirements on the system, and this is most likely to be achieved only in developed countries, while it is more difficult to achieve in developing and underdeveloped countries;
(4) The type of technology will change to be environment-friendly while economic growth promotes capital factors to replace environmental factors.

Among the above four points, the key to the formation of an EKC between environmental quality and economic growth is whether the environmental protection efforts of the latter three points can offset the environmental damage caused by the first point and also the negative impact of trade (the negative impact on the pollutant-importing countries) caused by the second point. In this regard, the traditional EKC research studies do not properly answer this question. Most of them only conduct a direct correlation analysis between income and environmental quality. As an important manifestation of the environmental protection efforts, what role does the government environmental public expenditure play in it?

Starting from the analysis of a typical EKC, this curve is often interpreted in the following formula:

$$e = a + by + c(y)^2 + \varepsilon, \quad \text{or} \quad E = a + by + c(y)^2 + \varepsilon,$$

where e is per capita emissions, E is total emissions, y is per capita income, ε is the interference item, and the quadratic power of y determines the final form of the curve, which is in an inverted U shape. Taking the derivative of the above formula, we can get $y^* = -b/2c$, this is where the highest point of the curve is located. Starting from this point, per capita environmental pollution or absolute environmental degradation will decrease as income grows.

Based on the above hypotheses of EKC, one of the accepted reasons for the decline of the curve from the apex is that the demand for environmental quality will begin to rise when income reaches the apex. Although different income groups have different demands for emissions reduction — for example, high-income groups are more willing to reduce emissions than low-income groups — the shape of EKC actually has little to do with differences in the willingness of different groups to reduce emissions. The key factor for the curve to move from low to high and then from high to low is that the demand for environmental quality is income elastic, that is, when income changes, people's demand for environmental quality and emissions reduction will change. As embodied in environmental expenditures, both private and public environmental expenditures have income elasticity. This is extremely valuable for explaining the latter segment of the EKC. As the economy grows and the income level of the whole society increases, due to the effect of income elasticity, the proportion of expenditure on environmental protection will increase, and both public and private environmental spending will rise at the same time.

As part of public goods which are non-competitive and indivisible, environmental products cannot be directly monetized like other private products. Therefore, in terms of environmental quality and the income elasticity of public environmental expenditures, the environmental value assessment method must be introduced. Usually when it comes to the scale of public goods supply, it is often defined by willingness to pay, that is, the environmental quality itself is the manifestation of value under the different levels of the willingness to pay. Compared with the direct concept of income, willingness to pay is not only positively related to income level but also related to other variables, including environmental awareness, education, gender, and equity (Freeman, 2002). However, overall, there is another factor that has a greater impact on environmental willingness to pay, and that is price. Therefore, after excluding other factors, environmental quality and public environmental expenditures that depend on the willingness to pay can be divided into two major parts: One is the income elasticity of environmental quality demand, and the other is the price elasticity of environmental quality demand. Ultimately, the elasticity of willingness to pay for environmental quality demand is equal to the ratio of income elasticity to negative price elasticity. Regarding the magnitude of the elasticity of demand for environmental quality, Garrod and Willis (1999) believe that the short-term price elasticity of environmental products is less than 1, and the income elasticity is positive and often greater than 1. The latter conclusion is consistent with the intuition that environmental products are "luxury goods."

So, what determines the growth of public environmental expenditures? Through the above breakdown of environmental quality demand, it can be seen that (1) with the increase of income, the elasticity of the willingness to pay for the environment increases, which can drive the increase of environmental public expenditure; and (2) higher income means an increase in the ability to pay. Once the apex of the curve appears, the country will invest more resources in environmental protection to offset the emissions accumulated during the growth process. In this regard, higher environmental expenditure reflects a higher degree of environmental degradation. In addition, the increase in public environmental expenditure reflects the increase in the society's awareness of environmental protection and the increase in environmental protection tendencies. Perhaps it is the change in social consciousness or environmental protection tendency after income rises that the above-mentioned correlation between income and expenditure appears. According to the public choice theory of Buchanan and Tullock (1975) and the transaction cost theory of Coase (1960), the demands of different stakeholders for environmental quality jointly promote the government to provide environmental public goods.

The above research conclusions lead to the next question, that is, since public environmental expenditures help explain the causes of EKC and are linked to income levels (including price levels), will public environmental expenditures harm economic growth while promoting the improvement of environmental quality?

10.3 Public Environmental Expenditures and Economic Growth

In order to answer the above questions, it is necessary to sort out the relationship between public environmental expenditures and economic growth.

A common view is that public environmental expenditures will weigh on economic growth, including industrial competitiveness. The reason is that while environmental regulation imposes costs on the private sector, its derived public expenditures will cause a crowding-out effect on private investment and output. The theory assumes that public environmental expenditures are embodied in the form of capital goods such as environmental protection infrastructure. In a general sense, this will have a negative impact on the level of input into the capital goods of the private and other sectors. In other words, public capital expenditures have a crowding-out effect on private investment, even though the spending of private sector could have been more effective to acquire scarce capital through fair market competition. Hence, the results of some studies show that the true cost of environmental expenditures is the long-term loss of economic growth and industry earnings due to the crowding-out effect. For example, when mandatory environmental protection standards limit the operation of new plants but let loose existing ones, it will place restrictions on the investment in new and effective technologies and increase operating costs of existing plants because emissions reduction rules will affect their production efficiency (e.g., the SO_2 emissions control will lower energy efficiency). Apparently, public environmental expenditures affect the cost structure in multiple ways and in turn affect economic growth.

Of course, there are opposite opinions, arguing that public environmental expenditures have the positive effect of decreasing the cost of private sector. First of all, mandatory public environmental expenditures can raise the environmental awareness of market players, urging them to save expenses on energy and materials. Second, environmental regulation that accompanies public environmental expenditure can improve production efficiency. In addition, in many literatures on corporate environmental management, the complementarity between benefits and expenditures is underlined; the most representative example in this regard is the "Porter Hypothesis" (Porter, 1990, 1991). According to this hypothesis, market players (companies) are, on the whole, not operating efficiently, while certain environmental regulations and public expenditures will function as catalysts that stimulate companies to increase output by raising resource utilization efficiency. This happens to be the win–win standpoint as endorsed in the afore-said literatures.

At the same time, Pearce also used OECD data to analyze the income elasticity of environmental expenditures. He analyzed and synthesized data over 1972–1995, finding that in absolute terms, the US was the biggest spender on the environment, followed by Germany, France, and Japan. However, in terms of income share, the public environmental expenditures of the US lagged behind other countries; such expenditures of Japan, Austria, the Netherlands and Ireland accounted for more than 1% of their GDP. In addition, the results of Pierce's study also show that there is a clear correlation between GDP and public environmental expenditures: When GDP increases, public environmental expenditures also increase. Although the study is a little bit simple, failing to take into account of other exogenous factors such as population, pollution, or environmental awareness that are independent of nationality or GDP, its conclusions indicate that public environmental expenditures and economic growth are positively correlated.

In order to further explain whether public environmental expenditure is detrimental or beneficial to economic growth, this section will, under the analysis framework of public economics on the impact of public expenditure on economic growth (i.e., by employing the traditional economic equilibrium model), divide all environmental investments into two parts as public expenditure and private expenditure. However, with respect to the output of investment, this book, instead of employing the previous analysis models, equates the potential net income of all investment projects with the average potential investment efficiency. This section will compare two types of economic equilibrium: economic growth with and without public environmental expenditure.

The analysis focuses on the difference between the output of private consumption and the output of public consumption on environment. The latter output is known as "nonproductive public environmental output." The basic conclusion of this section is that an economy with public environmental expenditure will grow faster than that without such expenditure. Of course, the analysis in this section is based on a precondition that the output efficiency of public environmental expenditure is the same as that of private expenditure, and there is no budget constraint to such public spending.

As mentioned before, economic growth is related to the level of public environmental expenditure. This section will further prove that the premise of this relationship is that the environmental consumption tendency in public sector is weaker than such tendency in private sector. Under these conditions, public environmental expenditure is related to economic growth, and the level of spending can contribute to economic growth at the same time.

In the traditional economic equilibrium model, the equilibrium economic growth rate of environmentally-free public expenditure is $g = s\sigma$ (Domar, 1946), where s is the propensity for private savings, and σ is the social average rate of return on investment, then there is $\sigma = dP/dt/I = P'/I$, so $P' = \sigma I$ ($dP/dt = P'$ indicates the potential growth level of investment). We take the economic growth rate g as the standard for comparison, that is, if there is a public environmental expenditure department in the process of economic growth, we can have the economic growth rate after purchasing environmental public goods and services through taxation.

For the sake of analysis, we can assume that all social investment is divided into two sectors: environmental protection (Ie) and private investment (Ip), and the growth level of investment P is the same in the two sectors, namely $P' = \sigma(Ie + Ip)$. In order to achieve economic equilibrium, the level of output growth must be equal to the level of investment growth, namely $Y' = dY/dt = dP/dt = P'$, while the growth level of total demand in the private sector is $C'p + I'p = (1 - s)(1 - t)\, Y' + I'p$, $C'p$ and $I'p$, respectively, represent the growth level of private consumption and private investment. The total environmental public expenditure of the society is the sum of capital environmental expenditure Ie and consumer environmental expenditure Ce. We can express consumer environmental public expenditure as $Ce = atY$, where t is the average tax rate, and a represents the proportion of consumer expenditure in the public environmental expenditure of the whole society. Therefore, the equilibrium condition for economic growth under environmental public expenditure is $Y' = (1 - s)(1 - t)\, Y' + I'p + atY' + I'e$, and a balanced growth level $g1$ can be obtained from it, $g1 = [(1 - t)s + t(1 - a)]\sigma$. Compared with g, if $a < (1 - s)$, then there will be $g1 > g$.

The above analysis shows that when the propensity to consume public environmental expenditures is lower than that of private expenditures, the economic growth that meets the conditions of public environmental expenditures will be faster than the economic growth without public environmental expenditures. In other words, in the overall public environmental expenditures, if the proportion of capital expenditure (i.e., the degree of capitalization) is higher than the proportion of private expenditures in private income, public environmental expenditures are conducive to economic growth. The economic significance of this conclusion is extremely obvious, that is, in equilibrium growth, if all savings are used for investment, then the public environmental sector supported by taxation will cause a decline in private savings and harm economic growth. However, as long as the degree of capitalization of the public environmental sector is higher than that of the private sector, the negative impact of taxation on the private sector can be offset, and overall economic growth will benefit from a higher tendency to capitalize public environmental expenditures.

10.4 Budget Constraints and Different Returns on Expenditures

10.4.1 *Introduce budget constraints*

Compared with reality, one of the biggest problems in the above analysis process is that it does not consider public sector budget constraints. Next, we will set budget constraints for public environmental expenditures, assuming that the tax rate is t, less than 1, and fixed. Here we do not consider the possibility of the public sector's issuance of bonds to break the budget constraints of public environmental expenditures; we only consider the situation of balanced budgets. The government budget is $B = G - T = Ie + (a - 1)tY$, where G and T are total public expenditure and revenue, respectively. Assuming that B is zero, then there is $B' = G' - T' = I'g + (a - 1)\, tY' = 0$, the condition to meet the budget constraints is $a = ab = 1 + qs\,(1 - 1/t)$, in which $q = Ie/Ip$, namely the ratio of environmental public expenditure to private expenditure scale. Because of $s(1 - 1/t) < 0$, the above formula can ensure that ab is less than 1, but it does not guarantee that a is positive. However, if a is allowed to be negative, it means that the tax rate can be increased, which is inconsistent with our assumption. In order to guarantee $0 < ab < 1$, there must be $q < t/s\ (1 - t)$, that is, if q does not exceed this value determined by the tax rate and private consumption propensity, then the government budget is balanced and the tax rate remains unchanged.

Budget constraints and fixed tax rates will also have an impact on the growth rate. The growth rate is the largest when $a = 0$ and the smallest when $a = 1$. It can be concluded that the condition for faster economic growth is $(1 - s) > 1 + qs\ (1 - 1/t)$, then there is $q > (1 - t)$. Therefore, to achieve a higher economic growth rate under the conditions of budget constraints and non-negative public consumption expenditures, it is necessary to meet $t/(1 - t) < q < t/s(1 - t)$, and both the left and right parts of it are indispensable.

In economy where public environmental expenditures do not have budget constraints, analysis shows that a higher level of economic growth can be obtained by increasing the capitalization of public environmental expenditures, that is, by reducing the consumption proportion of public environmental expenditure. Furthermore, a negative value can be given to a, that is, the level of economic growth can be increased by increasing the tax rate, but the problem is that the tax rate is not unlimited in the real economy.

10.4.2 *Introduce different rates of return on expenditure*

Previously, we assume that the rate of return on expenditure of different economic sectors is the same. Now we can further relax this condition, that is, the benefit of public environmental expenditure σe is different from that of private sector investment σp, then the average social benefit is $\sigma G = (Ip\sigma p + Ie\sigma e)/(Ip + Ie)$. Given other conditions, σG is positively proportional to Ie. Of course, when is given, σG is positively proportional to Ie ($\sigma e > \sigma p$), or is negatively proportional to Ie ($\sigma e < \sigma p$). For the sake of simplicity, assuming that the return on private investment remains unchanged and is independent of the scale and return on public investment, at this time, the return on economic growth is $g^2 = \sigma G\ [s(1 - t) + t(1 - a)]$, in order to make g^2 larger than g, there must be $a < (1 - s) + (s/t)(1 - \sigma/\sigma G)$, and whether this condition is more severe than the second part depends on σe.

If $\sigma e < \sigma$, then $\sigma G < \sigma$, namely $(s/t)(1 - \sigma/\sigma G) < 0$. In this way, this condition is higher than the requirements of the second part. Conversely, if $\sigma e > \sigma$, then $\sigma G > \sigma$, the condition is relatively relaxed. Even when the "propensity to consume public environmental expenditure" is higher than the propensity to consume private expenditure, the economy can grow at a faster rate. The larger σe is, the easier it is to realize the condition that the economic growth rate g^2 is higher than g.

10.4.3 *Include government budget constraints*

The government budget constraints are added again; in order to achieve budget balance when a is non-negative, the relevant conditions of the second part must also be met. So under the requirement that g^2 is greater than g, the condition for the public sector budget to achieve balance is $1 + qs(1 - 1/t) < (1 - s) + (s/t)(1 - \sigma/\sigma G)$. Taking into account the structural decomposition factors, it can also become $q > t/(1- t) \cdot \sigma/\sigma e$. If this condition is not met, then the economic growth rate of g^2 is less than g. Hence, the economic growth policy needed is to increase the ratio of capitalization of public environmental expenditure to private savings (that is to increase q). In order to make a positive, this ratio cannot be increased indefinitely. Therefore, the condition for balancing public consumption expenditure and budget in a non-negative environment is $t/(1 - t)\ \sigma/\sigma e < q < t/s\ (1 - t)$. Corresponding to the analysis in the second part, we can notice that a certain value of q is not necessarily required to achieve the above conditions. The condition for the above formula to be solvable is $t/s\ (1 - t) > t/(1 - t) \cdot \sigma/\sigma e$, namely $\sigma/\sigma e < 1/s$.

If $S < 1$, the right part of $t/(1 - t) \cdot \sigma/\sigma e < q < t/s\ (1 - t)$ is greater than 1, which means that when $\sigma < \sigma e$, there must be a solution. But if $\sigma/\sigma e > 1$, there may still be a solution, but there are restrictions on the ratio of private investment income to public investment income: The large income gap between the public and private sectors will prevent g^2 from being greater than g. Even if the above formula is satisfied, $\sigma/\sigma e$ must be used to determine whether the condition that the economic growth rate of g^2 is faster than g is more stringent than that of $g1$. If $\sigma < \sigma e$, the condition is more stringent; otherwise, if $\sigma > \sigma e$, the condition is more relaxed.

10.5 Summary

The analysis results of this chapter show that consumer expenditures in public environmental expenditures have a negative impact on economic growth, which means that the consumption part of public environmental expenditures must be restricted, while capital expenditures (degree of capitalization) in public environmental expenditures need to be encouraged. To some extent, this explains the cause of EKC, that is, in the early stage of economic growth, there are also public environmental expenditures, but from the perspective of expenditure structure, most of them are concentrated in the short-term consumer environmental expenditures while ignoring the long-term capitalized environmental expenditures, which has a crowding-out effect on other economic sectors and affects economic growth. Therefore, from the perspective of improving expenditure efficiency and economic growth, at this stage, the magnitude of public environmental expenditures is relatively low. Conversely, with the extension of the economic growth stage, in the later period, public environmental expenditures are more capitalized, which provides better support for output efficiency and economic growth. Under the effect of feedback mechanism, economic growth will begin feedback public environmental expenditures, thereby enabling the economy to obtain a higher environmental quality. This conclusion is obviously also proved by some empirical studies (Liu, 2012).

It should also be pointed out that although we have demonstrated the negative impact on economic growth from the consumer spending in public environmental expenditures, certain important expenditures are still necessary. Public consumption expenditures are actually exogenous, that is, it is inappropriate to deliberately reduce the consumer spending of public environmental expenditures in order to obtain higher capitalization of public environmental expenditures. To enable the capitalized public environmental expenditures to play a role in economic growth, it is necessary to ensure a sufficient scale of consumption, so it is impossible to continuously reduce the ratio of the two to promote economic growth. An excessively low consumption/capital ratio will actually impair output efficiency and public environmental expenditure efficiency, and will ultimately impair economic growth. Therefore, in the process of economic growth, there must be an optimal consumption/saving ratio of public environmental expenditures, which can optimize the output level of public environmental expenditures. This is also one of the important issues that need to be resolved in the next step of research.

Chapter 11

Comparative Analysis of Environmental Protection Investment and Economic Growth in the Yangtze River Delta

11.1 Introduction

As one of the regions with the largest economic aggregate in China, the Yangtze River Delta (YRD), which consists of Shanghai Municipality and another 15 cities in Jiangsu and Zhejiang provinces,[1] is well ahead in terms of socio-economic development and degree of marketization and opening-up. Such conditions have made the YRD climb over the peak of Environmental Kuznets Curve (EKC) to gradually realize coordinated development of environment and economy, and probably become the first region capable of doing so in China. However, on its way to harmonize the relationship between environment and economy, the YRD has to overcome huge obstacles such as a large size of immigrant population, highly homogeneous sub-regional industries, shortage of resources and energy, poor-quality foreign investments, repeated ecological construction, and weak links in environmental protection. In a bid to solve these problems,

[1]The composition of the YRD, namely Shanghai Municipality and another 15 cities of Nanjing, Suzhou, Wuxi, Changzhou, Yangzhou, Tàizhou, Nantong, Zhenjiang, Hangzhou, Ningbo, Jiaxing, Shaoxing, Huzhou, Zhoushan, and Tāizhou, is defined by the Forum for the Coordination of Urban Economy of the YRD which is a semi-official organization. But the YRD in a general sense is made up of Shanghai and all cities in Jiangsu and Zhejiang. The YRD discussed in this book is the latter one.

local governments shall, in addition to the existing environmental protection measures, play a leading role in further increasing investment, strengthening sub-regional cooperation, performing the positive radiation effect of investment, and intensifying regional economic integration. This chapter starts from the comparative analysis of environmental protection investment and economic growth in the YRD, then discusses the duty of local governments in coordinating environmental protection and economic growth, and finally puts forward suggestions.

11.2 Current Situation of YRD's Investment in Urban Environmental Protection

In recent years, major cities in the YRD have attached greater importance to environmental protection and reflected on the traditional economic growth model. They are not only promoting urban ecological planning but also stepping up construction of environmental protection infrastructure, showing their aspiration for coordinated development of environment and socio-economy. Moreover, most YRD cities have further increased investment in environmental protection (see Table 11.1) and set up supporting systems. A large number of studies have shown that expenditure on environmental protection is the most direct guarantee for coordinating the development of environment and socio-economy.

Table 11.1. Statistics of environmental protection investment across China and in YRD over 2000–2004 (Unit: billion yuan).[a]

	Region			
Year	National	Shanghai	Jiangsu[b]	Zhejiang
2000	106.098	14.191	1.31036	16.952
2001	110.660	15.293	1.03524	19.783
2002	136.340	16.239	0.75393	19.876
2003	162.73	19.153	1.729	26.01
2004	190.8	22.5	—	—

Notes: [a]All the data are excerpted from National, Shanghai, and Zhejiang *Bulletin of Environmental Statistics* (2001–2004) and *Jiangsu Statistical Yearbook* (2001–2004). [b]The environmental protection investment in Jiangsu Province is the amount of investment completed in industrial pollution control projects that year.

The government is the main provider of investment in environmental protection — a public product with huge externalities — that is why the expenditure on urban environmental protection is objectively inseparable from the government's dominance. Presently, the government mainly guides public investment in treatment of industrial pollution sources, construction of urban environmental infrastructure, and improvement of environmental management capability (see Table 11.2).

In terms of the relationship between the central and local governments in funding environmental protection, it is local governments that mainly and directly bear the investment in environmental protection, which is decided by China's public expenditure budget system. Therefore, the decisions for public spending on environmental protection are made at the local level to complement local economic growth and vice versa. However, this endogeneity will inevitably affect the scale and structure of such public spending. One of the prominent impacts is that the relatively independent investment in the YRD sub-region (individual cities in Zhejiang and Jiangsu provinces, and Shanghai) will conflict with the need for integration of environmental protection in the entire YRD. Apparently, environmental protection investment based on the eco-environment and economic development level of an individual city cannot meet the entire region's overall requirements for improving the environment.

In short, in the process of studying the scale and structure of environmental protection investment, we can learn about the extent to which the YRD's environmental quality has improved amid continuous economic growth and identify the problems caused by the existing system for environmental protection investment.

Table 11.2. Two types of environmental protection investment across China and in YRD in 2003 (Unit: billion yuan).

	Region			
Environmental types	National	Shanghai	Jiangsu	Zhejiang
Treatment of industrial pollution sources	21.28	2.891	3.328	6.955
Construction of urban environmental infrastructure	107.2	14.403	25.885	20.211

Source: *China Statistical Yearbook* (2004), National Environmental Statistics Bulletin (2004).

11.2.1 *Characteristics of YRD's environmental protection investment*

11.2.1.1 *The scale of investment keeps increasing year by year*

Grossman and other economists studied a large quantity of economic data of Western countries in 1995 and proved that the direct investment into environmental protection measures play a major role in improving environmental quality (Grossman and Krueger, 1995). After setting up environmental protection agencies in the 1960s, Western countries successively poured enormous funds into pollution control and construction of urban environmental protection facilities and have achieved positive results.

Since the late 20th century, the major cities in YRD have gradually increased investment in pollution control and environmental protection; both the total amount and proportion of such investment have remained relatively high. As shown in Table 11.3, the total amount of investment in pollution control in 16 YRD cities has increased significantly since 2000. It is normal to see ups and downs in the amount of investment in different years, because the pollution control projects have a long span of time, and a large investment in a certain year is to be digested in subsequent years. On the whole, the annual growth of investment is relatively fast, which can be seen in the mounting investment in environmental infrastructure in cities such as Shanghai (see Figure 11.1).

First, looking at the scale of investment in pollution control, the 15 YRD cities (excluding Shanghai) can be roughly divided into three categories (see Figure 11.2): (1) The first category of cities is those that invest more than 1 billion yuan annually, namely Hangzhou, Wuxi and Ningbo. (2) The second category includes the cities with an average annual investment between 500 million yuan and 1 billion yuan, namely Tāizhou, Shaoxing, Jiaxing, Changzhou, Yangzhou, Nanjing, and Zhenjiang. (3) The third category covers Huzhou, Tàizhou, Suzhou, Nantong and Zhoushan, whose average annual investment is less than 500 million yuan.

Second, in terms of the proportion of environmental protection investment in GDP, the YRD is far ahead of the national average (see Table 11.4). Such proportion in Shanghai and the provinces of Jiangsu and Zhejiang is basically at the same level, but Shanghai has been doing much better then other YRD cities, showing that Shanghai has paid greater attention to environmental protection in recent years.

Table 11.3. Investment in pollution control in 16 YRD cities over 2000–2004 (Unit: million yuan).

	Year					
City	2000	2001	2002	2003	2004	Annual average
Shanghai[a]	14,191	15,293	16,239	19,153	22,500	1,747,520
Hangzhou	3,070.68	2,611.81	4,139.45	655.54	3,020	2,177.135
Ningbo	3,226.134	147.459	298.74	284.26	2,260	1,186.4666
Jiaxing	756.05	724.716	1,511.92	2,448.54	1,477	893.9372
Huzhou	22.49	33.204	876.48	93.17	1,143	433.6688
Shaoxing	42.81	636.983	2,009.045	314.29	2,270	927.229
Zhoushan	34.57	6.35	0.18	4.14	133	34.378
Tāizhou	88.48	740.32	1,871.03	347.44	1,653	940.054
Nanjing	2,083.49	176.39	133.12	162.60	—	638.90
Wuxi	2,466.31	656.05	878.36	1,021.51	—	1,255.5575
Changzhou	69.86	1,362.18	1,584.19	364.39	—	845.155
Suzhou	290.23	3,229.83	175.09	205.40	—	167.68
Nantong	68.44	155.08	241.49	112.67	—	144.42
Yangzhou	88.93	1,166.20	1,211.65	380.69	—	711.8675
Zhenjiang	48.60	1,042.80	1,047.67	100.12	—	559.7975
Tàizhou	80.24	445.03	918.54	166.71	—	402.63

Note: [a]Shanghai's investment in environmental protection is spent on pollution control, construction of urban environmental infrastructure, and enhancement of environmental protection capacity.
Source: Shanghai *Bulletin of Environmental Statistics* (2000–2004), *Zhejiang Statistical Yearbook* (2000–2004), and *Jiangsu Statistical Yearbook* (2000–2003).

11.2.1.2 *Local governments play a major role in driving environmental protection investment*

Environmental protection investment, with its output as public products, is subject to public decision-making. The American economist Jeremy Stevens has pointed out that there are mainly four theoretical models for the supply of public goods: Good Fairy Model, Semi-good Fairy Model, General Model of Elected Suppliers, and Wicked Witch Model. The key criterion for distinguishing these models is the government's willingness and degree of intervention in public decision-making. According to Stevens, too much and too little government intervention is

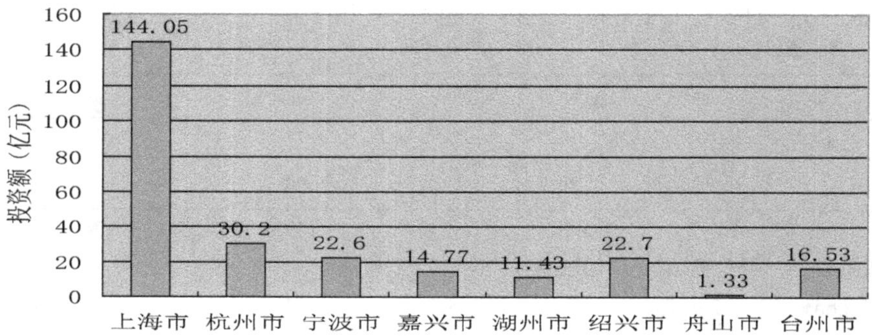

投资额（亿元）	Investment amount (billion yuan)
城市	City
上海市	Shanghai
杭州市	Hangzhou
宁波市	Ningbo
嘉兴市	Jiaxing
湖州市	Huzhou
绍兴市	Shaoxing
舟山市	Zhoushan
台州市	Tāizhou

Figure 11.1. Investment in construction of environmental infrastructure in Shanghai and other YRD cities in 2004.

not healthy, and the degree of intervention is judged by efficiency of supply. He holds that the government should withdraw from the supply of public goods in the fields where the market can guarantee effective supply. Data analysis shows that YRD's environmental protection investment is mainly driven by local governments, but the investment in different fields of environmental protection is differentiated.

(1) *The government serves as the main driving force in the fields with a strong public attribute*. At present, YRD's environmental protection investment is characterized by a government-led supply model, because such investment is mainly driven by local governments. In the expenditure on environmental protection investment (excluding the investment

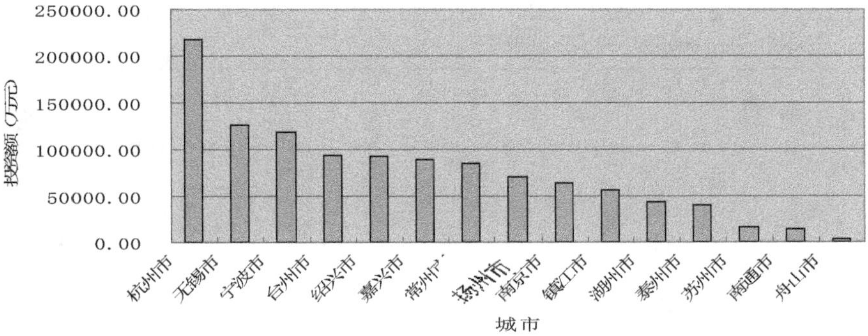

投资额（万元）	Investment amount (million yuan)
杭州市	Hangzhou
无锡市	Wuxi
宁波市	Ningbo
嘉兴市	Jiaxing
台州市	Tāizhou
绍兴市	Shaoxing
嘉兴市	Jiaxing
常州市	Changzhou
扬州市	Yangzhou
南京市	Nanjing
镇江市	Zhenjiang
泰州市	Tàizhou
苏州市	Suzhou
南通市	Nantong
舟山市	Zhoushan

Figure 11.2. Comparison of annual investment scale in pollution control among YRD cities.

for industrial pollution control with less government intervention), the construction of environmental infrastructure and building of environmental management capacity, which are of strong public externalities, are fully covered by government budget. Infrastructure investment occupies a large proportion of the total environmental protection investment (see Table 11.5). Such proportion in Shanghai and Zhejiang-based cities has been above 70% for years in a row, much higher than the national level in

Table 11.4. The proportion of environmental protection investment in GDP across China and in YRD over 1999–2003 (Unit: %).

Year	National (%)	Shanghai (%)	Zhejiang (%)	Jiangsu[a]
1999	1.14	2.77	2.27	—
2000	1.19	3.12	2.81	—
2001	1.14	3.09	2.93	—
2002	1.30	3.00	2.55	—
2003	1.39	3.06	2.83	2.35

Note: [a]The environmental protection investment in Jiangsu Province is the amount of investment completed in industrial pollution control projects that year.
Source: *China Statistical Yearbook* (2000–2004), *Shanghai Statistical Yearbook* and *Bulletin of Environmental Statistics* (1999–2004), *Zhejiang Statistical Yearbook* and *Bulletin of Environmental Statistics* (1999–2004), *Jiangsu Statistical Yearbook* and *Bulletin of Environmental Statistics* (1999–2004). Unless otherwise noted, the data presented below are also excerpted from the afore-said bulletins and statistical yearbooks.

Table 11.5. The proportion of environmental infrastructure investment in YRD's total environmental protection investment over 2000–2004 (Unit: %).

Year	National	Shanghai	Zhejiang
2000	0.528756	—	0.727209769
2001	0.538316	—	0.681329424
2002	0.575987	0.782006281	0.753573657
2003	0.65876	0.752101498	0.752101498
2004	0.597296	0.740461402	—

the same period, showing that YRD's local governments indeed play a decisive role in environmental protection.

(2) *The government plays a minor role in the fields with a weak public attribute*. Regarding the investment for controlling industrial pollution which is of weak public externalities, the local governments in YRD has been reducing its intervention. Theoretically, industrial pollution is a consequence of market-oriented production behavior of enterprises, therefore, it should be treated by the enterprises who have caused the pollution

Table 11.6. The proportion of investment for controlling industrial pollution in YRD's total environmental protection investment over 2000–2003 (Unit: %).

Year	National	Shanghai	Zhejiang	Jiangsu
2000	0.287755843	—	—	0.157819225
2001	0.298780711	0.077859249	0.023911871	0.28322901
2002	0.301303928	—	0.036068169	0.32463226
2003	0.140333889	—	0.074641148	—

according to the principle of "whoever causes pollution is responsible for its treatment." Relevant statistics show that the government does not play a major role in the treatment of industrial pollution and that both the central and local governments only contribute a small amount of funds for industrial pollution control (see Table 11.6), which is contrary to what they have done in supporting the construction of environmental protection infrastructure. As for the proportion of investment for industrial pollution control in total environmental protection investment, YRD falls behind the national average level: such proportion of Jiangsu-based cities is slightly higher, but that of Shanghai and Zhejiang-based cities is below 10% without exception.

11.2.1.3 *Local government expenditure for environmental purpose is mainly spent on the construction of urban environmental infrastructure*

While the market is becoming increasingly mature, the scale and scope of government public expenditure also experience changes, namely the government places different emphasis on items of expenditure. Especially for local governments, under the circumstance of mounting environmental pressure, they prefer injecting public budgets into the fields that can significantly improve local environment.

(1) *Local governments spend most of their environmental protection expenditure on the construction of urban environmental infrastructure.* The government investment in environmental protection has two sources: One is from the central government, and the other is from local governments. The former is mainly spent on treating pollution sources, while the

latter is mainly injected into construction of urban environmental infrastructure. In reference to the data in Table 11.5 and Figure 11.3, after deducting a small portion of state budgetary appropriation, YRD's local public expenditure on environmental protection is concentrated in the construction of urban environmental infrastructure, and the level of such investment is higher than that of the national average.

(2) *Local governments are not as passionate as the central government in pouring investment into environmental protection*. Compared with their enthusiasm for the construction of urban environmental infrastructure, YRD's local governments are not so active in control of industrial pollution, with their investment in this regard lower than the national level. Looking at the budget allocation of central and local governments for industrial pollution control (see Figures 11.3 and 11.4), local governments apparently lack the enthusiasm for investment, with the amount of public expenditure much lower than the state budgetary appropriation, which exactly reflects the attitude of YRD's local governments toward industrial pollution control.

11.2.2 *Motivation of YRD's investment in environmental protection*

EKC is proposed by environmental economists to illustrate the relationship between a country's economic development level and environmental condition. The main idea of this curve is that a country's environment is bound to deteriorate at the initial stage of economic boom, but it will get improved at a certain time point, namely when the per capita GDP reaches its critical value of US$5,000. Presently, owing to various constraints, this empirical relationship between economic growth and environmental quality as depicted by EKC has not been fully verified in China. However, looking at YRD's public expenditure on environmental protection, its environmental condition is substantially benefited from local economic success. A high level of economic development plays a key role in promoting environmental protection, while the mounting pressure on resources and environment and the stronger public awareness of environmental protection have stimulated YRD's local governments to intensify investment in environmental protection, for the purpose of satisfying the entire society's need for a better environment.

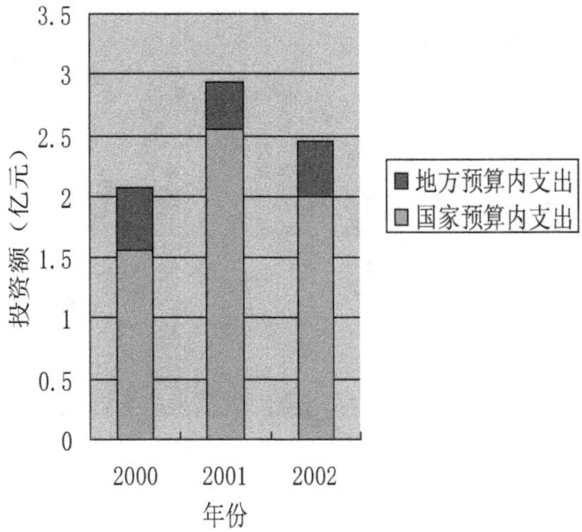

投资额（亿元）	Investment amount (billion yuan)
年份	Year
地方预算内支出	Local budgetary appropriation
国家预算内支出	State budgetary appropriation

Figure 11.3. Local and state budgets in industrial pollution control investment of Jiangsu Province.

11.2.2.1 *High-level economic development is the prerequisite and foundation for realizing environmental protection investment*

In both total amount and grade of environmental protection investment, YRD significantly outperforms the national average and many other provinces and cities, which is mainly attributed to its long-term rapid economic development. With continuously growing economy, YRD is increasingly capable of providing positive feedback to the environment. In short, a higher level of economic development is the material

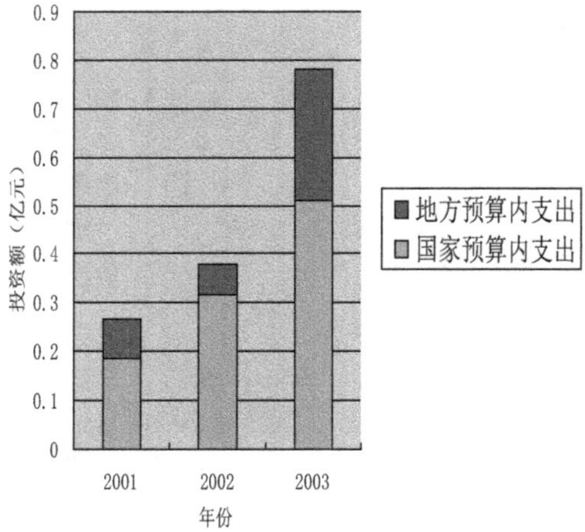

投资额（亿元）	Investment amount (billion yuan)
年份	Year
地方预算内支出	Local budgetary appropriation
国家预算内支出	State budgetary appropriation

Figure 11.4. Local and state budgets in industrial pollution control investment of Zhejiang Province.

prerequisite and foundation for realizing investment in environmental protection.

(1) *Horizontal comparison between the investment of YRD and that of the national average and other provinces and cities*. Regarding the level of environmental protection investment, YRD is far ahead of the national average and backward regions, but falls behind other more developed regions. We have selected seven provinces and cities across China as objects of comparison. We compared their per capita GDP (key indicator of economic development) and per capita environmental protection investment (key indicator of environmental protection investment). The result of comparison shows that these two indicators clearly have a

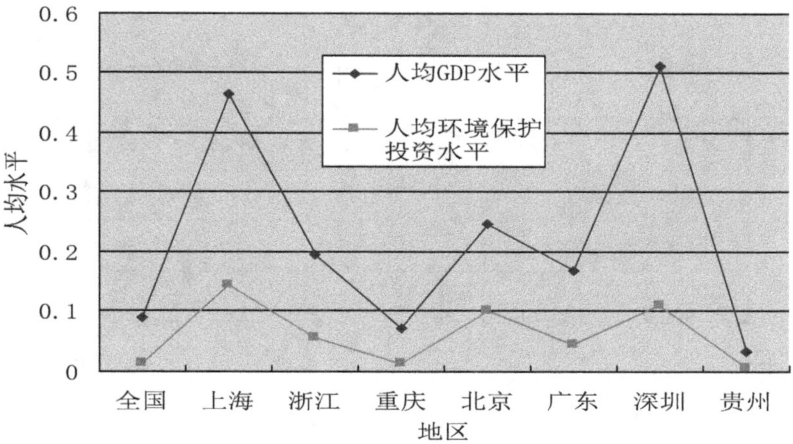

人均水平	Per capita (yuan)
人均 GDP 水平	Per capita GDP
人均环境保护投资水平	Per capita environmental protection investment
全国	National
上海	Shanghai
浙江	Zhejiang
重庆	Chongqing
北京	Beijing
广东	Guangdong
深圳	Shenzhen
贵州	Guizhou
地区	Province/city

Figure 11.5. Level of economic development and of environmental protection investment.

positive correlation (see Figure 11.5). For example, in 2003, Shanghai's per capita GDP ranked second among the seven provinces and cities, and its per capita environmental protection investment was top-ranked in the same period, while Zhejiang saw its per capita GDP and environmental protection investment both take the fourth place.

(2) *Vertical comparison between years' environmental protection investment in YRD*. The positive correlation between the level of economic development and the scale of environmental protection investment also

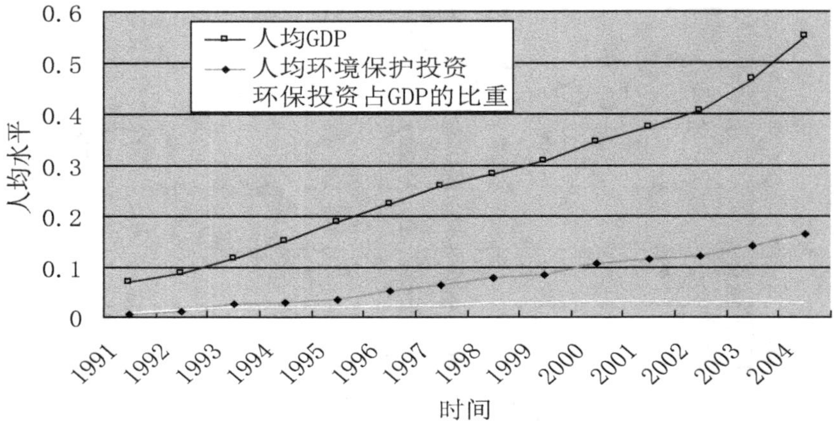

人均水平	Per capita (yuan)
人均 GDP	Per capita GDP
人均环境保护投资	Per capita environmental protection investment
环保投资占 GDP 的比重	Proportion of environmental investment in GDP
时间	Year

Figure 11.6. Level of economic development and of environmental protection investment in Shanghai over 1991–2004.

exists in YRD. The expanding scale of YRD's environmental protection investment is attributed to the year-by-year economic growth. It is economic success that provides sufficient funds to the construction of environmental protection infrastructure and treatment of pollution sources. As shown in Figure 11.6, Shanghai has maintained a double-digit growth rate in the past decade or so, which drives up its environmental protection investment from no more than 100 yuan per capita (accounting for less than 1% of GDP) in 1991 to 1,663 yuan (3.02% of GDP) in 2003.

11.2.2.2 *Mounting pressure on resources and environment and growing public environmental awareness drive up investment in environmental protection*

Although a relatively developed economy objectively provides material guarantee for realizing environmental protection investment, the above analysis tells that the ultimate realization of such investment in YRD is impossible without the dominant and catalytic role of the government, especially local governments. Well then, what is the incentive for the government to increase environmental protection investment? In terms of the relatively developed YRD, are there any factors that finally push the local governments to keep increasing such investment? It can be explained from two aspects: (1) The traditional industrialized economic growth model, coupled with a large population base, has exerted great pressure on local resources and environment and (2) while earning more income than before, local residents have become increasingly aware of environmental quality, thus requiring more and more to be done in environmental protection.

(1) *Mounting pressure on local resources and environment.* As far as YRD is concerned, its traditional economic growth model in more than 20 years' industrialization is mainly characterized by high input, high consumption, high pollution, and low output. In this process, enormous resources and energy were consumed, and a large number of highly polluting industries were built to boost the export-oriented industrial structure. That's why YRD's resources, energy, and environment have been under huge pressure. As shown in Table 11.7, in terms of the waste pressure indexes (representing waste water, exhaust gas, and solid waste) and resource pressure index, the numerical values of Shanghai, Jiangsu, and Zhejiang are above the national level, especially Shanghai, which fully demonstrates that their economic growth has caused great pressure on local resources and environment. This pressure keeps mounting under the influence of a large population base and increased population mobility, giving rise to a sustainable development synthesis pressure index (representing population,

Table 11.7. Gross pressure on YRD's ecological resources and environment in 2003.

Region	Wastewater discharge pressure index	Solid waste pressure index	Exhaust gas emission pressure index	Environmental pollution pressure index	Sustainable development synthesis pressure index	Resource pressure index
National	0.42	0.43	0.41	0.4	0.32	—
Shanghai	1	0.79	1	0.95	0.41	0.69
Jiangsu	0.49	0.49	0.47	0.45	0.37	0.29
Zhejiang	0.51	0.37	0.44	0.41	0.38	0.29

living space, and population quality) at a total value of 1. Such index of Shanghai, Jiangsu, and Zhejiang in 2003 is respectively 0.6, 0.36, and 0.24, with Shanghai far exceeding the national level of 0.39 (Department of Statistics, 2004).

Enormous pressure on resource and environment and on population has brought YRD's socio-economy to a crisis — only by vigorously increasing environmental protection investment can the region overcome the shortcomings of the traditional growth model and coordinate the local economic and social development.

(2) *Improved public environmental awareness*. As a significant result of economic growth, people have seen their disposable income remarkably increased. According to the research of foreign scholars, increased disposable income of residents and the resulting changes in their environment preference are an important micro-mechanism for the EKC to reach a turning point. In terms of environmental protection investment, increased resident income will lead to two consequences: (1) It raises people's environmental awareness and motivates them to pursue a better living environment, which is manifested in their pressing demand for funding environmental protection and (2) with growing environmental awareness, people are more willing to pay for environmental protection by themselves. The two consequences can ultimately increase environmental protection investment, the difference is that the former will increase public (government) spending in environmental protection, while the latter will encourage private investment (consumption) for this purpose.

As far as YRD is concerned, local residents have seen their income increase significantly in the past 20 years (see Table 11.8), which objectively motivates them to ask for a good eco-environment; however, their willingness to pay for environmental protection is not improved at the same time, thus resulting in a deviation between higher expectation for environmental protection and lower willingness to pay (WTP). Since the incremental resident income fails to be converted into large-scale private

Table 11.8. Per capita GDP in YRD over 1995–2004 (Unit: yuan).

Year	1995	1996	1997	1998	1999	2000	2001	2002	2003	2004
Jiangsu	7,299	8,447	9,344	10,021	10,699	11,773	12,922	14,391	16,809	20,852
Zhejiang	8,074	9,455	10,515	11,247	11,981	13,461	14,655	16,838	20,147	23,942
Shanghai	18,943	22,275	25,750	28,253	30,805	34,547	37,382	40,646	46,586	55,089

investment in environmental protection, the government is bound to play a leading role in funding this cause.

11.3 Analysis of the Problems in YRD's Environmental Protection Investment

As an intermediate variable between economic development and environmental quality, environmental protection investment is not only the result of economic development but also the material basis for improving environmental quality. When providing funds to environmental protection, investors must give consideration to two externalities:

(1) Transboundary nature of environmental pollution, that is, adjoining areas in a region usually constitute an entire ecosystem. Environmental pollution in one area may inflict (or do more harm to) another area in the same ecosystem, which means that the pollution arising from the economic growth of an area is not limited to itself.
(2) Transboundary nature of environmental governance, that is, within the same region, the environmental improvement of critical ecological areas will benefit the other areas and even the entire region, however, that of non-critical areas can only do good to themselves. This means that the environmental protection investment of the same scale has different effects on the regional environment.

The YRD (or the Pan-YRD) is a self-contained ecosystem to a certain extent. Either from the perspective of natural ecological resources and watershed or from the perspective of acquired social demography, economy, and industry, all areas in YRD are naturally and indivisibly interdependent. In the long run, the society, economy, and eco-environment across YRD will become more integrated. Given this, the above two externalities also exist in all YRD cities, and they must take these factors into account when making decisions for environmental protection investment to prevent wasted efforts.

Regarding the current situation in YRD, although its amount of environmental protection investment is somewhat satisfying, the poor coordination between areas have made such investment ineffective in mitigating environmental pollution and precluded the economic achievements from benefiting the improvement of environmental quality. Moreover, all sorts of factors, such as slow transition from the traditional economic growth model to the new path of industrialization, acceleration of urbanization, industrial isomorphism, backward technologies, and super-national treatment of foreign capital, have weakened the effect of environmental protection investment to varying degrees, thereby further exacerbating the environmental pollution in YRD.

11.3.1 *Existing problems*

11.3.1.1 *Environmental protection investment fails to vigorously improve YRD's overall environmental condition*

The analysis in Section 11.3 shows that YRD's environmental protection investment accounts for a large share of its GDP. For rational investors involved in this cause, their ultimate goal is to maximize the utilization efficiency of such investment and improve the regional environmental quality. However, in reality, the notable increase in YRD's environmental protection investment, which is dominated by local governments, has failed to significantly improve the regional environmental quality. Take Shanghai and Zhejiang as an example: Their environmental conditions have not improved in recent years, but continued to deteriorate to a certain extent, as evidenced by the air quality indexes such as total suspended particulate (TSP) concentration, inhalable particulate concentration, sulfur dioxide (SO_2) concentration, nitrogen dioxide (NO_2) concentration, acid rain frequency, and rainfall pH value (see Tables 11.9 and 11.10).

11.3.1.2 *Imbalanced distribution of environmental protection investment restrains the positive externality of environmental public goods*

Although YRD's environmental protection investment has kept increasing in scale, it has remained in imbalanced distribution, which exists not only at the sub-regional level but also between urban and rural areas. As a result, the critical ecological areas are not properly protected and the non-critical areas have consumed most of the environmental protection investment. Looking at YRD as a whole, such situation is far from being able to meet the requirements for optimizing allocation of resources. Owing to imbalanced distribution, the sub-regional environmental protection investment can only get half the result with twice the effort.

Table 11.9. Air quality in Shanghai over 1999–2004.

Index	1999	2000	2001	2002	2003	2004
Daily average SO_2 concentration (mg/m^3)	0.044	0.045	0.043	0.035	0.043	0.055
Daily average NO_2 concentration (mg/m^3)	0.099	0.090	0.063	0.058	0.057	0.062
Daily average inhalable particulate concentration (mg/m^3)	0.168	0.156	0.100	0.108	0.097	0.099
Rainfall pH value	—	5.2	5.2	5.4	5.2	4.92
Acid rain frequency (%)	—	26.0	25.2	10.9	16.7	32.7

Table 11.10. Air quality in Zhejiang over 2001–2003.

Index	2001	2002	2003
TSP concentration	0.137	0.141	0.148
Daily average SO_2 concentration (mg/m^3)	0.008	0.012	0.02
Daily average NO_2 concentration (mg/m^3)	0.024	0.027	0.03
Daily average inhalable particulate concentration (mg/m^3)	—	—	0.093
Rainfall pH value	5.6	5.6	4.5
Acid rain frequency (%)	75.5	83.7	84.3

(1) *Shanghai's per capita environmental protection investment is more than that of Jiangsu and Zhejiang.* Looking at the entire YRD and from the perspective of a natural eco-region, Shanghai is subordinate to Jiangsu and Zhejiang provinces, which means that it is not as important as Jiangsu and Zhejiang in the ecosystem; however, thanks to a better economic geographical location than the two provinces, Shanghai has achieved prominent economic success, thereby driving up its environmental protection investment. The per capita environmental protection investment of Shanghai is much higher than that of Jiangsu and Zhejiang (see Figure 11.5).

(2) *Urban areas inject more investment in environmental protection than rural areas.* In YRD's sub-regions (Jiangsu, Zhejiang, and Shanghai), a great portion of environmental protection investment flows to urban areas, with suburban and rural areas being ignored to a certain extent.

This is particularly prominent in the investment for environmental infrastructure construction. Take Jiangsu Province as an example. In 1993, its investment for environmental infrastructure construction was 25.885 billion yuan, of which 60.9% (15.765 billion yuan) was diverted to all urban areas.[2] This fully demonstrates that the local government attaches great importance to urban environmental protection since urban residents have been caring more about environmental quality. However, the overall effect of such investment is significantly weakened due to the neglect of vast rural areas.

(3) *The central area of the sub-regions has more environmental protection investment than the peripheral areas.* The environmental protection investment in the central area of the subregions is significantly higher than that in the peripheral areas. For example, the provincial capital, the city specifically designated in the state plan, and other developed areas have more investment for environmental protection but such investment in the border areas of the sub-regions is much lower, especially in the border areas of some watersheds, thus resulting in loopholes and weak links in protection of the entire ecosystem.

The imbalanced distribution of YRD's environmental protection investment has greatly weakened the external effects of environmental protection, obstructed transboundary pollution sources from being effectively contained, and worsened the environmental condition of key ecological areas that have an important impact on the regional ecosystem. This is one of the reasons why the environmental protection investment in sub-regions, central cities, and urban areas produces little effect in improving YRD's overall environmental quality.

11.3.2 *Why is YRD's environmental protection investment flawed?*

The reasons for the above drawbacks in YRD's environmental protection investment, because of either scale expansion or structural imbalance, can be summed up in the following three points:

[2] *Jiangsu Statistical Yearbook* (2004).

11.3.2.1 *Expansion of population size and economic aggregate keeps putting pressure on resources and environment*

The mounting pressure on YRD's resources is mainly caused by the growth of total population and economic aggregate. These two factors, from the aspect of resource consumption and production and from the aspect of pollutant discharge from households and plants, affect YRD's environmental quality and at the same time interact with each other over and over again to keep pressurizing the environment.

The population growth resulting from fertility and mobility presents higher requirements for YRD's economic development, while its rapid economic development continues to attract immigrants from other regions, which in turn expands the size of population. Consequently, the accelerating urbanization will further squeeze the narrow space of eco-environment. Since technologies and economic growth pattern can hardly be transformed in the short term, the environment is bound deteriorate. Once this degree of deterioration exceeds the environmental carrying capacity, the existing scale of environmental protection investment will be of no use to reverse the trend of environmental deterioration, but more or less alleviate the worsening situation.

11.3.2.2 *Repetitive construction due to low-level regional economic integration increases the pressure on resources and environment*

Through decades of development, the market economy of YRD has reached a high level. The composite index of marketization of Jiangsu, Zhejiang, and Shanghai reached 76.07%, 78.38%, and 73.48%, respectively, and the entire YRD is characterized by decentralized industrial development, similar economic development route, and comparable economic development level.

According to the research by Hong *et al.* (2003), the areas in YRD are prone to compete with each other, which has led to low-degree economic integration within the region, numerous low-level and repeated industrial layouts, vicious competition between industries, and highly isomorphic industrial structure of the secondary (manufacturing) industry. All of these factors will, when market players have less constraints from negative externalities, weaken the self-regulation of the region's overall eco-environment and cause a negative impact on water, soil, air, and other resources.

In addition, because of low-level repeated construction, the subregions in YRD find it hard to raise their Return on Investment (ROI), but they still desire for more investment. They have taken investment as the primary means to boost up local economic growth, which stimulates all areas to compete for foreign capital recklessly, even at the expense of local resources and environment. This has not only increased the pressure on YRD's resources but also brought in a large number of "sunset" industries that have left behind environmental pollution to local and surrounding areas.

11.3.2.3 *All areas in YRD have not done well in coordinated development*

Owing to their administrative system, the areas in YRD have not properly cooperated or coordinated in economic development and failed to carry out unified actions in providing public goods such as environmental protection investment. Their poor coordination is mainly reflected in two aspects.

(1) *Lack of coordinated planning in highly marketized manufacturing industry.* The lack of coordination in economic planning between local governments is the main reason for the low-level and repeated construction of industries. Due to poor horizontal communication and information asymmetry in the administrative system, local governments often have contradictions and conflicts when working out economic development plans, which has led to high-degree industrial isomorphism, more competition than cooperation, and more horizontal expansion of investment than vertical expansion of investment. Coupled with local protectionism, the cities in YRD are hard to complement each other's advantages at the industrial level, thus resulting in waste of resources and environmental products.

(2) *Lack of administrative coordination in providing public goods (less market-oriented) such as environmental protection investment.* The imbalanced investment for environmental protection between the areas in YRD fully demonstrates that local governments do not have an

administrative coordination mechanism. Local governments, which care about their performance examination, usually determine the investment scale and scope for their own environmental protection cause. As a result, there have been repeated construction of environmental infrastructure in central cities and urban areas and neglect of transboundary pollution sources and vital ecological areas such as rural areas and border areas.

Moreover, the environmental protection mechanism, which is built on the basis of environmental protection investment, lacks coordination between sub-regions and cities. The identical ecological planning makes all cities in YRD, either large or small, become independent ecological bodies, which is to ignore and violate their ecological dependence and complementarity, and make them unable to learn from each other and complement each other's advantages at the ecological level.

Finally, a separate fiscal budget system not only impedes cross-regional and cross-city investment in environmental protection, but also goes against the overall balance of YRD's internal and external ecosystems. As far as government public expenditure is concerned, the absence of an effective evaluation system has greatly lowered the efficiency of existing environmental protection investment.

11.4 Analysis of the Prospects of YRD's Environmental Protection Investment

Presently, YRD's investment in environmental protection has kept expanding in both scale and scope, and plays a positive role in regional environmental protection on the whole. In the long run, YRD should, in combination of its concrete conditions, solve the problems in its environmental protection investment from three aspects:

First, improve the utilization efficiency of the environmental protection investment at the sub-regional level. YRD's environmental protection investment is jointly undertaken and funded by all sub-regions. Before a unified sharing system is established, the existing system for environmental protection investment should be improved, so as to attract private capital, expand the overall scale of the investment, and further raise the utilization efficiency of the investment in improving the regional environmental quality.

Second, strengthen the cooperation and coordination among sub-regions and give full play to the radiating function of sub-regional environmental protection investment. The radiating function means that such investment can also fund the environmental protection in surrounding areas, in addition to be spent on improving the local eco-environment, which will achieve the effect of "back-feeding" the local eco-environment. By doing so, the regional ecological integration and efficiency of environmental protection investment will be greatly improved.

Finally, improve the cross-regional coordination between YRD and surrounding regions in environmental protection investment and mechanisms. From a macro perspective, YRD is only a component or a sub-system in the entire Yangtze River Basin Ecosystem, competent authorities shall play the functional role of YRD in the entire ecosystem, and at the meantime increase environmental protection investment to other sub-systems that help regulate the eco-environment of YRD. At present, such cross-regional coordination remains at the primary level led by the State, but YRD should, by taking advantage of its economic strength, take the initiative to provide more environmental protection investment to surrounding regions.

In a nutshell, YRD should further increase the regional environmental protection investment by doing a better job in transforming economic growth model, building up government leading capability, and improving government coordination mechanism.

11.4.1 *Economic development remains a strong guarantee for realizing investment in environmental protection*

Although EKC is not yet fully verified in China, the law it has revealed (industrialization co-exists with environmental degradation in the early stage of economic development) is reflected in YRD. So, we have reason to believe that, as the economy continues to develop, the economic achievement and technological progress will start to promote the environmental improvement after a certain period of time, and the effect of environmental protection investment will become increasingly apparent. Therefore, sustaining rapid and healthy economic development is the only basis for realizing larger-scale environmental protection investment and an important prerequisite for enhancing the investment effect.

11.4.1.1 *Expand the scale of environmental protection investment by relying on economic growth*

(1) *Economic growth can build up the government's ability to invest in environmental protection.* Under the government-led public goods

investment system, the absolute and relative scale of environmental protection investment largely depends on the government fiscal expenditure capacity. On one hand, from a macro perspective, economic growth can increase the government fiscal revenue. With more financial resources, the governments, especially local governments, will be more capable of taking part in environmental affairs and playing a decisive role in approving the construction projects that benefit the local eco-environment. On the other hand, after its economic development has reached a certain level, the local governments in YRD have gradually withdrawn from intervention in the non-public goods sector, so that they can divert more financial resources to environmental protection.

(2) *Economic growth strengthens the will of residents to pay for ecology, thus expanding sources of investment in environmental protection.* Environmental protection investment is generally a kind of public goods which should be provided by the government. However, from a micro perspective, as residents are direct beneficiaries of improved eco-environment, they ought to, more or less, join in the supply of such public goods. As result of continuous economic growth, residents have earned higher disposable income and become more capable of taking part in environment protection. In a word, economic growth has motivated residents to be more willing to pay for environment protection. On one hand, residents can join in the supply of some quasi-environmental public goods through different channels, such as urban green space construction and water environment improvement. On the other hand, they can participate in some environmental protection undertakings for public good, such as buying environment-related lottery tickets and funds. The private capital from these two sources can complement the public investment in environmental protection.

11.4.1.2 *Maintain healthy economic development to reduce the pressure on resources and environment and improve the effect of environmental protection investment*

While increasing its economic aggregate, YRD must transform its own economic growth model and structure, so as to mitigate the pressure of economic growth on resources and environment and improve the practical effect of environmental protection investment.

(1) *Transform the growth model to pursue more scientific development.* YRD should first transform the traditional economic growth model, adjust industrial structure, and optimize the economic structure layout. In

addition to a reasonable division of labor system within the region, YRD should encourage cooperation between the financial service industry of Shanghai and the manufacturing and modern agricultural industries of Jiangsu and Zhejiang, so as to upgrade its industrial grade both internally and externally. Besides, YRD should give full play to its geographical advantages, let technological innovation play a guiding role, and reduce and transfer high-input, high-consumption, and high-polluting industries. Only when the traditional investment-oriented model is replaced by the new efficiency-oriented model can YRD's resource and environmental pressure be fundamentally relieved.

(2) *Improve the degree of integration of economic development.* In addition to cooperation in the division of labor, all areas in YRD should also increase the degree of integration in the fields such as market access, technological innovation, infrastructure construction, absorption of foreign investment, and product standardization. A high degree of integration will improve the effectiveness of economic development and produce an effect of "one plus one is greater than two," which will not only reduce the resource consumption per unit output, but also raise the utilization efficiency of environmental protection investment and create conditions for expanding the sources of such investment.

11.4.2 *Government should keep playing a leading role in environmental protection investment*

Experiences at home and abroad show that when the level of economic development is low, the government should play a leading role in dealing with the investment for public goods such as infrastructure construction (the market has no "home court advantage" in this regard) so as to propel economic development. As determined by China's existing environmental protection investment system, the local governments of YRD will remain as the main investor of environmental protection for a long time to come. In the context where economic growth keeps increasing pressure on resources and the environment, the local governments of YRD should continue to play a leading role in expanding the scale of environmental protection investment and absorbing private capital through institutional innovation to further build up the environmental protection capability.

11.4.2.1 *Continue to increase investment in environmental protection*

The government's leading role in environmental protection investment is first reflected in the continuous increase in the investment. The analysis in Section 11.2 shows that YRD's investment for environmental protection is at the forefront of China in terms of total amount and per capita amount but it remains ineffective in dealing with deteriorating environmental quality (Tables 11.1 and 11.2) and rapidly growing pollution, partly because the investment in certain fields of environmental protection is far from enough. In the total environmental protection investment, both public and private, only a small portion is spent on the treatment of pollution sources (including industrial pollution). As far as the public or government investment is concerned, the spending for treatment of pollution sources is even less. In the context where people's environmental awareness and payment capacity cannot be rapidly improved, the neglect of treatment of pollution sources by local governments is sure to weaken the effect of environmental protection investment.

From a regional perspective, the environmental protection investment in non-central cities, rural areas, and border areas is quite limited. However, these areas are usually of vital importance in YRD's entire ecosystem. Local governments should provide these areas with more investment for environmental protection, which will have a positive impact on the existing environmental protection undertakings. Local governments may stipulate the annual growth rate of the investment by law or specify a proportion of the investment in GDP. For example, Shanghai released a Three-Year Action Plan for Environmental Protection to fix a proportion of GDP to be spent on environmental protection.

11.4.2.2 *Enhance public awareness of environmental protection*

The government's leading role in environmental protection investment is also reflected in the improvement of the investment effect by enhancing public awareness of environmental protection. While caring more about environmental quality, people are willing to act as consultants in the process of making environment-related decisions, supervising the construction of environmental protection projects, protecting environmental facilities after they are built, and raising their use efficiency. Moreover, people are more willing to pay for environmental protection, which will diversify the sources of the environmental protection funds.

There are common measures to stimulate public interest in environmental affairs: intensify publicity on environmental protection, establish a hearing system for environmental protection investment, sell environmental lottery tickets, and set up a special environmental protection fund.

11.4.2.3 *Improve the public goods investment system to create favorable conditions for absorbing private capital*

The government's leading role in environmental protection investment is finally reflected in the improvement of public goods investment system with more flexible policies in a bid to attract private investors that are interested in environmental protection. With limited financial resources, the government itself cannot greatly expand the scale of environmental protection investment in the short term. So, the government should spend public funds on protecting the pure eco-regions which are of vital importance and encourage private capital owners to invest in the environmental protection fields which are market-oriented and to which people are willing to pay. The government also needs to create conditions for private investors to receive satisfying ROI and tax preference; for example, the government may try to integrate real estate development with urban green space construction or landscape construction, and introduce the build–operate–transfer (BOT) operations for urban environmental infrastructure construction.

11.4.3 *Governments of sub-regions should coordinate with each other in environmental protection investment*

As mentioned above, a prominent drawback in YRD's environmental protection investment is the lack of effective coordination between local governments. Since the eco-environments of sub-regions in YRD are interdependent, the disjointed environmental protection measures introduced by local governments will weaken the investment effect. At present, the inter-governmental coordination in YRD is only for communication or information exchange, instead of facilitating substantial cooperation and integration in various fields. Their coordination in environmental protection investment is especially disappointing. As a result, local governments have been doing things in their own way, making the sub-regional investment for environmental protection neither scientific nor reasonable, which is a waste of investment. Local governments may try to improve their coordination in environmental protection investment by employing three measures as follows.

11.4.3.1 *Build an inter-governmental working group dedicated to cross-regional environmental protection*

In order to improve their coordination on environmental protection investment, local governments may first build a special working group to integrate the sources of the investment. This working group can imitate the workstyles of some international organizations in the United Nations, that is, maintain the control of each government in environmental protection investment, strengthen communication between all local governments, and unify their cross-regional actions. This working group is a dedicated institutional platform for local governments to coordinate environmental protection investment. At the beginning, it can play a coordinating role in publicity and education on environmental protection, environmental quality survey, ecological protection planning, environmental protection scientific research, supervision of pollutant discharge, and reform of environmental protection investment system, so as to create a basis for the unified distribution of environmental protection investment through administrative means. Besides, this working group shall also take charge of unified communication between YRD's local governments and their counterparts in surrounding regions to further enhance the overall effect of environmental protection investment.

11.4.3.2 *Develop a unified environment protection plan and an action program*

After an inter-governmental working group dedicated to environmental protection is set up, the next step is to work out a unified environmental protection plan and a detailed action program within the scope of YRD. At present, all of YRD's sub-regions, cities, districts, and counties have formulated their own ecological development plans, setting a goal of developing ecological provinces, cities, districts, counties, towns, and villages in years to come. Such objective sounds encouraging, but in fact these local plans are more or less the same. Ecological imitation will lead to repeated ecological construction in YRD in a few years, which obviously violates the basic requirements for diversification of regional ecosystem and reduces the efficiency of environmental protection investment. Therefore, in order to protect the ecosystem from the ecological law itself, competent authorities must formulate ecological development plans at the regional (or even cross-regional) level and introduce a unified action program that covers the scale and scope of environmental protection investment. In the process of implementing these plans under the guidance of the action program, competent authorities must invest some areas with certain ecological functions in combination of local conditions, so that all areas will be both partners and competitors in environmental protection, which is good for YRD's ecological diversity and for raising the efficiency of environmental protection investment.

11.4.3.3 *Unify the allocation of public investment in environmental protection*

The last measure to establish and improve the inter-governmental coordination on environmental protection investment is to unify the allocation of investment resources in all areas. As determined by the existing fiscal expenditure system, the environmental protection investment of an area is approved by the local government in an independent decision-making process, which obviously violates the wholeness requirements of the ecosystem and significantly offsets the positive effects of environmental protection investment. After the inter-governmental working group has formulated the regional ecological development plan, local governments shall strive to gradually break the administrative division when handling the environmental protection investment, pool together investment resources of all areas according to the plan, and then start unified allocation of the investment (giving priority to key areas and weak links) to benefit the entire regional ecosystem, in a bid to maximize the positive radiation capability of the investment, and give full play to the role of the investment in improving environmental quality.

11.5 Summary

Environmental protection investment is an important leverage that coordinates economic growth and environmental quality. As for YRD's environmental protection investment, it is caught in a dilemma between limited government fiscal capacity and aggravating environmental pollution. Only by improving the efficiency of the investment can YRD, while sustaining the current economic growth, effectively improve environmental quality based on the existing scale of investment. As far as YRD is concerned, the most effective way to raise the efficiency of environmental protection investment is to maintain the leading role of the government in this regard and strengthen inter-governmental cooperation and coordination in regional environmental protection undertakings.

Chapter 12

Practice and Theory of Corporate Environmental Information Disclosure*

12.1 Introduction: The Origin of Corporate Environmental Information Disclosure

As one of the effective means to achieve sustainable development, corporate social and environmental information disclosure can be traced back to the early 1970s. From the initial employee report, social report, environmental report, and to the final triple bottom line report (Buhr, 2007), companies in developed countries have voluntarily disclosed social and environmental information for more than three decades (Tilt, 2001). They have diversified forms of disclosure, such as news, announcements, annual reports, and independent environmental reports. In China, the issue of environmental degradation is also of great concern; the incidents of industrial pollution have been exposed one after another, forcing China to prioritize corporate environmental information disclosure (EID) in its environmental policies protection regulation.

Environmental information can be used as a reference for investors and financial analysts to provide an overall assessment and environmental risk prediction of the concerned company. Besides, it can also serve as a basis for the government to exercise effective environmental policies and for the people to safeguard their rights and interests. Therefore, for companies themselves, EID is not only a requirement presented by the

*This chapter is co-authored by Cai Jianan.

financial market but also an opportunity for them to establish a good corporate image.

After going through relevant materials about the EID of Chinese and foreign-listed companies, we have found that there is a gap between them in both the academic research and the content and form of disclosure. In terms of academic research, Chinese research on the correlation between EID and environmental performance remains in their infancy; such research studies, particularly the empirical research on correlated variables, could be counted on one's fingers before 2008. However, foreign scholars have also not arrived at a consensus on this issue, and there are even four propositions as "insignificant correlation," "negative correlation," "positive correlation," and "U-shaped correlation" (Meng and Chu, 2013) (the last proposition, although recognized extensively in literature, still needs to be further tested). In terms of the specific content of EID, most of its information is not convenient for the public to interpret since it is disclosed by companies at the request of the government. For example, how can general people access to all sorts of environmental data when there are diversified forms of disclosure? Since the government has never shared the disclosed information with the public on its own initiative, thus restricting the further use of such information and causing the asymmetric distribution of environmental data, how can we change this situation?

This chapter combs through both Chinese and foreign literatures, with focus placed on the status quo of corporate EID, design of the disclosure mechanism, and correlation between EID and different variables, for the purpose of probing into the development process of corporate EID and paving way for follow-up research.

12.2 Status Quo of Corporate EID in Major Developed Countries

12.2.1 *Japan*

Japanese companies usually release EID reports of their own free will under the guidance of the government and applicable laws. The Ministry of the Environment of Japan has issued norms and guidelines to regulate the release of corporate environmental reports. In the *Master Plan for the Promotion of Sustainable Social Development* issued by the Cabinet of

Japan in 2003, the goal for the year 2010 is that more than 50% of listed companies and more than 30% of unlisted companies with over 500 employees should publish their environmental reports.

Although Japan has not yet institutionalized the third-party review of corporate environmental reports, a great number of third-party review agencies (e.g., accounting firms, consulting firms, and environmental research institutes) have already emerged. Almost 50% of these reports passed the third-party review in 2001. The content of this kind of report mainly includes project overview, environmental protection policies, objectives, performance overview, environmental management status, and environment load reduction.

In addition, Japan has set up an "Environmental Reporting Award" to encourage companies to develop environmental quality reports or environmental activity plans. The *Basic Environment Law of Japan* has provided for the government role in EID. The main idea of this law is that the environmental protection work and the improvement of public environmental awareness are inseparable from the collection and disclosure of environmental information by the government, and environmental information is part of public information (Zhang, 2009).

12.2.2 *UK*

The UK started recording air and water pollution as early as the 14th century. The *Environmental Protection Act* is known for its main idea "Integrated Pollution Control" (IPC) and the two concepts "Best Practicable Environmental Option" (BPEO) and "Best Available Technology of No-extra Expenditure Cost" (BATNEEC) (Holland and Yee, 2003).

According to the environmental disclosures summary released by the UK Environment Agency in 2013 (Table 12.1), all of the 443 FTSE all-share companies more or less had environmental disclosures in their 2011~2012 annual reports; 93% of them qualitatively disclosed their environmental information in the section of director's report; 80% (up from 56% in 2006) talked about their pollution; 49% made public the data about the three key environmental indicators, i.e., greenhouse gas (GHG) emissions, water resources, or waste discharge; and 40% revealed their GHG emissions under the 2006 government guidance.

Table 12.1. Proportion of FTSE companies that had environmental disclosures in their annual reports.

	2004	2006	2009–2010	2011–2012
Total number of FTSE all-share companies	506	537	458	443
Proportion of all-share companies with qualitative EID	89%	98%	99%	100%
Proportion of small-cap companies with qualitative EID	80%	97%	98%	100%
Proportion of small-cap companies whose annual reports contain partial EID after auditing	10%	35%	36%	61%
Proportion of all-share companies with quantitative EID related to three key environmental indicators	27%	42%	67%	70%
Proportion of all-share companies with quantitative EID related to three key environmental indicators at the government guidance	10%	15%	28%	49%
Proportion of all-share companies with EID covering three key environmental indicators at the government guidance	—	3%	6%	9%

Source: Environment Agency (2013).

12.2.3 *US*

The US started disclosing environmental information since the early 1970s when the Securities and Exchange Commission (SEC) proposed that listed companies are obliged for EID in accordance with the *National Environmental Policy Act*.[1] In 1970, the Environmental Protection Agency (EPA) was set up to lay down the laws for EID.

According to relevant regulations, the US-listed companies can explain their environmental affairs through news, bulletin boards, press conferences, annual reports, and independent environmental reports. They may talk about their environmental issues in the section of "management discussion and analysis" in their annual reports, or in the "notes" appended

[1] SEC Release No.33-5170 (July 19, 1971) [36 FR 13989].

to their financial statements and the section of "health, safety and environment" of their social responsibility reports. The EID mainly consists of three parts: environmental policies, environmental costs, and environmental liabilities. Mainly in the form of quantitative disclosure, EID may be supplemented by qualitative disclosure; and EID is also a mandatory content of the balance sheet, income statement (including its note), or Toxic Release Inventory (TRI) of listed companies.

The EPA issued the TRI Program in 1986, requiring relevant industries to regularly report their environmental information. This report should include the name of company; the amount of toxic chemicals discharged into the atmosphere, land, and water; the frequency of discharge; and the discharge amount at each specific site.

Regarding the EID of listed companies, the SEC has laid down rules for their compliance with environmental laws, and the pending litigation or allegation arising therefrom; the impact on capital expenditure, profitability, and competitive position; and a detailed plan for future investment in environmental protection equipment. Any company that fails to abide by these rules shall be fined more than US$500,000 and face media scrutiny.

In addition, the EPA and the SEC are close partners in guaranteeing corporate EID. Before carrying out any law enforcement action, the EPA must provide the SEC with a list of companies with potential environmental liabilities, so as to remind the latter to keep a close eye on the environmental responsibilities and risks of certain companies. When enforcing the provisions of the *Comprehensive Environmental Response, Compensation and Liability Act* (CERCLA) and the *Resource Conservation and Recovery Act* (RCRA), the EPA must inform the SEC in advance, then the latter will, in accordance with these two acts, review the annual financial statements of concerned listed companies to find out whether they have noticed the contingent liabilities that may be caused by environmental issues and whether these issues are fully disclosed, and ask these companies to explain in their financial statements the impact of environmental issues on their financial status or competitive position, as well as the environment-related costs and the amount of liabilities (in fact, it is the SEC that checks the authenticity, adequacy, and comprehensiveness of corporate EID). If the SEC believes that the data in a company's financial statement are not accurate or fully disclosed, it has the right to ask this company to revise its financial statement or explain the reasons for inadequate disclosure. Moreover, the SEC also needs to submit the list of companies with environmental problems to the EPA for corresponding management or sanction.

In accordance with the clauses 101, 103, and 303 of the *Securities Exchange Act*, the EID of US-listed companies shall include the following contents: the company's enforcement of relevant environmental acts and the pending litigation or allegation arising therefrom; the impact on the company's capital expenditure, profitability, and competitive position; the company's future investment plan for environmental protection equipment; and the grave consequences from either known or unknown factors (e.g., the environment) on the company's asset liquidity and capital sources (Ren, 2007).

12.3 China's Policies and Practices on Corporate EID

China began formulating laws and regulations for corporate EID since the year 2003 when the *Announcement on Corporate Environmental Information Disclosure* (No. 156) came out. According to this announcement, local environmental protection agencies should regularly make public a name list of heavy polluting companies, and the companies that are not included in the list can voluntarily disclose their environmental information. This announcement also specifies in detail the content of EID that must be disclosed and voluntarily disclosed, as well as the forms of disclosure.

According to the *Notice on Further Doing a Good Job in the Founding of National Environment-friendly Enterprises* (No. 27), which was issued by the General Office of the State Environmental Protection Administration (SEPA), local environmental protection agencies at all levels should guide and urge environment-friendly companies to implement the *Agreement on Voluntary and Continuous Reduction of Pollutant Discharges* (signed with provincial environmental protection agencies) through positive disclosure of environmental information and release of annual report on environmental protection. The content of corporate EID is specified in the *Announcement on Corporate Environmental Information Disclosure* (No. 156).

Later, the SEPA released the *Opinions on Accelerating the Promotion of Corporate Environmental Behavior Evaluation* (No. 125), which sets out the requirements for the evaluation of corporate environmental behavior. For example, the environmental protection agency shall assign ratings to the companies based on the results of their environmental behavior evaluation; the combined main pollutants discharge of the companies subject to evaluation shall exceed 80% of the total discharge of the local industry; and the results of evaluation should be made public and respectively marked in green, blue, yellow, red, and black for easy identification.[2]

According to the *Guiding Opinions on Strengthening the Environmental Protection Supervision and Management of Listed Companies* (Huanfa No. 24), the provincial environmental protection authorities shall strengthen coordination and cooperation with securities regulatory agencies and establish a notification mechanism so that the environmental protection inspection of listed companies can be promptly reported to the competent securities regulatory agency. The EID of listed companies is divided into two forms: mandatory disclosure and voluntary disclosure. In case of a major event that may have a great impact on the trading prices of listed companies' securities and derivatives and have something to environmental protection, listed companies should immediately disclose it; and the State encourages these companies to regularly and voluntarily disclose other environmental information (Table 12.2).

China put into effect the *Measures for Environmental Information Disclosure* in 2008, with an aim to encourage ordinary companies to voluntarily disclose their environmental information to the whole society through media and annual reports; mandatory disclosure is only applicable to the companies that discharge pollutants in excess of standards. In order to further encourage corporate EID, the *Guidelines for Environmental Information Disclosure of Listed Companies* were released two years later. The

[2]"Green": The company meets national or local pollutant discharge standards and environmental management requirements, passes ISO: 14000 certification or clean production audit, and sets a good example to comply with environmental protection laws and regulations. "Blue": The company meets national or local pollutant discharge standards and environmental management requirements, and has no violation of environmental protection laws. "Yellow": The company meets national or local pollutant discharge standards, but exceeds the index of total quantity control or has violations of environmental protection laws. "Red": The company has made efforts to control pollution, but fails to meet national or local pollutant discharge standards, or has experienced general or major environmental incidents. "Black": The pollutant discharge of the company far exceeds or repeatedly exceeds the pollutant discharge standards and thereby causing a relatively serious impact on the environment, or it has major violations of environmental protection laws, or experienced major or particularly major environmental incidents.

Table 12.2. Some laws and regulations related to corporate EID in China.

Year of issuance	Department of issuance	Name	Key content
2003	SEPA	Announcement on Corporate Environmental Information Disclosure	Carry out nationwide corporate EID according to the *Law of the People's Republic of China on the Promotion of Clean Production.*
2005	SEPA	Notice on Further Doing a Good Job in the Founding of National Environment-friendly Enterprises	To ask these companies to fulfill their social responsibilities, and set out their "EID measures" in the preparation outline of the *Technical Report on Founding National Environment-friendly Enterprises;* guide and encourage these companies to take the lead and set an example in voluntary EID.
2005	SEPA	Opinions on Accelerating the Promotion of Corporate Environmental Behavior Evaluation	Corporate EID is an important means to protect the public's right to know about the environment and also a helpful tool for promoting the prevention and control of industrial pollution. Efforts must be made to improve the evaluation of corporate environmental behavior and develop the *Technical Guidelines for Evaluation of Corporate Environmental Behavior.*
2006	SEPA	Interim Measures for Public Participation in Environmental Impact Assessment	In the phases of newly building, rebuilding, and expansion before the start of production or operation activities, the company shall entrust its construction unit or consulting agency to disclose its environmental information in a manner accessible to the public.
2007	SEPA, People's Bank of China (PBC), China Banking Regulatory Commission (CBRC)	Opinions on Implementing Environmental Protection Policies and Regulations to Prevent Credit Risks	Carry out credit control over the companies or projects that do not comply with industrial policies or environmental protection laws; and curb the blind expansion of energy-intensive and high-polluting industries. The environmental protection authorities at all levels shall, by working together with financial institutions, establish an information communication mechanism.

2007	SEPA	Measures for Environmental Information Disclosure (Trial)	The environmental protection authorities shall, by following the principles of justice, fairness, convenience, and objectivity, disclose the environmental information of the government in a timely and accurate manner. Companies shall disclose their environmental information in a timely and accurate manner either through voluntary or mandatory disclosure as the case may be.
2008	SEPA	Guiding Opinions on Strengthening the Environmental Protection Supervision and Management of Listed Companies	Make active explorations to establish an EID mechanism for listed companies. In case of a major event that may have a great impact on the trading prices of listed companies' securities and derivatives and have something to environmental protection, listed companies should have it immediately disclosed.
2008	Ministry of Environmental Protection (MEP), CSRC	Guiding Opinions on the Environmental Protection Supervision and Management of Listed Companies, Notice on IPO Application Documents for Production and Operation Companies in Heavy Pollution Industries	The system for "environmental protection inspection of listed companies" was put into place. At the request of this system, companies in 13 heavy pollution industries (e.g., metallurgy) must obtain a "green pass card" by passing the MEP's environmental protection inspection, otherwise their IPO application will not be accepted by the CSRC.
2010	CSRC	Guidelines for Environmental Information Disclosure of Listed Companies	Encourage disclosure of environmental information.

(*Continued*)

Table 12.2. (*Continued*)

Year of issuance	Department of issuance	Name	Key content
2013	MEP	Measures for the Self-monitoring and Information Disclosure of National Key Monitoring Enterprises (Trial)	For national key monitoring companies, as well as large-sized livestock and poultry farms (areas) that directly discharge sewage into waters and are included in local annual emission reduction plans, they are required to disclose their environmental self-monitoring work and results to the public; the objects of monitoring include many environmental factors such as water, atmosphere, and noise.
2015	MEP	Environmental Information Disclosure Measures for Enterprises and Institutions	The key pollutant-discharging units should disclose their environmental information within 90 days after the environmental protection authority makes public the list of key pollutant-discharging units. The key pollutant-discharging units that have altered their environmental information should have it disclosed within 30 days after making the change.
2015	National People's Congress (NPC)	Environmental Protection Law of the People's Republic of China	If any key pollutant-discharging unit fails to disclose its environmental information truthfully, the local environmental protection authority shall order this unit to do so, impose a fine upon it, and make this matter known to the public.

Source: Chen H. (2011).

comprehensive and systematic provisions for EID are included in the *Environmental Information Disclosure Measures for Enterprises and Institutions* (MEP Order No. 31), which came into force as of January 1, 2015. According to this order, the key pollutant-discharging units should disclose their environmental information within 90 days after the environmental protection authority makes public the list of key pollutant-discharging units; and the key pollutant-discharging units that have altered their environmental information should have it disclosed within 30 days after making the change.

The revised *Environmental Protection Law of the People's Republic of China* was also brought into effect on January 1, 2015. Article 53 of this law states that citizens, legal persons, and other organizations have the right to obtain environmental information, participate in, and supervise environmental protection in accordance with the law. Article 62 states that if any key pollutant-discharging unit fails to disclose its environmental information truthfully, the local environmental protection authority shall order this unit to do so, impose a fine upon it, and make this matter known to the public. Article 68 states that local environmental authorities will be severely punished for their dereliction of duty.

Generally speaking, Chinese-listed companies has been disclosing their environmental information in a scattered way for a long time, for example, in the notes to their financial statements. The EID is neither mandatory nor legally binding, and its form and content are not unified and standardized. Besides, the review procedures and departmental linkage mechanism for EID are imperfect. With reference to the corporate EID policies and practices in developed countries, we believe that China's competent authorities (e.g., SEPA and CRSC) must take the lead in working out more mandatory and transparent rules for EID. More than that, they also need to investigate listed companies to verify whether they comply with EID-related laws and regulations and find out the determinants that affect their information disclosure and how EID affects their business performance. All of these practices will provide valuable references for competent authorities to formulate policies.

12.4 Corporate EID: Content, Incentives, and Effects

12.4.1 *Content of corporate EID*

As the research on EID continues to deepen, foreign scholars have defined the content of EID. For example, M. Ali Fekrat and Carla Inclan divide the content of EID into four parts: accounting and financial information, environmental litigation information, environmental pollution information, and other information. In the US, the Coalition for Environmentally Responsible Economics (CERES) designed the first standardized corporate EID report in the early 1990s. Later, thanks to the joint efforts of the SEC, the EPA, and the Financial Accounting Standards Board (FASB), a relatively systematic EID system came into being. Since then, the US corporate EID is required to cover two aspects of content: (1) In the financial aspect, companies shall disclose their environmental costs and liabilities and (2) in the aspect of business performance, companies should disclose their environmental responsibilities and policies, descriptions for environmental management system and compliance with international standards (e.g., ISO), and rules for energy use and waste disposal. In Japan, according to the *Environmental Accounting Guidelines* issued by the Ministry of the Environment, the corporate EID should cover environmental preservation costs which fall within the financial scope, as well as the non-financial environmental goals, policies, compliance with environment-related regulations, consumption of raw materials and energy, waste discharge and recycling, environmental management system and standards, and renewable energy utilization.

In contrast, the EID research in China remains at the exploratory stage. According to Shen Hongtao and other scholars, the content of EID mainly involves environmental protection policies, total annual resource consumption, development of environmental protection technologies, construction and operation of environmental protection facilities, and expanses on environmental protection. Li Lianhua and other scholars hold that the basic environmental information should include background introduction, pollutant discharge, environmental performance, environment-related financial matters, and quality assurance of environmental information.

Besides theoretical research, China is also a late starter in EID practice. The most representative EID norm in China is the *Guidelines for Environmental Information Disclosure of Listed Companies* issued by the Shanghai Stock Exchange (SSE) in May 2008. As required by the guidelines, listed companies can, according to their own needs, disclose environmental information in their annual social responsibility report or in a separate report; the content of EID should include environmental protection policies, objectives and results, total annual resource consumption, environmental protection investment, development of environmental protection technologies, type, quantity, concentration and destination of discharged pollutants, construction and operation of environmental protection facilities, waste treatment and disposal, recycling and integrated utilization of waste discharge, the agreement signed with the environmental protection authority to voluntarily improve their environmental behavior, the reward given by the environmental protection authority, and other environmental information to be disclosed voluntarily.

12.4.2 *Factors influencing corporate EID*

The development of corporate EID has been under the influence of three factors, that is, institution and society, companies, and individuals. Therefore, companies have to think about why to disclose, when to disclose, and how to disclose.

(1) *The factor of institution and society*. Studies have shown that laws and regulations have a significant impact on corporate EID. Without laws and regulations, EID is a kind of voluntary behavior, and there will be no uniform standard for comparing environmental information of different companies. On one hand, the provisions of laws and regulations affect companies to make decisions for EID. Blossom points out that both EID-related laws and regulations and environmental due diligence investigation are indispensable. In addition, he continues to stress that "full disclosure of the information about existing and potential environmental problems" is urgently needed. Hutchison reminds that the EID-related laws and regulations must to be diversified, because each country implements a set of unique laws and regulations. On the other hand, the wording and translation of laws and regulations also have an impact on corporate EID. Vague wording of laws and regulations or people's misunderstanding and manipulation may cause biases in corporate EID reports. Many literatures contain analyses of the ambiguities of laws and regulations, blaming the ambiguities for causing preferences or prejudices in corporate EID. In 2006, in a first by Chinese researchers, He Limei and other scholars, by taking the 2008 social responsibility reports of 112 Chinese heavily polluting and listed companies as a sample, made a quantitative evaluation of the EID of these companies with the index method and by following the *Sustainability Reporting Guidelines* issued by the Global Reporting Initiative (GRI). They found that the SSE listed companies, which are under intensified external supervision, are doing much

better in EID than their counterparts in the Shenzhen Stock Exchange (SZSE).

In addition, the public demand for the right to know and impartiality has increased pressure on companies to disclose their environmental information and affected their decision-making in this regard. According to Toms, the annual EID report does have certain impact on companies' environmental reputation. He takes "Community and Environmental Responsibility" (CER), which is a benchmark for Britain's Most Admired Companies, as a symbol of environmental reputation and concludes that the quality of EID (measurability and verifiability) and the risks taken by companies are somewhat associated with high-grade CER. Guthrie and Parker examined the social reports of an Australian mining company, finding that corporate EID report is correlated with public pressure within a certain period of time. In their follow-up study in 1990, they investigated the differences in EID of the companies in the UK, US, and Australia, finding that almost all of their information disclosure is to comply with government policies and respond to public pressure.

(2) *The factor of companies*. A large number of studies have revealed the relationship between corporate EID and companies or characteristics of companies. These characteristics mainly indicate the company's ownership structure, business size, and industry background. Cormier and Godon (2001) believe that the identity of business owners can affect the company's environmental report — for example, public utility companies usually disclose more environmental information. Teoh and Thong interviewed managers with some Malaysian companies and learned that larger companies take more responsibilities to deal with environmental issues. He Limei and other scholars have found that the size of listed companies has significant positive correlation with the sufficiency of corporate EID, while the asset-liability ratio, profitability, nature of actual shareholder, and site for business operation have little impact on the sufficiency of corporate EID.

Hackston and Milne examined the annual reports of the top 50 companies in New Zealand and found that companies engaged in eco-friendly business or those with a strong public awareness usually disclose more environmental information. Bragdon holds that pollution control and profitability coexist and benefit each other, and he has found that the environmental rating of paper-making companies is positively correlated with their price-to-earnings ratio (P/E ratio). By taking six accounting indexes as the manifestation of economic performance, Freedman *et al.* have failed to refute the null hypothesis that there is no significant relationship between EID and economic performance. According to Richardson, EID is different from general financial disclosure from the perspective of corporate capital cost: more profitable companies have to pay more fines for disclosing more social information, including environmental information.

In addition, lots of studies have shown that information cost is associated with the depth of information disclosure. Cormier and Magnan (2003) examined the factors that affect the depth of EID reports of French companies and found that information cost and media visibility are closely related to EID report, because these two factors give companies more contacts with the outside world.

(3) *The factor of individuals*. First, culture is able to affect corporate EID through legitimate claims and by influencing individuals' attitudes towards relevant information disclosure. Matthews and Reynolds explored the moral attitude of the residents in Scandinavia and the US toward the sustainability of timber industry and environmental accounting and happened to discover the cultural differences regarding public pressure and confidentiality. Buhr and Freedman compared the EID of American and Canadian companies and found that an increasing number of companies have joined EID as time goes by, and Canadian companies prefer voluntary disclosure. Besides, there are many examples showing that the attitudes of managers (e.g., how to look at the obligations of their companies and how to deal with the environmental problems caused by their companies) have varied manifestations in different countries, and all of which are attributed to cultural differences.

Second, attitude also affects corporate EID. According to Trotman and Bradley, if managers pay more attention to long-term corporate interests, they are likely to disclose environmental information; and the more they care about long-term interests, the more content the EID report will have. This shows that corporate EID is affected by the company's own attitude, its intention to influence public perception, and its desire for shaping a long-term image and pursuing long-term benefits. However, there are studies showing that the company's attitude is not necessarily related to information disclosure. Cowen *et al.* found that corporate EID is free from being affected by the company's social responsibility committee.

12.4.3 *The main effects of EID*

After taking into account various factors, companies will take actions to disclose their environmental information in accordance with the law and the public demand. However, corporate EID will exert influence on certain factors, and studies have shown that corporate EID mainly affects companies' stock price, environmental performance, and pollution control.

(1) *Stock price fluctuation*. Corporate EID will affect investors' expectations of the future profitability and costs of the concerned company, which may lead to changes in the company's stock price. Certain pieces of information mainly affect the company's expected costs. After such information is released, investors may expect that the company to become the object of government regulation in the future and withstand the dual pressure from government and communities to reduce emissions. As a result, the company has to inject more resources into pollution control, which is sure to push up its production costs. The intra-industry comparative information mainly affects the company's expected earnings. On one hand, consumers will prefer the companies with better environmental performance, while investors expect that the company will have a smaller market in the future. On the other hand, environmental efficiency is usually related to the company's overall production efficiency, and the company ranking behind may trigger investors to suspect its production capacity. From the perspective of environmental rewards and punishments, some studies have revealed that the American companies in the sample, which get enmeshed in environmental litigation, see their market value shrink by 1.2% on average; in contrast, environmental rewards can boost up their market value by 0.82%. From the perspective of comparative information, in the environmental performance rankings published by the government, the lower-ranking companies will experience a significant decline in their market value.

(2) *Environmental performance*. For decades, there have been many studies on the correlation between the environmental performance of listed companies and the degree of their EID. On one hand, companies with good environmental performance can save budget on environmental affairs, which is encouraging news for investors. These companies are willing disclose more quantitative and qualitative environmental information voluntarily. On the other hand, companies with poor environmental

performance may be sued for environmental incidents, so they prefer disclosing as little negative information as possible. The empirical studies on the correlation between corporate environmental performance and degree of EID have led to four conclusions: "insignificant correlation," "negative correlation," "positive correlation," and "U-shaped correlation." Most studies support the conclusion of "negative correlation," while certain studies stand for "insignificant correlation." For example, some researchers compared companies' EID with their Corporate Environmental Management (CEP) rating results, finding that companies with either good or poor environmental performance like to disclose more environmental information to spruce up their image and reach investors' expectation, it is the companies with average environmental performance that prefer less disclosure. In short, the "U-shaped correlation" is regarded as a synthesis of the prior three correlated relationships.

There are mainly two types of theories to predict and explain corporate environmental performance and information disclosure, namely voluntary disclosure theory and socio-political theory. The voluntary disclosure theory is that environmental performance is positively related to EID: Companies with good environmental performance voluntarily disclose environmental information to distinguish themselves from those with poor environmental performance. The socio-political theory implies that there is a negative correlation between the two items: Higher social and political pressure may lead to better corporate EID. To be specific, companies with poor environmental performance are eager to improve their EID so as to show stakeholders of the improvements in their environmental performance, thereby shoring up investors' confidence in them.

(3) *Pollution control.* Relevant researches have shown that corporate EID can, to a certain extent, help reduce pollutant discharge and control environmental pollution. As the first mandatory database in the US, the TRI provides the public with a channel to learn information about the toxic substances discharged by companies. In the 1980s, several major accidents of toxic chemical leaks took place in the US, forcing the EPA to create an inventory (i.e., TRI) of 300 chemical substances and 20 toxic substances and have it enforced, which has greatly reduced corporate pollutant discharge and leakage of toxic substances. In terms of the companies in China, Indonesia, the Philippines, and Vietnam that have joined in the Green Watch Program (i.e., to disclose corporate environmental performance to the public), all of them have reduced pollutant discharge and

performed better in complying with environmental protection regulations, proving that public disclosure plays an important role in pollution control.

12.5 Summary

In a nutshell, so far there have been in-depth researches on the factors affecting corporate EID, but the effects of corporate EID need to be further explored. In the future, more research needs be undertaken on the following two aspects: (1) The analysis of the factors affecting corporate EID needs to be enriched, so as to pave way for establishing a corporate EID system and (2) the elaboration of the effects and consequences of corporate EID, so as to lay a basis for improving the corporate EID system.

Chapter 13

Impact of Different Corporate Environmental Information Disclosures on Credit Scale — An Empirical Study on Shanghai-Based Listed Companies in High-Polluting Industries*

13.1 Introduction

Since China implemented the reform and opening-up policy in 1978, its economy has achieved a compound growth rate of 14.9% in four decades. However, social problems such as environmental degradation and resource depletion have kept cropping up during the same period. The extensive economic growth pattern has caused long-lasting environmental problems across the country, mainly represented by air pollution, water pollution and solid waste pollution. In view of this, domestic listed companies — which are the major contributors to China's economic development — have more work to do to help alleviate environmental pollution. They should actively disclose their environmental information under the guidance of the Ministry of Environmental Protection (MEP), which not only fulfills their social responsibility but also satisfies the demand of key stakeholders for environmental information (Song, 2010). All the information disclosed can serve as a basis for evaluating their environmental risks and responsibilities.

---

* This chapter is co-authored by Cai Jianan and Jiang Ping.

The environmental information disclosure (EID) of Chinese listed companies started relatively late, with relevant laws and regulations dated back to the year 2003. The *Guidelines for Environmental Information Disclosure of Listed Companies* issued by the MEP in 2010 is the most influential and enforceable policy so far, specifying that listed companies in high-polluting industries shall regularly disclose their environmental information in annual reports and also in provisional reports (for any emergent environmental incident), while list companies in other industries can do so voluntarily. This provides not only an operation guide for listed companies to disclose environmental information but also a basis for researchers to measure the quality of disclosed information. However, while relevant laws and regulations have been introduced and improved constantly, the practice still lags behind. In 2015, only about 27% of Chinese listed companies released environmental information,[1] performing worse than their counterparts in developed countries.

In recent years, Chinese bricks-and-mortar companies have been doing better in equity and bond financing, but bank loans remain their main source of funding. However, information asymmetry is still a serious drawback in the credit market, making it difficult to optimize allocation of credit resources. As one of the major creditors of listed companies, banks have an increasing demand for corporate EID to assess the environmental risks and credit default risks of the companies applying for a loan. Currently, banks are consulting with corporate annual reports, social responsibility reports, and environmental reports to obtain companies' environmental information and assess their environmental risks.

Green credit involves the banks having to review the environmental information of a project or company in the process of loan approval, so as to approve the loans that are beneficial to green development (Chen, 2010). Internationally, the concept of green credit stemmed from the Equator Principles (EPs) (Zhu C. Y., 2010) in the early 21st century and has been adopted by 90 financial institutions in 37 countries around the world, including China's Industrial Bank and Bank of Jiangsu. In July 2007, the PBOC, CBRC, and State Environmental Protection Administration (SEPA) jointly issued the *Opinions on Implementing Environmental Protection Policies and Regulations to Prevent Credit Risks*, marking the official launch of China's green credit business. Since

[1]China Forum of Environmental Journalists. 2017.

then, Chinese banks, represented by Industrial Bank, have been making explorations in credit granting and management of environmental and social risks. By the end of June 2017, the green credit balance of 21 major banks in China had amounted to 8.2 trillion yuan, accounting for more than 9% of their combined loans, and maintained a low non-performing loan ratio. Currently, against the backdrop of economic downturn both home and abroad, domestic industrial restructuring and basically completed marketization of interest rates, green credit is highly likely to become a new profit growth point and competitive edge for commercial banks.

There are rich studies on EID at home and abroad, but most of them are quantitative research on statistics, descriptions, and influencing factors, and those concentrated on the economic consequence of EID are quite limited. Besides, among the studies on corporate EID and financing capability, equity financing studies are much more than debt financing studies. Among the studies on corporate financing through bank loans, a majority of them analyze interest rate on loans and term structure of loans, but the focus of this chapter is placed on the scale of bank loans, which is not yet a popular topic. By building a multiple regression model and selecting 204 Shanghai-based companies in high-polluting industries as samples, this study examines the impact of EID on the scale of bank loans, the relationship between the two and the impact of other factors on their relationship, so as to enrich the research results in this field and inspire more scholars.

The innovation of this research is mainly reflected in three aspects:

(1) It has established a set of indexes for environmental disclosure evaluation, namely environmental disclosure index (EDI), which is compliant with MEP's requirements and is more objective. This set of indexes, covering five first-level indexes and 20 second-level indexes, differ from previous studies which only focus on whether companies have done information disclosure and from other similar evaluation indexes that are based on subjective criteria.
(2) When scoring the EDI of each research sample, this research has evaluated all the properties and data of the sample itself, so that it contains detailed descriptive statistics on EID. In addition to the conventional comparison of industries and annual changes, this research also takes account of diverse information disclosure performances of listed companies (both state-owned and non-state-owned) in regions with different levels of economic development.

(3) This research splits the EDI into five categories (vision, economy, pollution, governance, and carbon emissions) and then evaluates their combined impact on corporate application for bank loans. In contrast, most previous studies do not have categorized evaluation indexes, or their indexes are only available for qualitative and quantitative evaluation.

13.2 Literature Review and Research Hypotheses

There is a wealth of research on EID at home and abroad. The qualitative researches evaluate the development background, current situation, and prospects of EID or explore its influencing mechanism. The quantitative researches are more common, with focus placed on content evaluation and influencing factors of EID, but few of them are dedicated to studying the economic consequences of disclosure.

Foreign research studies on green credit mainly revolve around the EPs. An empirical study by Scholtens and Dam (2007) shows that the banks that adopt the EPs bear more cost than non-adopters, but they can earn a higher reputation and mitigate loan risks. Such research studies in China started relatively late, and most of them are mainly about policy review or the impact on commercial banks. In their studies, Zhang *et al.* (2012) reviewed the evolution of China's green credit policies and their background and put forward policy recommendations such as strengthening the sense of responsibility and environmental awareness of banking industry and promoting the sharing of environmental information among regulators. Besides, there are also researches that have analyzed the impact of green credit policies on the profitability of commercial banks (Wang and Zhu, 2017; Li, 2015). Li (2015) set the scoring standards for green credit indicators of listed banks by following the EPs. And the empirical study done by Li (2015) shows that implementation of green credit policies can help banks mitigate loan risks, cultivate green reputation, and improve their operating performance.

Regarding the researches on the correlation between corporate EID and bank borrowing, lots of them focus on the relationship between corporate EID and bank loan's interest rates and term structure or financing ratio. Most scholars believe that companies with insufficient information disclosure have to bear higher loan interest rates and accept shorter life of loan to make up for the environmental risks borne by creditors. But a small number of scholars hold that, under the premise of limited funds, excessive environmental investment may occupy the resources of companies to develop their core business, then increase the risk of banks recovering credit funds in full and on time, so the relationship between the two is exactly opposite or there is no significant correlation between them.

Among the existing research literatures, most of them focus on the term structure and interest rates of bank loans, while those examining the impact of corporate EID on the scale of bank borrowing remain scarce. Ni and Kong (2016), with the Shanghai- and Shenzhen-based companies in heavily polluting industries (2012–2013 statistics) as a study sample, controlled possible endogenous problems by employing the propensity score matching method, and found that companies that disclosed environmental information could obtain more bank loans than their counterparts that did not do so, but they failed to analyze the impact of the quality of information disclosure on corporate financing. Li and Wang (2011) have found that, when the monetary policy is tightening, companies with higher-quality information disclosure are able to ease their financing constraints to a certain extent due to reduction of information asymmetry, thereby obtaining larger-scale bank borrowings. According to Cormier and Magnan, a lower financial leverage is a symbol of stronger financing and capital operating capabilities, and the main purpose of EID is to shape a good corporate image and maintain a financing advantage. In her study with the Shanghai- and Shenzhen-based companies in heavily polluting industries (2007–2011 Statistics) as a sample, Long (2013) found that listed companies with higher-level corporate governance can obtain larger-scale bank loans, but this positive effect will be weakened when the quality of EID is high. In summary of the above conclusions, two hypotheses are proposed as follows:

H1: *Higher scores of EDIs, weaker ability to apply for bank loans*. The EDI is divided into five categories: vision, economy, environmental governance, carbon emissions, and pollution discharge. Companies that put forward more visions in environmental protection may encounter more risks in this regard. More information disclosure about carbon emissions and pollution discharge will make companies take on more environmental responsibilities. High scores of economy and environmental governance EDIs indicate that companies spend resources on the purchase and operation of environmental protection facilities, which may affect the development of their main business and hamper their application for loan.

H2: *The negative impact of information disclosure on corporate borrowing capacity will weaken when there is financing demand.* When they need financing, companies are usually in a situation where they are about to invest a new project or short of cash flow for normal operation. At this time, when banks are going through the loan approval procedure, they tend to pay more attention to the expected return on investment (ROI) of the project itself or companies' own business and financial conditions, and downplay the environmental risks demonstrated in the environmental information disclosed by companies.

13.3 Research Design and Descriptive Statistics

13.3.1 *Sample selection*

According to the definition of high-polluting industries in the *Directory of Listed Companies under Environmental Protection Inspection by Industry* issued by the MEP, the author preselected a bunch of sample companies in 14 high-polluting industries (mining, coal, steel, thermal power, cement, textile, brewing, papermaking, metallurgy, building materials, chemicals, petrochemicals, pharmaceuticals, and fermentation), then excluded 10 companies that have no bank loans within the research period, and finally decided on a study sample of 204 companies listed on the Shanghai Stock Exchange (SSE). The disclosed environmental information of each company can be found in its annual report, sustainable development report, social responsibility report, or environmental report. But most of these companies prefer disclosing environmental information in the notes to their annual reports and the reports of the board of directors. The EDIs are manually scored according to the established indicator system. The aforesaid corporate reports are retrieved from the websites of the SSE (http://www.sse.com.cn/), Cninfo (http://www.cninfo.com.cn/new/index), while the corporate financial data comes from the iFind (http://www.51ifind.net/) and Wind (https://www.wind.com.cn/NewSite/wft.html). Data descriptive statistics and regression analysis are processed with Stata 12.

13.3.2 *Definitions of variables*

(1) *Explained variable*. By drawing on the approach of Ye *et al.* (2010), the author uses the "cash received from borrowings" in the cash flow

statement of the following year to represent the scale of new bank borrowings and standardizes it according to the corporate asset size.

(2) *Explanatory variables*. Explanatory variables involve aggregate EDI and five categories of EDI (mission, economy, governance, carbon, and emission). Internationally, EDI is usually used to describe the level of EID, but there is not yet any uniform standard for the specific content of EDI in both China and other countries. So, the author has constructed an EDI system by referring to the *Guidelines for Environmental Information Disclosure of Listed Companies* issued by the MEP (now the Ministry of Ecology and Environment, referred to simply as "MEE"), which lays down requirements for the environmental information that must be disclosed by listed companies in high-polluting industries. This EDI system is made up of five primary indexes and 20 secondary indexes.

(3) *Control variables*

(i) *Company size*. Studies have shown that larger companies, with sufficient cash flow and better debt solvency, are more likely to try debt financing. Other things being equal, it is easier for larger companies to gain trust of banks for their lower credit risk, so as to obtain a loan at a favorable rate (Wang, 2014). In order to make independent variables closer to normal distribution and eliminate heteroscedasticity, the author refers to similar research practices and takes the natural logarithm of companies' total assets to measure their size.

(ii) *Company ownership*. In the course of economic transformation, the government monopoly on certain resource allocation makes state-owned enterprises (SOEs) more closely related with state-owned banks than private companies. SOEs (enterprises whose actual controller is the state or state-owned legal person) depend on government endorsement, that is, the government either provides implicit guarantee to these companies through financial subsidy and tax incentive or intervenes in bank credit directly, which may undermine the reference value of their regular information disclosure in applying for bank loans. Learning from the research techniques of Li and Xia (2008), the author distinguishes state-owned (valued as "1") and non-state-owned (valued as "0") listed companies according to the ownership of their actual controller.

(iii) *Profitability*. Companies with stronger profitability usually have more sources of funds for repaying principal and interest and lower risk of debt default (Jin, 2007), so they are more likely to obtain larger amount of bank borrowings. In this chapter, Return on Equity (ROE) is used in the master model to represent the profitability of companies, and Return on Asset (ROA) is used in the robustness test to represent the profitability of companies.

(iv) *Growth ability*. Fast-growing companies have faster expansion speed and better profit prospects, which may generate more future cash flow guaranteeing their own operation and repayment of loans, and building up their borrowing capacity (Chen, 2011). With both profitability and development potential, companies are more likely to repay principal and interest and obtain larger amount of bank borrowings and less likely to commit credit default or encounter financial risk. In this chapter, the year-on-year (YoY) growth rate of operation revenue is used in the master model to represent the growth ability of companies, and the YoY growth rate of total operation revenue is used in the robustness test to represent the growth ability of companies.

(v) *Solvency*. According to the trade-off theory on capital structure, too much debt will cause companies to fall into financial distress and suffer from the direct, indirect, or agency cost brought by the possible bankruptcy. Creditors will adopt higher borrowing rates for companies with higher financial leverage. Generally, indicators such as debt-to-asset ratio, current ratio, and quick ratio are used to show the debt situation and solvency of companies. In this chapter, the debt-to-asset ratio (total debts/total assets) is used to measure the long-term solvency of companies, and the current ratio (current assets/current debts) is used to measure the short-term solvency of companies.

(vi) *Liquidation value ratio*. When a company fails to repay in cash or goes into bankruptcy, the bank can force its repayment through auction of its mortgaged properties. By drawing on the research of Liu (2013), the tangible asset ratio (fixed assets/total assets) is used in this chapter to represent the liquidation value ratio of companies.

(vii) *Financing demand*. With a greater financing demand, companies are more likely to apply for more bank loans. In this chapter, by drawing on the approach of Ran Dan, supposing that when the sum of operating cash flow and investment cash flow of a company is less than 0, the company has a refinancing demand; otherwise, such refinancing demand does not exist.

The symbols and definitions of all research variables in this chapter are shown in Table 13.1.

13.3.3 *Model building*

This chapter mainly analyzes the relationship between companies' EID in a given year (and other variables) and their borrowing behavior in the following year. In the process of writing this book, the 2017 annual reports of most sample companies were not yet released, so the analysis model is built on the basis of the corporate borrowing data over 2015–2016 and other corporate data over 2014–2015; as a result, all explanatory variables are balanced short panel data with first order lag. Although there are only two-year panel data, they can still appropriately reduce the possibility of collinearity, which is convenient for controlling individual heterogeneity.

As for the selection of panel data models, because of short time span of study samples and multiple measured values, the individual effect is regarded as a fixed factor that does not change with time. In addition, the measured values involved in this chapter represent the entire parent body of SSE-listed companies in high-polluting industries, so the fixed effect model is adopted. In Section 13.5.3, the results of Hausman Test and F Test will show that the fixed effect model is better than the random effect model and mixed regression model. The unit root test and cointegration test are not performed because of short time span of study samples. In order to distinguish the impacts of five categories of EDIs (mission, economy, governance, carbon, and emission) on the borrowing capacity of listed companies, the following five models are built:

In order to better display the regression results, the individual variables are amplified or minified (specifically, "loan" is amplified by ten times, "edi" and "guaranty" are minified by ten times, and "roe," while "debt," "growth" and "currentratio" are minified by 100 times), but it does not affect the model interpretation, significance of variables, and other results.

$$\text{Loan}i, t+1 = \beta_0 + \beta_1\text{EDIecon}i, t + \beta_2\text{ Lnasset}i, t + \beta_3\text{ Nature}i, t + \beta_4\text{ ROE}i, t + \beta_5\text{ Debt}i, t + \beta_6\text{ Growth}i, t + \beta_7\text{ Guaranty}i, t + \beta_8\text{ Currentratio}i, t + \beta_9\text{ EDIecon} * \text{cash}i, t + \varepsilon i, t \quad (13.1)$$

Table 13.1. Interpretation of research variables.

Symbol	Name	Interpretation
Explained variable		
Loan	New short-term borrowings for unit assets	Cash received from borrowing/total assets at the end of the year
Explanatory variables		
EDI	Environmental information disclosure index	Total score of environmental information disclosure (%)
EDIecon	Economic environmental information disclosure index	Total score of economic environmental information disclosure (%)
EDImission	Vision environmental information disclosure index	Total score of vision environmental information disclosure (%)
EDItreat	Governance environmental information disclosure index	Total score of governance environmental information disclosure (%)
EDIcarbon	Carbon emission environmental information disclosure index	Total score of carbon emission environmental information disclosure (%)
EDIemit	Pollutant emission environmental information disclosure index	Total score of pollutant emission environmental information disclosure (%)
EDI × Cash	Intersection of information disclosure and financing demand	To separately examine the impact of environmental information disclosure on bank loans when companies have or don't have financing demand
Control variables		
lnasset	Corporate scale	Logarithm of total assets at the end of the year
Nature	Corporate attributes	Dummy variable, state-owned enterprise = 1, non-state-owned enterprise = 0
ROE	Corporate profit	ROE
Growth	Corporate growth	Operating income growth rate for the year
Currentratio	Short-term solvency	Current ratio (current assets/current liabilities)
Debt	Long-term solvency	Asset-liability ratio (total liabilities/total assets)
Guaranty	Liquidation value ratio	Fixed assets/total assets at the end of the year
Cash	Financing demand	If the operating cash flow + investment cash flow at the end of the year is less than 0, it is considered that there will be a need for borrowing and financing in the next year, and Cash = 1; otherwise, Cash = 0
Year	Year	2014–2015, dummy variable

$$\text{Loan}i,\ t+1 = \beta_0 + \beta_1\ \text{EDImission}i,\ t + \beta_2\ \text{Lnasset}i,\ t + \beta_3\ \text{Nature}i,\ t + \beta_4\ \text{ROE}i,\ t + \beta_5\ \text{Debt}i,\ t + \beta_6\ \text{Growth}i,\ t + \beta_7\ \text{Guaranty}i,\ t + \beta_8\ \text{Currentratio}i,\ t + \beta_9\ \text{EDImission}i * \text{cash}i,\ t + \varepsilon i,\ t \quad (13.2)$$

$$\text{Loan}i,\ t+1 = \beta_0 + \beta_1\ \text{EDItreat}i,\ t + \beta_2\ \text{Lnasset}i,\ t + \beta_3\ \text{Nature}i,\ t + \beta_4\ \text{ROE}i,\ t + \beta_5\ \text{Debt}i,\ t + \beta_6\ \text{Growth}i,\ t + \beta_7\ \text{Guaranty}i,\ t + \beta_8\ \text{Currentratio}i,\ t + \beta_9\ \text{EDItreat} * \text{cash}i,\ t + \varepsilon i,\ t \quad (13.3)$$

$$\text{Loan}i,\ t+1 = \beta_0 + \beta_1\ \text{EDIcarbon}i,\ t + \beta_2\ \text{Lnasset}i,\ t + \beta_3\ \text{Nature}i,\ t + \beta_4\ \text{ROE}i,\ t + \beta_5\ \text{Debt}i,\ t + \beta_6\ \text{Growth}i,\ t + \beta_7\ \text{Guaranty}i,\ t + \beta_8\ \text{Currentratio}i,\ t + \beta_9\ \text{Edicarbon} * \text{cash}i,\ t + \varepsilon i,\ t \quad (13.4)$$

$$\text{Loan}i,\ t+1 = \beta_0 + \beta_1\ \text{EDIemit}i,\ t + \beta_2\ \text{Lnasset}i,\ t + \beta_3\ \text{Nature}i,\ t + \beta_4\ \text{ROE}i,\ t + \beta_5\ \text{Debt}i,\ t + \beta_6\ \text{Growth}i,\ t + \beta_7\ \text{Guaranty}i,\ t + \beta_8\ \text{Currentratio}i,\ t + \beta_9\ \text{EDIemit} * \text{cash}i,\ t + \varepsilon i,\ t \quad (13.5)$$

In the above five models, β_i (i = 1, 2, 3, 4, 5, 6, 7, 8, 9) represents the regression coefficient of each variable, β_0 represents a constant term, and ε represents a random error term. The definition of each variable is shown in Table 13.1.

13.4 Descriptive Statistics

13.4.1 *Descriptive statistics of EID index*

Based on the 2014–2016 statistics about the EID of 204 SSE-listed companies in high-polluting industries, the subsequent content analyzes the differences in five categories of EDI and the variation trend of aggregate EDI in these three years; compares the information disclosure by industry, region (developed and underdeveloped), and listed company (state-owned and non-state-owned); and explains the reasons for these differences (see Tables 13A.1–13A.3 in Appendix A for detailed analysis).

13.4.1.1 *Comparison of five categories of EDI*

Figure 13.1 shows the descriptive statistics of EDIs of 204 companies in 14 industries over 2014–2016 (taking 612 measured values as blended data). All the five categories of EDIs are scored on the 100-point scale.

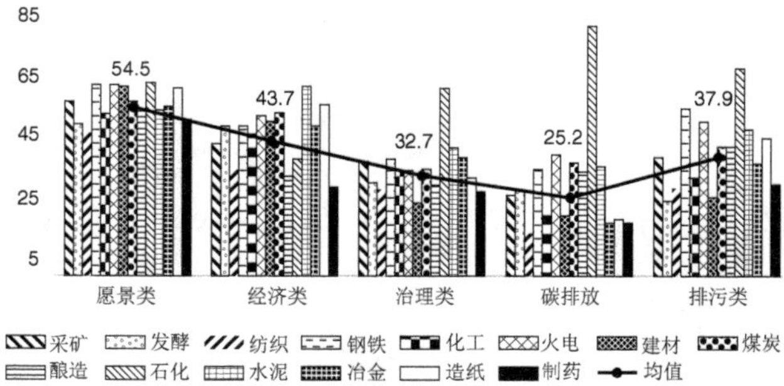

愿景类	Mission
经济类	Economy
治理类	Treat
碳排放	Carbon
排污类	Emission
采矿	Mining
发酵	Fermentation
纺织	Textile
钢铁	Steel
化工	Chemical
火电	Thermal power
建材	Building materials
煤炭	Coal
酿造	Brewing
石化	Petrochemical
水泥	Cement
冶金	Metallurgy
造纸	Papermaking
制药	Pharmacy
均值	Mean value

Figure 13.1. Comparison of corporate EDIs in 14 industries over 2014–2016.

The three-year average scores of the five categories of indexes from high to low are as follows: Vision (54.49) > Economy (43.71) > Mean Value (37.45) > Emission (37.92) > Governance (32.71) > Carbon (25.24), showing that most companies prefer disclosing general information such as overall environmental protection goals, followed by economic information that affects their business development; they do not pay great attention to the disclosure of carbon emissions information.

Mission EDI is scored on basis of environmental policies, guidelines and ideas, as well as environmental protection goals for the next year. Companies are more willing to disclose their Mission EDI since it is not a key index for assessing their environmental performance. Economy EDI is related to pollution discharge fee, greening fee, and government funds and subsidies for environmental protection, which are fixed contents of corporate annual reports. Since Economy EDI is able to act as a guide, its disclosure has remained satisfying. Moreover, the information related to the expenses on environmental protection facilities and R&D is actively disclosed by companies.

13.4.1.2 *Annual changes in EDIs*

Figure 13.2 shows the changes in the aggregate EDI of 204 companies in 14 industries over 2014–2016. The three-year average scores of the aggregate EDI by industry from high to low are as follows: Petrochemical (59.75) > Steel (45.66) > Thermal Power (44.42) > Coal (42.40) > Papermaking (40.80) > Metallurgy (38.80) > Mining (38.75) > Mean Value (37.45) > Chemicals (35.44) > Brewing (35.02) > Fermentation (34.17) > Building Materials (32.83) > Pharmaceutical (29.11) > Textile (29.07), showing that there is a big gap in the level of EID of listed companies in different high-polluting industries.

The top-ranking petrochemical industry is far ahead of the other 13 industries, but its industry average score over 2014–2016 (50.00, 62.26, and 66.99, respectively) barely meets the requirements in the *Guidelines for Environmental Information Disclosure of Listed Companies*. Although the average score of the lowest-ranking textile industry has risen for three years in a row, such score in 2016 is merely 34.20, which is still far below the pass level. This shows that the level of aggregate EDI of listed companies in high-polluting industries remains low, and there is much room for them to make improvement.

Among the 14 industries, seven of them (petrochemical, cement, papermaking, metallurgy, chemical, brewing, and textile) see their aggregate EDI rising for three consecutive years; while the aggregate EDI of

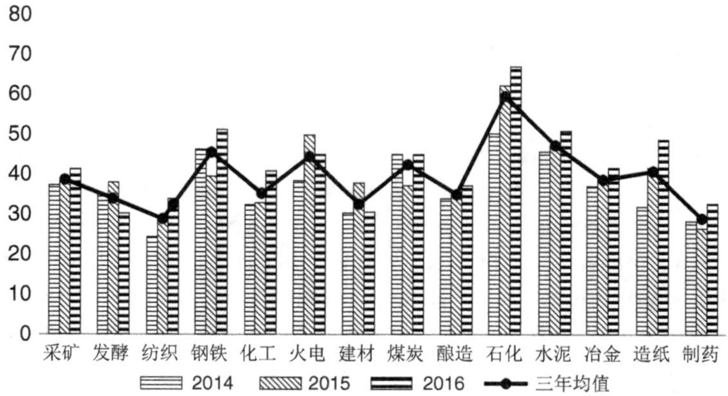

三年均值	Three-year mean value
采矿	Mining
发酵	Fermentation
纺织	Textile
钢铁	Steel
化工	Chemical
火电	Thermal power
建材	Building materials
煤炭	Coal
酿造	Brewing
石化	Petrochemical
水泥	Cement
冶金	Metallurgy
造纸	Papermaking
制药	Pharmacy

Figure 13.2. Annual changes of corporate EDIs in 14 industries over 2014–2016.

remaining industries keeps fluctuating. No industry has a constantly declining aggregate EDI, showing that the overall situation of EID of listed companies in high-polluting industries has been gradually improving.

13.4.1.3 *Regional differences in EDIs*

As for the EDI of sample companies involving 30 provinces and municipalities over 2014–2016, the EDI by region (province and municipality) shows fluctuations in different years. The EDI in Tibet, Shaanxi, and Guizhou has remained unsatisfactory, with a score of lower than 30 in three years; while the EDI in the Beijing–Tianjin–Hebei Region and the Yangtze River Delta looks better on the whole.

In order to elaborate on the relationship between economic development and EID of each region, the 30 provinces and municipalities where the sample companies are located are divided into developed and underdeveloped regions according to their per capita GDP ranking in 2014. With reference to the practice of Sun (2012), this study classifies 13 provinces and municipalities with per capita GDP above the national average as developed regions, and classifies the remaining 17 provinces and municipalities with per capita GDP below the national average as underdeveloped regions. Table 13.2 show that, compared with underdeveloped regions, developed regions have a higher average EDI and bigger differences in the quality of disclosure within regions (larger variance). The quality of EID in developed regions has been improving year by year, with the mean value of EDI over 2014-2016 scored as 35.75, 37.72, and 42.27, respectively. In underdeveloped regions, the mean value of EDI in those three years is 34.25, 33.68, and 39.15, respectively. This shows that the level of corporate EID may be related to the market environment and the level of economic development in the region where they are located, and the information disclosure may be more standardized under a more standardized market environment.

Table 13.2. EDIs in developed and underdeveloped regions over 2014–2016.

	Underdeveloped regions				Developed regions			
Year	2014	2015	2016	Total	2014	2015	2016	Total
Mean value	34.25	33.68	39.15	35.69	35.75	37.72	42.27	38.58
Standard deviation	16.02	17.34	16.50	16.74	19.14	19.90	19.58	19.68
Number of samples	80	80	80	240	124	124	124	372

13.4.1.4 *Differences in EID of companies of different nature*

Table 13.3 shows the comparison between the EDIs of listed companies of different ownership over 2014–2016: The EDI of non-state-owned companies first drops from 31.25 to 30.63 and then rises to 35.70; that of state-owned companies have achieved a steady increase for three consecutive years, with the average annual score being 37.68, 39.61, and 44.43, respectively. In general, the EDI scores of state-owned companies are four to six points higher than those of non-state-owned companies. With relatively close standard deviations, the EDI scores of the two types of companies have similar degrees of dispersion. The reason for this difference may be that state-owned companies have a stricter management system and more standardized implementation of EID rules, or it may be that these companies themselves have done a good job in environmental protection and pollution control, so they are confident to disclose more environmental information and deliver more positive information to investors and the public, which is a way that helps them enhance corporate image and increase information transparency.

13.4.2 *Descriptive statistics of other variables*

Table 13.4 shows the descriptive statistical results of all variables. The mean value of standardized borrowing scale of all samples is 0.26, with the minimum value as 0 and the maximum value as 1.76 (i.e., the company's borrowing in that year is 1.76 times of its total assets, which is a relatively high amount), showing a big gap between them. The average debt-to-asset ratio is 51.64, which is a moderate leverage level. The mean values of profitability (ROE) and growth rate are both negative, marking a poor operating condition of listed companies in high-polluting industries

Table 13.3. EDIs of state-owned and non-state-owned companies over 2014–2016.

Ownership	Parameter	2014	2015	2016	Total
Non-state-owned	Mean value	31.25	30.63	35.70	32.52
	Standard deviation	16.44	18.83	17.00	17.52
State-owned	Mean value	37.68	39.61	44.43	40.58
	Standard deviation	18.49	18.34	18.60	18.64
Total	Mean value	35.16	36.13	41.05	37.45
	Standard deviation	17.95	19.00	18.45	18.62

Table 13.4. Descriptive statistics of explained and control variables.

Variables	Number of samples	Mean value	Standard deviation	Min value	Median	Max value
Floan	408	0.250	0.210	0.000	0.220	1.530
lnasset	408	22.98	1.460	19.40	22.80	28.50
Nature	408	0.610	0.490	0	1	1
ROE	408	−6.540	159.1	−3106	4.700	55.70
Debt	408	52.21	19.19	9.300	51.45	108.1
Growth	408	−0.280	22.74	−57.40	−0.750	217.4
Guaranty	408	0.370	0.170	0.000	0.360	0.860
Currentratio	408	1.360	1.410	0.130	1.000	12.98
Cash	408	0.450	0.500	0	0	1
EDI	408	35.65	18.47	1.890	32.08	86.79
EDImission	408	53.53	22.57	0.000	60	100.0
EDIecon	408	41.58	25.43	0.000	41.67	100.0
EDIcarbon	408	31.50	19.10	0.000	29.41	94.12
EDItreat	408	25.44	31.61	0.000	14.29	114.3
EDIemit	408	34.10	28.12	0.000	25.00	100.0
ROA	408	4.970	6.670	−23.90	4.380	29.68
Growth2	408	−316.2	1609	−19000	−3.260	4737

Note: The "ROA" and "growth2" in the table are the variables used to replace "ROE" and "growth" in the robustness test in Section 13.5.3.

over 2014–2015. The mean values of all types of EDIs are below 60 points, showing that the level of EID of these companies is not high.

13.5 Analysis of Empirical Results

13.5.1 *Correlation test of variables*

Table 13.5 shows that the EDIs of companies are significantly correlated to their borrowing scale (5%). Corporate assets, ROE, debt-to-asset ratio, collateral, current ratio, and financing demand are all related to the scale of borrowing. The correlation coefficients among the variables are not greater than 0.616, and their multicollinearity is almost nonexistent.

Table 13.5. Correlation coefficient matrix of main research variables.

	EDI	Floan	lnasset	Nature	ROE	Debt	Growth	Guaranty	Currentratio	Cash
EDI	1									
Floan	0.111*	1								
lnasset	0.431*	0.117*	1							
Nature	0.204*	0.055	0.327*	1						
ROE	0.063	−0.094	0.049	0.032	1					
Debt	0.117*	0.478*	0.360*	0.248*	−0.217*	1				
Growth	−0.098	−0.046	−0.15*	−0.35*	0.078	−0.119*	1			
Guaranty	0.227*	0.205*	0.23*	0.258*	−0.095	0.409*	−0.181*	1		
Currentratio	−0.179*	−0.331*	−0.322*	−0.122*	0.066	−0.604*	0.125*	−0.410*	1	
Cash	−0.024	−0.025	−0.080	−0.084	0.042	−0.041	0.077	−0.223*	−0.013	1

Note: * Indicates a significant correlation at 5%.

13.5.2 *Regression result*

The empirical results of models (1)–(5) are shown in Table 13.5. It is the three indexes (EDIecon, EDIcarbon, and EDIemit) that are scored above 5%, which has a negative impact on the scale of borrowing and accords with Hypothesis 2. It is probably because EDIecon exposes that the company bears more environmental expenditures, thus occupying the resources required for its core business development, while EDIcarbon and EDIemit reveal that the company may be fined for environmental violations and then increase expenses on pollution reduction and governance, thus causing creditors to worry about its profitability and reduce the scale of loans. The score of EDImission is irrelevant to the scale of borrowing, which is inconsistent with Hypothesis 2. It may be because this index is closely associated with corporate environmental policy at the macro and holistic level and of little impact on the company's economic benefit and overall development, and thereby hard to be transmitted to the company's borrowing behavior. The score of EDItreat is not related to the scale of borrowing, which is inconsistent with Hypothesis 2. The possible explanation is that the environmental governance can mitigate the company's environmental risks in the future but also increase the expenses for doing so. The positive and negative effects cancel each other out to some extent, thereby not affecting the company's borrowing and repayment behaviors.

In order to confirm whether the impact of EID on bank loans is disturbed by other factors, we have introduced various cross terms between EDI and corporate financing demand in their study. The result shows that the cross terms between all categories of EDI and financing demand have a positive impact on corporate borrowing capacity, which is consistent with the hypotheses (Table 13.6). Take the aggregate EDI as an example: EID has a negative impact on corporate borrowing capacity (the EDI coefficient is negative), while the cross items between them have a positive impact on corporate borrowing capacity (the EDIcash coefficient is positive), indicating that when the company has a financing demand, the negative impact of aggregate EDI on its borrowing capacity will be weakened (the sum of EDI and EDIcash coefficients represents the impact of EDI on bank loans when the company needs financing). It is probably because when the cash flow is insufficient, banks pay greater attention to more obvious factors such as project Internal Rate of Return (IRR) or corporate financial condition when going through the credit approval procedure and play less attention to the secondary factors such as environmental risks or environmental protection expenditures, hence weakening the impact of EID on corporate bank loans.

Table 13.6. Regression result of the fixed effect of EDIs on corporate borrowing capacity.

	(1) Econ	(2) Mission	(3) Treat	(4) Carbon	(5) Emit
Variables	F. loan	F. loan	F. loan	F. loan	F. loan
lnasset	−0.427 (−1.36)	−0.428 (−1.21)	−0.412 (−1.20)	−0.371 (−1.13)	−0.375 (−1.18)
Nature	−0.097 (−0.08)	−0.089 (−0.05)	0.188 (0.16)	0.203 (0.18)	−0.254 (−0.24)
ROE	0.195*** (7.16)	0.185*** (3.63)	0.182*** (7.47)	0.177*** (8.52)	0.176*** (7.34)
Debt	1.207 (0.87)	1.634 (1.45)	1.400 (0.91)	1.231 (0.81)	1.541 (1.06)
Growth	0.628** (2.16)	0.650 (1.54)	0.703** (2.34)	0.667** (2.42)	0.645** (2.31)
Guaranty	1.998 (0.17)	7.750 (0.54)	5.235 (0.45)	5.772 (0.51)	7.189 (0.65)
Currentratio	−7.830 (−1.35)	−4.526 (−0.38)	−6.636 (−1.12)	−7.237 (−1.28)	−4.465 (−0.78)
EDI					
EDIcash					
EDIecon	−1.291** (−2.27)				
EDIeconcash	1.027*** (2.79)				
EDImission		−0.531 (−1.20)			
EDImissioncash		0.580* (1.82)			
EDItreat			−0.692 (−1.40)		
EDItreatcash			1.119** (2.32)		
EDIcarbon				−0.833** (−2.34)	
EDIcarboncash				1.154** (2.38)	

Table 13.6. (*Continued*)

Variables	(1) Econ	(2) Mission	(3) Treat	(4) Carbon	(5) Emit
EDIemit					−1.054** (−2.54)
EDIemitcash					0.888** (2.11)
Constant	12.182* (1.84)	11.507 (1.49)	11.132 (1.51)	10.273 (1.46)	10.562 (1.55)
Observations	408	408	408	408	408
R-squared	0.149	0.105	0.111	0.124	0.123
Number of id	204	204	204	204	204
Adj. R-squared	0.104	0.104	0.104	0.104	0.104

Note: Robust t statistics in parentheses; *** $p < 0.01$, **$p < 0.05$, *$p < 0.1$.

Among the control variables in six models, ROE, which characterizes profitability, has a positive effect on the scale of borrowing at a significant level of 1%. This is because profitability is the guarantee for a company to generate cash flow and continue to repay its principal and interest. Companies with stronger profitability also have stronger borrowing ability. The variable Growth (YoY growth rate of the company's operation revenue in the previous period) has a positive effect on the company's borrowing capacity at a significant level of 5%, because the growth of operation revenue indicates more cash flow and more certainties of punctual repayment.

13.5.3 *Robustness test*

This chapter performs a robustness test of models by replacing their control variables: Replace ROE (characterizing corporate profitability) with ROA, and replace Growth that characterizes YoY growth of operation revenue with Growth of total operation revenue. After replacing those control variables, the aggregate EDI has a significant negative impact on corporate borrowing capacity at 5% (which is 1% of the original model), while EDImission and EDItreat still have no significant correlation with corporate borrowing capacity. The other three EDIs have a significant correlation with corporate borrowing capacity at 5%, which is basically consistent with the original model. On taking account of the cross terms between EDIs and corporate financing demand, their significant correlation with corporate borrowing capacity is the same with the original model (see Table 13.7), except that the

Table 13.7. Regression result of the fixed effect of EDIs on corporate borrowing capacity with substituted key control variables.

Variables	(1) Econ	(2) Mission	(3) Treat	(4) Carbon	(5) Emit
	F. loan	F. loan	F. loan	F. loan	F. loan
lnasset	−0.318 (−0.90)	−0.331 (−0.91)	−0.291 (−0.81)	−0.258 (−0.73)	−0.267 (−0.75)
Nature	−0.899 (−0.50)	−0.910 (−0.49)	−0.747 (−0.41)	−0.789 (−0.43)	−1.154 (−0.63)
ROA	3.523* (1.68)	3.499 (1.64)	3.234 (1.52)	3.342 (1.58)	3.318 (1.58)
Debt	1.437 (1.20)	1.797 (1.48)	1.635 (1.35)	1.461 (1.21)	1.761 (1.47)
Growth2	−0.011** (−1.99)	−0.010* (−1.88)	−0.010* (−1.84)	−0.009* (−1.74)	−0.009 (−1.62)
Guaranty	−2.305 (−0.16)	−1.849 (−0.12)	−0.005 (−0.00)	0.844 (0.06)	2.194 (0.15)
Currentratio	−8.887 (−0.74)	−7.716 (−0.63)	−8.118 (−0.67)	−9.128 (−0.76)	−6.180 (−0.51)
EDI					
EDIcash					
EDIecon	−1.065** (−2.60)				
EDIeconcash	0.010*** (2.82)				
EDImission		−0.269 (−0.60)			
EDImissioncash		0.005* (1.66)			
EDItreat			−0.411 (−0.67)		
EDItreatcash			0.010* (1.92)		
EDIcarbon				−0.829** (−2.13)	
EDIcarboncash				0.011** (2.48)	

Table 13.7. (*Continued*)

Variables	(1) Econ	(2) Mission	(3) Treat	(4) Carbon	(5) Emit
	F. loan	F. loan	F. loan	F. loan	F. loan
EDIemit					−1.014** (−2.43)
EDIemitcash					0.009** (2.09)
Constant	9.904 (1.28)	9.613 (1.21)	8.737 (1.11)	8.183 (1.05)	8.488 (1.09)
Observations	408	408	408	408	408
R-squared	0.088	0.050	0.055	0.070	0.070
Number of id	204	204	204	204	204
Adj. *R*-squared	−0.941	−0.941	−0.941	−0.941	−0.941

Note: Robust *t* statistics in parentheses; *** $p < 0.01$, **$p < 0.05$, *$p < 0.1$.

cross terms between EDItreat and corporate financing demand have a 1% significant correlation with corporate borrowing capacity (which is 5% of the original model), showing that the conclusions of this study are robust.

13.6 Summary

13.6.1 *Research conclusion*

The literature review shows that there are a large number of empirical studies on corporate EID in China and other countries, but most of them take EID as a dependent variable rather than an independent variable. Although both bank-side and enterprise-side studies exist, most of them focus on the factors influencing bank loans' term structure and interest rate, and studies on the scale of corporate borrowing remain scarce.

The descriptive statistics of EDI over 2014–2016 show:

(1) The score of aggregate EDI remains low, barely reaching the passing level, and there are problems such as incomplete information disclosure, scattered disclosure positions, subjectivity, and arbitrariness.

(2) The scores of different categories of EDI vary greatly, and they are ranked from high to low as EDImission > EDIecon > EDIemit > EDItreat > EDIcarbon. Companies prefer disclosing general information such as environmental protection targets but pay little attention disclosing carbon and emission information.
(3) There is a large gap between the scores of EDI of different industries. Petrochemistry, steel, and thermal power are on top three of 14 high-polluting industries, while textile, pharmacy, and building materials industries come in last. Over 2014–2016, half of the 14 industries have seen their quality of EID improving constantly, and deteriorating quality of disclosure does not exist at all, showing that the quality of EID is getting improved on the whole.
(4) There are regional differences in EDI. The information disclosure in remote southwestern areas remains unsatisfactory, while the Beijing–Tianjin–Hebei Region and the Yangtze River Delta are doing better in this regard. The overall disclosure level in developed regions is higher, but their internal differences are more prominent.
(5) The level of EID of state-owned companies is significantly higher than that of non-state-owned companies (the average EDI score of the former is four to six points higher than that of the latter every year). Over 2014–2016, the EDI scores of non-state-owned companies first decline and then go up, while those of state-owned companies keep rising at a steady pace.

The multiple regression result shows that:

(1) The three indexes (EDIecon, EDIcarbon, and EDIemit) have a negative impact on the scale of bank loans. It is probably because they can reveal the existing or potential environmental risks or environmental protection expenses of companies, thus weakening the bank loan intention.
(2) The two indexes as EDImission and EDItreat have no significant impact on the scale of bank loans, because the former only conveys general environmental information and the latter implies that environmental risks and increased investment in environmental protection can cancel each other out, making them not the focus of banks when going through the procedure of loan approval.
(3) The corporate financing demand will weaken this negative impact, because banks usually pay great attention to the profitability and solvency of a given project or company when it applies for a loan, instead of caring about its environmental risks exposed by EDIs.

(4) Among the control variables, both corporate profitability and growth ability can guarantee a cash flow in the future, which has a positive effect on the borrowing capacity of companies.

The two policies of EID and green credit go hand in hand, forming synergy between environmental protection and financing. On one hand, EID can promote the development of green credit, not only reducing the cost of banks in collecting information about the environmental protection work of borrowing companies and evaluating their environmental risks but also promoting the upgrading of financial products and adoption of new analysis methods (e.g., classify borrowing companies into green, light green, and dark green ones according to their pollutant discharge, thereby improving the financing efficiency of green companies and making financial better serve the real economy). On the other hand, the development of green credit has a positive effect on EID. When banks pay more attention to all aspects of corporate environmental performance, it will force companies to optimize their EID, improve their environmental awareness and behavior, and strive for sustainable development, which will ultimately benefit the financial industry. In addition, the implementation of EID and green credit policies can generate spillover of positive benefit. For example, it can promote the construction of a legal system related to corporate environmental protection; strengthen public attention to environmental protection; and promote a more comprehensive, coordinated. and sustainable development of society.

13.6.2 *Policy suggestions*

First, financial institutions and competent authorities need to strengthen cooperation. There are a wide range of users of environmental information, including creditors, shareholders, regulatory agencies, and social groups. Therefore, environmental protection departments, Central Bank, CSRC, and CBRC shall strengthen cooperation; build an environmental information credit system, so as to motivate and supervise companies to fully and truthfully disclose their environmental information, which will reduce the degree of information asymmetry for all stakeholders; improve work efficiency; and optimize resource utilization. Moreover, the independent verification of environmental information by third parties (e.g., accounting firms) is encouraged, and inter-disciplinary talents in environmental auditing shall be cultivated, which will make EID more authentic and reliable.

Second, the banking industry shall strengthen the application of corporate EID in environmental risk control as follows:

(1) It is necessary to formulate quantitative environmental risk rating standards, develop more feasible environmental supervision indicators, unify the statistical caliber of green credit, and explore the EPs that are in line with China's national conditions.
(2) Financial institutions must build up their ability to identify environmental risks and do a better job in risk management such as environmental risk assessment and handling. Moreover, they must pay attention to continuous innovation of green credit products; learn from the innovative models of developed countries; try financial innovation tools such as credit derivatives and insurance to transfer environmental risks (Green Credit Research Group of CBRC Shanghai Office, 2016); give green credit more room for trial and error; guide the flow of capital to green, energy conservation, and environmental protection industries; facilitate industrial restructuring; and promote the development of a green economy.

Third, economic incentives for green credit shall be strengthened. At present, there are not yet enough economic incentives for the government, banks, and enterprises to implement green credit policy, thus holding back the further development of green credit. The green GDP performance appraisal shall be gradually improved to demonstrate the government's high attention to green development. A special fiscal fund for environmental protection shall be set up to subsidize companies that are compliant with environmental requirements and banks that provide green credit. Competent authorities shall learn from the financial institutions in developed countries (e.g., the German KFW Bankengruppe) to provide impetus for the development of green credit by means of discounts and guarantees, and use public and private funds to jointly develop green credit under the operation of a professional management team. Since green credit is a kind of Pigou means that subsidizes energy-saving and environmental protection industries by providing preferential borrowing interest rates, it is regarded as innovative application of environmental economic theory in the financial field, which can play an important role in green development and innovation of industrial financial sectors.

13.6.3 *Research outlook*

In the future, this study may further develop in the following directions:

(1) Lengthen the time frame of this study longitudinally (trace the data in earlier years and acquire the latest available data) and go over the changes of the impact of corporate EID on the scale of bank loans from the day when the EID and green credit policies were introduced.
(2) Expand the scope of study samples horizontally (from companies in high-polluting industries to manufacturing companies, from Shanghai Stock Exchange (SSE)-listed companies to SZSE-listed companies, and even to Hong Kong or US listed companies), and analyze the impact of institutions and market environments on corporate EID and the scale of bank loans.
(3) Expand or modify the control variables used in analysis models and take more consideration of the influences of internal and external factors on the enterprise side, as well as the influences of factors on the bank side; try to take into account of the cross variables between factors despite of corporate financing demand and EID; and explore the influences of these factors on the relationship between EID and the scale of bank loans.
(4) Use more methods to conduct robustness testing to make analysis models more convincing.

Appendix A: EIDs in 14 Industries

Table 13A.1. Descriptive statistics of various EIDs in 14 industries over 2014–2016.

Industry	Parameter	Aggregate EDI	EDImission	EDIecon	EDItreat	EDIcarbon	EDIemit
Mining	MV	38.75	56.34	42.52	36.63	25.73	38.25
($N = 36$)	SD	17.73	22.03	21.56	18.54	31.23	27.62
Fermentation	MV	34.17	48.89	48.15	30.07	26.98	24.07
($N = 9$)	SD	19.71	26.67	19.88	18.71	36.03	27.78
Textile	MV	29.07	46.33	34.10	27.30	14.05	28.12
($N = 30$)	SD	16.84	24.98	22.02	17.67	20.76	26.53
Steel	MV	45.66	61.67	48.18	37.87	34.52	53.99
($N = 48$)	SD	19.95	22.91	22.97	20.66	38.63	30.75
Chemistry	MV	35.44	52.05	44.94	33.00	19.27	31.89
($N = 129$)	SD	15.34	20.97	23.79	18.75	27.87	23.06
Thermal power	MV	44.42	61.72	51.75	32.47	39.18	49.87
($N = 66$)	SD	21.18	22.47	28.11	21.66	33.78	32.54
Building materials	MV	32.83	60.89	49.81	23.27	19.37	25.56
($N = 15$)	SD	13.81	20.76	24.48	14.44	26.60	24.08
Coal	MV	42.40	56.08	52.89	34.02	36.46	41.57
($N = 51$)	SD	17.40	18.34	22.05	17.78	31.12	27.55
Brewing	MV	35.02	49.58	31.68	29.04	33.78	41.49
($N = 24$)	SD	18.51	22.69	21.43	17.09	33.45	26.02
Petrochemistry	MV	59.75	62.22	37.50	60.78	80.95	67.13
($N = 6$)	SD	14.74	18.70	24.01	17.71	23.33	19.98

Cement	MV	47.67	53.33	61.39	41.76	35.24	47.22
(*N* = 15)	SD	16.10	22.25	15.78	18.61	36.47	25.57
Metallurgy	MV	38.80	54.96	48.21	38.09	16.77	36.51
(*N* = 45)	SD	18.59	22.08	24.84	23.34	23.29	30.63
Papermaking	MV	40.80	60.64	55.32	31.50	17.95	44.52
(*N* = 27)	SD	17.90	18.51	17.53	19.33	26.04	33.88
Pharmacy	MV	29.11	49.50	29.04	27.52	17.21	29.90
(*N* = 111)	SD	17.59	22.24	24.01	19.00	25.77	27.94
Total	MV	37.45	54.49	43.71	32.71	25.24	37.92
(*N* = 612)	SD	18.62	22.06	24.95	19.80	30.99	28.99

Table 13A.2. Annual changes of EDIs in 14 industries over 2014–2016.

Industry	Parameter	2014	2015	2016	Three-year average
Mining	MV	37.27	37.58	41.40	38.75
	SD	13.68	19.96	20.07	17.73
Fermentation	MV	34.59	37.73	30.19	34.17
	SD	23.89	28.49	11.32	19.71
Textile	MV	24.34	28.68	34.20	29.07
	SD	14.33	12.92	22.07	16.84
Steel	MV	46.34	39.51	51.12	45.66
	SD	20.32	17.61	21.23	19.95
Chemistry	MV	32.34	32.99	40.98	35.44
	SD	16.38	14.16	14.17	15.34
Thermal power	MV	38.25	49.91	45.10	44.42
	SD	21.90	21.60	19.23	21.18
Building materials	MV	30.19	37.74	30.57	32.83
	SD	13.34	20.01	6.59	13.81
Coal	MV	45.06	37.07	45.08	42.40
	SD	16.41	39.39	16.00	17.40
Brewing	MV	33.84	33.96	37.27	35.02
	SD	19.68	22.82	14.47	18.51
Petrochemistry	MV	50.00	62.26	66.99	59.75
	SD	17.34	13.34	17.35	14.74
Cement	MV	45.66	46.41	50.95	47.67
	SD	16.25	11.67	22.01	16.10
Metallurgy	MV	37.11	37.61	41.69	38.80
	SD	9.74	21.99	22.24	18.59
Papermaking	MV	31.87	41.93	48.60	40.80
	SD	13.78	17.92	19.25	17.90
Pharmacy	MV	28.25	26.57	32.52	29.11
	SD	18.55	17.08	17.03	17.59
Total	MV	35.16	36.13	41.05	37.45
	SD	17.95	19.00	18.45	18.62

Table 13A.3. EDI in regions/provinces/municipalities over 2014–2016.

	Underdeveloped					Developed				
Variable	Province (region/ municipality)	2014	2015	2016	Total	Province (region/ municipality)	2014	2015	2016	Total
MV	Anhui	41.51	23.11	37.42	34.01	Beijing	47.45	44.15	48.16	46.59
SD		23.52	21.20	24.22	22.39		22.64	20.65	18.36	20.34
Sample		4	4	4	12		20	20	20	60
MV	Gansu	33.02	33.96	36.79	34.59	Fujian	31.45	37.53	39.27	36.08
SD		1.334	16.01	14.68	9.888		15.36	19.62	22.27	18.85
Sample		2	2	2	6		9	9	9	27
MV	Guangxi	27.36	37.42	48.58	37.79	Guangdong	19.50	36.48	28.93	28.30
SD		25.53	20.23	19.98	22.56		9.682	24.62	7.143	15.56
Sample		6	6	6	18		3	3	3	9
MV	Guizhou	23.90	22.01	29.35	25.09	Hubei	28.30	39.62	41.51	36.48
SD		11.37	7.625	5.844	8.142		14.04	15.63	13.69	14.44
Sample		3	3	3	9		4	4	4	12
MV	Hainan	23.90	35.22	22.64	27.25	Jiangsu	30.57	31.04	40.77	34.12
SD		8.508	29.97	8.646	17.24		16.32	19.84	17.90	18.09
Sample		3	3	3	9		10	10	10	30

(*Continued*)

Table 13A.3. (*Continued*)

	Underdeveloped					Developed				
Variable	Province (region/ municipality)	2014	2015	2016	Total	Province (region/ municipality)	2014	2015	2016	Total
MV	Hebei	40.97	40.97	38.41	40.12	Liaoning	30.50	29.87	40.88	33.75
SD		12.64	16.62	13.19	13.58		7.586	17.14	27.33	18.71
Sample		7	7	7	21		6	6	6	18
MV	Henan	36.57	29.46	40.03	35.36	Inner Mongolia	30.82	38.99	39.52	36.44
SD		15.70	16.20	18.67	17.05		10.98	22.97	10.25	15.44
Sample		13	13	13	39		6	6	6	18
MV	Heilongjiang	39.25	35.47	33.96	36.23	Shandong	32.02	35.26	48.44	38.57
SD		14.82	10.62	16.72	13.42		13.54	19.13	18.03	18.18
Sample		5	5	5	15		16	16	16	48
MV	Hunan	38.49	35.47	36.10	36.69	Shaanxi	21.70	25.47	19.81	22.33
SD		16.15	19.49	4.074	13.77		9.339	20.01	25.35	15.25
Sample		5	5	5	15		2	2	2	6
MV	Jiangxi	33.33	30.82	43.40	35.85	Shanghai	45.28	37.66	49.73	44.22
SD		19.36	6.626	18.00	14.80		24.10	21.58	24.53	23.45
Sample		3	3	3	9		15	15	15	45
MV	Ningxia	24.53	26.42	41.51	30.82	Tianjin	23.59	50.00	37.74	37.11
SD		0	0	0	9.307		6.671	25.35	8.005	17.03
Sample		1	1	1	3		2	2	2	6

MV	Qinghai	38.36	30.19	52.20	40.25	Zhejiang	37.74	39.36	38.09	37.40
SD		12.28	23.19	22.51	19.79		19.93	20.45	18.51	19.51
Sample		3	3	3	9		29	29	29	87
MV	Shanxi	33.73	41.51	44.81	40.02	Chongqing	33.02	21.70	20.75	25.16
SD		17.10	13.03	11.94	14.37		20.01	14.68	8.005	13.16
Sample		8	8	8	24		2	2	2	6
MV	Sichuan	31.45	30.19	38.16	33.26					
SD		15.22	19.57	25.18	19.50					
Sample		6	6	6	18					
MV	Tibet	15.09	3.773	16.98	11.95					
SD		18.68	2.668	8.005	11.17					
Sample		2	2	2	6					
MV	Xinjiang	28.68	40.75	40	36.48					
SD		14.52	21.20	14.70	16.83					
Sample		5	5	5	15					
MV	Yunnan	44.34	44.81	42.92	44.03					
SD		11.78	13.46	11.77	11.22					
Sample		4	4	4	12					
MV	Total	34.25	33.68	39.15	35.69	Total	35.75	37.72	42.27	38.58
SD		16.02	17.34	16.50	16.74		19.14	19.90	19.58	19.68
Sample		80	80	80	240		124	124	124	372

Chapter 14

The Environmental Information Sharing Mechanism in Zhejiang Province in the Context of Green Finance Reform*

14.1 Introduction

The 19th National Congress of the Communist Party of China (CPC) convened in 2017 had the important thought of "lucid waters and lush mountains are invaluable assets" written into the Party Constitution, and since then the concept of green development has become a vital part of Xi Jinping's Thought on Socialism with Chinese Characteristics for a New Era. As the birthplace of this important thought, Zhejiang Province has taken green development as the keynote of its development and has set about developing green finance, which is an essential requirement of this important thought and also a necessary means to promote green development in the new era.

Xi Jinping, General Secretary of the CPC Central Committee, pointed out at the 27th Meeting of the Central Leading Group for Comprehensively Continuing the Reform in 2016 that we should, by innovating financial system arrangement, guide and encourage more social capital to invest in green industries and strictly restrict investment

---

* The compilation of this chapter is ascribed to the strong support from the Zhejiang Green Finance Youth Research Group.

in polluting industries, and we should employ financial tools and supporting policies (e.g., green credit, green consumption, green stock index and related industries, green development fund, green insurance, and carbon finance) to facilitate green development. Later in 2017, "green finance" was repeatedly stressed in the National Financial Work Conference and the Report to the 19th CPC National Congress. In June of the same year, the State Council decided to set up pilot zones for green finance reform and innovation in the provinces of Zhejiang, Jiangxi, Guangdong and Guizhou, and the Xinjiang Uygur Autonomous Region ("Xinjiang" for short). This pilot program is to diversify the main bodies of green finance, enrich green financial products, improve market infrastructure, strengthen policy support, and establish a green financial risk prevention mechanism, thereby accumulating reproducible experiences for promoting green finance across the country. The official launch of these pilot zones marks that the development of green finance has entered the stage of practical operation, which is characterized by "top-level design and grassroots experiment" (market-based operation with the government playing a leading role), and also shows that the timetable and roadmap for green finance reform are getting clearer and green finance is to play an active role in advancing China's economic transformation and upgrading and green development. Here, from the meso-microscopic perspective, what needs to be explored is how green finance can cater to the economic development and environmental protection of urban and rural areas, and how the tasks and principles of financial work can be applied to the development of green finance.

A system for disclosing and sharing corporate environmental information is one of the key micro-mechanisms for effective development of green finance. In this regard, the Report to the 19th CPC National Congress clearly presents to "establish a mandatory environmental information disclosure system," and the *G20 Green Finance Synthesis Report* takes the utilization and sharing of public environmental data (or information) as the key development direction of green finance, because corporate environment information disclosure (EID) is a critical infrastructure for green finance, and sharing of environmental information is a driving force for promoting the development, reform, and innovation of green finance. In short, it is of vital importance to build a system for disclosing and sharing environmental information, which is a means to raise the use efficiency of environmental information.

14.1.1 *A system for disclosing and sharing environmental information is the groundwork for effective resource allocation in green financial market*

As shown in the *G20 Green Finance Synthesis Report* (2017), the value of corporate environmental information manifests in four aspects as follows:

First, without appropriate corporate environmental information, investment, credit, and insurance institutions can hardly assess the impact of investment-related environmental and climatic factors on their finance. The resulting underestimation of environmental risks and absence of risk pricing and management may lead to decision-making misplay, thereby causing fluctuations in their asset value, including sudden and unexpected impairment of assets.

Second, the absence of corporate environmental information may undermine effective communication between investors and target companies on substantive environmental issues. In addition to investors who strive for business returns and avoiding risks, users of environmental information also include an increasing number of institutions interested in "sense of value investment." These institutions care about the consistency of their investment with long-term policies and social goals, especially the Sustainable Development Goals (SDGs) and the Paris Agreement. They cannot have any investment inclination if appropriate environmental information is unavailable.

Third, government departments are also users of environmental information. If companies fail to disclose their environmental information and estimate their environmental costs and benefits, there will be no eligible entity to receive government incentives for green investment, even if the government intends to do so.

Fourth, in the context of green development, companies will accept various types of environmental risk analysis, and companies or their industries are to be subject to "risk exposure" evaluation based on their disclosed environmental information.

Therefore, valid disclosure and sharing of environmental information is an important basis for green finance pilot reform and an urgent need of financial institutions to develop green credit and innovate service models. Moreover, it is also a vital means for financial institutions to prevent and control environmental compliance risks and credit risks, and a factor that directly affects the professionalism and effectiveness of Zhejiang-based pilot zone for green finance reform and innovation.

14.1.2 *Uneven and inadequate disclosure and sharing of corporate environmental information impede development of green finance*

The above analysis shows that corporate environmental information is crucial to the development of green finance; however, the disclosure and sharing of such information are still unbalanced and inadequate. On one hand, financial institutions need sufficient environmental information to quantify environmental risks. On the other hand, the government and companies fail to fully disclose and share such information. Such conspicuous contradiction between supply and demand is mainly reflected in three aspects:

First, the sources of corporate environmental information are not transparent enough. Relevant statistics show that listed companies are not active in EID, although they are the most representative enterprises. There are both objective reasons (e.g., imperfect information disclosure system) and subjective factors (e.g., companies themselves are not good at it). Because of their inactive disclosure behavior, the available environmental information is far from enough to vigorously support the development of green finance.

Second, in terms of information circulation, the corporate environmental information is not effectively transformed and shared. Without the constraint of a sound information disclosure system, the limited environmental information disclosed by companies cannot “flow” in the market. On one hand, the original environmental information and data cannot be professionally processed, digested, and absorbed, thus unable to support the development of green finance. On the other hand, there is not yet a platform for exchanging and sharing the environmental information scattered in industrial sectors and government departments, and the presentation of such information is inorganized, resulting in “overlapped” collection and sorting of such information and certain “resistance,” which will obstruct banks and other financial institutions from further use of such information.

Third, as for information sharing in the end, banks and other financial institutions — one of the main users of environmental information — are not skilled in the efficient use of environmental information, because they have not fully prepared in governance mechanism, incentive mechanism, and reserve of professionals; moreover, they are constrained by imperfect systems in this regard. Consequently, even though financial institutions themselves attach great importance to collection of environmental information, they must raise efficiency in utilizing such information.

To sum up, in order to support Zhejiang's development of green finance and its "run-once-most-again" reform of banking industry, the disclosure and sharing of corporate environmental information needs to be further improved. To this end, the Zhejiang Green Finance Youth Research Group organized a special sample survey of the province-wide banks (including their legal persons and branches) and listed companies (mainly in high-polluting industry). This special survey is made up of group discussion, questionnaire survey, and field trip; in this process the research group learned about the current situation and challenges of the survey subjects, and then managed to present suggestions and solutions to help them overcome these challenges.

14.2 Achievements of Zhejiang-Based Banks in Collecting and Sharing Corporate Environmental Information

According to the survey, Zhejiang-based banks are, on the whole, active participants in green financial practices. They not only have an accurate understanding of the importance of corporate environmental information but also have higher requirements for the collection and sharing of such information. However, owing to the absence of an effective information collection and sharing mechanism, Zhejiang-based banks fail to possess adequate and high-quality corporate environmental information, which is a stumbling block for them to develop green finance. They can hardly keep abreast of the operations of companies in a timely and comprehensive manner, evaluate their true status, and adjust their credit line. Moreover, without enough corporate environmental information, banks are unable to accurately evaluate the effectiveness of green finance business, which greatly weakens the financial leverage of green finance in environmental protection.

14.2.1 *Wide coverage of green credit*

The results of this survey show that Zhejiang-based banks are quite active in joining in various green financial practices, which is proved by their vigorous credit support for green development projects. Among the

210 banks that were surveyed, most of them have taken part in green credit projects in different industries: There are 174 banks joining in "energy saving and environmental protection" projects, 159 in "clean energy" projects, and 144 in "five water governance" projects (see Figure 14.1). Since the State has intensified efforts in promoting green finance reform and innovation, banks are motivated to develop green financial business. They have become sponsors of not only market-led profit-oriented projects but also government-led environmental protection infrastructure projects.

Zhejiang-based banks have been active in carrying out green credit business: 31% of them have a green credit proportion of above 20%, far exceeding the national average. However, 28% of them have a green credit proportion of lower than 5%, showing that the green credit business structure of Zhejiang-based banks is not well-balanced (see Figure 14.2).

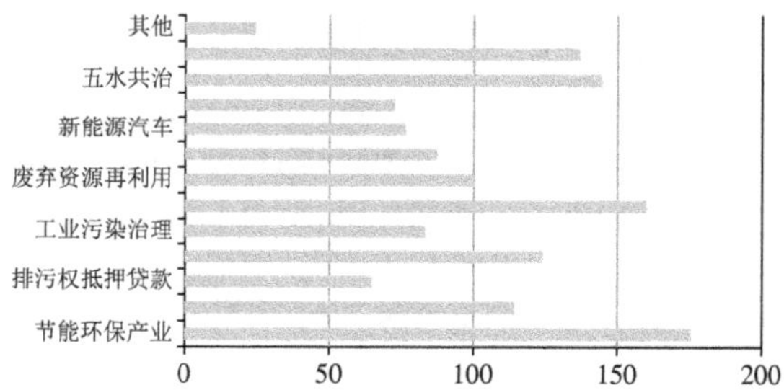

其他	Others
五水共治	Five water governance
新能源汽车	NEVs
废弃资源再利用	Reuse of waste resources
工业污染治理	Industrial pollution control
排污权抵押贷款	Emission allowance mortgage loan
节能环保产业	Energy saving and environmental protection

Figure 14.1. Green credit distribution by industry in Zhejiang.

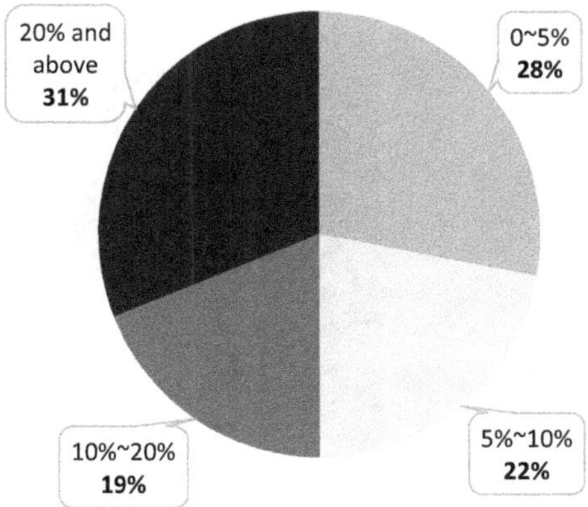

Figure 14.2. Proportion of green credit in Zhejiang-based banks.

14.2.2 *Pay attention to the organization and management of green finance*

Zhejiang-based banks have been actively making organizational preparations and creating innovations for developing green finance (see Figure 14.3). Among the banks that were surveyed, about 20% of them have set a "green finance business unit" and nearly 40% of them have set a high-level division, such as the "board of directors" or "credit committee," to take charge of green credit, showing that Zhejiang-based banks have attached great importance to the green finance business and its management.

14.2.3 *Listed companies become more active to disclose environmental information*

According to the survey of Zhejiang-based listed companies (mainly in pollution-intensive industries), while the entire society attaches great importance to ecological protection, companies have become more active in disclosing their environmental information. According to the *Report on Corporate Environmental Information Disclosure Index* produced by the Center for Environmental Economic Studies, Fudan University for three consecutive years, as affected by various factors, Zhejiang-based listed companies are more willing to disclose environmental information and also more capable of doing so, with the average score of green transparency going up from 36.34 points in 2014 to 41.52 points in 2016 (see Figure 14.4), demonstrating a relatively positive momentum.

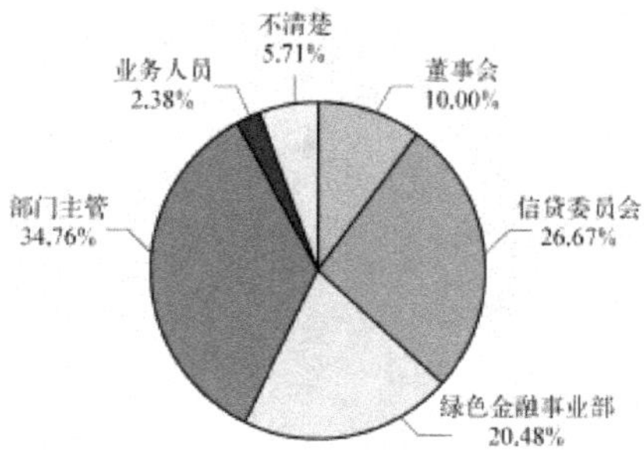

部门主管 34.76%	Department head (34.76%)
业务人员 2.38%	Business personnel (2.38%)
不清楚 5.71%	Not clear (5.71%)
董事会 10.00%	Board of directors (10.00%)
信贷委员会 26.67%	Credit committee (26.67%)
绿色金融事业部 20.48%	Green finance business unit (20.48%)

Figure 14.3. Green finance departments in Zhejiang-based banks.

The statistics have shown the content of EID report released by most of the listed companies that were surveyed. Such report mainly includes corporate environmental protection policy; annual goals and results of environmental protection; total resource consumption per year; investment and technological development for environmental protection; name, type, quantity, concentration, and discharge mode of pollutants (including excessive discharge); construction and operation of environmental protection facilities; waste treatment and disposal during production, waste recycling and integrated utilization; agreement signed with environmental protection authority on voluntary environmental enhancement; and rewards presented by environmental protection authority. All of this shows that corporate EID has created more possibilities and favorable conditions for banks to obtain and analyze companies' environmental information and data.

14.2.4 *Banks should do their best to collect and use corporate environmental information*

There is still much room for banks to make better use of corporate environmental information and data. The results of survey show that while

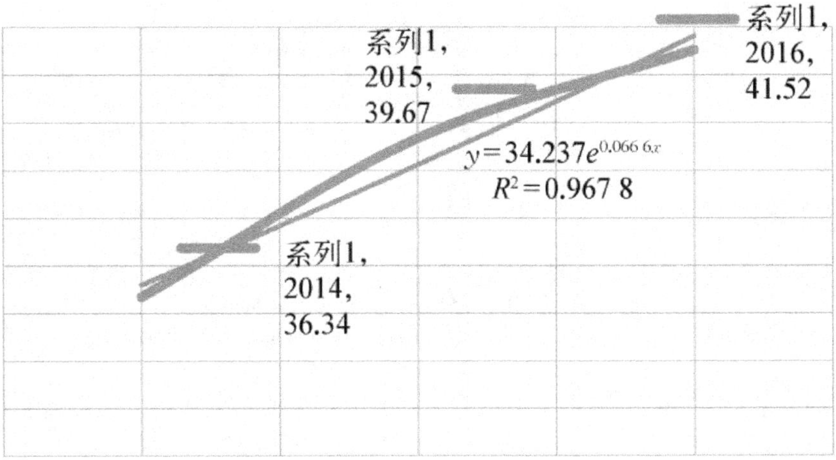

系列 1, 2014, 36.34	Series1, 2014, 36.34
系列 1, 2015, 39.67	Series1, 2015, 39.67
系列 1, 2016, 41.52	Series1, 2016, 41.52
$y = 34.237e^{0.0666x}$	
$R^2 = 0.09678$	

Figure 14.4. Corporate EID Index over 2014–2016.

banks have been active in taking on green financial practices, they must learn to make environmental information and data "interactive" and use them more efficiently, which is their top priority to further promote the development of green finance.

On one hand, most banks speak highly of the value of corporate environmental information and have been quite active in collecting and sharing such information (see Figure 14.5).

Most of the banks that were surveyed agree that "public environmental data and information are important for their financial business." When answering the question of "importance degree of environmental data and information," 99% of the banks choose "very important" or "important"; followed by those who vote for the data and information from other fields (taxation, customs, industry and commerce, and intellectual property). None of them consider environmental information "not important" or "least important" (see Figure 14.6).

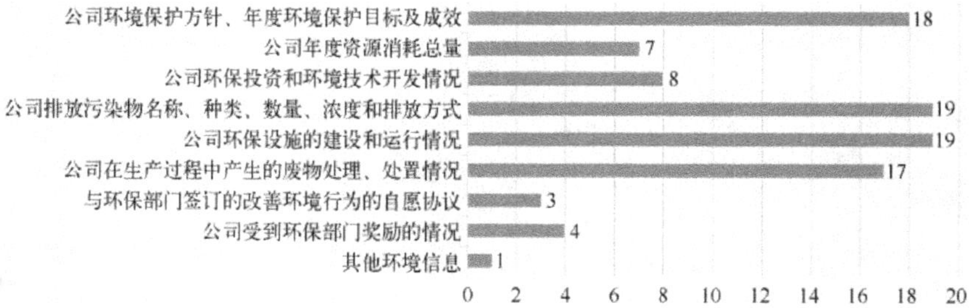

公司环境保护方针、年度环境保护目标及成效	Corporate environmental protection policy, annual goals and results of environmental protection
公司年度资源消耗总量	Total resource consumption per year
公司环保投资和环境技术开发情况	Investment and technological development for environmental protection
公司排放污染物名称、种类、数量、浓度和排放方式	Name, type, quantity, concentration and discharge mode of pollutants
公司环保设施的建设和运行情况	Construction and operation of environmental protection facilities
公司在生产过程中产生的废物处理、处置情况	Waste treatment and disposal during production
与环保部门签订的改善环境行为的自愿协议	Agreement signed with environmental protection authority on voluntary environmental enhancement
公司受到环保部门奖励的情况	Rewards presented by environmental protection authority
其他环境信息	Other environmental information

Figure 14.5. Types of corporate environmental information to be disclosed.

On the other hand, banks are fully aware of the importance of environmental data and information. They believe that such data and information can help them "identify, prevent, measure, monitor and control" the environmental and social risks in their credit business, which happens to coincide with the judgment in the *G20 Green Finance Synthesis Report* (2017) (see Figure 14.7).

Banks have made various efforts and attempts actively to obtain environmental information and data, which are mainly reflected in three levels: internal governance mechanism, tools and means for obtaining

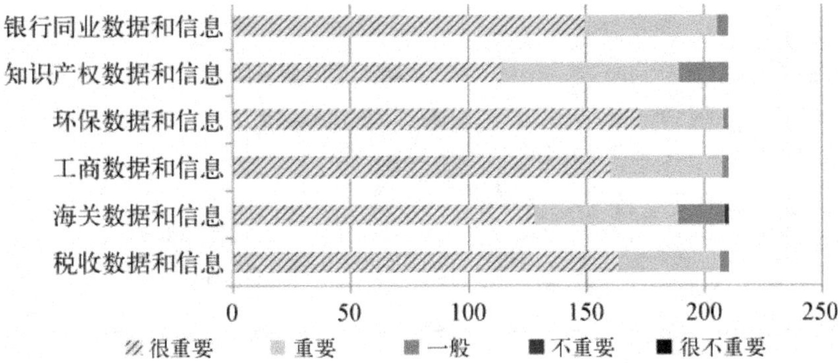

银行同业数据和信息	Banking
知识产权数据和信息	IP
环保数据和信息	Environmental protection
工商数据和信息	Industry and commerce
海关数据和信息	Customs
税收	Taxation
很重要	Very important
重要	Important
一般	General
不重要	Not important
很不重要	Least important

Figure 14.6. Importance of all kinds of data and information to banks' financial business.

environmental information, and information/data processing and analysis.

First, in terms of internal governance mechanism, many banks have laid down rules and regulations for collection of environmental information and data. For example, more than 50% of the banks that were surveyed have special regulations for the collection, review, analysis, and management of corporate environmental information, while some banks have the board of directors or council to discuss and deal with such information (see Figure 14.8).

Second, in terms of tools and means for collecting environmental information, banks have made attempts in doing credit business due diligence, obtaining corporate social responsibility report, accessing to the databases of banking authority and environmental protection authority,

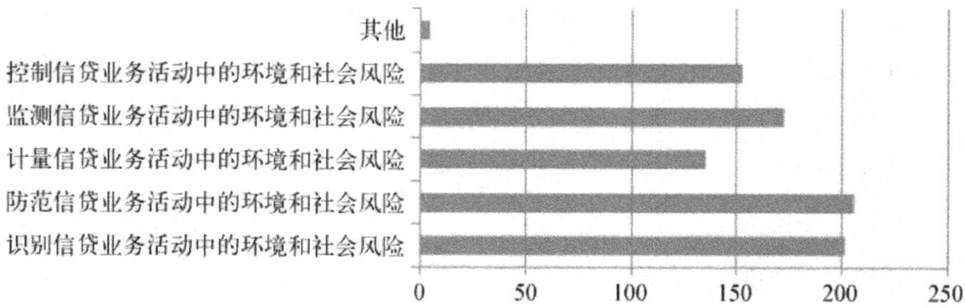

其他	Others
控制信贷业务活动中的环境和社会风险	Control the environmental and social risks
监测信贷业务活动中的环境和社会风险	Monitor the environmental and social risks
计量信贷业务活动中的环境和社会风险	Measure the environmental and social risks
防范信贷业务活动中的环境和社会风险	Prevent the environmental and social risks
识别信贷业务活动中的环境和社会风险	Identify the environmental and social risks

Figure 14.7. Significance of corporate environmental information and data on banks' credit business.

and cooperating with third-party professional organization. Among the banks that were surveyed, 204 of them prefer "credit business due diligence," 97 rely on the "database of banking authority," and 117 rely on the "database of environmental protection authority." This shows that the means and tools for banks to obtain environmental information and data are "fragmented." In general, banks are not quite skilled in efficient use of these information and data, so they need to make improvement in this regard.

Finally, after obtaining corporate environmental information and data, banks shall actively process and analyze these information and data by "building an environmental risk/event database," "making environmental big data analysis," "using corporate green rating tool," "carrying out corporate ESG (Environmental, Social and Governance) rating," or "evaluating and analyzing corporate carbon footprint and emissions reduction." However, the survey results show that banks must build up their ability to process and analyze corporate environmental information and data and make more efforts to compensate their weakness in docking with the internationally accepted ESG Disclosure Standards.

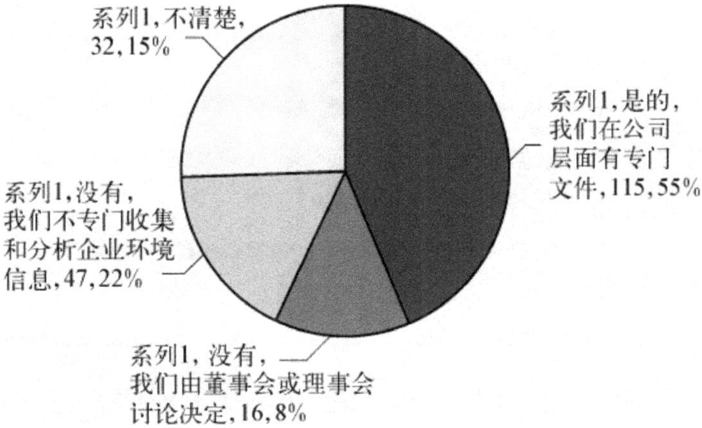

系列 1，不清楚，32 (15%)	Series 1, not clear, 32 (15%)
系列 1，没有，我们不专门收集和分析企业环境信息，47(22%)	Series 1, none, not collect and analyze corporate environmental information specially, 47 (22%)
系列 1，没有，我们由董事会或理事会讨论决定，16 (8%)	Series 1, none, the board of directors or council deals with corporate environmental information, 16 (8%)
系列 1，是的，我们在公司层面有专门文件，115 (55%)	Series 1, yes, special regulations at the corporate level, 115 (55%)

Figure 14.8. Regulations of banks for collection, review, analysis, and management of corporate environmental information.

14.2.5 *Government departments help build an environmental information sharing platform*

By relying on the existing local area network, the Banking Regulatory Bureau and Environmental Protection Department of Zhejiang Province started working together in building a green credit information sharing platform since 2011 and put this platform into trial operation about six months later. Thanks to this platform, banks can immediately learn about energy-saving and environmental protection policies and corporate environmental behaviors, while environmental protection authorities can receive timely feedback from banks so as to evaluate the effects of environmental protection policies and adjust relevant policies and measures if

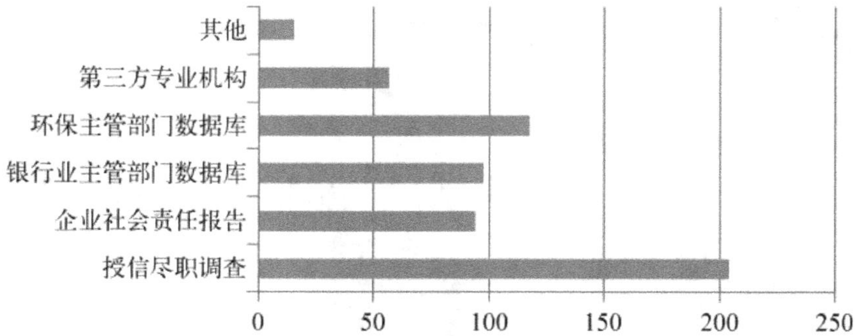

其他	Others
第三方专业机构	Third-party professional organization
环保主管部门数据库	Database of banking authority
银行业主管部门数据库	Database of environmental protection authority
企业社会责任报告	Corporate social responsibility report
授信尽职调查	Credit business due diligence

Figure 14.9. Ways for banks to collect corporate environmental information.

necessary, and banking regulatory authorities can provide guidance to the green credit policies via this platform, monitor the green credit business of banks, and organize supervision and assessment accordingly (see Figure 14.9).

14.3 Main Problems of and Challenges to Zhejiang-Based Banks in Collecting and Sharing Corporate Environmental Information

In the process of this survey, we found that some banks still have a lot of confusion about the collection and sharing of corporate environmental information, and there are many difficulties and challenges for them to overcome.

14.3.1 *A vague understanding of the definition and connotation of corporate environmental information*

According to the survey, most banks usually identify and evaluate the environmental risks of companies based on the fact that whether they are fined for environmental violations and whether there is negative news about their environmental behaviors. More than 90% of the banks that were surveyed take an interest in this type of information, but they fail to pay enough attention to positive environmental information, and they cannot screen out the companies or green projects (or assets) that may benefit the environment. According to the author's research (see Figure 14.10), corporate environmental information is associated with the environmental protection process and results of a company; the environmental risks of the company are closely related not only to the environmental protection standards and requirements but also to its environmental protection efforts in the course of business operation. However, the banks, which are the main beneficiaries of corporate environmental information, have failed to fully absorb the value of this information and tap its potential productivity. Their understanding of this information is one-sided, that is, they only identify companies' environmental risks from their penalty for environmental violations but ignore the positive effects of this information on the synthetic judgment and prediction of companies' environmental risks.

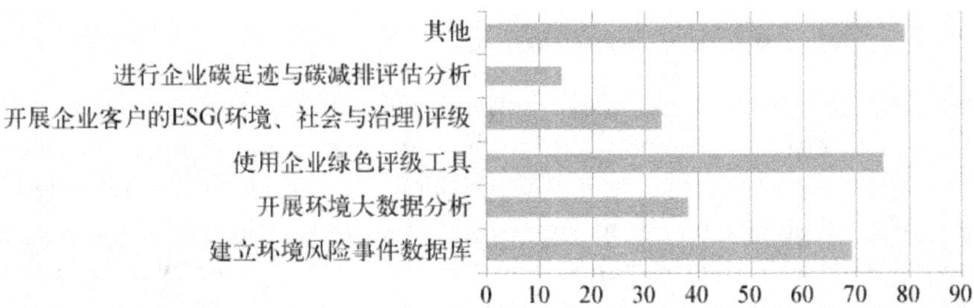

其他	Others
进行企业碳足迹与碳减排评估分析	Evaluate and analyze corporate carbon footprint and emissions reduction
开展企业客户的 ESG（环境、社会与治理）评级	Carry out corporate ESG rating
使用企业绿色评级工具	Use corporate green rating tool
开展环境大数据分析	Make environmental big data analysis
建立环境风险事件数据库	Build an environmental risk/event database

Figure 14.10. Tools for banks to process and analyze corporate environmental information and data.

14.3.2 *Greatly different standards for identifying green finance*

While actively carrying out green financial practices, Zhejiang-based banks are facing the challenges of non-uniform standards for green rating, and the problem of blurring the differences between "dark green," "light green," and even "fake green." For example, when banks are about to conduct green rating of loan companies or projects, their understandings and practices in this regard are greatly different. Among the banks that were surveyed, 149 of them (accounting for 70% of the total) refer to the green rating standards developed by relevant government departments, 122 of them employ the industrial standards, and 117 of them follow the standards established by banks. Moreover, statistics also show that many banks have double or multiple standards for green rating of loan companies and projects (see Figure 14.11). In short, the banking industry does not have unified identification standards for green credit, which is undoubtedly detrimental to the long-term and stable development of green finance.

14.3.3 *Not doing very well in collection of corporate environmental information*

The above analysis shows that Zhejiang-based banks have made various attempts to collect, process, and analyze corporate environmental information and data. However, most of the banks that were surveyed said that they often feel powerless to obtain these information and data due to internal and external constraints, and they cannot fully satisfy the requirements for developing green finance. Compared with the collection of corporate environmental information and data, it is easier for banks to obtain other types of public data. Among the banks that were surveyed, only 40% of them believe that the acquisition of environmental data is "good" or "very good," but most of them find it more efficient to obtain data from other sources, such as taxation, customs, industry and commerce, and other banks (see Figure 14.12).

There are obstacles that hold back banks from obtaining environmental information and data, such as "non-cooperative companies," "banks themselves not professional enough," "lack of third-party professional organizations," "absence of a formal EID system," and "insufficient information

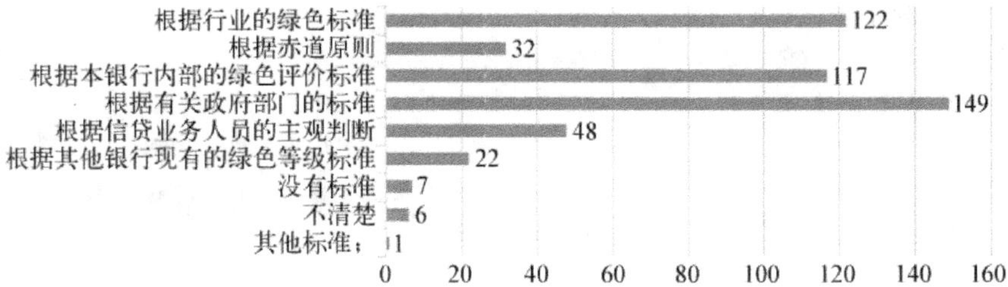

根据行业的绿色标准	Industrial standards
根据赤道原则	Equator Principles
根据本银行内部的绿色评价标准	Internal standards of the bank
根据有关政府部门的标准	Standards developed by government departments
根据信贷业务人员的主观判断	Subjective judgment of credit officer
根据其他银行现有的绿色等级标准	Standards of other banks
没有标准	No standard
不清楚	Not clear
其他标准	Other standards

Figure 14.11. Rating of green enterprises and green projects by banks.

sharing among government departments." Amon them, the "absence of a formal EID system" is the major challenge, which to some extent illustrates the urgency for the State to establish and improve a mandatory EID system.

14.3.4 *Insufficient information sharing among government departments*

We also need to pay great attention to the "insufficient information sharing among government departments," which is mainly because the environmental information sharing platforms and mechanisms (between government departments and also between government and banks) fail to play their proper role.

As shown in Figure 14.13, the number one obstacle keeping banks from obtaining corporate environmental information is "absence of a formal EID system," which is followed by "insufficient information sharing among government departments." In the process of our survey, we also

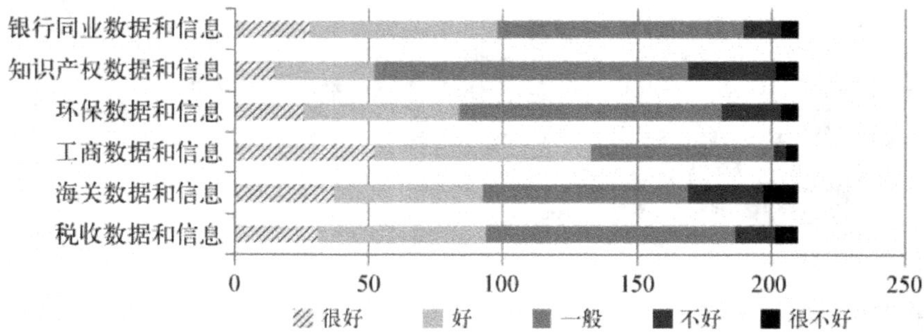

银行同业数据和信息	Banking industry
知识产权数据和信息	IP
环保数据和信息	Environmental protection
工商数据和信息	Industry and commerce
海关数据和信息	Customs
税收数据和信息	Taxation
很好	Very good
好	Good
一般	General
不好	Bad
很不好	Very bad

Figure 14.12. Banks' accessibility of external information and data by source.

noticed that some banks are lagging behind the collection of environmental information and the authenticity of their green credit information is unwarranted (such information mainly comes from the official reply to the project environmental impact assessment or from companies themselves), since there is no third-party authority capable of verifying this information. Moreover, local government departments at all levels have not integrated or unified the information on industry, investment, environmental protection, and safety supervision, making the information on environmental violations scattered in national, provincial, municipal, and county-level environmental protection authorities. Banks have to spend time and energy retrieving data from each authority, showing that the environmental information inquiry channel must be improved. Besides, government departments, financial institutions, and third-party organizations do not have a valid information-sharing mechanism, making the green credit data on the existing platform far from enough for Zhejiang-based banks to develop their green financial services.

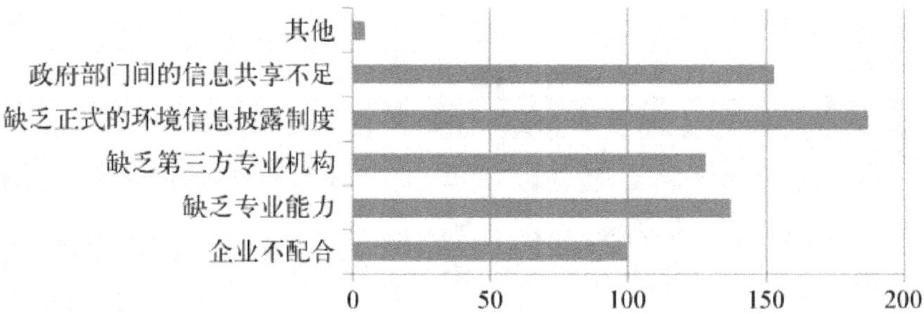

其他	Others
政府部门间的信息共享不足	Insufficient information sharing among government departments
缺乏正式的环境信息披露制度	Absence of a formal EID system
缺乏第三方专业机构	Lack of third-party professional organizations
缺乏专业能力	Banks themselves not professional enough
企业不配合	Non-cooperative companies

Figure 14.13. Main obstacles keeping banks from obtaining corporate environmental information.

14.3.5 *Inter-bank environmental information sharing mechanism needs to be improved*

While obtaining public environmental information and data from the outside, banks themselves are also an important source of such information and data. Most banks attach great importance to their own information disclosure. In addition to regularly submitting green finance development reports to the banking regulatory bureau, some banks directly make public environmental information in annual report, social responsibility report or sustainable development report (see Figure 14.14).

The environmental information disclosed by banks, which is mainly about the status quo and development strategies and policies of green credit, has greatly improved the communication between investors and the public (see Figure 14.15).

However, without uniform regulations at present, each bank has been "sharing" the information and data on green finance and environment in its own way, so they are less motivated or active to exchange these information and data with each other. For example, only about 30% of the

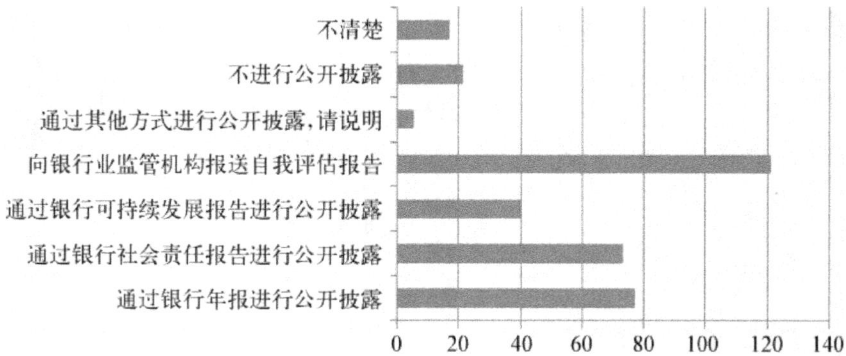

不清楚	Not clear
不进行公开披露	No public disclosure
通过其他方式进行公开披露，请说明	Other means of public disclosure (to specify)
向银行监管机构报送自我评估报告	Self-assessment report submitted to the regulator
通过银行可持续发展报告进行公开披露	Sustainable development report
通过银行社会责任报告进行公开披露	Social responsibility report
通过银行年报进行公开披露	Annual report

Figure 14.14. Ways of banks to disclose green financial information.

banks that were surveyed have a public information disclosure mechanism for green financial credit business (see Figure 14.16).

14.3.6 *Some companies need to improve their EID*

According to the survey, banks cannot obtain environmental information and data from all companies, because some of them are not active in doing so for the following reasons:

(1) Some companies concern about the "cost effect" of information disclosure. Since China does not have uniform and specified mandatory standards and formats for corporate EID, companies have no idea what should they abide by for information disclosure. Moreover, the high cost sometimes forces companies to give up disclosure or only disclose a small amount of information.

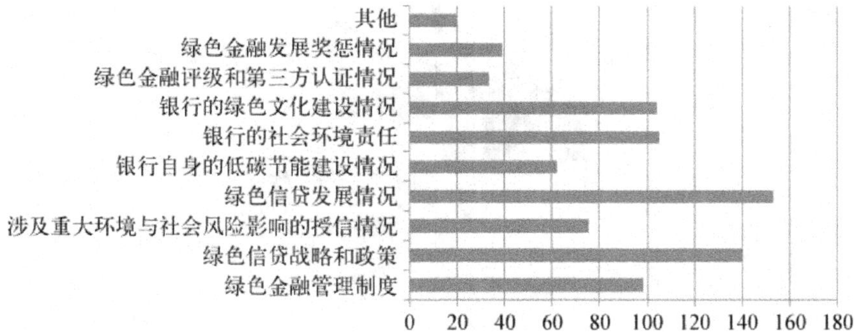

其他	Others
绿色金融发展奖惩情况	Rewards and punishments for green finance development
绿色金融评级和第三方认证情况	Green finance rating and third-party certification
银行的绿色文化建设情况	Green culture development of the bank
银行的社会环境责任	Social and environmental responsibilities of the bank
银行自身的低碳节能建设情况	Low-carbon and energy-saving development of the bank
绿色信贷发展情况	Green credit development
涉及重大环境与社会风险影响的授信情况	Credit granting involving major environmental and social risks
绿色信贷战略和政策	Green credit strategy and policy
绿色金融管理制度	Green financial management system

Figure 14.15. Types of green financial information disclosed by banks.

(2) The "competitiveness" of corporate EID has yet to be brought into play, and the positive incentive effect of information sharing has yet to be formed.
(3) Both the internal and external environmental information disclosure is not professional.
(4) Some banks themselves are not skilled in collecting and utilizing corporate environmental information, hence unable to guide companies to disclose information.
(5) The information-sharing mechanism between the government and the market, between government departments, and between banks and companies is not perfect.

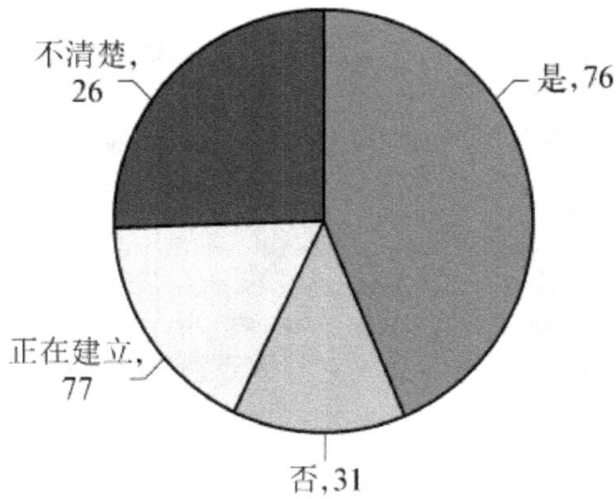

不清楚，26	Not clear, 26
正在建立，77	Being built, 77
否，31	No, 31
是，76	Yes, 76

Figure 14.16. Available green financial information disclosure mechanism in banks.

14.4 Solutions and Suggestions

In order to help banks overcome the challenges in collecting and using corporate environmental information, we suggest that, on the basis of existing practices, they should take specific measures in terms of information sources, sharing, and utilization to make the best use of corporate EID for the development of green finance. Thanks to the favorable opportunity for promoting information sharing as required by the "run-once-most-again" reform, efforts should be made to strengthen the cooperation among the departments for banking regulation, environmental protection, water conservancy, and land and resources administration, and give full play to the role of banks, companies, experts and scholars, and market players, for the purpose of creating a pilot "Five Ones" information-sharing mechanism. The so-called "Five Ones" is made up of "one minimum standard and negative list of corporate EID"; "one classification and grading mechanism and positive list of green enterprises"; "one green credit information sharing platform"; "one incentive and restraint mechanism for environmental information sharing," and "one monitoring and rating mechanism for green information, green credit, and green banking."

14.4.1 *Establish an information source governance mechanism combining mandatory and voluntary disclosure*

According to statistical analysis, the primary and the biggest challenge faced by most banks in the process of collecting and sharing corporate environmental information is "they can't make brick without straw." No matter whether it is their due diligence or a government-led information platform, they cannot provide a large amount of high-quality data for utilization, mainly because companies are not interested in EID in the case of immature market economy and ineffective external regulations. Given this, various measures shall be taken to encourage and force companies to disclose environmental information at the source, such as setting corporate EID standards, developing a corporate environmental transparency index, rewarding the companies that actively disclose environmental information and punishing those who are passive to do so, combining mandatory and voluntary disclosure, and increasing corporate environmental transparency.

14.4.2 *Press ahead with the "run-once-most-again" reform, create and upgrade the platform for disclosing and sharing environmental information*

It is important to keep improving the ability of banks to process the original corporate environmental information, prevent the information sources from being simplified or fragmented, increase their willingness to share information, and build up their ability to do so. In practice, banks are both "consumers" and "providers" of corporate environmental information. As "consumers," banks neither have effective tools nor abilities to absorb and digest first-hand environmental information from various sources, so their data processing is quite superficial. As "providers," banks are handling environmental information separately and unwilling to share it with each other or with other institutions. In addition to banks, the information platform built by the government and third-party authorities are not capable enough to process information, let alone have the environmental information "circulate" widely for larger-scale sharing.

Companies, government departments, and banks should break all kinds of information barriers, strengthen communication, press ahead with the "run-once-most-again" reform, and improve the information-sharing platform between financial institutions and environmental protection departments. The third-party authorities shall be cultivated so that corporate environmental information can be properly processed by market players, which is beneficial to the green finance development.

14.4.3 *Create and improve the green credit rating mechanism and improve the use efficiency of corporate environmental information*

In addition to their weakness in obtaining and processing corporate environmental information, banks cannot use such information and data efficiently. It is mainly because most banks have not linked corporate environmental information with their green finance business, that is, they cannot make use of such information to serve their businesses such as green credit. In view of this, some banks have made attempts to develop systematic green rating standards and systems for loan companies and projects based on existing corporate environmental information, including the "negative list" and different identification colors. Although these attempts are worth encouraging, they still have shortcomings such as non-uniform standards and poor execution, which render corporate environmental information unable to facilitate the development and evaluation of green credit business.

For this reason, a unified evaluation system for green information, green credit, and green banks should be established. In this way banks will be forced to make full use of corporate environmental information, data resources, and Energy Information Administration (EIA) results under the supervision of competent departments; promote the evaluation and rating of green information and credit to the maximum extent; and integrate them with risk pricing, prevention, and control.

Chapter 15

Green Development and Transformation — Hard Constraints Based on Energy and Environment

"Economic downturn" and "environmental storm" are hot phrases nowadays. As far as China is concerned, the implications of these two phrases are of great importance: One is economic transformation associated with economic growth pace and quality, and the other green transformation associated with eco-environmental quality. Both of them have become the biggest challenges in front of China's socio-economic development and give rise to two major issues: How to achieve transformation separately? And more importantly, how to achieve balanced development between them? The latter issue seems more intricate. For example, at the time of an economic downturn or economic circle, an economy can easily fall into a rebound in "resources and environmental utilization," which is reflected in large-scale infrastructure investment influenced by Keynesian economic thinking and development of heavy chemical industry, hence weakening the role of technological progress. For another example, when there is an economic downturn, intensified protection of resources and environment will lead to transfer of industries between regions. As a result, even if positive effects of economic transformation are shown in some regions, the country as a whole is to be dragged down by the inefficient economic transformation of other regions. Such examples have kept us from properly dealing with the above two issues.

15.1 Reshape the Cognitive Basis of China's Economic Transformation

China's economic transformation has been a hot topic for years. The CPC Central Committee put forward the slogan as "rejuvenating the country through science and education" (Wu, 2013) as early as in 1995. At that time, China's economic development and reform were at a stage when the old driving force was depleting and the new driving force remained in the bud. A new growth model was badly needed for national economic transformation. As a result, the entire society begun to contemplate on and discuss about the transformation of economic growth pattern, hence starting a new round of "economic transformation."

However, economic transformation is hard to fully comprehend and even harder to achieve. Today, the Chinese economy is still faltering on the road of transformation. Why?

(1) For a long time, economists dedicated to studying economic transformation focus on the economic structure itself, believing that improving the efficiency of economic growth, such as promoting technological progress and improving economic system, is enough to transform the extensive economic growth Pattern into the intensive one, and ignoring the particularity of energy environment utilization in this process. The biggest particularity lies in the scarcity of energy environment and the constraints it brings. To a certain extent, the economic transformation arising from the needs of economic growth does not pay attention to these constraints. At best, it only treats them as a boundary condition. Therefore, for a long time, the economic transformation has been proceeding under the condition of "soft constraints of energy environment." Looking back, this kind of economic transformation cannot be truly successful. Under the soft constraints of energy environment, governments at all levels do not have enough motivation to promote economic transformation.

(2) Most experts engaged in energy environmental protection research only focus on their own technical fields. Of course, they can understand the challenges and difficulties faced by China's energy and environmental fields more accurately and put forward strategies to strengthen energy environmental protection. For example, corresponding laws and regulations can be introduced to raise the standards of energy and environmental protection and clarify the rewards and punishments for environmental

behaviors. However, from the perspective of the entire life cycle of energy and environmental protection, these laws and regulations can only be governance in the "end-point sense." This is because we can strengthen the protection of energy resources and the environment from the technical level, but we must know whether such protection measures can be effectively transmitted to the source (i.e., energy, resources, and environment) and what kind of measures will really affect economic transformation; there is obviously a long and complicated transmission path. If we simplify this transmission path to "rule of law," it is definitely not enough to protect the energy, resources, and environment. As a result, from the end point of view, the energy, resources, and environment have not been protected, while from the source point of view, the economic structure is still extensive, and economic transformation is far away.

The problems caused by the two extreme perspectives are obvious. Considering the strong correlation between economic transformation and energy, resource, and environmental protection, what perspective do we need most? It should be the comprehensive perspective of economy–energy–environment, which is called the perspective (or method) of general equilibrium in economics. To put it simply, it is to examine the effectiveness of economic development under the constraints of the energy environment. This perspective can help avoid detours when carrying out studies in this regard.

In fact, to understand economic transformation based on the (constraints) perspective of energy, resources, and environment, the key is to incorporate the need for energy and environmental protection into the strategy and decision-making process of economic transformation, especially the internal relationship between the two. For example, the cost of energy and environment needs to be calculated and converted into shadow prices, and then included into economic policies in various ways. This is also the best bridge between economic research and energy environmental protection. According to the well-known environmental economist Nordhaus, this is also the best choice to "make a balance between economy and environmental protection."

15.2 China's Economic Transition Under the Constraints of Energy and Environment

After determining the basic cognitive methods, the next question is how to fully understand the meaning of economic transformation. In Wu Jinglian's

The Choice of China's Growth Model (2013), the CPC Central Committee noticed the shortcomings of the original economic growth model by around 1995, began to formulate policies on transforming the mode of economic growth (changed to the "economic development pattern," which essentially means the same thing), and achieved phased results. Although the fundamental transformation of the economic development pattern has not manifested as expected, and there are even some setbacks, it is undeniable that the entire academia and industry have accepted the concept of transforming the economic development pattern and realized the great necessity of economic transformation for the sustainable development of China's economy. However, the understanding of the connotation of economic transformation or the transformation of economic development pattern still appears to be slightly inadequate and quite controversial.

In a review of the development history of the concept of economic transformation itself, we can find that in the initial stage, it was completely equivalent to "transforming the mode of economic growth." In combination with the economic situation at that time, we estimate that the first or primary meaning of the so-called "economic transformation" is to determine how to keep consolidating this institutional transformation after the initial success of the reform and opening up in 1978 and the transition from a planned economy to a market economy, and then release new productivity through further reforms. In other words, after the planning system was gradually replaced by the market economy system, owing to inadequate experience in market economy construction, there had been serious inefficiency in social and economic development, which had weakened the motivation to press ahead. This is reflected in the fact that we mainly rely on extensive economic growth mode rather than intensive mode to promote economic development (Wu, 2013). This is obviously an unsustainable development mode under the absolute law of diminishing economies of scale and therefore has become the main source of economic transformation. It should be said that such an understanding is not inaccurate at that time. However, compared with the global trend of protection of energy, resources, and environment, such judgment is also biased. That is, if only from the perspective of efficiency and diminishing returns to scale, the direction of economic transformation will remain in the efficient use of all economic resources (including energy, resources, environment, and labor capital); as long as these resources are effectively utilized and a variety of industries are developed on this basis, the economic transformation will be successful. And we are indeed working hard in this direction through various efforts, such as curbing the irrational "investment hunger."

However, the problem is not that simple. Only a few years later, the efforts to transform the economic growth mode began to become futile. Why? When China joined the WTO in 2001, there was a strong global demand for Chinese-made products, and China became the "world factory." In this process, we continue to increase efforts to achieve the transformation of economic development pattern, especially to promote technological progress and industrial upgrading to increase the added value of industrial products. A considerable number of mainstream economists firmly believe that as long as China adheres to the path of open economy, technological progress, and industrial upgrading, we will surely achieve economic transformation soon. Unfortunately, after more than 20 years of hard work, our economic transformation did not arrive as expected (Wu, 2013). The reason is that the economic transformation actually has an important second meaning.

The second meaning of economic transformation is precisely related to globalization. If the reform and opening up after 1978 benefited from globalization, then after 2001, while benefiting from the global free trade, Chinese economy is also subtly changing the connotation of economic transformation. As mentioned above, after joining the WTO, China's economic development has overcome many shortcomings and achieved greater results in related industries, such as a larger global market share and stronger international competitiveness, with the total factor productivity (TFP) of the national economy maintaining a relatively high level. The outcome is, however, environmental devastation. It is attributed to the enormous economic scale, that is, even if we improve the efficiency of each unit of resources and environment to the utmost, we cannot stop the huge pressure on the limited resources and environment brought by the global market demand for Chinese manufactured goods in just 10 years. Moreover, at the beginning of the promotion of economic transformation, we did not include the marketization of energy, resources, and environment into the scope of reform, which means that from the beginning, economic transformation has evolved in an unbalanced state. As a result, despite the partial success of technological transformation, the transformation of resources and the environment lags behind economic efficiency and eventually drags down the effectiveness of the entire transformation. As mentioned in Chapter 2, "there are four major driving factors that drag down economic efficiency, namely capital deepening, energy intensity, industrial structure, and energy structure" (Chen, 2013).

In his book *Energy, Environment and Economic Transformation in China* (2013), Chen Shiyi takes energy intensity as the key analysis object, which is of great significance. If we only keep the connotation of economic transformation at the level of capital deepening (the scale remains diminishing), then our understanding of economic transformation is not comprehensive enough and unable to "advance with the times." If we cannot change the main constraints of economic transformation from efficiency constraints to resource and environmental constraints as quickly as possible, then even if we can promote technological transformation and industrial upgrading in the manufacturing industry in a short period of time, we cannot really respond to the latest trends in global energy, resources, and environment changes, thus losing the opportunity to solve the problem of economic transformation. I think the understanding of this point is very helpful for the theoretical circles and industry professionals to re-understand the relationship between economic transformation and environmental protection and thus accelerate the adjustment of economic transformation strategies and countermeasures.

After understanding the second meaning of economic transformation, we can understand that the current economic transformation is under the constraints of resources and environment, but it has embarked on an economic growth path of "soft constraints on energy, resources and the environment." As a result, the direction of economic transformation has gradually become clear, that is, turning the soft constraints of resource environment into "hard constraints" and incorporating economic growth into the framework of these hard constraints.

15.3 The "Green Road" of China's Economic Transformation

China's economic transformation is facing hard constraints from energy and environment, but hard constraints do not mean "hard policies" or "rigid policies" to achieve economic transformation through environmental protection. For one thing, this is not in line with the law of economic transformation. Moreover, the social economy will pay a great price for this. To achieve hard constraints and soft landing at the same time, the key is to gain a deep understanding of the interaction relationship between environment and economic growth, and then use an organic relationship to achieve a balanced development between them.

(1) *The root of the soft constraints on energy, resources, and environment lies in the lack of an effective and precise pricing mechanism.* Regarding the relationship between environment and economic development, the most classic theory in the world is the Environmental Kuznets Curve (EKC). Although the Kuznets Curve (KC) is mainly derived from scenarios in developed countries, the theoretical explanation behind it is also applicable to developing countries. However, as the largest developing country, China has a relatively special system, mechanism, and reform path. This greatest particularity is reflected in the fact that in the past 30 years, China has been committed to replacing the planning mechanism with a market mechanism (this can also be called the first round of economic transformation), that is to say, in the long process of economic transformation, we really attach great importance to the role of the market-based pricing mechanism, and in fact, we have also tried to incorporate all factors (including some energy and environmental factors) into this pricing mechanism through various policies, so as to let prices play a role in clearing the market and improving the efficiency of factor resources allocation. In this regard, all sectors of society have a broad consensus. However, the question is, compared with ordinary factors, do energy, resources, and environmental factors obey ordinary pricing mechanisms and principles? Judging from the utilization process and results of energy, resources, and environment, it is obviously different from ordinary factors.

Among them, the biggest difference is that the use of environment will produce negative externalities, that is, the direct market price cannot really reflect and then clear this imbalance caused by negative externalities. This determines that the use of market mechanisms in the field of energy and environment has its special features, that is, to find the "real price" (Chen, 2013) behind it through the analysis of its negative externalities, and to analyze the factors that determine this price. In this regard, we can try to find this "real price" from the perspective of the shadow price of carbon emissions. I think this is a theoretical breakthrough that truly applies the principles of marketization to the coordination of the relationship between China's environment and economic development. The main reason why this is a theoretical breakthrough is that only by finding this real price can it be enough to determine the economic rationality of various energy and environmental policies. That is to say, no matter what method is adopted to promote environmental protection, we must adhere to the principle of reasonable prices and make the use of energy environmental protection (or sewage discharge) cost-equivalent. Only in this way can the energy and environmental sector be able to play a role in influencing the transformation of economic development pattern and use its hard constraints to force economic transformation.

Of course, it is not easy to use shadow prices to reflect the actual costs of the energy and environmental sector and force economic transformation. The biggest difficulty is that the level of shadow prices varies greatly among different industries and regions. Therefore, the motivation to cut emissions, of course, varies from person to person. If we do not pay enough attention to this "actual situation" and deal with it in accordance with the "actual situation," then the result will be a one-size-fits-all approach to energy and environmental protection, and result in "hard landing of environmental protection." The coexistence of overexertion and underperformance will undermine the effectiveness of economic transformation. The question is, what are the differences? Chen Shiyi conducted an in-depth analysis in this regard. Through the distinction and comparison of 38 different types of industries, she found that the shadow price of carbon emissions from heavy industry is lower than that of light industry, and the shadow price of carbon emissions in economically backward areas is lower than that in developed areas. Such a conclusion is of course completely tenable in theory, but there is still a long way to go before it can be implemented in practice. The biggest sticking point is how to overcome the interest groups behind industries and regions, so that the emission reductions of different regions and industries truly obey the laws behind them. Because, in theory, we can take the national welfare output as the overall objective function, but in reality, different industrial sectors and different regions often give priority to the welfare output of their own sectors and regions. In this case, it is inevitable that there will be some kind of interest game, and then change the optimal decision. Despite this, Chen Shiyi's views still have a lot of application space, that is, our policies should be based on the basic principle of achieving coordinated development of energy, environment, and economy at the lowest cost and achieve the economic transformation under the constraints of energy and environment at a smaller cost.

(2) *How to realize the hard constraints of energy environment on economic transformation*? To achieve hard constraints, in addition to hard

methods, more attention should be paid to "soft landing," especially the study of the organic relationship between energy environmental utilization and emission change trends and economic development and transformation, and then on the basis of fully understanding and respecting the laws, let energy environmental protection and economic transformation achieve the effect of synergistic development. The source of China's economic growth can generally be divided into factorial and non-factorial. The latter can also be simply summarized as TFP, which is the residual part that cannot be explained clearly by factor contribution. In general, the proportion of non-factorial parts determines the quality and stage of a country's economic growth and also affects the effectiveness of economic transformation. With the deepening of research, the non-factorial driving force is divided into three parts, namely technological change, scale effect, and structural change. According to relevant research, technological change and structural change have a great influence on China's economic growth in the past 40 years, but the scale effect is small (Chen, 2013). Moreover, in recent years, as the effects of structural changes have fluctuated and weakened, TFP has shown a downward trend as a whole, which has substantially affected the process of economic transformation. The question is, what factors make the effect of structural change sometimes weak and sometimes strong? Chen Shiyi's research found that the structural change effect remained strong from 1981 to 2001 and made greater contribution to economic growth. After that, the structural change effect gradually weakened from 2001 to 2006. So, what had happened during this period?

In fact, the meaning of so-called structural changes ostensibly refers to the internal industrial structure of the economy, such as the ratio of heavy industry to light industry, but behind it is the level of factor input. In general, heavy industry is naturally energy, resource, and environment intensive, while light industry is labor intensive. In other words, changes in the industrial structure are driven by factors, especially the factor allocation mechanism, which is inseparable from China's economic reform process. If we examine China's economic reform process in depth, we can find that all major reform strategies will affect the factor market to varying degrees. For example, the rural agricultural reform that began in 1978 improved agricultural productivity and released a huge amount of rural labor. This created a labor factor foundation for the subsequent industrial economic development, especially the labor-intensive, export-processing industrial economy. For another example, the reform of urban SOEs that began in 1984 focused on "delegating powers" and "transferring profits," which caused a large number of heavy industrial enterprises to consider turning to produce profitable light industrial products that are urgently needed by the market. Later, as the SOE reform entered the "deep-water zone," China began to implement the strategy of "invigorating large enterprises while relaxing control over small ones," thus closing down a large number of small and medium-sized inefficient and energy-intensive enterprises. These have loosened the energy and environment consumption on the economic level and altered the mechanism of factor allocation to create incentives for structural transformation. However, after this process entered the 21st century, as large SOEs have regained their strength, they ventured into various fields and re-launched "high-quality" construction projects, which have greatly increased their dependence on energy and environmental consumption and dragged down the effectiveness of structural transformation.

From the above process, it can be seen that the fluctuations in energy environmental consumption are closely related to the various economic policies that are developed for the factor allocation mechanism, and the energy environmental consumption will have an impact on the economic structure and eventually affect the economic transformation effect. When talking about the relationship between economic transformation and energy environmental protection, we should focus neither only on the end-of-life pollution control nor only on the construction of the so-called "environmental protection system." More importantly, it is necessary to understand the linkages and logic from the perspective of economic policy lever and to pay more attention to the use of "green" economic policies to promote environmental protection and economic transformation.

In short, if the above-mentioned inherent logical relationship exists between energy environment and economic transformation, then according to this logical relationship, we can at least carry out the next steps in the following aspects to promote economic transformation and green development. First, promote ownership reforms including the reform of SOEs to further stimulate the efficiency of factor allocation. Second, further adjust industrial policies to make industrial development more suitable for the characteristics and needs of the development stage. After all, the current pressure on the energy environment is excessively concentrated on the heavy chemical industry. Third, further improve energy conservation and environmental protection policies, improve laws and regulations in the field of environmental protection, and play a positive role in the formation of "hard constraints" by the system.

Chapter 16

Free Trade Zone Construction and Economic Transition from the Perspective of Green Development

The main purpose of free trade zone construction is to promote the liberalization of trade and investment, which will affect the environmental quality of host countries and bring a variety of impacts. For the sake of environmental protection, the free trade zone must be brought into full play, which requires the transformation of the existing development pattern through effective institutional design and arrangement. In particular, we must change the factor endowment structure that relies solely on low-cost environmental factors, so as to let environmental factors continue to restore their original prices and values along with the liberalization of trade and investment. Only in this way can China (Shanghai) Free Trade Zone (or "Shanghai FTZ" for short) truly play its role in improving trade efficiency, promoting green development, and fulfilling the grand strategic goal of building a beautiful China.

16.1 The Background of Free Trade Zone Construction

Under the guidance of the *China (Shanghai) Pilot Free Trade Zone Overall Plan* issued by the State Council, the Shanghai FTZ was established in October 2013, becoming the first free trade zone of this kind in China. It shoulders great missions such as "accelerating the transformation of government functions in the new era, exploring the ways for innovating management mode, promoting trade and investment facilitation, and accumulating experiences for comprehensively deepening the reforms and opening wider to the outside world the State Council, China (Shanghai) Pilot Free Trade Zone Overall Plan, 2013." However, in the tide of constructing a new global free trade order dominated by the US, China has to cope with new challenges and re-establish its position in the international trading system, which determines the top priority of Shanghai FTZ to be "promoting trade and investment facilitation." In order to profit from the economic benefits generated by free trade and investment, China has no other choice but to press ahead with reforms in all aspects and devote itself into the globalization of resource allocation (Yuan, 2013). To this end, China must deepen reforms and promote development by further liberalizing trade and investment. The construction of Shanghai FTZ is only one step to achieve this goal. However, things are never quite as simple as that. There is no doubt that the liberalization of trade and investment can benefit both the society and economy, but some issues are indeed controversial. The most typical one is whether the liberalization of trade and investment will affect environmental quality, particularly the environmental quality of developing countries that are exporters of trade.

This typical issue was first raised in the 1990s. At that time, the North American Free Trade Agreement (NAFTA) was just signed and brought into effect. Later, Grossman and Krueger (1993) noticed a dramatic decline in the environmental quality of Mexico — the largest developing country among the contracting parties — which sparked economists to probe into the relationship between free trade and environmental quality, and then came up with several important theories including the Environmental Kuznets Curve (EKC), Pollution Haven Effect (PHE), and Pollution Haven Hypothesis (PHH). Up to this day, developing countries have been suffering from intensified environmental problems, such as the large-scale air pollution (i.e., fog and haze weather) in China, which are more or less attributed to international trade. Well then, how should we look at the relationship between free trade and environmental protection? As far as the Shanghai FTZ is concerned, will it affect China's environmental quality in the process of promoting trade and investment liberalization? Is it possible for us to transform China's traditional development pattern by taking advantage of the Shanghai FTZ, thereby making it contribute to the national green development?

16.2 The Relationship Between Free Trade and Environmental Protection: Theory and Practice

With respect to the relationship between free trade and environmental protection, there are two opposite opinions in the international academic community. One opinion is that free trade goes against environmental protection, because "under different levels of environmental regulation, the worldwide trade and flow of goods will inevitably increase environmental risks and endanger environmental quality" (Gallagher, 2008), and "international trade will accelerate excessive exploitation and utilization of various resources. For example, the ivory trade endangers the survival of elephants, the export-oriented Chinese economy seriously affects air quality, and the export of timber from tropical rainforests interrupts the sustainable forest development" (Copeland and Taylor, 1994). According to this opinion, the greatest impact of free trade on environmental quality is that countries are likely to weaken their environmental regulation in order to gain more competitive edge in free trade, therefore accelerating their environmental degradation. This process seems like to "race to the bottom," with the "bottom" here referring to the "bottom line of environmental protection."

Contrary to the above opinion, some economists hold that free trade can improve the eco-environment of trading countries instead of destroying it. That is to say, trade can produce an "income spillover effect," making the wealth effect spread to environmental protection and other fields. As for the impact of free trade on the environmental quality of developing countries, the argument of this opinion is that free trade enables developing countries to obtain clean and eco-friendly technologies more easily, pursue innovation more firmly under the pressure from increasingly strict environmental regulation, and ultimately make environmental protection and trade liberalization complement each other (Porter and Van der Linde, 1995). In this case, what free trade brings is not "racing to the bottom" but "racing to the top."

Both the above two opinions are convincing to a certain extent. So, how about the effect of free trade on environmental quality? A variety of studies have divided such effect into three types: Scale effect, technology effect, and structure effect (Korves, 2011). The reason for opposite opinions is due to the contrasting relations of these three effects. First, when the scale effect of free trade is predominant, its negative impact on environmental quality will be more prominent, because larger-scale economic output is sure to consume more resources. Second, when the technology effect of free trade is predominant, the environmental impact of free trade appears to be positive, because technological progress will improve the environmental output effect and level of protection. Third, when the structure effect of free trade is predominant, the impact on environmental quality will be unknown, which is attributed to two scenarios: If free trade reinforces the existing resource endowment of a country, it tends to expand the use of low-cost environmental pollutions when the environmental regulation is not strict, thereby deteriorating its environmental quality. However, when its environmental regulation becomes strict, the country tends to adjust up the price of environmental resources to change its trade endowment advantage, hence optimizing its environmental quality.

From the above analysis, it can be seen that whether and how free trade affects the environment actually depends on the type of dominant effect of free trade, that is, environmental quality is neither positively nor negatively related to free trade itself. The key point is that, in the process of promoting free trade and construction of free trade zones, we must choose an appropriate development path or pattern and try to give full play to the positive effect of free trade, such as technology effect and structure effect.

From the perspective of resources and environmental protection, based on various understandings of sustainable development, the West has two main ideas in the choice of social and economic development models. One is to continue to follow the resource-intensive development path (known as "Model A"). As the most extreme theory of growth supremacy, this road has basically no market in Western developed countries, and the concept of sustainable development has been deeply rooted in the hearts of the people. As a result, as early as the 1970s, the environmentalist movement in Western countries gave birth to a second concept of development, that is, to take the path of "green" growth, especially represented by the concept of "sustainable development" proposed by the UN in 1988. Since then, Western countries have basically agreed with this concept and have effectively adopted various policies and actions to carry out tangible "green governance" and achieved remarkable results.

Today, the overall environment of Western countries is better than that of developing countries. One of the indispensable conditions for the success of such a development model is the transfer of the country's high-polluting and energy-consuming industries with the help of increasingly convenient international trade and investment and, at the same time, export of their own "green and clean resources" (i.e., energy, resources, and the environment) in a limited or selective way (e.g., in the agreement of inter-regional trade integration, the trade varieties of specific regions are limited). Although the results show that this seems to be caused by the participation of various factors in the global division of labor in the background of globalization, if all trade is truly two-way and freely flowing, developing countries will not accept such a high proportion of polluting industries and will completely ignore the introduction of clean industries, and the environmental governance of developed countries will not be so smooth. Among them ,a factor that cannot be ignored is how to strengthen technical effects and structural effects.

On one hand, the free trade zone, as the name suggests, must increase the degree of liberalization of trade and investment, allowing goods and factors to truly flow in the international market through this pipeline, and then promote the domestic endowment to obtain the greatest degree of return in the international market. However, this is not the full content of the free trade zone. To this day, we have begun to study the so-called "negative list management," which was something that we did not dare to do or think about at the beginning of China's reform and opening up more than 30 years ago. At that time, what we were worried about was lack of foreign investment and foreign trade. However, more than 30 years ago, the US and other Western countries set up a large number of "negative lists" for the free trade zone and devised many regulations on trade objects and types. From an economic point of view, this is actually a "distorted allocation of resources," that is, in the process of trade liberalization, the cost of certain traded goods has been raised through various policies, and at the same time the relative cost of other traded goods has been reduced through the "free trade zone," thereby creating and highlighting the so-called endowment advantage of certain traded goods. In fact, everyone now understands (perhaps most people do not really understand) that such costs should have been restored through domestic price signals. However, it is difficult to reverse the price signals of factors such as resources and environment in the country. For example, the government and the market need to play repeated games. However, if the negative list of the free trade zone is used to act as a price signal, it will reduce a lot of social game costs, and at the same time achieve a certain control over the flow of trade and investment. This is the second significance of the free trade zone construction to the choice of social and economic development mode, and it can also be understood as the so-called "anti-driving mechanism." A broader understanding is that the free trade zone is not only forcing the government, enterprises, and other subjects. If the policy is reasonable and effective, it will directly force the "price formation in the field of resources and environment."

In this regard, in view of the current highly free-flowing and unreasonable international division of labor system, in the design of the "negative list management" of the free trade zone, various resources and environmental protection control policies should be continued, and more constraints should be imposed to makes the outflow of resources and environmental factors increasingly difficult, while promoting the active inflow of these factors. It is important to avoid repeating previous mistakes, so that high-pollution and high-energy-consuming industries are barred from continuing to flow inward through the free trade zone under the name of "freedom and openness."

16.3 Analysis on the Environmental Effect of Free Trade Zone Construction

In addition to the above-mentioned Model A and Model B, Prof. Zhu Dajian of Tongji University also proposed another development model, namely Model C (Zhu, 2010). This model emphasizes "appropriate" sustainable development and focuses on gradually increasing the greenness of the national economy by expanding economic increments. Its essence is to provide a "gradual approach" to sustainable development, take a "medium value"; it believes that the pace of environmental protection should not be too hasty and should be adapted to the stage of social and economic development. When "development and backwardness" remain the main contradictions, we should not completely transfer our attention and energy to the field of resources and environment. It should be said that such a model (or theory) is more in line with China's practical experience of reform and opening up in 1978, that is, incremental reforms are used to gradually eliminate distortions in the market and solve structural problems in stocks through incremental reforms.

The problem is that, from the perspective of foreign practice, once the trend of sustainable development is enlightened, it will be extremely "radical" in the initial stage. For example, in the US, the environmentalist movement opens the gates to the US, after that, the government and all walks of life all used "green" to advertise themselves, so that any policy in any field will be resisted if it conflicts with "environmental protection," including the "free trade zone" policy. Conversely, there are also some countries that have not really started the sustainable development process, and if the resources and environmental conditions continue to deteriorate, they will basically end up in a dismal state. As far as the current situation is concerned, stimulated by factors such as globalization and informatization, our sustainable development can be said to have reached a very important selection threshold, that is, on the issue of resource and environmental protection, should we proceed at a "constant speed" or at an "accelerated speed?"

Viewed in an objective manner, the domestic environmental protection field looks very lively. However, fundamentally, we still have a long way to go before achieving "true environmentalist enlightenment," and we have not yet reached the stage of distinguishing who is "dark green" and who is "light green." It must be admitted that many government officials, scholars, and entrepreneurs are still bound by the traditional thinking of growth supremacy. It is hoped that the starting point of all work should be based on economic growth, and the evaluation of all work should also be based on GDP. In this context, it is difficult to say that the relevant reforms of the Shanghai FTZ do not have such considerations, that is, to optimize the allocation of resources through institutional reforms and the opening of related fields, introduce external capital, improve international competitiveness, and inject freshness into the economy. If this is the case, the opening and construction of the free trade zone is more in line with the development concept of the above-mentioned Model C: On one hand, let the economy continue to accelerate; on the other hand, the utilization speed of resources and environment is relatively slow, and the current resource and environment dilemma can be resolved through a gradual approach.

In fact, judging from the will and deployment of the Central Government, if the free trade zone only stays at such a goal and stage, it will obviously not be able to meet the urgent needs of the development of the current situation. Among them, structural adjustment is obviously the top priority. For this reason, whether it is the development positioning of the "five in one," the "joint prevention and joint governance of pollution," or the "action plan for the prevention and control of air pollution," it can be seen that the Central Government is responding to the new developments that may emerge in the next stage. Various preparatory work started with a round of "environmental protection appeals," If the development trend of the free trade zone is still only to promote growth, it will conflict with such efforts, and it does not conform to the Central Government's administrative intentions.

Finally, how should the free trade zone use its own development to assist the goal of structural adjustment and transformation of the growth model? In addition to the concept of "burden alleviation," there is another important possibility that through the construction of a free trade zone, free trade can be used to obtain the "structural effect" that is beneficial to environmental protection, which is to promote factor endowment transformation, using free trade zones to attract capital and promote the formation of global or regional "capital highlands" in some regions of China, allowing capital to gradually become our new competitive edge, and replacing relatively "cheap" resources and environment with more "cheaper" capital. In this way, without forcing "burden alleviation" (avoiding polluting industries), social and economic competitiveness and "sustainable development" can go hand in hand, or it can be understood as a kind of "burden alleviation" based on competitive advantage. In fact, this is the key to why we must promote the integration of finance, trade, and shipping to fight external competition.

16.4 How Can Free Trade Zones Collaborate with "Green Development" Synergies? Policies and Prospects

From the perspective of the choice of development model, in the above three models, the strategic space available for us to move has actually become smaller and smaller; even if the Model C of "progressive sustainable development" currently has the approval of the government, it could not hold on for a few more years. As the experience of other countries has shown, the enlightenment and appeal of environmentalism is not a "gradual" development process. Under the increasingly tight environmental degradation situation, it is very likely that it will rise overnight from the central to the local level. There are at least some signs to prove it. At that time, all strategies, policies, and measures to improve efficiency will have to face a challenge, that is, how to synergize with the endogenous nature of "building a beautiful China?" As far as the fundamental issue of coordination is concerned, the key lies in how to open up the common point of "optimizing resource allocation" between different policies.

From the perspective of allocation efficiency, the essence of "green development" is to optimize the allocation of resources and environment, and the direct manifestation is to restore the underestimated prices of resources and the environment. How to do so? Under the socialist market economy system, the easiest way is to gradually increase their use prices through control, until the quality of the resource environment is restored to a normal level. In fact, compared with the European and American market economy systems, we should have a greater advantage in this regard. However, the complexity of the problem lies in the fact that the invisible hand of the "market" does not make environmental control efforts fulfill its wishes. It will use its own power to offset the government's environmental protection efforts. For example, the most typical one is to "vote with feet" to resist countries and regions that strictly enforce environmental regulations, which is to form a so-called "pollution paradise," that is, industries are shifting to countries and regions with "less pollution control and lower costs." This is precisely the essence of our repeated control of the environment for more than 30 years. To put it bluntly, it is because our resources and environmental products and services are not as expensive as those of developed countries in Europe and America. This is reflected in the global trading system, that is, there has been a large-scale flow of resources and environmental elements from China to other countries. After a long period of accumulation, resulting in the internal and external environment quality imbalance. In the end, even European and American developed countries, which are importing countries of resources and environment, must introduce policies to oppose this imbalance in the environmental field (e.g., various regional trade integration agreements specifically stipulate environmental protection).

Therefore, in line with the needs of "green development," it is urgent to solve the internal and external imbalances in the field of resources and the environment. At the same time, whoever started the trouble should end it — since international trade is the cause of this imbalance, it is necessary for us to improve the terms of trade on the basis of strengthening internal environmental control to reverse the imbalance. Here, the free trade zone should make a difference.

Similarly, in accordance with the need to optimize the allocation of resources, the starting point of setting up a "free trade zone" is itself to eliminate various internal and external differences and imbalances, such as the internal and external differences in institutional costs, the internal and external costs of goods and services, and capital and technological elements. It is worth noting that, in general, for most commodities and factors, internal costs are higher than external costs, but the opposite is true for the resources and environment alone. This is actually enough to provide us with an important enlightenment for the development of the free trade zone and the volatile foreign and bilateral free trade agreements, that is, how can we bring the costs and prices of our resources and environment into line with international standards while further enhancing the freedom of trade and investment and reducing the costs of investment and trade? In other words, can the free trade zone and free trade agreement serve to solve the imbalance in the field of resources and environment? This is in fact the biggest point of synergy between the reform of the "free trade zone" and the demand of "green development."

On the surface, it is difficult to do this, but in fact, as long as there is a long-term imbalance (inconsistency between cost and price), all theories tell us that the market can clear this imbalance. The only problem is how we will reasonably use various methods, including the free trade zone, to improve our terms of trade and strive for a more free and equal market basis for resource and environmental factors.

Specifically, how do we build a bridge between the free trade zone and "green development?" If we can understand the free trade zone as a certain functional zone that further promotes free trade, then the essence of this problem lies in how to correctly understand and resolve the relationship between free trade and environmental protection. As mentioned above, there is a dilemma between the two. There is a certain correlation between free trade and the environmental degradation of developing countries, especially the expansion of free trade, so that the result of the introduction of global competition has been a relaxation of environmental governance and constraints and a decline in quality in the so-called "race to the bottom" for developing countries, but this is not the full effect of free trade in the environmental field. In addition to the abovementioned "evil" side, free trade also has a positive side to the environment.

There are also many theories to explain the advantages, including the promotion of economic growth through free trade, which has greatly improved the investment capacity of developing countries in environmental infrastructure, that is, improved capacity building for sustainable development. If free trade truly realizes the free flow of factors, then while resources and environmental factors flow out of developing countries, it will also help developing countries introduce environmental protection technologies and services at a lower cost. In addition, the marketization results driven by free trade will also greatly improve the efficiency of resource and environmental utilization in developing countries from the institutional level, that is, increase environmental productivity. Finally, the free flow of goods and services will inevitably drive the flow of "thoughts," including sustainable development ideas and concepts, which is particularly important in the long-term environmental governance of developing countries. In fact, the development model and cognition, including "sustainable development" itself, are actually related to the establishment and expansion of global markets (In the 19th century, the famous British economist Milton Friedman once asserted that "A free market of goods correspond to a free market of ideas). It now appears that the "ideas" include both non-commodity "services" (such as environmental consulting) and non-commodity "ideas and cognitions." It can be seen from this that although the disadvantaged developing countries have caused environmental pollution due to free trade, free trade and "green development" are still mutually complementary. Without seeing this, we will not be able to take full advantage of the reform opportunity of "reopening" to improve our environment.

In this way, as far as the free trade zone is concerned, in order to protect the resources and environment in the pattern of further opening up, it is necessary to exploit its strengths and avoid weaknesses and give full play to the positive aspects of free trade. On one hand, it is necessary to adhere to the principle of marketization to allocate resources and environmental elements, that is, to cancel various policies that artificially suppress the prices of resources and the environment. Under the premise of ensuring national economic security, resources and environmental factors should be allocated through financial, trade, and other means. Circulation in the international market is extremely necessary for improving the utilization efficiency or productivity of our domestic resources and environmental elements. At the same time, it is also conducive to allow the dynamics of the international market to smooth the price gap between us and developed countries in terms of resources and environmental factors. On the other hand, a more realistic question is how to further use the free trade zone to bring into play its active role in introducing resources and environmental services, technology, knowledge, and ideas, to further promote our skill building in sustainable development. In this way, it can be combined with the "negative list management" of monitoring "environmental pollution discharge," and truly exert the influence and role of the free trade zone in "building a beautiful China."

16.5 Summary

The construction of the Shanghai FTZ is already started as scheduled, offering the biggest development opportunity for Shanghai. On the front line of China's reforms, Shanghai not only takes on the mission of deepening the national reform and opening up but also benefits from the dividends from all reforms. For this reason, in addition to discussing Shanghai FTZ construction from the perspectives of finance, economy, trade, and system, we also need to make further examination to confirm whether this free trade zone has any value in the sense of sustainable development. That is, from the perspective of resource conservation and environmental protection, how will Shanghai FTZ affect China's "five-in-one" strategy and "green development" target?

Since Shanghai FTZ is to shoulder the historical mission of deepening the reform and opening up, does it "increase" or "alleviate" the burden on Chinese development? According to the author, after going through the rapid "low-quality" growth for more than 30 years, our society and economy have accumulated a lot of "negative assets," including overweight industrial structure, and less effective systems and mechanisms, resulting in inefficient resource utilization and serious environmental pollution. These developments, which seem like "negative energy," have been seriously eroding our economy and society. In this context, the way to continue reforms and advance socio-economic development has become clear, that is, "burden alleviation." It is time to clear away some of the "negative assets" that are detrimental to the healthy and comprehensive development of society and economy — all possible means are worth a try as long as they can help China get rid of the drawbacks in its economic structure. This is the core of building an upgraded version of Chinese economy and the major background for the construction of Shanghai FTZ. If we are only about to traipse on the same old road taken over the past 30 years, why should we promote the construction of a FTZ with great fanfare?

If the free trade zone is a kind of reform and in-depth development of the finance, trade, and industry policies, the essential difference between it and the 1978 reform and opening up and the 2001 WTO accession is that the latter two events are a kind of "outside-to-in" development, while the free trade zone is "inside-to-out" development. It seems like digging a hole in a wall for the purpose of "dredging" rather than "absorbing," thereby channeling the internal "negative assets" to the outside and lightening the internal heavy burden, namely "alleviating burdens" on the national economy.

Based on this understanding, it will be easy to interpret all the policies set by the Central Government for the free trade zone. These policies seem like "increments," that is, clearing some institutional and industrial obstacles; but compared with previous policies, we are not sure how many "siphon effects" these new policies will have on the international market and capital. Nevertheless, with these policies, a large number of domestic capital and industries can find a path of "outflow" more easily. From the perspective of policy effect, a so-called "anti-driving mechanism" is formed; but from the perspective of efficiency, the most extensive domestic sectors, markets and industries are going to be squeezed. If the market has long-term expectations for the free trade zone policies, the degree of such squeeze will gradually increase. In other words, such "burden alleviation" seems to be detrimental to domestic capital accumulation and efficiency improvement. However, in the long run, "burden alleviation" will help us squeeze out the bubble, treat the "investment hunger" that Chinese government and market have formed in the past, and turn to "efficiency hunger" instead. In view of this, the "burden alleviation" effect brought about by the free trade zone construction will help us to free up our hands to truly improve the environment, increase energy efficiency, and achieve green development from a structural perspective.

Chapter 17

Legal and Economic Analysis of the Lawsuit of Xiaoling Cement Plant Against the Ministry of Environmental Protection

"Small Cement Plant v. Ministry of Environmental Protection" was once the headline news of major environmental media and columns. In fact, everyone is equal before the law, or there are only rights and wrongs before the law. In the opinion of the author, this lawsuit has typical significance in the special period when the whole society is carrying out extraordinary environmental protection. It reflects the complicated relationship between environmental protection and socio-economic development. An analysis of this lawsuit may help us fully understand the current situation of China's environmental protection and do a better job in this regard in the future.

17.1 Why did Xiaoling Cement Plant Sue the MEP

The cause of this lawsuit is not complicated. A reconstruction project of Xiaoling Cement Plant, based in Harbin City, Heilongjiang Province, had passed the environmental assessment acceptance of the Heilongjiang Provincial Department of Environmental Protection, but the Ministry of Environmental Protection (MEP) rejected this decision, because this project did not cover any plan for relocating the residents within 500 m of the plant (later revised as 300 m) as required by the national health department, and seven resident representatives applied to the MEP for administrative reconsideration, hence leading to the rejection of the project.

This lawsuit is of some referential value for other similar cases. Xiaoling Cement Plant was built in 1935, much earlier than the duration of residence of the surrounding residents, and the reconstruction project was planned on the original site, instead of expanding the scope. Because of this, Xiaoling Cement Plant argued that residents should move out of the scope of possible impact by themselves, but this reason did not become the focus of dispute between the prosecution and the defense. Based on his understanding of the project transformation technology, the author finds that the environmental impact of the transformed cement production is even lower than that of the original project (which can be measured by pollutant emissions). In other words, residents around the cement plant are to be benefited from the reconstruction project. Even so, the reconstruction project is a "latecomer" relative to the residents, and it is more likely to be regarded as an "infringing party" in the law, which means that as far as the law is concerned, Xiaoling Cement Plant will most likely lose the lawsuit. Anyway, is the "first come, first come" rule so important from the perspective of welfare? Moreover, will the possible loss of this plant have any adverse welfare effect? All of these issues will be explained in this chapter.

17.2 Analytical Perspective

Regarding the above-mentioned cause of action, it can be analyzed from two perspectives: Legal perspective and economic perspective, the former emphasizes fairness, while the latter stresses efficiency (welfare).

(1) From a legal perspective, whether there are definite legal provisions on the standard for the living environment at the periphery of the reconstruction project is the main basis for judging this lawsuit. If it is clearly specified, the case shall be decided in accordance with the law. In this case, should the residents first report the inaction of the Heilongjiang Environmental Protection Department? However, if there are no applicable legal provisions, the principles of legal fairness and acquiescence shall prevail, that is, the reconstruction project is rightful despite its impact on the lives of residents.

(2) From an economic perspective, the situation may be a little more complicated. First of all, if there are definite legal provisions on the scope of living around the cement plant, then should the plant bear the relocation cost of residents? The court must examine the ownership of environmental rights and interests, that is, the residents moved into the surrounding area of the cement plant long after it was built, so they are deemed to have given up their environmental rights and interests. This is actually the key to this the outcome of this lawsuit. Second, if the ownership and definition of environmental rights and interests are not legally prescribed, then the basis for determining the relocation of residents around the construction project will be "reasonability," that is, the principle of efficiency. This principle is not just for the cement plant as the main body but for the benefit of the entire society; specifically, no matter whether the residents bear the relocation expenses on their own or the cement plant pays for them, the outcome of the case shall do good to the social welfare.

17.3 Welfare Analysis

The analysis from the economic perspective focuses on the rational definition of the results of resource allocation. The criterion of reasonability is whether the influence of the law and the litigation result on the parties to the litigation will change the effectiveness of resource allocation, distort the resource allocation, and form a knock-on effect to reduce the total social welfare.

17.3.1 *Economic significance of 500 m/300 m sanitary protection belt*

(1) According to relevant regulations, the health department has set up a "500 m/300 m sanitary protection belt" around the cement plant/project. This is obviously a restriction on the environmental impact of the cement plant, that is, the pollution emitted by the cement production will cause external effects on public health and damage their welfare. Although such restriction will bring additional costs to the cement plant/project (e.g., increasing the transportation cost of the cement plant), compared with the economic loss caused by the impact of public health, it is of social significance for the cement plant to bear this cost. The above is obviously "cost-effective." Although it is not clear whether the distance of 500 m/300 m

just meets the requirements of the above-mentioned cost/benefit analysis at the margin, this is precisely the way to obtain the most effective allocation of land resources around the cement plant. On this basis, the value of the land around the cement plant will be "cleared" through the market under this restriction. There is reason to believe that the optimal equilibrium price under market allocation should be lower than the equilibrium price without this restriction, and this also reflects the "negative externality" of pollution emissions to a certain extent.

(2) From another perspective, the "500 m/300 m sanitary protection belt" also embodies a kind of protection for the "pollution right" of cement plants. From the perspective of enterprise production, due to technical limitations, the production process emits certain pollutants, which will inevitably cause environmental impact within a certain range. If the limit on the scope of environmental impact is expanded indefinitely, for example, the protection distance is expanded to 10 km, the environment or public health will be protected to the maximum, but the company will also greatly increase production costs, and this cost is transmitted through the product market and ultimately hurts the public and social welfare itself. Therefore, setting up a protection belt within a certain distance, rather than expanding it indefinitely, is in fact a definition of the boundary between the allocation of the "pollution right" (and its environmental impact) between the cement plant and the public, and the theoretical basis for this definition also comes from the need to maximize welfare.

17.3.2 *Economic analysis of infringement*

The above discussion only provides a framework for static analysis. In reality, there will be two situations: One is that the cement plant/project meets the requirements of "500 m/300 m sanitary protection belt," the second is that the cement plant/project does not meet the requirements of "500 m/300 m sanitary protection belt." The scenario worth discussing is the latter, especially whether the dynamic evolution process formed in the social and economic development meets the relevant regulations and requirements, which itself is constantly changing and evolving.

(1) From a legal point of view, in cases where the cement plants/projects do not meet the requirements of "500 m/300 m sanitary protection belt," legal issues of infringement will naturally arise, just like the relationship

between the residents and the cement plant, and the relationship between the cement plant and the MEP involved in this lawsuit. The core lies in whether the project construction of the cement plant violates the law and infringes the residents' right of residence. There is no doubt about this. Whether it is built first or built later, the reconstruction plant has violated the laws and regulations related to health protection, thus constituting infringement.

(2) Our focus is to analyze the welfare impact after being identified as infringement As mentioned earlier, since the "500 m/300 m sanitary protection belt" requirement contains welfare value, violating this requirement will naturally damage welfare. However, the problem is not so simple. As shown in this lawsuit, the situation of infringement is not static, but dynamic.

First, the cement plant was built before resident settlement, and it also met the protection requirements set by the health department, that is, there are no residents (or willing to live) with the "500 m/300 m sanitary protection belt." After passing the Environmental Information Administration, if any residents still dwell in or move into the "500 m/300 m sanitary protection belt," this means that residents have accepted the "environmental impact" of the cement plant and refused to move from the "500 m/300 m sanitary protection belt." This is actually a normal market choice under the condition of information symmetry, and a market-based decision made after judging the value of real estate and the cost of living in the "500 m/300 m sanitary protection belt." At this time, the residence of inhabitants in the "500 m/300 m sanitary protection belt" obviously does not involve infringement issues (voluntary waiver of rights), and social welfare is also balanced and maximized in this selection process.

Second, the reconstruction project of this existing cement plant is equivalent to a new project according to relevant regulations, and the environmental assessment must be conducted again. In other words, at this time, the requirement of "500 m/300 m of sanitary protection belt" was reintroduced and demonstrated. At this time, what is different from a new project is that a group of residents have moved into the protection belt before the reconstruction project is launched. According to the analysis of the first point, it can be assumed that these residents have given up their corresponding rights (pollution discharge rights) when they moved in. So, how should we define the rights that they have already waived? Or can they reapply for these rights? Obviously, laws and regulations do not provide a clear explanation of the changes in rights under this dynamic condition. Can it be equivalent to a "secondary contract?"

From an economic point of view, behind the waiver of rights is the balance of costs and benefits, that is, choosing to live in the "500 m/300 m sanitary protection belt" has achieved the maximum welfare of the actor in its consideration. However, afterward, with the acceleration of urbanization, a possible market result is that the appreciation of the land within the "500 m/300 m sanitary protection belt" is much lower than that of the appreciation of the land outside the "500 m/300 m sanitary protection belt." This means that residents who choose to live in the "500 m/300 m sanitary protection belt" have their assets relatively depreciated. However, this point is the result of market selection, which is in line with the law of dynamic deduction between economic development and environmental value, that is, the value of real estate is low around the pollution source. If this is the case, should this right be redefined after the cement plant reconstruction project?

The redefinition means that residents living in the "500 m/300 m sanitary protection belt" of the cement plant regain their "pollution discharge rights" they have given up. Leave aside whether this reallocation of resources itself is justified or legally defensible. The result of this is that the reconstruction project of the cement plant infringes on the residents' right to discharge and housing. According to the law, when the residents did not move away from the "500 m/300 m sanitary protection belt," the cement plant's reconstruction project could not obtain the production permit (it could not pass the EIA). In this case, a new market equilibrium condition will appear, which is attributed to two reasons: First of all, the cost of moving away from the "500 m/300 m sanitary protection belt" is higher compared to new projects (rising property prices in surrounding areas). Second, the game relationship has changed. When the cement plant was building a new project, there were no residents in the "500 m/300 m sanitary protection belt," so its construction did not need to consider the cost of moving the residents, but when the reconstruction project is to be implemented, there are already residents in the "500 m/300 m sanitary protection belt." At this time, once the residents are given the right to "move out," then, according to the relevant research results of behavioral economics, their willingness to accept compensation (WTA) for relocation will be higher than their willingness to pay (WTP) for improving the living environment. In addition, because the reconstruction project is built on the original plant site, there is a certain initial investment cost, which also makes the cost of reconstruction higher than that of the new project. Both of these costs mean that if the emission rights in the "500 m/300 m sanitary protection belt" after the project are rebuilt are allocated to the residents, the cement plant will bear additional cost.

In other words, a new market equilibrium will be formed under conditions of higher external costs. First, residents who are sensitive to the environment and wish to move away from the "500 m/300 m sanitary protection belt" need to be compensated. Second, residents who have previously given up their environmental rights, under the demonstrative effect, propose additional compensation that is slightly equivalent to the requirement of moving away from the "500 m/300 m sanitary protection belt" (in this case, appropriate compensation will be provided for this part of the residents, and it is still cost-effective). Third, once the right of residence within the "500 m/300 m sanitary protection belt" obtains the corresponding compensation of different scales, it will bring expectations to the land and real estate market, that is, by continuing to live or move into the "500 m/300 m sanitary protection belt" to wait for the next reconstruction to obtain new relocation compensation. Fourth, stimulated by additional compensation, the land and real estate market of the "500 m/300 m sanitary protection belt" has a higher relative price level, and its value is not lower than that of the land and real estate in the "500 m/300 m sanitary protection belt." On the contrary, driven by expectations, it may be higher than the land and real estate outside the "500 m/300 m sanitary protection belt" (including high prices in absolute and relative terms). Therefore, the result is inconsistent with the actual value, resulting in a misallocation of resources.

Of course, the result of resource misallocation not only harms the direct stakeholders related to the reconstruction project, such as the income of the cement plant. What is more serious is that the result of misallocation of resources in a place will spread to the whole society through various channels, affecting the maximization of social welfare. First, due to the misallocation of resources, the relative appreciation of the land and real estate around the cement plant actually means the relative depreciation of the land and real estate in other areas, which is a welfare loss. Second, due to the misallocation of resources, cement plants bear a higher production cost. This production cost is transmitted to consumers through the product market, increasing the purchase cost of consumers; if this cost cannot be digested by the market, it may be digested inside the cement plant, resulting in production cuts or shutdowns, which may result in unemployment and loss of social welfare. Third, once the mismatch effect spreads on a larger scale, it will result in a large amount of inefficient use of resource elements such as capital, labor, and land.

17.4 Enlightenment from This Case

First, the environmental impact of enterprise production is neutral, and its welfare effect depends on the pricing of environmental impact. Only pricing at a balanced level can maximize social welfare.

Second, in the context of the rising level of environmental impact pricing, the market pricing mechanism should be improved to create a symmetrical information, fair competition, and access market environment for environmental impact pricing. Only pricing formed on the basis of market equilibrium is sufficient to accurately allocate resources.

Third, in the process of "de-capacity," strengthening the constraints on "excess capacity" from the environmental field is only one way. Exaggerating or underestimating the environmental constraints on production will not be conducive to our correct evaluation of the environmental value and will also be detrimental to our protection of the ecological environment.

Chapter 18

Research on Residential Step Tariff and Elasticity Ratio of Electricity Consumption*

18.1 Introduction

The setting of electricity tariff in China has long been under the purview of government regulation, rather than a choice based on free market competition. Consequently, the rise in on-grid electricity tariff pushed up by rising coal prices is not passed on to end-consumers, resulting in power companies accumulating deficits due to serious cost inversion and distortion of the price adjustment mechanism, leading to inefficient resource allocation and a sharp increase in residential energy consumption. On July 1, 2012, the step tariff was piloted nationwide. As a product of electricity tariff reform in the transitional stage, step tariff — although a form of administered price — has relieved the intensive cross subsidization for industry power consumption to some extent and saved power companies from excessive loss.

By drawing on the mature experiences in other countries, China introduced the step tariff policy to respond to its huge energy demand and gradual deterioration of the ecological environment. However, step tariff is not simply about raising electricity prices and reducing electricity consumption but also involves the setting of block tariff in different regions, estimation of the elasticity of residential electricity demand, prediction of the

* This research was backed up by Jinglan Society, Fudan University.

impact on different income groups, and coordination with related policies. All of these factors can affect the implementation effect of step tariff.

18.2 Literature Review

18.2.1 *Elasticity of residential electricity demand*

For residents earning different levels of income, the elasticity of their electricity demand differs greatly. According to the Ramsey Pricing, for low-income groups that have larger elasticity of demand, a lower tariff is set, while high-income groups with smaller elasticity of demand are imposed with a higher tariff. Both the setting and implementation of step tariffs must be based on the elasticity of residential electricity demand.

Romero-Jordán *et al.* (2014) examined the panel data over 1998–2009 in Spain and, by employing the Dynamic Partial Adjustment Model, performed a regression analysis of the explanatory variables (including household electricity usage, income, electricity tariff, climate-related variables, household appliances, and other socioeconomic factors). They determined that residential electricity demand is significantly positively correlated with some explanatory variables, however, the previous year's electricity consumption, income, temperature changes, electric water heating, and number of cooling and heating equipment are significantly negatively correlated with the variables such as the number of elderly and electric heaters in the family; the impact of electricity tariff and resident income on electricity consumption is very limited; and policies cannot greatly reduce electricity consumption.

By employing the Generalized Method of Moments (GMM), Fell *et al.* (2014) examined some empirical data and estimated that the elasticity of electricity tariff in American households is −0.5, and their income elasticity is 0.01, which are lower the estimated value in other studies. For example, they also estimated the elasticity parameters with the Ordinary Least Square (OLS) method, and found that the results are greatly different from those based on the GMM.

After examination of the electricity consumption data of Taiwan, China over 1955–1996, (Holtedahl and Joutz, 2004) modified the Two-Stage Model proposed by Fisher and Kaysen (1962), and assumed that this modified model was applicable to developing countries. Based on the explanatory variables of the model, including population, income, electricity tariff, oil price, urbanization and weather, they estimated the elasticity of electricity tariff and resident income in Taiwan as −0.15 and 1.57, respectively, and the cross-price elasticity of substitute oil as 0.18.

Alberini *et al.* (2011) conducted a statistical analysis of the elasticity of electricity tariff and income in American households. Based on the panel data at the household level in the US from 1997 to 2007, they calculated the elasticity of electricity tariff to fall between −0.860 and −0.667, and it will decrease slightly with the increase of income. The short-term cross-price elasticity of electricity to gasoline is 0.265, but it is insensitive to the changes in income.

Based on the survey data of urban households in Sichuan Province over 2007–2009, Zhou and Teng (2013) performed a regression analysis of residential electricity consumption with the regressors including income, electricity tariff, and lifestyle (family size, living area, and usage of household appliances). The results show that, no matter which measurement model was employed, the elasticity of electricity tariff and income respectively falls between 0.35 and 0.5 and between 0.14 and 0.34, demonstrating that electricity is one of daily necessities. When many lifestyle-related variables are controlled, their impact on electricity tariff and income becomes even less insignificant.

A report released by the National Academy of Development and Strategy, Renmin University of China, which introduces an empirical analysis of the unbalanced panel data of Chinese cities over 2006–2009 based on the OLS and FGLS regressions, reveals a conclusion that per capita electricity consumption of urban resides is elastic to their wage, but inelastic to electricity tariff (Yu and Che, 2014).

The results of existing studies vary greatly in the influencing factors and electricity of residential electricity consumption, which is attributed to the choice of explanatory variables and model settings and to the temporal and spatial nature of data. In different regions, residential behavior of electricity consumption, family structure, and electricity market are not the same; therefore, it is the empirical research for specific regions that has reference value for the setting and implementation of step electricity tariff.

18.2.2 *Theory and practice of step electricity tariff*

The step tariff policy has triggered in-depth research by scholars at home and abroad. Some of them went over the design procedures of step tariff in light of the situation in China, and hold that multiple factors shall be taken into account, such as number of grades, electricity consumption per grade, household grouping, electricity consumption of people in different income ranges, and electricity tariff per grade. They have also pointed out that electricity consumption elasticity is an important factor for estimating the welfare changes brought about by the step tariff, and the key indicator of improved fairness and efficiency is the subsidy distributed to poverty-stricken households.

Reneses *et al.* (2011), with electricity tariff design of transitional economies as the research object, proposed that the electricity tariff design must cover the supply cost and send correct economic signals to consumers to ensure that the electricity service can be effectively used. Moreover, the government price regulation should follow three principles: (1) Business sustainability (power companies should not suffer loss for providing residential electricity); (2) economic efficiency (minimum production costs and maximum efficiency of transmission and utilization); and (3) fair treatment to all consumers (the same price pays for the same service). In their research report, they also introduced the methodology for electricity tariff design, and an empirical analysis with Libya as an example.

Sun and Lin (2013) carried out a research study on the nonlinear pricing of electricity. They analyzed the impact of step tariff on the effectiveness of electricity consumption with economic models, stating that a reasonable step tariff can improve the effectiveness of most residents' electricity consumption and also improve the level of social welfare. Besides, they pointed out certain problems with the step tariff. For example, the first-grade low tariff also subsidizes wealthy families, which is a kind of "welfare spillover." However, for large-sized families, step tariff seems like a punishment; a practical solution to this dilemma is to allow these families to install multiple electricity meters or enjoy government subsidy.

Liu and Yang (2010) divided the step electricity tariff into degressive tariff and incremental tariff and interpreted related policy objectives. In their research paper, they analyzed the feasibility for China to implement incremental electricity tariff and explored the corresponding design procedures and paths for doing so. Zhu C. Z. (2010) elaborated on the harms of China's cross-subsidization for electricity tariff from four perspectives: resource value, equitable burden sharing, development of electricity industry, and reform of electricity market, compared the advantages and disadvantages of three patterns of step tariff, and recommended that these patterns may be combined to perform their functions in light of local conditions.

In terms of the impact and effect of step electricity tariff, Zeng *et al.* (2011), based on the utility theory of microeconomics, developed a model for evaluating the plans for residential progressive step electricity tariff and compared the power-saving effect of different plans. They took Beijing's step tariff as an example for calculation, and drew a conclusion that the tariff difference of 1:3:6 works best.

(Houqing *et al.*, 2012) evaluated the step electricity tariff from three aspects: residents, power companies, and energy-saving and emissions reduction targets. They believe that the step tariff can ensure normal electricity consumption of low-income earners and guide all residents to use electricity reasonably; reduce the electricity purchase cost paid by power grid companies; smooth the upstream, midstream, and downstream price transmission; encourage more households to use energy-saving appliances; and reduce peak electricity consumption through technological upgrading and intellectualization.

Wu Chaoyang (2011) probed into the problems in the implementation of step electricity tariff — for example, the rationality of determining basic electricity consumption by household, the overall level of residential electricity tariff remains low, users unwilling to cooperate with modifications of electricity meters, and existence of financing gap.

In addition to multi-angle evaluation of step electricity tariff, some scholars also care about the impact of step tariff on power supply companies. Cui and Liu (2012) pointed out that the implementation of step electricity tariff has forced the electricity metering system, electricity bill settlement, power grid operation, and corporate business operation to make corresponding adjustments. Moreover, they suggested that all supporting measures, such as an electricity data collection system, time-of-use step tariff, and institutional improvement, shall be adopted at the same time.

18.3 Survey of Resident Electricity Consumption in Shanghai

Through a review of previous studies, we can find that after China put the step electricity tariff policy into trial implementation and then promoted it across the nation, most Chinese researchers only analyzed the effect of this policy at the macro level. Even if there are data from certain cities as supporting evidence, the indicators for measuring the effect of this policy have remained abstract. In order to evaluate this policy at the micro level and obtain timely feedback from households on this policy, a survey team by the name of "Energy Observer," which was mainly comprised undergraduates from Fudan University, conducted a household survey known as "The Impact of Step Electricity Tariff on Residents' Power Consumption Behaviors" in Shanghai.

18.3.1 *Sample description*

Considering the diversity and extensiveness of respondents and the difficulties in conducting a household questionnaire survey, the survey team decided to interview the residents in six districts of Shanghai, that is, Yangpu, Pudong (New District), Minhang, Hongkou, Baoshan, and Zhabei and recovered a total of 132 valid questionnaires in the end. These respondents reside in "villages" inside city or high-grade residential buildings, with total family income ranging from 1,000 to 100,000 yuan per month. Among the interviewed families, 40.8% of them have three members, 13.6% of them are extended families with four or more members, and 45.6% of them only have one or two members.

18.3.2 *Residents' attitude toward step electricity tariff and corresponding actions*

18.3.2.1 *Attitude of residents*

In recent years, many regions in China have seen "electricity shortage." However, when asked if electricity is a scarce resource, quite a number of respondents say they have seldom experienced electricity shortage and believe it is unlikely. The results of the survey show that less than 50% of the respondents believe that electricity is a scarce resource, while 34.13% of them hold the opposite view (see Figure 18.1).

In order to determine why many respondents have no idea of electricity shortage, the survey team had them grouped by monthly income and educational background:

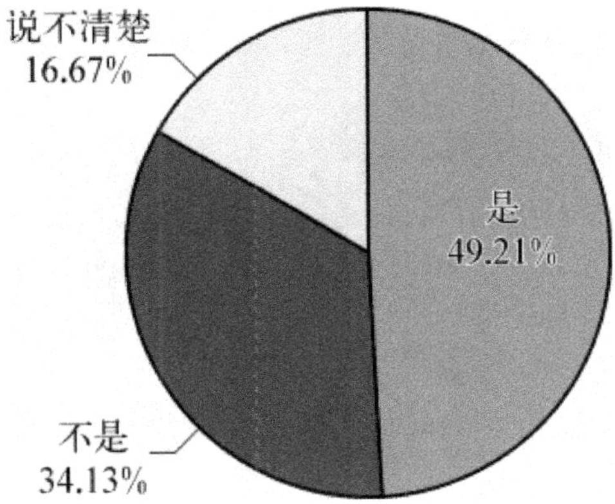

说不清楚 16.67%	Not clear, 16.67%
不是 34.13%	No, 34.13%
是 49.21%	Yes, 49.21%

Figure 18.1. Respondents' reply to the question "whether electricity is a scarce resource."

(1) The respondents with per capita monthly income of above 10,000 yuan were divided into Group 1, while those earning less than 10,000 yuan were divided into Group 2. The questionnaires show that 60% of the respondents in Group 1 believe electricity is a scarce resource, and 54.83% of the respondents in Group 2 hold the same view. In the two groups, roughly the same proportion of respondents have a negative opinion (see Figure 18.2). It demonstrates that high-income earners usually have a better understanding of electricity shortage.

(2) When interpreting the relationship between one's educational background and his attitude towards electricity shortage, the survey team divided the respondents into five groups, that is, junior high school and below, high school/secondary school/vocational high school, junior college, university undergraduate, postgraduate and above. The survey results (see Figure 18.3) show that people's awareness of electricity shortage is positively correlated with the level of education, except for those with a junior college degree.

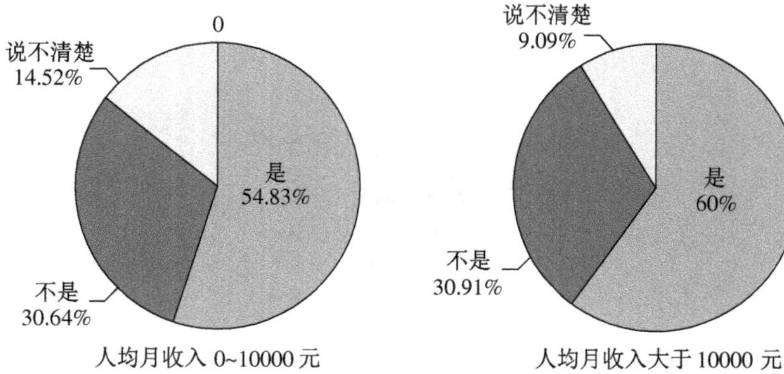

人均月收入 0~10000 元	Per capita monthly income of 0~10,000 yuan
说不清楚 14.52%	Not clear, 14.52%
不是 30.64%	No, 30.64%
是 54.83%	Yes, 54.83%
人均月收入大于 10000 元	Per capita monthly income of above 10,000 yuan
说不清楚 9.09%	Not clear, 9.09%
不是 30.91%	No, 30.91%
是 60%	Yes, 60%

Figure 18.2. The influence of per capita monthly income on awareness of electricity shortage.

All respondents do not have a deep understanding of the step electricity tariff — 89.68% of them only hear of this, but none of them knows the exact three-grade cutoff point of the step tariff. Besides, the survey team also noticed that a large number of respondents often confuse the step tariff with the peak-valley tariff, which may be caused by insufficient publicity for the step tariff policy.

Regarding their attitude toward the step electricity tariff, most of the respondents support it (see Figure 18.4), mainly because this policy is able to "save electricity consumption" and embodies the principle of equality and efficiency (i.e., "those who consume more energy shall pay more"). Those who do not like this policy is for the reason that "the increased electricity tariff is an additional burden for them." Among the respondents in two groups, which are divided by their income level, the proportion of

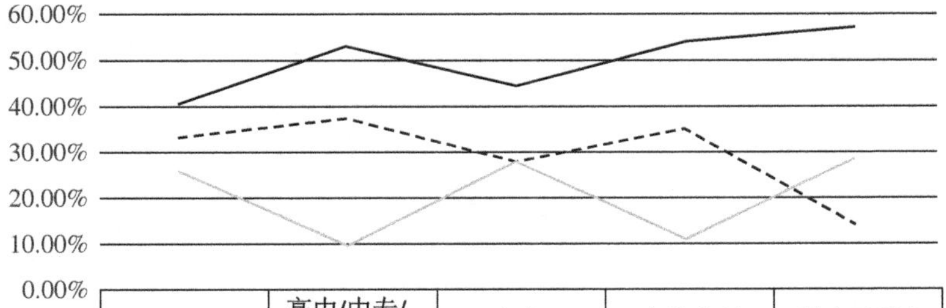

	初中及以下	高中/中专/职高	大专	大学本科	硕士及以上
——是	40.73%	53.13%	44.44%	54.05%	57.14%
----不是	33.33%	37.50%	27.78%	35.14%	14.29%
——说不清楚	25.93%	9.38%	27.78%	10.81%	28.57%

—— 是 ----不是 —— 说不清楚

是	Yes
不是	No
说不清楚	Not clear
初中及以下	Junior high school and below
高中/中专/职高	High school/secondary school/vocational high school
大专	Junior college
大学本科	University undergraduate
硕士及以上	Postgraduate and above

Figure 18.3. The influence of educational background on awareness of electricity shortage.

those who support this policy is roughly the same. The analysis of 105 valid samples shows that the difference in approval rate between the respondents earning more than 10,000 yuan per month and those earning no more than 10,000 yuan is as small as 1.4%.

Although only a few respondents oppose the step electricity tariff, most of them are not satisfied with the current grade pricing for the step tariff: Grade 1: 0~3,120 kWh annually per household (260 kWh per month). Grade 2: 3,120~4,800 kWh annually per household (400 kWh per month). Grade 3: more than 4,800 kWh annually per household (more than 400 kWh per month). Only 46.56% of the respondents endorse such grade pricing, while 24.43% of them believe it is

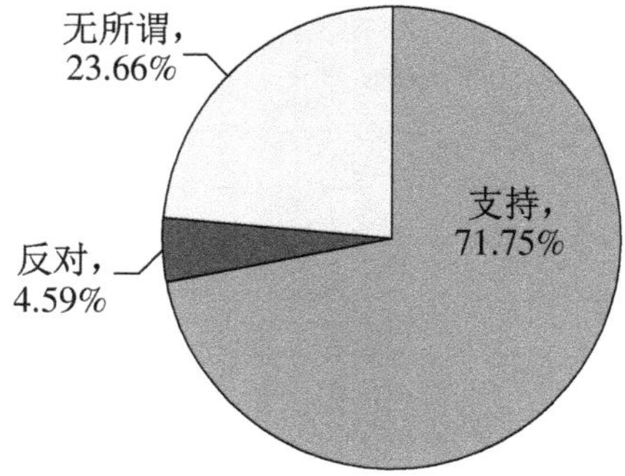

无所谓，23.66%	Not interested, 23.66%
反对，4.59%	Oppose, 4.59%
支持，71.75%	Support, 71.75%

Figure 18.4. Respondents' attitude toward the step electricity tariff.

unreasonable. Among the respondents who hold a negative view, 17.24% of them say that the grade pricing should be canceled, and 59.26% of them hope that the electricity quota of each grade should be increased appropriately.

18.3.2.2 *Electricity consumption of residents*

For all residents, the direct purpose of saving electricity is to save expenses, so the survey team evaluated the impact of step electricity tariff on their electricity consumption behaviors from five dimensions: (1) Whether they have spent less time using certain electrical appliances? (2) Whether they have changed the period of time for electricity use? (3) Whether they have replaced electrical appliances to save electricity? (4) If the electricity consumption of this month is over the limit, will they use less electricity the next month? (5) Whether they have thought about using other types of energy to replace electricity? These five dimensions correspond to the questions 20, 22, 24, 25, and 28 in the questionnaire (see Table 18.1) — selecting "Yes" scores 1 point, while selecting "No" scores 0 point.

Table 18.1. Impact of step tariff on respondents' electricity consumption behaviors.

Question	Yes (1)	No (0)	Average score
20. Have you spent less time using certain electrical appliances?	17 (12.88%)	115 (87.12%)	0.129
22. Have you changed the daily time frame for electricity use?	38 (28.79%)	94 (71.21%)	0.288
24. Have you replaced electrical appliances to save electricity?	5 (3.79%)	127 (96.21%)	0.038
25. If the electricity consumption of this month is over-high, will you use less electricity the next month?	22 (16.67%)	110 (83.33%)	0.167
28. Do you think about using other types of energy to replace electricity?	5 (3.79%)	127 (96.21%)	0.038
Total score	—	—	0.659

It can be seen from Table 18.1 that the impact of step electricity tariff on residents' electricity consumption behaviors has the following characteristics.

The average score of each yes-or-no question shows that the step electricity tariff has little impact on residents' electricity consumption behaviors; the most important manifestation of the impact is that they have adjusted the daily time frame for electricity use to save expenses without reducing the amount of electricity consumption.

The total score is lower than 1 (the full score is 5), and the distribution of all scores is clearly right-skewed (most respondents have a total score of 0), indicating that the step electricity tariff has not significantly changed the electricity consumption behaviors of the respondents.

In order to further explore the reasons for the poor effect of step electricity tariff, we should first use the utility maximization theory of economics to analyze how residents rationally choose electricity consumption. Regardless of their income level, all residents desire for maximum utility. However, for different income groups, the marginal utility of money is different. MU_1 and MU_2, respectively, represent the marginal utility of money for high-income groups and low-income groups ($MU_1 < MU_2$, see Figure 18.5). Residential electricity consumption depends on the marginal utility brought by the last unit of electricity. MU_A and MU_B, respectively,

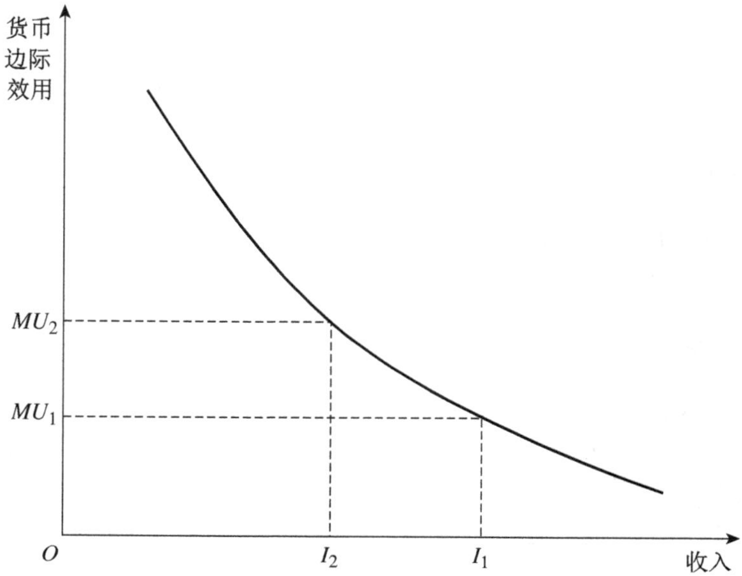

货币边际效用	Marginal utility of money
收入	Income

Figure 18.5. Marginal utility of money changes with income.

represent the marginal utility of electricity consumed by high- and low-income groups. For rational residents, when the marginal utility ratio between money and electricity is equal to the ratio between their prices, the marginal utility of money is the greatest. Suppose the price of base currency is 1, and the price of unit electricity is P_E. Well then, the condition for maximizing the utility of high-income group is $MU_1/1 = MU_A/P_E$, while that for low-income group is $MU_2/1 = MU_B/P_E$. From $MU_1 < MU_2$, we can infer the conclusion as $MU_A = MU_B$. According to the law of diminishing marginal utility, the electricity consumption Q_A of high-income groups should be higher than the electricity consumption Q_B of low-income groups (see Figure 18.6). However, the step electricity tariff policy pushes up the electricity price for large electricity consumers, that is, the P_E goes up, which will increase the MU_A of the electricity consumption of high-income groups under the condition of maximum utility, implying that residents will reduce their electricity consumption.

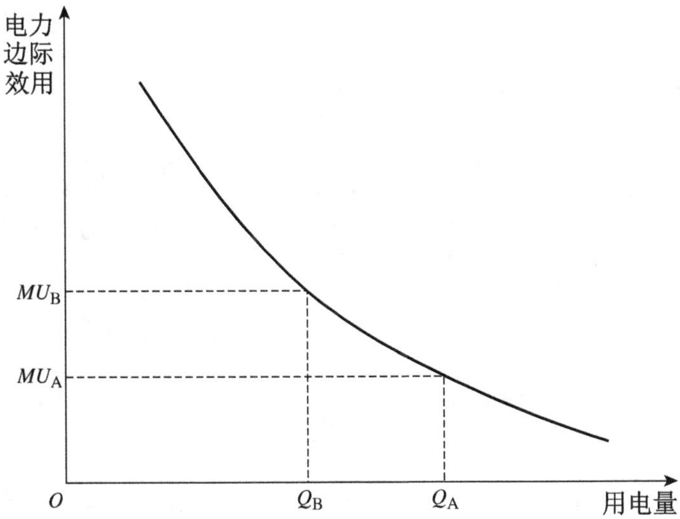

电力边际效用	Marginal utility of electricity
用电量	Electricity consumption

Figure 18.6. Marginal utility of electricity changes with income.

The survey results show that the step electricity tariff fails to motivate people to greatly reduce electricity consumption. Based on the above analysis, we put forward two hypotheses to explain the reasons:

H1: The pricing of step electricity tariff is not reasonable enough, that is, the level of block tariff is too high and the level of unit tariff is too low;

H2: The respondents are low- and middle-income earners with elasticity of electricity demand excessively small.

In order to verify the validity of the above two hypotheses, we first screened out the respondents that answered "No" to question No. 24 (see Table 18.1) as the research sample, and then started data analysis based on their questionnaires. About 75% of these respondents express that they seldom use any techniques in electricity consumption, so we can preliminarily infer that the pricing of electricity tariff is not high enough, so residents do not pay attention to saving electricity. If H2 is tenable (i.e., the reason why step electricity tariff is of little impact is for rigid residential demand for electricity), it is to say that residents have already done well in saving electricity in their daily lives, which apparently conflicts with the survey results. In our opinion, the reason why step electricity tariff fails to weigh on residential electricity consumption is because its pricing needs to be further adjusted up in a reasonable manner.

Further, when step electricity tariff is set to a higher level, how will it affect residents' electricity consumption behaviors? To learn about the opinions of respondents, we interviewed with some of them from both high-income and low- and middle-income groups. We learned that many high-income earners have many high-energy-consuming luxury appliances in their homes, like central air-conditioning, central floor heating, intelligent sweeping robots, and side-by-side refrigerators. These high-income respondents say that if electricity tariff rises to a certain level, they may choose to reduce the comfort of luxury living to reduce electricity consumption. For example, they may turn off some unnecessary lighting equipment (they have been used to switch on all lighting equipment) or reduce the use of some entertainment electrical equipment; while the low- and middle-income groups said that all their electricity consumption behavior will turn into rigid demand, and any increase in electricity bills by then will be equivalent to a direct tax burden, which will not only produce further energy-saving effect but also lower people's quality of life.

18.3.3 *Conclusions*

The survey results show that residents do not have a clear knowledge of step electricity tariff, and the implementation of this policy fails to have any broad or significant impact on their electricity consumption behaviors, because the current pricing for step tariff remains at a low level. In the future, the level of step tariff needs to be further adjusted up, but in this process competent authorities must think about the different electricity-saving effects arising from varied elasticity of electricity demand of all income groups.

The main conclusions drawn from the survey are as follows:

(1) Residents are not fully aware of electricity shortage. With stronger awareness of electricity shortage, residents will be more willing to support the step electricity tariff. Given this, it is quite important to enhance the publicity of the scarcity of power resources.
(2) Residents do not have a deep understanding of the step electricity tariff, and quite a number of them have only heard of this policy.
(3) Residents are on the whole supporting the step electricity tariff, but many of them are not satisfied with the current block tariff.
(4) The step electricity tariff has not brought significant changes to the electricity consumption behaviors of the interviewed residents.
(5) Since the step electricity tariff has little restrictive impact on residents' electricity consumption behaviors, its pricing level needs to be reasonably adjusted up in the future.
(6) In urban villages, low-income earners usually pay their electricity bills to landlords at a fixed price, so they are hardly affected by the step electricity tariff. However, self-employed people, who are large electricity consumers, are greatly affected by the step tariff, since they have to pay for a high block tariff as ordinary residents.

18.4 Outlook for Step Electricity Tariff

As a part of China's electricity tariff reform, the step tariff has its significance at a given time. Compared to the single pricing plan that has been implemented for years, the step tariff responds to the rising cost of upstream producers, slows down the depletion of fossil energy, and broadens the space for new energy research and development. However, at the same time, endless problems have kept cropping up in the implementation of step tariff. For example, is it true that all high-income earners are large electricity consumers? Can low-income earners receive electricity tariff subsidies? After the step electricity tariff policy was put into force, its drawbacks have been exposed one after another due to the complexity of actual situations. Changes in electricity tariff can affect the interests of multiple parties, and step electricity tariff cannot satisfy all parties at the same time — it is a specific product born in the current environment of energy, ecology, and economy and also a buffer for the market-oriented reform of electricity tariff.

Bibliography

Chinese Literature

Bai Y. F. & Wang G. Q. (2011). The evolution, reform and improvement of China's pollutant charging system. *Academic Exchanges*, 11, 79–82.

Bi Q. & Yu L. C. (2016a). Environmental tax, media supervision and corporate green investment. *Finance and Accounting Monthly*, 20, 66–70.

Bi Q. & Yu L. C. (2016b). Research on the effect of tax on corporate green investment: An empirical study based on panel quantile regression. *Chinese Journal of Population Resources and Environment*, 26(3), 76–82.

Cao X. F. (2016). Two issues that should draw attention in the "fee-to-tax reform" of environmental protection. *China Environment Supervision*, 10, 26–27.

Cao G., Yang Z. J., & Wang Y. H. (2001). Quantitative discussion on the Kuznets relationship between environmental quality and economic growth. *Environmental Assessment*, 6, 21–24.

Chen H. (2011). Research on the quality of EID of listed companies based on their social responsibility reports. PhD Thesis, Jiangsu University.

Chen H. R. (2010). Summary and prospect of green credit research. *Financial Theory & Practice*, 8, 90–93.

Chen R. (2011). Study on the impact of reputation on corporate financing capability. PhD Thesis, Yangzhou University.

Chen W. (2012). Research on dynamic CGE model construction and policy evaluation of China's water pollution control. PhD Thesis, Hunan University.

Chen X. S. & Fan D. C. (2009). Empirical research on China's industrial water pollution status and its treatment efficiency. *Statistics & Information Forum*, 24(3), 30–35.

Chen J., Mao H. P., & Huang G. Z. (2015). A brief discussion on the current situation of Zhejiang Province's environmental and economic policy system construction and the development priorities in the "13th Five-Year Plan." *Environmental Science and Management*, 9, 12–15.

China Forum of Environmental Journalists (2017). Evaluation report on environmental responsibility information disclosure of listed companies in China.

Cui X. M. (2011). The driving mechanism of corporate green investment and its realization path. Collected papers from the Third Cross-Strait Academic Accounting Seminar between Accounting Society of China and National Chengchi University, 13–21.

Cui X. M. (2013). The driving mechanism of corporate green investment and its realization path — Analysis based on value creation. *Jianghai Academic Journal*, 3, 85v91.

Cui X. M. & Liu J. (2012). Do or not do: Research on the driving mechanism of corporate green investment — Analysis based on questionnaire. Proceedings of 2012 International Annual Conference of Environmental Accounting Committee in ASC & the 1st Chinese CSEAR, pp. 197–210.

Dong W. F. & Fu D. Q. (2008). Study on the status quo, existing problems and countermeasures of urban sewage treatment plants in China. *Environmental Science Survey*, 3, 40–42.

Dong Z. F., Ge C. Z., Wang J. N., & Gao S. T. (2012). Assessment and prospect of the current situation of China's lake environmental and economic policies. *Environmental Protection and Circular Economy*, 1, 4–6.

Dong Z. F., Ge C. Z., Wang J. N., Gao S. T., & Li X. L. (2012). Evaluation of the implementation of environmental and economic policies in the 11th Five-Year Plan — Based on statistical analysis of policy documents. *Environmental Economy*, 10, 22–31.

Freeman A. M. (2002). *Measurement of Environmental and Resource Values: Theory and Methods*. Beijing: China Renmin University Press.

Gong Y., Ruan X. H., & Hu X. D. (2003). Research progress on non-point source pollution of urban surface water environment in China. *China Water & Wastewater*, 3, 21–23.

Green Credit Research Group of CBRC Shanghai Office (2016). Research on the financial innovation and industrial restructuring supported by green credit. *Financial Regulation Research*, 5, 98–108.

He S. W. & Cui X. M. (2014). Green investment: Passive and active choice. *Corporate Finance*, 9, 53–55.

Hong Y. X. & Liu Z. B. (2003). *The Model and Mechanism of Economic Development in the Yangtze River Delta*. Beijing: Tsinghua University Press.

Hou W. L. (2005). *Research on China's Economic Growth and Environmental Quality*. Beijing: China Environmental Science Press.

Hu W. (2015). China's water pollution fee-to-tax reform: Foreign experiences and system conception. Thesis, Anhui University of Finance and Economics.

Hu Y. (2015). Analysis of China's tax reform of waste gas discharge fees. *Journal of Tongling University*, 14.

Industry and Information Technology Department of Jiangsu (2016). Completion of industrial and technological transformation investment in Jiangsu province from January to September 2016. Retrieved from http://gxt.jiangsu.gov.cn/art/2016/10/18/art_6285_3713579.html.

Jiang Z. H. (2014). Speech at the Press Conference of the Information Office of the State Council.

Jiang H., Xu H. Q., Huang H. Q., Fan X. M., Wang L., & Ji Y. H. (2014). The status quo and development strategies of the ecological public-good forests compensation system in Jiangsu Province. *Journal of Jiangsu Forestry Science & Technology*, 4, 54–57.

Jiangsu Provincial Forestry Bureau (2016). Overview of the forestry in Jiangsu Province in 2015. Retrieved from http://jsf.jiangsu.gov.cn/art/2016/4/19/art_7084_3017601.html.

Jin W. (2007). Thoughts on the debt evaluation in the new "Debt Restructuring Standards." *Research of Financial & Accounting*, 6, 22–23.

Li S. J. (2013). Establishment of the evaluation index system of corporate green investment efficiency. *Foreign Investment in China*, 18, 202.

Li S. S. (2015). The impact on the operating performance of China's listed banks from implementation of green credit policies. Thesis, Zhejiang Gongshang University.

Li Z. Q. (2012). Development of Shanghai's carbon finance, Shanghai Financial White Paper (2011). Shanghai: Shanghai People's Publishing House.

Li Z. Q. (2013a). Urban "hydraulic power" and new urbanization. *Dongfang Daily*, July 1.

Li Z. Q. (2013b). "Beautyism" and new urbanization. *Wenhui Daily*, May 6.

Li Z. Q. (2017). Adopting a market-based environmental economic policy. *China Environment Daily*, January 6.

Li Z. J. & Wang S. P. (2011). Monetary policy, information disclosure quality and corporate debt financing. *Accounting Research*, 10, 56–62.

Li D. M. & Xia L. J. (2008). The nature of equity, institutional environment and R&D intensity of listed companies. *Journal of Finance and Economics*, 4, 93–104.

Li T., Shi L., & Ma Z. (2016). Analysis and evaluation of China's sewage discharge fee policy amid collection of environmental tax. *Journal of Central University of Finance & Economics*, 9, 20–28.

Ling K., Wang H. C., & Liu T. (2001). Statistical research on the relationship between urban economic development and environmental pollution — Taking Nanjing City as an example. *Statistical Research*, 10, 46–52. doi:10.19343/j.cnki.11-1302/ c.2001.10.008.

Liu S. J. (2012). Research on regional environmental protection investment and sustainable economic development — Based on comparative analysis of China's regional panel data. *Enterprise Economy*, 1, 136–140. doi:10.13529/j.cnki.enterprise.economy.2012.01.015.

Liu Y. G. (2013). Research on the debt cost of listed companies under the institutional background of China. Thesis, Southwest University of Finance and Economics.

Liu Y. Y. (2007). Research on the application performance of economic means of environmental protection in China. Thesis, Ocean University of China.

Liu S. J. & Yang J. (2010). Research on tiered electricity tariff. *Price: Theory & Practice*, 3, 12–14.

Liu L. M., Niu Y. F., & Wang Y. Q. (2017). The impact of green credit on the profitability of China's commercial banks — Based on panel data analysis of 14 listed banks. *West China Finance*, 3, 28–33.

Liu J. H., Zhou Z. B., & Liu Y. (2015). Research on the construction of China's environmental tax system from the perspective of "double dividend" — Based on international comparative analysis. *Macroeconomics*, 2, 68–77.

Long J. (2013). Environmental information disclosure, corporate governance and financing with bank loan. *Finance and Accounting Monthly*, 20, 6–9.

Lu M. (2012). Agglomeration and emission reduction: An empirical analysis based on China's provincial panel data. Collected Papers from the Annual Meeting of Fudan University Environmental Economic Research Center.

Malthus T. R. (2008). *An Essay on the Principle of Population*. Beijing: Peking University Press.

Mao X. Q. & Yang L. (2006). Swedish environmental tax — Policy effect and its enlightenment to China. *Environmental Protection*, 2, 90–95.

Marx K. (1953). *Capital*, Vol 3. Beijing: People's Publishing House.

Meng Y. (2006). Research on green investment issues. Thesis, Dongbei University of Finance and Economics.

Meng X. J. & Chu J. (2013). A literature review of the research on the correlation between environmental performance and EID of listed companies. *Productivity Research*, 9, 193–196.

Ministry of Environmental Protection (1995). *China's Environmental Protection Agenda for the 21st Century*. Beijing: China Environmental Science Press.

Moffatt I. (2002). *Sustainable Development: Principles, Analysis and Policies*. Beijing: Economic Science Press.

National Environmental Economic Policy Research and Pilot Project Technical Team, Dong Z. F., Li H. X., Ge C. Z., Wang J. N., & Cheng C. Y (2015a). Progress assessment of national environmental and economic policies (2013). *Chinese Journal of Environmental Management*, 3, 12–19.

National Environmental Economic Policy Research and Pilot Project Technical Team, Dong Z. F., Li H. X., Ge C. Z., Wang J. N., & Cheng C. Y (2015b).

Progress assessment of national environmental and economic policies (2014). *Chinese Journal of Environmental Management*, 3, 5–11.

National Environmental Economic Policy Research and Pilot Project Technical Team, Dong Z. F., Li H. X., Ge C. Z., Wang J. N., & Cheng C. Y. (2016). Progress assessment of national environmental and economic policies (2015). *Chinese Journal of Environmental Management*, 3, 9–13.

Ni J. & Kong L. W. (2016). Corporate EID, bank credit decisions and debt financing cost: Empirical evidence from Shanghai and Shenzhen-based A-share listed companies in heavily polluting industries. *Economic Review*, 1, 147–156.

Niu H. P., Du W. C., & Zhu Y. C. (2012). Pollution fee collection, technological innovation, and pollution discharge. *Review of Economy and Management*, 28, 51–56.

PBOC, The Nanjing Branch (2016). The financial support for the corporate transformation and upgrading of Nanjing's manufacturers has achieved positive results, November 23.

Peng Y., Zhou T., & Xu Y. A. (2013). Analysis of the impact of environmental protection investment on industrial waste gas emission reduction under environmental regulation — The GMM method based on China's provincial industrial panel data. *Journal of Industrial Technological Economics*, 32, 123–131.

Piketty, T. (2014). *Capital in the Twenty-first Century*. Beijing: CITIC Press.

Qin C. B., Wang J. N., Ge C. Z., Gao S. T., & Liu Q. Q. (2015). The impact of environmental tax on economy and pollution emissions. *Chinese Journal of Population Resources and Environment*, 25, 17–23.

Ren Y. N. (2007). Research on China's Corporate EID. Master Thesis, Sichuan University.

Shen J. J. (2007). Environmental tax theory and practice and its application in China. Thesis, Southwest University of Finance and Economics.

Shen L. (2014). Environmental protection fee-to-tax reform: Whoever causes pollution is responsible for its treatment. *Environment*, 3, 64–66.

Shen M. H. & Xu Y. H. (2000). A new type of EKC: An economic research on economic growth and environmental changes in Zhejiang Province's industrial process. *Zhejiang Social Sciences*, 4, 53–57.

Si Y. W. & Li J. (2007). The realistic thinking and theoretical conception of China's fee-to-tax reform of pollution discharge. *Statistics & Decision*, 4, 53–57.

Song Y. N. (2010). Research on the content of corporate environmental information disclosure based on core stakeholders. Thesis, Ocean University of China.

Song G. J., Jin S. Q., & Feng S. (2011). On the general model of environmental policy evaluation. *Environmental Pollution & Control*, 5, 100–106.

Song G. J., Ma Z., & Jiang N. (2003). Environmental policy assessment and its significance to China's environmental protection. *Environmental Protection*, 12, 34–37.

Su Z. K. (2016). Necessity of "fee-to-tax" reform for China's water pollution prevention and control measures. *Journal of Harbin University*, 39, 24–27.

Sun L. (2012). Empirical analysis of the impact of regional employment structure on China's regional economic differences. *Commercial Times*, 22, 131–133.

Sun L. (2018). CBRC discloses the green credit situation of 21 banks. Securities Times. Retrieved from http://finance.sina.com.cn/roll/2018-02-10/doc-ifyrkzqr1024839.shtml.

Tang Y. Q. (2015). Research on the taxation system of China's industrial waste water pollution treatment. Thesis, Liaoning University.

Tian L. L., Lin C. M., & Zhao L. W. (2014). The status quo and problems of Tianjin's environmental economic policies and its countermeasures. *Future and Development*, 4, 99–104.

Wang M. (2009). Limitations and reform of China's pollution charging system. *Taxation Research*, 7, 28–31.

Wang Q. (2014). Empirical study on the influencing factors of credit financing ability of listed manufacturing companies. *Communication of Finance and Accounting*, 24, 86–88.

Wang J. (2017). Research on green investment issues — Based on the micro perspective of enterprises. *Economic & Trade*, 15, 27–28.

Wang X. N. & Zhu G. Y. (2017). Does the implementation of green credit in commercial banks affect their profitability? — Based on panel data analysis of 12 listed banks. *Journal of Finance and Economics*, 6, 41–46.

Wang J. F., Wu Y. Q., Guan L. S., & Qiu Y. (2016). Research on foreign environ mental policy evaluation system — Based on the comparison of such system in the United States and the European Union. *Environmental Protection Science*, 1, 41–47.

Wu C. Y. (2011). Problems in the implementation of resident tiered electricity tariff in Zhejiang Province and countermeasures. *Energy Technology and Economics*, 23, 48–52.

Wu J. L. (2013). *The Choice of China's Growth Model* (4th edn.). Shanghai: Shanghai Far East Publishers.

Xu Q. X. (2010). Study on problems and measures in the collection of pollutant discharge fees in China. Proceedings of the Annual Conference of the Chinese Society of Environmental Sciences, 2, pp. 368–371. Beijing: China Environmental Press.

Yu J. (2013). "Double dividend" of environmental tax and China's environmental taxation reform orientation. *Macroeconomics*, 8, 3–7.

Yu Y. H. & Che Z. Z. (2014). Is it sure that raising electricity tariff will reduce urban residents' electricity demand? Report Series of National Academy of Development and Strategy, RUC, 1.

Yuan X. H. (2012). Comparative study of pollutant discharge fee and pollution tax. *China Population Resources and Environment*, 22, 40–43.

Yuan Z. G. (2013). *China (Shanghai) Pilot Free Trade Zone — New Strategy Research*. Shanghai: Truth & Wisdom Press.

Zeng M., Li N., & Liu C. (2011). Evaluation of electricity saving effect of resident tiered electricity tariff scheme based on utility function. *East China Electric Power*, 39, 1215–1219.

Zhang F. (1998). *Environment and Natural Resource Economics*. Shanghai: Shanghai People's Publishing House.

Zhang L. (2009). Research on the legal issues of governmental EID. Master Thesis, Kunming University of Science and Technology.

Zhang X. H. (1989). *Productivity and Economic Laws*. Shanghai: Fudan University Press.

Zhang X. H. (2001). *Exploration of Economic Laws — Selected Works of Zhang Xunhua*. Shanghai: Fudan University Press.

Zhang Y. (2016). What does environmental protection tax bring? *China Report*, 10, 34–35.

Zhang P. D. & Zhang X. Y. (2017). The construction and development of China's green credit policy system. *Environmental Protection*, 19, 7–10.

Zhang B., Zhang Y. L., & Bi J. (2012). Jiangsu's path of environmental economic policy in the "12th Five-Year Plan" — One of the annual reports on environmental economy. *Environment Economics*, 3, 30–39.

Zhang J. J., Yu L. C., Bi Q., & Pan J. (2016). Media supervision, environmental regulation and corporate green investment. *Journal of Shanghai University of Finance and Economics*, 18(5), 91–103.

Zheng H. Q., Jin Y., & You P. P. (2012). Evaluation and prospect of residents' tiered electricity price. *Energy Technology Economics*, 24, 6–9.

Zheng P. N., Chen X. G., Li M. G., Zhou D. B., & Wu J. L. (2007). Research on the relationship between pollutant charging system and pollutant emission reduction — Taking Guangdong Province as an example. *Ecology and Environment*, 5, 1376–1381.

Zhou X. H. (2012). Corporate green investment decisions facing circular economy: Status quo, dilemma and way out. *Journal of Hunan Business College*, 19, 29–34.

Zhu C. Y. (2010). On the social responsibilities of financial intermediaries. *Tsinghua Law Review*, 1, 6–21.

Zhu C. Z. (2010). Proposals and ideas on the implementation of tiered electricity tariffs in China. *Sino-Global Energy*, 5, 13–17.

Zhu D. J. (2010). From Brown model B to model C for China's development. *Shanghai & Hongkong Economy*, 6, 17.

Zhu G. H. (1997). *Sustainable Development: Decisions for China's Modernization — Research on the Relationship between China's Population,*

Resources, Environment and Economic Development. Fujian: Fujian People's Publishing House.
Zhu Q. (2013). Research on the micro dynamic mechanism of suburbanization of urban population in China. Undergraduate Thesis, Fudan University.

English Literature

Alberini A., Gans W., & Velez-Lopez D. (2011). Residential consumption of gas and electricity in the U.S.: The role of prices and income. *Energy Economics*, 33(5), 870–881. doi: 10.1016/j.eneco.2011.01.015.
Aschauer D. A. (1989). Is public expenditure productive? *Journal of Monetary Economics*, 23(2), 177–200. doi: 10.1016/0304-3932(89)90047-0.
Barde J. (1994). Economic instruments in environmental policy: Lessons from the OECD experience and their relevance to developing economies. Working Paper No. 92, 92(92), 5.
Barrett S. (1998). Political economy of the Kyoto Protocol. *Oxford Review of Economic Policy*, 14(4), 20–39. doi: 10.1093/oxrep/14.4.20.
Blanchard O. J. & Fischer S. (1989). *Lectures on Macroeconomics*. Cambridge, USA: The MIT Press.
Bo N. & Mahar D. J. (1987). Rapid population growth and human carrying capacity, two perspectives. *Population* (French Edition), 42(2), 394. doi: 10.2307/1533097.
Boahene K., Snijders T. A. B., & Folmer H. (1999). An integrated socioeconomic analysis of innovation adoption: The case of hybrid cocoa in Ghana. *Journal of Policy Modeling*, 21(2), 167–184. doi: 10.1016/s0161-8938(97)00070-7.
British Petroleum (2011). BP Annual Report 2011.
Buchanan J. M. & Tullock G. (1975). Polluters' profits and political response: Direct controls versus taxes. *American Economic Review*, 65(1), 139–147. doi: 10.4324/9781315197296-24.
Buhr N. (2007). Histories of and rationales for sustainability reporting. In *Sustainability Accounting and Accountability*. London and New York: Routledge, pp. 57–69. doi: 10.4324/noe0415384889.pt2.
Butler E. & Friedman M. (2011). *A Concise Guide to the Ideas and Influence of the Free-market Economist*. Petersfield: Harriman House Ltd.
Chen S. (2013). *Energy, Environment and Economic Transformation in China*. London: Routledge. doi: 10.4324/9780203374627.
Chenery H. B. & Taylor L. (1968). Development patterns: Among countries and over time. *The Review of Economics and Statistics*, 50(4), 391. doi: 10.2307/1926806.
Coase R. H. (1960). The problem of social cost. *The Journal of Law and Economics*, 3(3), 1–44. doi: 10.1086/466560.

Cobb J. B. & Daly H. E. (1989). *For the Common Good: Redirecting the Economy toward Community, the Environment, and a Sustainable Future.* Boston: Beacon Press.

Cohen J. E. (1995). Population growth and earth's human carrying capacity. *Science*, 269(5222), 341–346. doi: 10.1126/science.7618100.

Copeland B. R. & Taylor M. S. (1994). North-South trade and the environment. *The Quarterly Journal of Economics*, 109(3), 755–787.

Cormier D. & Magnan M. (2003). Environmental reporting management: A continental European perspective. *Journal of Accounting and public Policy*, 22(1), 43–62.

D'arge R. C. & Kogiku K. C. (1973). Economic growth and the environment. *Review of Economic Studies*, 40(1), 61–77. doi: 10.2307/2296740.

de Bruyn S. M. (2000). *Economic Growth and the Environment: An Empirical Analysis*. Boston: Kluwer Academic Publishers.

Domar E. (1946). Capital expansion, rate of growth, and employment. *Econometrica*, 14(2), 137–147. Retrieved from https://www.jstor.org/stable/1905364.

Dong Z. F., Wang J. N., Ge C. H., & Gao S. T. (2010). Evaluation and prospect of lake environmental and economic policies in China. *Environmental Protection and Circular Economy*, 2010(01), 4–6.

Easterly W. & Levine R. (1997). Africa's growth tragedy: Policies and ethnic divisions. *Quarterly Journal of Economics*, 112(4), 1203–1250. doi: 10.1162/003355300555466.

El-Demellawy D. (2010). Economic growth and the environment. In *A Handbook of Environmental Management*, pp. 359–407. doi: 10.1201/b17299-9.

Fagin D. (2013). *Toms River: A Story of Science and Salvation.* USA: Random House LCC.

Fedderke J. & Klitgaard R. (1998). Economic growth and social indicators: An exploratory analysis. *Economic Development and Cultural Change*, 46(3), 455–489. doi: 10.1086/452354.

Fell H., Li S., & Paul A. (2014). A new look at residential electricity demand using household expenditure data. *International Journal of Industrial Organization*, 33(1), 37–47. doi: 10.1016/j.ijindorg.2014.02.001.

Fisher F. M. & Kaysen C. (1962). *A Study in Econometrics: The Demand for Electricity in the United States*. Amsterdam: North-Holland Publishing Co.

French D. (1998). Kyoto protocol to the United Nations framework convention on climate change. *Journal of Environmental Law*, 10(1), 215–224. doi: 10.1093/jel/10.1.215.

Gallagher K. P. (2008). *Handbook on Trade and the Environment*. Cheltenham: Edward Elgar Publishing. doi: 10.4337/9781848446045.

Garrod G. & Willis K. G. (1999). *Economic Valuation of the Environment: Methods and Case Studies*. Cheltenham: Edward Elgar.

Gillis M., *et al.* (1992) *Economics of Development*. WW Norton & Company, Inc.

Goulder L. H. & Mathai K. (2010). Optimal CO_2 abatement in the presence of induced technological change. In *Technological Change and the Environment*. Routledge, pp. 216–256.

Grossman G. & Krueger A. (1993). Environmental impacts of a North American Free Trade Agreement. In Garber P. M. (Ed.), *The Mexico-U.S. Free Trade Agreement*. National Bureau of Economic Research, pp. 13–56. Retrieved from https://www.nber.org/papers/w3914.

Grossman G. M. & Krueger A. B. (1995). Economic growth and the environment. *Quarterly Journal of Economics*, 110(2), 353–377. doi: 10.2307/2118443.

Grubler A. & Gritsevskyi A. (1998). A model of endogenous technological change through uncertain returns on learning (R&D and investments). IIASA Working Paper, pp. 1–50. Retrieved from http://www.iiasa.ac.at/Research/TNT/WEB/endog.pdf.

Hardin G. (1968). The tragedy of the commons. *Science*, 162(3859), 1243–1248.

Hartwick J. M. (1978). Investing returns from depleting renewable resource stocks and intergenerational equity. *Economics Letters*, 1(1), 85–88. doi: 10.1016/0165-1765(78)90102-7.

Holland L. & Foo Y. B. (2003). Differences in environmental reporting practices in the UK and the US: The legal and regulatory context. *British Accounting Review*, 35(1), 1–18. doi: 10.1016/S0890-8389(02)00127-0.

Holtedahl P. & Joutz F. L. (2004). Residential electricity demand in Taiwan. *Energy Economics*, 26(2), 201–224. doi: 10.1016/j.eneco.2003.11.001.

Hotelling H. (1990). The economics of exhaustible resources. In *The Collected Economics Articles of Harold Hotelling*, Darnell A. C. (Ed.) pp. 64–92. New York, NY: Springer. doi: 10.1007/978-1-4613-8905-7_5.

Houqing Z., Yi J. I. N., & Peipei Y. O. U. (2012). Analysis and prospect of residential block tariff. *Energy Technology and Economics*, 24(1), 6–9.

IPCC (2007a). Fourth assessment report: Synthesis, report. Retrieved from http://www.ipcc.ch/%5Crpdf/assessment-report/ar4/syr/ar4_syr.pdf.

IPCC (2007b). Climate change 2007-impacts, adaptation and vulnerability: Working group II contribution to the fourth assessment report of the IPCC. Cambridge University Press.

Kedzie C. R. (1997). Communication and democracy: Coincident revolutions and the Emergent Dictator's Dilemma. p. 106. Retrieved from http://www.rand.org/publications/RGSD/RGSD127/.

Korves N., Martinez-Zarzoso I., & Monika A. (2011). Is free trade good or bad for the environment? New empirical evidence. In *Climate Change — Socioeconomic Effects*. doi: 10.5772/23008.

Kremer M. (1993). Population growth and technological change: One million B.C. to 1990. *Quarterly Journal of Economics*, 108(3), 681–716. doi: 10.2307/2118405.

Kuznets S. S. (1965). *Economic Growth and Structure: Selected Essays*. New York: Norton.

Lewis W. A. (1954). Economic development with unlimited supplies of labor. *The Manchester School*, 72(5), 139–191.

Lewis T. R. (1979). The exhaustion and depletion of natural resources. *Econometrica*, 47(6), 1569. doi: 10.2307/1914021.

Lin B. & Jiang Z. (2012). Designation and influence of household increasing block electricity tariffs in China. *Energy Policy*, 42, 164–173. doi: 10.1016/j.enpol.2011.11.062.

Manne A. S. & Richels R. G. (1999). The Kyoto protocol: A cost-effective strategy for meeting environmental objectives? *Energy Journal*, 20(SPEC. ISS.), 1–23. doi: 10.5547/issn0195-6574-ej-vol20-nosi-2.

Mansfield E. (1961). Technical change and the rate of imitation. *Econometrica*, 29(4), 741. doi: 10.2307/1911817.

McCormick J. (2017). *Carrots, Sticks & Sermons*. Bemelmans-Videc M.-L., Rist R. C., & Vedung E. (Eds.). Routledge. doi: 10.4324/9781315081748.

McGinnis R., *et al*. (1973). The limits to growth: A report for the club of Rome's project on the predicament of mankind. *Demography*, 10(2), 295. doi: 10.2307/2060820.

Meadows D. H. & Club of Rome (Eds.) (1972). *The Limits to Growth: A Report for the Club of Rome's Project on the Predicament of Mankind.* New South Wales, Australia: Universe Books.

Meijers H. H. M. (1994). On the diffusion of technologies in a vintage framework: Theoretical considerations and empirical results.

Messner S. (1997). Endogenized technological learning in an energy systems model. *Journal of Evolutionary Economics*, 7(3), 291–313. doi: 10.1007/s001910050045.

Mickwitz P. (2006). *Environmental Policy Evaluation: Concepts and Practice*, p. 78. The Finnish Society of Sciences and Letters, Finland.

Munasinghe M. (1995). Making economic growth more sustainable. *Ecological Economics*, 15(2), 121–124. doi: 10.1016/0921-8009(95)00066-6.

Murray C. J. & Lopez Alan D. (1996). The Global burden of disease : A comprehensive assessment of mortality and disability from diseases, injuries, and risk factors in 1990 and projected to 2020. Harvard School of Public Health, pp. 1–46. Retrieved from https://apps.who.int/iris/bitstream/handle/10665/41864/0965546608_eng.pdf?sequence=1&isAllowed=y.

Newman P. (2006). The environmental impact of cities. *Environment and Urbanization*, 18(2), 275–295. doi: 10.1177/0956247806069599.

Nordhaus W. (2008).). *A Question of Balance: Weighing the Options on Global Warming Policies*. Newhaven, USA: Yale University Press.

Nordhaus W. (2010) 'Economic aspects of global warming in a post-Copenhagen environment. *Proceedings of the National Academy of Sciences of the United States of America*, 107(26), 11721–11726. doi: 10.1073/pnas.1005985107.

Nordhaus W. (2013). Integrated economic and climate modeling. In *Handbook of Computable General Equilibrium Modeling*, 1, 1069–1131. doi: 10.1016/B978-0-444-59568-3.00016-X.

North D. C. (1990). *Institutions, Institutional Change and Economic Performance*. doi: 10.1017/cbo9780511808678.

Panayotou T. (1993). Empirical tests and policy analysis of environmental degradation at different stages of economic development. ILO Technology and Employ Programmed Working Paper, WP238.

Panayotou T. (1994). Economic instruments for environmental management and sustainable development. United Nations Environment Programme's Consultative Expert Group Meeting, pp. 1–72. Retrieved from http://classwebs.spea.indiana.edu/kenricha/Classes/V600/Spring2009ClassReadings/Frameworks/panyouto_econ_instru.pdf.

Pearce D. W. (1993). The economic value of externalities from electricity sources, Paper read to Green College, Oxford, Seminar on Environment and British Energy Policy.

Pearce D. W. (1996). *Blueprint of Green Economy*. Beijing, China: Beijing Normal University Press.

Pearce D. & Palmer C. (2003). Public and private spending for environmental protection: A cross-country policy analysis. *The Economics of Public Spending*, 22(4), 267.

Peiyuan G. (2015). Corporate environmental reporting and disclosure in China 1. *CSR Asia*, pp. 1–72.

Pizer W. A., Shih J.-S., & Morgenstern R. D. (1997). Are we overstating the economic costs of environmental protection? (97–12). Retrieved from http://ideas.repec.org/p/cen/wpaper/97-12.html.

Porter M. E. (1991). America's green strategy. *Scientific American*, April, 168.

Porter M. E. (1990). The competitive advonioge of notions. *Harvard Business Review*, 40(4), 292. Retrieved from http://scholar.google.com/scholar?hl=en&btnG=Search&q=intitle:Copyright+©2001.+All+Rights+Reserved.#0%5Cnhttp://scholar.google.com/scholar?hl=en&btnG=Search&q=intitle:Copyright©+2001+All+Rights+Reserved#0.

Porter M. E. & Van der Linde C. (1995). Toward a new conception of the environment-competitiveness relationship. *Journal of Economic Perspectives*, 9(4), 97–118.

Rees W. E. (2019). Ecological footprints and appropriated carrying capacity: What urban economics leaves out. In *The Earthscan Reader in Rural–Urban Linkages*, pp. 285–297. doi: 10.4324/9781315800486-15.

Reneses J., *et al.* (2011). Electricity tariff design for transition economies. Application to the Libyan power system. *Energy Economics*, 33(1), 33–43. doi: 10.1016/j.eneco.2010.04.005.

Romero-Jordán D., Peñasco C., & Del Río P. (2014). Analysing the determinants of household electricity demand in Spain. An econometric study. *International Journal of Electrical Power and Energy Systems*, 63, 950–961. doi: 10.1016/j.ijepes.2014.06.005.

Scholtens B. & Dam L. (2007). Banking on the Equator. Are banks that adopted the Equator principles different from non-adopters? *World Development*, 35(8), 1307–1328. doi: 10.1016/j.worlddev.2006.10.013.

Serageldin, I. & Steer A. (Eds.) (1994). Epilogue: Expanding the capital stock. In *Making Development Sustainable: From Concepts to Action*. Environmentally Sustainable Development Occasional Paper No 2. Washington, DC: World Bank.

Shafik N. (1994). Economic development and environmental quality: An econometric analysis. *Oxford Economic Papers*, 46, 757–773. doi: 10.1093/oep/46.Supplement_1.757.

Solow R. M. (1974). The economics of resources or the resources of economics. In *Classic Papers in Natural Resource Economics*, pp. 257–276. doi: 10.1057/9780230523210_13.

Solow R. M. (1986). On the intergenerational allocation of natural resources. *Scandinavian Journal of Economics*, 88(1), 141–149.

Solow, R. M. (1999). Notes on social capital and economic performance. In *Social Capital — A Multifaceted Perspective*, Dasgupta P. & Serageldin I. (Eds.), (pp. 6–10). Washington, DC: World Bank.

Stavins R. N. (2003). Experience with market-based environmental policy instruments. In *Handbook of Environmental Economics*. Oxford: Elsevier, pp. 355–435.

Stern N. (2007). *The Economics of Climate Change: The Stern Review*. Cambridge: Cambridge University Press. doi: 10.1017/CBO9780511817434.

Sterner T. & Coria J. (2010). *Policy Instruments for Environmental and Natural Resource Management*, 2nd edn., London: Routledge, pp. 1–638. doi: 10.4324/9781315780894.

Sun C. & Lin B. (2013). Reforming residential electricity tariff in China: Block tariffs pricing approach. *Energy Policy*, 60, 741–752. doi: 10.1016/j.enpol.2013.05.023.

Tietenberg T. H. (1990). Economic instruments for environmental regulation. *Oxford Review of Economic Policy*, 6(1), 17–33. doi: 10.1093/oxrep/6.1.17.

Tilt C. A. (2001). The content and disclosure of Australian corporate environmental policies. *Accounting, Auditing & Accountability Journal*, 14(2), 190–212. doi: 10.1108/09513570110389314.

Tol R. S. J. (2001). Estimates of the damage costs of climate change. *Environmental and Resource Economics*, 21, 135–160.

Tol R. S. J. (2002). Estimates of the damage costs of climate change. Part 1: Benchmark estimates. *Environmental and Resource Economics*, 21(1), 47–73. doi: 10.1023/A:1014500930521.

Tol R. S. J. (2009). The economic effects of climate change. *Journal of Economic Perspectives*, 23(2), 29–51. doi: 10.1257/jep.23.2.29.

Toman M. A. (1997). A framework for climate change policy. In *Resources*, 11.

Turner R. K. (1991). Municipal solid waste management: An economic perspective. In Bradshaw A. D., Southwood S. R., & Warner S. F. (Eds.) *The Treatment and Handling of Wastes*. Bradshaw A. D., Southwood S. R., & Warner S. F. (eds.). Boca Raton, FL: Chapman and Hall, pp. 85–104.

United Nations Development Programme (UNDP) (2011). Human Development Report 2011.

UN Habitat (2013). *State of the World's Cities 2012/2013: Prosperity of Cities*. Oxford: Routledge. doi: 10.4324/9780203756171.

UN Habitat (2008). *State of the World's Cities 2008/9: Harmonious Cities* (1st edition). London, Sterling, VA: Routledge. https://doi.org/10.4324/9781849772624.

van Brabant J. M. (1995). The economics of collective choice. *Comparative Economic Studies*, 37(2), 112–115. doi: 10.1057/ces.1995.13.

World Bank (2010). Cities and climate change an urgent agenda. Urban Development and Local Government, 10, p. 279. Retrieved from http://books.google.es/books?id=mDTsgiMgnHwC.

World Commission on Environment and Development (1987). Report of the World Commission on Environment and Development: Our Common Future. Oxford: Oxford University Press. Retrieved from http://www.ask-force.org/web/Sustainability/Brundtland-Our-Common-Future-1987-2008.pdf.

Ye K. T., Zhang R., & Xu H. P. (2010). Reputation, institutional environment and debt financing: Evidence from private-owned listed firms in China. *Journal of Financial Research*, 362(8), 171–183.

Zhou S. & Teng F. (2013). Estimation of urban residential electricity demand in China using household survey data. *Energy Policy*, 61, 394–402. doi: 10.1016/j.enpol.2013.06.092.

Index

Q

R

S

T

www.ingramcontent.com/pod-product-compliance
Lightning Source LLC
LaVergne TN
LVHW011701200926
848484LV00004B/1019